The
Productive
Edge

THE PRODUCTIVE EDGE

*How U.S. Industries
Are Pointing the Way
to a New Era of
Economic Growth*

Richard K. Lester

W.W. NORTON & COMPANY
New York   London

For information about permission to reproduce selections from this book, write to Permissions, W. W. Norton & Company, Inc., 500 Fifth Avenue, New York, NY 10110.

The text of this book is composed in Melior with the display set in Umbra, Gill Sans Light Italic, and Eurostile Bold Condensed. Composition and manufacturing by the Haddon Craftsmen, Inc.

Book design by Charlotte Staub

Library of Congress Cataloging-in-Publication Data

Lester, Richard K. (Richard Keith), 1954–
    The productive edge : how U.S. industries are pointing the way to
a new era of economic growth / Richard K. Lester.
      p. cm.
    Includes bibliographical reference and index.
    ISBN 0-393-04574-9
    1. Industrial productivity—United States.   I. Title.
HC110.I52L47   1998
338.0973—dc21   97-35029
                                CIP

W. W. Norton & Company, Inc., 500 Fifth Avenue, New York, N.Y. 10110
http://www.wwnorton.com

W. W. Norton & Company Ltd., 10 Coptic Street, London WC1A 1PU

1 2 3 4 5 6 7 8 9 0

To My Parents

CONTENTS

ACKNOWLEDGMENTS

The Alfred P. Sloan Foundation provided the principal financial support for the preparation of this book, as part of its base grant to the MIT Industrial Performance Center (IPC). I am tremendously grateful to Foundation President Ralph Gomory and Vice President Hirsh Cohen for their continuing support and encouragement. Their vision in establishing a nationwide network of university-based Centers for the Study of Industry, of which the IPC is a part, helped to create the intellectual framework within which this book could take shape. As a member of this network, I have benefited greatly from my interactions over the years with fellow Sloan-supported researchers at several universities, including Berkeley, Carnegie Mellon, Harvard, the Wharton School at the University of Pennsylvania, the University of Pittsburgh, Stanford, and, of course, MIT. Thanks also go to the many other experts in industry, government, and academia, too numerous to mention by name, whom I have consulted and from whom I learned so much during the course of this work. Coopers and Lybrand provided important additional sponsorship of the research on product development and human resource management described in the book, and I am grateful to Vice Chairman Vin O'Reilly for his and Coopers' help. At Norton, editor Joe Wisnovsky got the ball rolling and shepherded the project to its conclusion with his usual patience, good humor, and wise counsel. I owe a great deal to Joe, to Don Lamm, chairman of Norton, and to everyone at the company for their support and their many valuable contributions along the way.

At the IPC itself, I am indebted in any number of ways to as fine a group of colleagues as one could wish for. Among those whom I have been fortunate to learn with and from: Erik Brynjolffson, Charles Fine, Tom Kochan, and Ed Roberts. I am especially grateful to Suzanne Berger, Frank Levy, Richard Locke, Michael Piore, and Harvey Brooks of Harvard for their careful readings of sections of the manuscript. Bob Solow has been a continuing source of inspiration and a central figure in my intellectual development. I have also been privileged to

9

work with many talented students during the course of this project; Kamal Malek, Rohit Sakhuja and Micky Tripathi are among those who have made valuable contributions. I particularly want to thank my superb research assistant, Joe Bambenek, whose careful calculations, conceptual contributions, indefatigable sleuthing and trolling through vast quantities of data, and acute critical faculties were crucial to the entire enterprise. Last, but certainly not least, my administrative assistant, Anita Kafka, and IPC administrator Betty Bolivar served with distinction throughout the project; this dedicated, generous, and highly professional team assisted in the research in countless ways and kept the Center running smoothly during my long absences. To them, and to everyone mentioned above, I express my deep appreciation.

PREFACE

This book grows out of a decade-long research program based at the MIT Industrial Performance Center, but its conception can be traced to a particular moment. It was the first day of spring classes in early 1992, and as is my usual practice at the beginning of term I walked into the classroom armed with an exercise for my new students. Their task was to unmask the identity of two countries, which I referred to as A and B. Country A, I told the class, was in poor economic health. I recounted its dismal performance over the preceding decade. Many of its manufacturing firms had been devastated by foreign competition, and large numbers of high-paying manufacturing jobs had been lost. Years of huge trade deficits had turned Country A into the world's largest debtor nation. Its high-technology industries, once widely admired, had fallen behind in key fields. The rate of savings had fallen far below historical levels, and investment in new plant and equipment and research and development was lagging badly relative to other industrialized countries. Moreover, the shortcomings of the economy were falling unevenly on the population. Inequalities in the distribution of wealth and income had been growing for some time. While most of A's best-paid workers were somewhat better off than they had been a decade earlier, for the majority of the workforce real incomes had been gradually declining. And however bad things were, most people seemed to think that they would only get worse. A leading opinion poll suggested that only 20 percent of Country A's population expected their children to be better off than they were.

Country B, on the other hand, had compiled an enviable economic record over the past decade. Once again I summarized the main points. Just then, like most industrialized nations, it was struggling through a recession, but this had been preceded by an unusually long expansion, and during the 1980s Country B's economy had created more new jobs than any other country. The ravaging inflation of the 1970s and early 1980s had been brought to heel, and for the last decade the inflation rate had hovered around 4 percent, a level not seen for a quarter of a century. The population of Country B enjoyed the highest per capita income in the world, and its manufacturing industries, widely dismissed only a short time before as backward and uncompetitive, more recently had achieved impressive gains. Manufacturing exports had nearly doubled between 1987 and 1992, and the country's firms had managed to maintain or even slightly increase their share of world markets.

Quite a contrast, the class agreed. But which were these two countries? Only one student guessed correctly. They were both the United States.

The point of my little exercise had been to show how easily a unscrupulous practitioner can manipulate a given set of economic facts to get a desired result. But underlying it was a more fundamental question: Which of these alternatives—the United States as A or B— was closer to the truth? The prevailing view, echoed in countless editorials and expert commentaries, was that U.S. industry, overwhelmed by foreign competitors, was in rapid and perhaps terminal decline. But was this really the case? I was doubtful. Even though, just a few years earlier, I had participated in a scathing critique of American industrial performance, my subsequent research had focused on the extraordinary efforts many American firms were making to address their competitiveness problems. From this perspective, the jeremiad of popular commentary seemed overdrawn. I told my students that our main goal for the semester would be to discover what had really been happening in American industry since the mid-1980s, when the problem of industrial competitiveness had first invaded the nation's consciousness. Our discussions that spring became the starting point for this book.

Within a remarkably short time the prevailing mood swung from despair to exultation, as a powerful economic recovery, buoyant export performance, and exciting news from the high-technology frontier restored American business confidence and helped propel the stock market to record heights. Meanwhile, the formerly high-flying Japanese economy—for years the benchmark against which Americans had unfavorably compared themselves—was mired in recession, its once supremely confident industrialists and government officials enveloped in a cloud of uncertainty and self-doubt.

In 1996, America's vigorous economic performance helped elect President Clinton to a second term, and by mid-1997 the economy was firing on all cylinders, with continued strong job growth, unemployment and inflation at historically low levels, and the troublesome federal budget deficit seemingly finally under control. In the verdict of *Fortune* magazine that June, the economy was "stronger than it's ever been."

Optimism always peaks at the crest of the business cycle, and some of the current good feeling will fade when the economy heads into the inevitable downturn. But has there been a more permanent improvement in the economy's capacity to generate wealth, a lasting change in patterns of microeconomic activity that transcends the vicissitudes of the business cycle? Some observers have begun to proclaim the arrival of a new golden age for the U.S. economy, a new era of prosperity related to global integration, deregulation, and rapid advances in technology. Yet there has been no discernible improvement lately in the nation's rate of productivity growth—the single most important indicator of any nation's economic performance in the long run. And the median household income in America in 1996 was still below its level in 1989, after adjusting for inflation; indeed, it was barely above what it had been in 1979. So, although the context has obviously changed, the question I posed to my class earlier in the decade—how well is American industry *really* doing?—is still germane. Are we confusing media hype with real changes in economic capabilities? Or is the nation still selling itself short? If real improvements have indeed taken place, what are the most important causes? And what must be done to ensure that the gains can be sustained? These are the questions at the core of this book.

The first goal is to try to present the facts of the current situation as clearly as possible. We begin by examining recent U.S. industrial performance in the aggregate. A top-down perspective has important advantages. It allows us to keep in view the performance of the economy as a whole, and it makes possible a focus on those factors that affect the behavior of the economy in the large, especially the fiscal and monetary policies that influence overall levels of employment, income, savings, and investment. Here we pay particular attention to America's indifferent productivity performance for more than two decades. Unless the United States can improve on this record, the prospect of sustainable improvements in the standard of living for most Americans will remain out of reach. This is the single most important fact about current American industrial performance.

In the second part of the book, we switch to a "bottom-up" perspective. To understand what has been happening to American industry, it is also necessary to know what has been taking place on the ground—on the factory floors, in the offices, in the laboratories, and in the classrooms. It is here, on the front lines of industry, that the struggle to improve productivity is being won and lost.

This is the focus of Part II. This part of the book tells a story not told by the disappointing productivity statistics, the story of America's recent industrial revival. Actually, it tells five separate stories, about five different industries. These five cases illustrate the tremendous variation in the processes of industrial transformation that are at work in the economy today. In chapter 3 we examine the U.S. auto industry, the scene of one of the most intriguing (and unanticipated) industrial transformations of the past decade. Chapter 4 tells the story of how another traditional American industry, steel, has renewed itself. The revival of the American semiconductor industry, described in chapter 5, offers an opportunity to reflect on the impact of government intervention on an industry that was widely considered to have been 'too important to fail'. What was the actual effect of government policy, and how did it compare with the other forces that were simultaneously bearing on the industry?

In chapter 6 we explore a policy phenomenon of a very different kind: deregulation. During the last fifteen years, starting with the airlines, then spreading to the oil and gas industries, truck and rail transportation, banking, and telecommunications, the deregulation movement has cut a wide swath across the American industrial landscape, directly affecting huge numbers of people both as employees and consumers. Chapter 6 tells the story of the American electric-power industry, one of the most recent—and the largest—to undergo deregulation. Finally, chapter 7 explores still another mechanism of renewal: the creation of an entirely new industry from scratch. We consider the case of wireless telecommunications.

Together, these five case studies form a sort of mosaic of renewal. Obviously it is only a partial mosaic; other industries would have their own, unique stories to tell. But even these five cases suffice to demonstrate the inadequacies of some of the most popular claims about the causes of America's industrial recovery—claims that single out one particular factor or another. The evidence in Part II makes clear that any credible explanation must take account of the considerable variation in the experiences of different industries.

Part III of the book revisits the empirical evidence from a different perspective. It asks whether, in the face of all this diversity, there are nonetheless certain fundamental patterns that are common to the most successful companies in these industries. It is at this point that we examine the contribution of well-known managerial tools like total quality management and reengineering. The evidence here highlights a critical distinction between the techniques that the leading corporations use, which very often are imported from elsewhere, and the character of these corporations and the values they hold, which never are. The advocates of many of the new techniques stress the need to break with the past, to wipe the slate clean. Yet we shall see that one of the most striking features of the leading firms has been their enduring, deep-seated commitment to a handful of basic ideas or beliefs. By embracing and constantly reaffirming these core ideas, they have been able to communicate clearly and consistently who they are and what they stand for to their employees, their customers, their suppliers, and their shareholders. And this knowledge has helped engender the trust and mutual commitment that have been so important to their success. The latest management ideas, to the extent that they figure in these developments, are consciously and explicitly used and adapted in support of the more fundamental objectives of the firm.

Many of the industries and firms described in this book are engaged in manufacturing. If our goal is to understand the origins of industrial renewal, this is a proper focus. It is in the manufacturing sector that the transformation of production processes has gone farthest and fastest over the past decade. (Between 1990 and 1996, manufacturing productivity grew at an average rate of nearly 3 percent per year, about three times the productivity growth rate of the economy as a whole.) But how relevant are the lessons drawn from manufacturing for the rest of the economy—especially the huge services sector, which today employs more than 70 percent of the workforce?

As we shall see, the traditional boundary between manufacturing and services is fast becoming obsolete. Manufacturing has traditionally meant the production of tangible goods, but for today's customers it is the bundling together of the tangible object with an array of intangible services that makes for the most desirable, "service-enhanced" product. Conversely, information technology is allowing many services to be stored and transported over long distances, and as their production and consumption come to be separated geographically and in time, these services take on many of the attributes of manufactured products. So we might indeed expect that the lessons learned from the transformation of the manufacturing sector will be germane to the service industries too.

Finally, in Part IV we examine the implications of these case studies for America's future growth. It is no coincidence that the three powerful driving forces of economic change that together hold such tremendous promise for growth—globalization, deregulation, and technological change—are also each associated with uncertainty and disruption in the shorter term. Investment is essential for growth, and in periods of rapid change investment in the creation of intangible assets—more flexible organizations, more competent employees, ideas for new products and processes, knowledge of new market possibilities—takes on special importance. Yet it is also during these periods that such investments come under the greatest pressure. How to increase the rate of investment in these intangible assets is one of the most important issues facing American industry today.

For American society, too, there are critical questions. The turbulent energies released by globalization, deregulation, and rapid technological change are inspiring fear as well as hope among millions of ordinary Americans. How much stomach do people have for change? How much tolerance will they have for the costs and uncertainties that are an integral part of the new processes of economic growth?

The evidence in this book points toward the need for a new national agenda for economic growth, tailored to the volatile, unpredictable conditions that seem certain to persist for the foreseeable future, and focused on the problem of investing in knowledge and skills. At the heart of this agenda is a new vision of the role of work in our society. If people are to embrace change rather than resist it, if they are to open themselves up to economic forces that will sometimes seem arbitrary and out of control, they must have a positive reason to do so; they must have a sense of direction and purpose. The book concludes with a proposal for a "new economic citizenship"— a new view of the rights, responsibilities, and resources that should be accorded to those who will contribute their ideas and labor to the economy of the new century.

PART I

Introduction

CHAPTER 1

Introduction

It was a job the First Lady could hardly have savored. Moments earlier, her husband, George Herbert Walker Bush, had regurgitated the contents of his meal into the lap of the distinguished dinner companion to his left. The prime minister of Japan, President Bush's neighbor and host at the state banquet in Tokyo, moved swiftly to create some breathing space for the ashen American leader, but not before scores of cameras had captured the unfortunate scene. In the unkind words of one wag, it was "the barf heard around the world." Barbara Bush, standing in for the president, was left to salvage the occasion with a brief, gracious response to the welcoming toast.

Though obviously unintended, the symbolism was lost on no one. The president had come to Tokyo on a mission to open Japanese markets to U.S. exporters. Flanked by the captains of American industry, among them the chief executives of Detroit's Big Three automobile manufacturers, Bush had sought concrete commitments from Japan's leaders to reduce the big trade imbalance between the two countries. It was not a successful visit. The president, attempting to play the role of cheerleader for American industry, found himself cast in a much less flattering role—part poodle of U.S. business interests, part neighborhood bully, and part supplicant pleading for handouts. The Japanese press made much of the enormous salaries commanded by Chrysler's chairman, Lee Iacocca, and the chiefs of other supposedly struggling American firms. Pundits in both countries had a field day. The president's illness seemed to be a metaphor for the entire trip, and indeed for the sick, wobbly state of the U.S. economy as a whole—a humiliating display of American weakness in the face of Japanese industrial might.

The Bush visit, in early 1992, marked the nadir of a decade of growing despondency over the health of American industry. As evidence of America's competitive problems had accumulated during the 1980s, many had come to believe that the nation's industrial decline was irreversible. A best-selling book by the Yale historian Paul Kennedy ominously cataloged the parallels between present-day America and the twilight years of lost empires of the past. The collapse of the Soviet Union, far from raising America's spirits, had seemed only to magnify the country's preoccupation with its domestic weaknesses. Pessimism about the economy would later cost George Bush the 1992 presidential election.

Yet already by the time of the president's trip to Tokyo some dissonant facts were beginning to intrude on the conventional wisdom. For much of the previous decade, American analysts had been drawing unfavorable comparisons with other countries—Japan especially, but also Germany—and arguing vigorously for the adoption of the management strategies, public policies, and institutional structures pioneered in those countries. The logic of Japanese "lean production" and German "flexible specialization" had begun to seem unassailable, even if it was not entirely clear whether these were distinct models or variants of the same thing.

But by 1992 business confidence in both countries was not what it had been. And by the following year it was obvious to all that Japan, the economic juggernaut of the 1980s, was a diminished giant—its economy stumbling through the worst recession since World War II, its once all-conquering manufacturing firms grappling with falling profits, big layoffs, and a disastrously overextended banking system, and its biggest and long-dominant political party disintegrating amid political scandal and corruption. As firm after firm shifted production out of Japan to try to offset the rapid rise in the value of the yen, prominent business leaders began to worry publicly about the "hollowing out" of the Japanese industrial base, to American ears an ironically familiar echo of fears that had so often been voiced at home.[1]

In Germany, too, the loss of confidence was palpable. In 1991, with German reunification a *fait accompli* and the European Community striding toward full political and economic integration, the future had seemed extraordinarily bright. An American economist's prediction that the twenty-first century would be the Century of Europe, a new economic powerhouse with Germany at its heart, perfectly captured the mood of the moment.[2] Yet within two years the mood had been transformed. Nineteen ninety-two, the Year of European Unity, turned out to be nothing of the sort. In country after country voters went to the polls to register their disquiet about the whole undertaking. A complete unraveling seemed unlikely, but with war raging in the Balkans, unemployment soaring, and social and ethnic tensions flaring up across the continent, the Century of Europe looked much further away than it had only a year or so earlier. In Germany itself, the euphoria of reunification rapidly gave way to despondency over the staggering costs of absorbing the failed East German economy, and rioting, anti-immigrant violence, and previously unimaginable levels of unemployment began tearing at the social fabric.

Meanwhile, as their Japanese and German role models were looking increasingly shopworn, American manufacturers quietly began recouping some of their losses of the 1970s and 1980s. At first the gains were barely perceptible, but before long they became too obvious to ignore. The breadth of the recovery was striking. It encompassed traditional manufacturing industries like steel and automobiles, as well as high-technology industries like semiconductors, whose slide in the 1980s had been particularly shocking to many Americans. American firms were also competing successfully in the rapidly expanding global markets for banking, entertainment, and telecommunications services. And in important new industries like software, biotechnology, and Internet services, U.S. firms often seemed to have the field to themselves.

"The American Economy, Back on Top," proclaimed the *New York Times* in early 1994, as the flood of good news about international competitiveness and profits buoyed hopes of a fundamental turnaround in the United States.[3] Perceptions were also shifting overseas. Japanese commentators, long dismissive of America's industrial prowess, began making admiring references to the "Rising Sam in the West," while Japanese managers, reversing a familiar traffic pattern across the Pacific, were now to be seen flying east to study the techniques of leading U.S. corporations.[4] American reengineering consultants, claiming credit for the U.S. turnaround, began to gain a worldwide following for their ideas. In 1993 the World Economic Forum, best known for its prestigious annual gatherings of world political and business leaders in Davos, Switzerland, named the United States the world's most competitive industrial nation in its annual rankings, the first time it had done so for nearly a decade.

On the macroeconomic front, too, the good news was pouring in. Inflation and interest rates both remained at reassuringly low levels, even as millions of new jobs were being created. By mid-1997, inflation in the United States was at its lowest level in decades, unemployment was heading down below 5 percent, lower than at any time in the last quarter of a century, and more than 10 million new jobs had been added to the economy since the end of the 1990–91 recession. The federal budget deficit had fallen 75 percent from its peak, and as a share of economic output was now the lowest of all the major industrial economies. In the private sector, American corporations were reporting record profits. On Wall Street investors registered their approval by driving the stock market to unprecedented heights.

Serious-minded economists and business leaders began speaking euphorically of a new golden age for the U.S. economy. Declared the well-known Wall Street economist Allen Sinai in 1997, "I think this may be the best economy in U.S. history and probably the world."[5] More than a year earlier, deputy treasury secretary Lawrence Summers had already remarked that "the U.S. economy has perhaps the most solid macroeconomic foundation for growth that I've seen in my lifetime."[6] Others predicted that large, well-capitalized U.S. corporations would lead the way to a new era of steady growth and productivity gains related to global integration and technological advance. Some even went so far as to suggest that the ability of information technology to link customers and suppliers more closely would cause the normal cycles of boom and bust in the economy to fade away.

What happened? How can we explain all this good news, so close on the heels of predictions of irreversible decline? Were things never really as bad as they once seemed? Or did we only seem to be doing so much better because countries like Germany and Japan were looking so much worse? Or had American industry indeed staged a miraculous recovery? If so, what was responsible? Was it the cumulative effect of total quality management, reengineering, and the other new business management techniques of the last decade? Was it the entrepreneurial energies unleashed by America's dynamic capital markets, personified by the brash young multimillionaires of the Internet? Or was it rather the result of sound fiscal and monetary policies—a return to macroeconomic stability after nearly two decades of turbulence? Finally, what had happened to the economic malaise that had apparently been afflicting so many Americans just a short while earlier? For even as America's competitiveness problems receded after the early 1990s, commentators had begun to focus on other economic concerns, including the growing income gap between rich and poor, the widely shared belief that the living standards of many Americans were declining, and the epidemic of demoralizing corporate "downsizings." Each week seemed to bring new announcements of mass layoffs by blue-chip companies like IBM, AT&T, and General Motors. "We're Number 1. And It Hurts," ran a *Time* magazine cover story in 1994 highlighting the ambiguity in the nation's economic performance.[7] A crescendo of similar reports appeared over the next year, culminating in a much-discussed special series in the *New York Times* during March 1996 analyzing in exhaustive detail the devastating impacts of corporate downsizing on laid-off workers and their families. (*The Economist* of London later reported that the *Times* had devoted more space to this issue than to any other since Watergate.) Opinion surveys revealed deep anxieties about the future, with many Americans seemingly increasingly unsure of their place in the new global economy. An NBC News/*Wall Street Journal* poll taken in January 1996 reported that only 41 percent of the respondents thought that their children's generation would enjoy a standard of living higher than theirs. By the spring of 1996, many political commentators were confidently predicting that "economic insecurity" would be the central issue in the coming presidential election campaign.

But here, too, the real story was more complicated. The same NBC News/*Wall Street Journal* poll had also asked the following question: "Would you say that you and your family are better off or worse off than you were four years ago?" Nearly 75 percent answered either that they felt better off or that they were holding their own. Now, the fact that a quarter of the respondents felt their economic situation had clearly deteriorated was certainly no cause for celebration, but neither was it consistent with the more alarming accounts in the popular press of widespread economic hardship and disappointment.

Nor were things quite as bad as they seemed on the employment front. Despite the intense preoccupation with downsizing, it remained a matter of debate among the experts as to whether the real risk of job loss had actually risen at all. Henry Farber, a labor economist at Princeton University, estimated that the job tenure of a typical male worker aged forty-five to fifty-four had fallen only slightly between 1983 and 1993, from about thirteen years to a little less than twelve.[8] Other studies reported that the rate of job destruction during the recession of the early 1990s was no greater than it had been during previous recessions.[9]

Some things *did* seem to have changed. Unexpectedly, the rate of job displacement continued to rise even after the recession of the early 1990s had ended—a radical departure from the usual pattern. On the other hand, a preliminary analysis of the post-recession data indicated that people who had lost their jobs were taking less time to find a new one, and that although they typically had to accept a paycut in their new jobs, this was smaller than before. In other words, even though the probability of losing one's job had risen on average, the economic impact had declined.[10]

Why, then, did the issue of downsizing attract such an extraordinary amount of attention? A likely reason is that the feeling of vulnerability had become more widespread. As a 1996 report by the President's Council of Economic Advisors pointed out, although the overall probability of being laid off had not changed significantly over the past decade, middle-aged men, who had previously been relatively secure, now faced an above-average risk of being displaced. Moreover, what used primarily to be a blue-collar issue had now spread to the ranks of managerial and other white-collar employees. Of this period it was often said, with only a slight exaggeration, that almost everybody knew someone who had been laid off.

Yet as the powerful economic expansion of the mid-1990s gained strength these anxieties also faded, and by the fall of 1996 the question of economic insecurity had largely disappeared from the presidential campaign. What happened? Was it a chimera all along, the media-amplified confection of a few ill-informed pessimists? Or were the concerns real—eclipsed temporarily in the euphoria of the expansion's later stages but sure to reappear with the next downturn? Or had there been a more fundamental change for the better in the economy's long-term prospects that had swept away the concern over economic insecurity once and for all?

Looking at an economy as vast and complex as that of the United States is a bit like looking through a kaleidoscope. There is an almost limitless number of angles of view, each suggesting its own interpretation. So it is no surprise that the facts of America's industrial performance should be so hard to pin down. Even so, the industrial situation today is strangely out of focus. There is certainly no shortage of good news. But it is hard to say exactly how well we have been doing, or why we have been doing better, or what we must do to succeed in the future.

The End of Mass Production

Ten years ago, such questions were easier to answer. The issue of performance was not in doubt. American industry was clearly ailing. And to find successful models one had only to look at the impressive achievements of leading foreign firms, especially the Japanese. In 1986, when a group of MIT researchers (the MIT Commission on Industrial Productivity) embarked on a major assessment of American industrial performance, there was little argument about the magnitude of the problem the United States was facing. The challenge was to sort out which of the many competing theories and interpretations was most important in explaining its origins.

The findings of the MIT Commission serve as a useful point of reference against which to measure more recent progress. By studying the practices and performance of almost two hundred firms in eight large industries in the United States, Europe, and Asia, the commission constructed a picture, from the ground up, of the strengths and weaknesses of the U.S. industrial sector at that time. The differences among these industries and firms were great: there were aging steel and apparel makers and sleek young computer companies; huge airframe manufacturers and small, family-owned machine-tool shops; process-oriented businesses like chemicals as well as discrete parts manufacturers like auto assembly firms. Despite this diversity, the evidence from the case studies had much in common. Everywhere, the forces of international competition and technological change were transforming the industrial landscape. The rules of the game were changing in fundamental ways, and simply trying to do harder what had worked well in the past was no longer adequate. The commission's 1989 report, *Made in America: Regaining the Productive Edge,* concluded that American industry as a whole needed to accelerate its historic shift away from the system of mass production of low-cost, standard products—the system that had been developed early in the century, initially by Henry Ford and Alfred Sloan for automobile manufacturing, and later extended to a wide range of other industries.

The mass production system had been enormously successful in serving—indeed, in a very real sense creating—the huge domestic consumer market, and had brought great prosperity to American firms and their employees. But the age of traditional mass production was ending, and a new system of production was emerging, capable of producing smaller volumes of high-quality products tailored to different segments of an increasingly demanding, sophisticated, and global market. In the new system, success would go to those who combined the traditional emphasis on keeping costs low with a new focus on product quality and design, customer service, and the ability to bring new products rapidly to market. More flexible and less bureaucratic organizations; cross-functional teams; closer ties to suppliers and customers; intelligent use of information technology; global reach: all of these practices took on greater significance in the new competitive environment.

Most important, success in this new system of production hinged on the knowledge that people at each level of the organization were acquiring and bringing to bear in the course of their work. In the traditional mass production model, managerial control in the workplace was exercised through steeply hierarchical organizational structures.

Most jobs were defined narrowly, and were relatively easy to learn. A sharp separation was made between "thinking" work, reserved for the higher echelons of the management hierarchy, and the remaining jobs, whose main purpose was the unthinking execution of someone else's instructions. Training for the second category of jobs—much the larger of the two—often could hardly be dignified by the name, amounting to little more than following a more experienced colleague around. Since the jobs required only limited skills, managers could adjust to fluctuations in demand by hiring and firing workers with little fear that the firm's stock of knowledge would be dissipated. In short, labor was seen essentially as a cost to be minimized.

But in the new model, the workforce was perceived as an asset to be cultivated. Especially where markets were changing rapidly, where product quality commanded a premium, and where increasingly complex technologies were dominating the production process, the leading firms seemed to have recognized the need for motivated, skilled, engaged, and adaptable workers in every part and at every level of the organization. *Made in America* argued that these firms offered a model for the nation as a whole:

> Under the new economic citizenship that we envision, workers, managers, and engineers will be continually and broadly trained, masters of their technology, in control of their work environment, and involved in shaping their firm's objectives. No longer will an employee be treated like a cog in a big and impersonal machine. From the company's point of view, the work force will be transformed from a cost factor to be minimized into a precious asset to be conserved and cultivated.[11]

Nor was it only individual firms and their workers that stood to gain from this scenario. The "new economic citizenship" seemed to offer a way out of one of the most feared consequences of globalization: the risk of low-wage competition from abroad driving down wages at home. In this view, highly skilled, adaptable, motivated American workers wouldn't be impoverished by the low-paid workers of the Third World because they wouldn't be competing with them. They would instead be engaged in an altogether different set of enterprises, producing and delivering high-quality products and services for markets lying beyond the reach of the huge pools of low-skilled labor in the Third World. They would be a source of sustainable competitive advantage for the nation. Beyond even this, a strategy of "putting people first" also seemed consonant with the core values of a democratic society. In the new world of work, participation, opportunity and commitment would replace control, regulation, and alienation.

Thus, at the height of the concern over American competitiveness, *Made in America* offered an optimistic vision of the future. It was, moreover, a vision with precedents. The MIT researchers could point to American firms in a wide range of industries that had embraced these ideas and that were competing successfully against the best of their foreign rivals.

Puzzles, Not Paradigms

Nearly ten years later, the world seems a great deal more complicated. Signs of progress abound. But how well is the American economy really doing? The competitiveness of its industries has improved. But, as we shall see in chapter 2, there has been no significant improvement in the rate of productivity growth—the single most important measure of any nation's economic performance. For the last quarter of a century labor productivity has edged up at an average rate of about 1 percent per year. No other advanced economy has done as poorly. (There would be no comfort even if this were not so; the American standard of living is not centrally affected by productivity trends in other countries, but to the degree that there is a dependency we tend on the whole to benefit from higher productivity growth overseas.) Nor has the picture changed during the 1990's: in spite of all the corporate restructuring and the wave of excitement about the possibilities of new technology, between 1990 and 1996 productivity continued to grow at an average rate of 1 percent each year. Even the latest flurry of attention to the difficulties of measuring productivity accurately (see chapter 2) doesn't fundamentally alter this conclusion. So how well are we *really* doing?

Much of what we thought we knew about how to succeed in the new competitive environment also seems less certain. Some of America's most successful corporations over the past decade—firms like Hewlett Packard, Levi Strauss, and Motorola—exemplify the ideal of a "new economic citizenship" laid out in *Made in America,* albeit each in a somewhat different way. Yet many other American firms point to aggressive downsizing and restructuring as the main reason for their increased competitiveness—hardly an advertisement for the idea of the workforce as "a precious asset to be conserved and cultivated."

The earlier ideas about the international division of labor have also been thrown into question. How sustainable is the advantage of a highly skilled American workforce at a time when tens of millions of well-educated workers from Eastern Europe and the former Soviet Union are entering the global labor market? And when Chinese garment workers can produce top-of-the-line Escada fashion apparel, and U.S. computer firms can hire highly trained software engineers in Bangalore, India, at less than a fifth the cost of American programmers, the distinction between First World and Third World labor markets no longer seems so clear. According to one recent estimate, 1.2 billion Third World workers will enter the global labor market over the next twenty or thirty years, most of them earning only a tiny fraction of the average wage in the advanced economies. Many in the West are deeply apprehensive about the prospect.

These vast armies of workers and their families will also present huge new opportunities for growth, of course—opportunities that large American corporations, well capitalized and sophisticated in the use of technology, seem well positioned to exploit. Yet the degree to which American workers will share in these benefits depends on the outcome of corporate location decisions that today can only be guessed at. At a time when advances in communications and transportation technologies are creating unprecedented opportunities for companies to distribute their operations around the world, remarkably little is known about how these choices will be exercised. Where will the jobs go? What will be the impact on the number and quality of jobs remaining at home? Ten years ago, an American auto worker could focus on his highly efficient counterpart in Toyota City or elsewhere in Japan as the primary threat to his job security. Today, the threats seem to come from all over—a Mexican auto worker in a Big Three plant across the border, an American worker in a Japanese-owned plant in Tennessee, a nonunion employee of one of his own company's subcontractors, and on and on.

For managers, too, globalization presents extraordinary risks and uncertainties as well as opportunities. Is it possible to break up production systems and redistribute the functions of research, product conception and design, development, production, and marketing across the world without sacrificing efficiency and innovative capabilities? Which activities can be separated and moved and which need to be retained in close proximity to preserve the capacity for future innovation and growth?

The implications of continuing innovation in information technologies are also profoundly uncertain. Change here has been particularly rapid. New computer and communications technologies are transforming relations between firms, and may eventually work even more profound changes in the relationships between consumers and producers. Already in many industries, information technologies are promoting a shift away from "selling what you can make" toward the demand-driven principle of "making what you can sell," and in the process creating the potential for enormous gains in value and productivity. In this sense, the earlier picture of a transition away from mass production seems very much on target. But other patterns are much more difficult to discern. Firms are confronting the prospect of radical changes in products, delivery systems, and competitors with no roadmap to guide them.

There is certainly no shortage of candidates. Indeed, it is as though the uncertain climate draws them out. Just within the past few years the business literature has been swept by successive waves of prescriptions for improving corporate performance—total quality management, lean production, reengineering, the learning organization, the networked corporation, to name only a few. All of these prescriptions are notable for the breadth of their ambition. Each rejects incrementalist solutions and insists on the need for fundamental, systemic change. And each has gained a very sizable following in the ranks of American industry. It is surely no exaggeration to say that experimentation with new ways of organizing and managing business activity has reached a level not seen in decades. On the one hand, all this ferment points to a welcome openness to new ideas and change, a vigorous searching for new sources of competitive advantage. But the rapidity with which each new prescription has shouldered past its predecessors may also indicate a lack of conviction on the part of practitioners, a hasty and indiscriminate search for a quick fix. Beyond a certain point, enthusiastic experimentation risks curdling into protean irresolution. How many enterprises have crossed that line? And what has been the role of those on whom they rely for advice, the management consultants and the academic gurus? Do their articulate diagnoses and persuasive prescriptions perhaps mask a deeper failure to grasp the fundamental principles of production in the new economic environment? In any case, as each new management technique has flashed into view the effect has frequently been only to add to the general sense of instability and confusion.

The scare over "economic insecurity" in the mid-1990s was no chimera. It was rooted in real and fundamental changes in the nature of the economy. To dispel it will take more than the expansion phase of one business cycle. Rather, our society must accept the inevitability of a significantly higher level of economic ambiguity and volatility than in even the recent past; we need to recognize that this will be a normal condition of our economic existence for the foreseeable future. The challenge is to find a way to grow and flourish in such an environment, rather than wishing it away. As I will try to show in this book, success will require a basic rethinking of many of our most cherished business practices and public policies—a formidable task that is only just beginning.

CHAPTER 2

American Industrial Performance: A Top-Down View

Of all the possible explanations for why the real state of America's industrial health seems so elusive, surely the least convincing is that there is not enough information. On the contrary, we are inundated by it. Dispatches from the front arrive constantly: interest rates are down, then up; the stock market has peaked; the dollar is rallying; the latest figures on inflation, trade, factory orders, jobs gained, jobs lost, the money supply, the discount rate, consumer confidence—the list goes on and on. But what does it really mean? How can we make sense of it all?

In truth, the blizzard of economic statistics is actually part of the problem. It mostly neither tells us where we've been nor where we're going. If anything, the opposite is true; the figures tend to confuse more than inform. There is one small difficulty here, and a much bigger one. The small one is simply the lack of historical perspective. Too often, the information that would allow the latest figures to be placed in context is omitted. Sometimes there is a comparison with last quarter's results, or with "this time last year." But trying to infer long-term trends from such crumbs of information is a bit like trying to infer long-term climatic patterns from last week's weather.

Even with a more complete chronicling, however, most of these indicators would still reveal next to nothing about long-term trends. That is because they are useful only for monitoring business cycles, the not-very-regular fluctuations around the long-term trends in national income, employment, and output that characterize all modern economies. Compared with the great depressions of the past, contemporary business cycles are relatively tame affairs. Nevertheless, the existence of these cycles remains a central fact of economic life. Every business—from the local storeowner restocking for the coming quarter to the steelmaking giant planning the production schedule for its mills—wants and needs to know where the economy is in the current business cycle. A large proportion of all economic decisions taken by businesses and individuals hinge on such knowledge. And one of the main economic functions of government is to manage these cycles. Government officials and central bankers are continually adjusting the levers of macroeconomic policy in an effort to prevent the cyclical fluctuations from becoming too large and destabilizing. Political considerations are never absent from these calculations, of course, since political fortunes themselves frequently ride on the outcome. When slumps coincide with elections, incumbents seldom do well. (The voters' unhappiness about the recession played a large role in President George Bush's defeat in 1992; ironically, it later became clear that the recovery had already begun by the time of the election.)

So it is perfectly understandable that there should be such a preoccupation with the indicators that measure these cycles. The problem is that there is something hypnotic about the ups and downs of the economy. It is as if a driver were to become so absorbed in keeping his car in the middle of the road that he lost track of where he had come from and where he was going.

Keeping the car on the road is certainly a necessary achievement, but it is also a limited one. The former British chancellor of the exchequer Roy Jenkins once reflected on the ephemeral nature of much of what is involved in the conduct of that high office—in American terms a combination of treasury secretary and budget director. A chancellor's achievements in economic management, wrote Jenkins in his memoirs, are like "footprints in the sand," soon washed away by the tide of events.

Productivity Growth

To see how well an economy has been performing at a more fundamental level, we must look for footprints of a more durable kind. Over the long term, the single best indicator of how well a nation's economy is performing is its productivity—simply defined, the value of the outputs produced per unit of labor (labor productivity) or per unit of capital goods (capital productivity), averaged over the economy as a whole. In the long run, a nation's workforce cannot be paid more than the real value of what it is producing. Similarly, owners of capital plant and equipment cannot keep earning returns greater than the true value of the use to which these are put. Productivity is thus the critical link between how we work and how we live, and the mark of a national economy in robust health is a high and steadily rising level of productivity.

In the short run, of course, the link between the standard of living and productivity is not rigid. There are any number of ways that an individual worker, even one whose sole source of income is his (or her) job, can enjoy a standard of living that is unrelated to the real value of his output, at least for a while. He might, for example, persuade his employer to pay him more than his labor is worth. Or he might persuade a sympathetic aunt to lend him money. In the short run he will probably feel better off, but this cannot last. Eventually the aunt will have no money left to lend and may even ask to be repaid, or his firm will be driven out of business by a rival that is not overpaying its employees.

The same is true of a national economy. In the short run the population of a country would feel better off if, say, its government borrowed from abroad and the money was used to pay for increased domestic consumption. But eventually the bills would come due and living standards would have to decline as the loans were paid back. Another short-term fix would be for the central bank to reduce interest rates; the additional cash that would then become available to consumers and businesses would fuel an increase in demand and hence more rapid growth for a while. But if the economy were already operating at (or close to) full employment, this would not be sustainable for long. The increase in demand would lead to wage and price inflation and the central bank would be forced to raise interest rates again, thus terminating the growth spurt.

Productivity Growth and Economic Growth

There is a very close relationship between productivity growth and economic growth, but the two are not the same, and the distinction helps us to see why productivity is so fundamental to the standard of living. In the long run, an economy cannot grow any faster than the rate at which its underlying productive capacity grows. And if the existing supply of labor and capital is already being fully utilized, there are only two possible ways for productive capacity to grow. One is to add new inputs of labor and capital. The other is to increase the productivity of the existing inputs. Of the two, only productivity-driven growth has the potential to make everyone truly better off. Adding new workers would not in general increase the hourly wages of the existing workforce; indeed, it might even reduce them. Similarly, additional infusions of capital might reduce and certainly wouldn't normally increase the returns to existing capital resources.

Here, though, there is a complication. Increasing the amount of capital available to each worker (the capital/labor ratio) *will* generally increase labor productivity, whether or not the capital is efficiently used. Installing new, higher throughput machinery in a factory, for example, will usually raise the average output of the factory's workers. So, if the goal is to increase the living standards of workers, more investment in capital stock is an effective approach, even though it might also depress the returns to capital. (Some economists argue that very large infusions of capital, orchestrated and sometimes subsidized by governments, account for much of the rapid rise to prosperity of several leading East Asian economies.) It is partly for this reason that economists make a distinction between labor productivity and "multifactor" productivity, a composite measure of how efficiently an economy makes use of both labor and capital. The latter is a purer measure of productivity, in the sense that it is the better index of the combined efficiency with which both inputs are used. Put differently, multifactor productivity measures that portion of economic growth that isn't caused by increases in the amount of labor and capital inputs. Labor productivity, on the other hand, is the better measure of the potential *outcome* of the productive process for its human participants, because it is a measure of the income, or consumption, that can be promised as the reward for an hour of labor.

In the long run, a country cannot enjoy sustained growth in its standard of living unless it also achieves a healthy rate of productivity growth. As the MIT economist Paul Krugman has observed, "productivity isn't everything, but in the long run it is almost everything."[1] Or as his fellow economist William Baumol and colleagues put it, "for real economic miracles you have to look to productivity growth. . . . In terms of human welfare, there is nothing that matters as much *in the long run"* (emphasis in the original).[2]

Productivity Trends

For more than a century, productivity growth did in fact work a kind of miracle. Between 1870 and 1979, the output produced per hour of labor, averaged over the U.S. economy as a whole, grew at a rate of about 2.3 percent per year—enough to cause a twelvefold increase in productivity over this period. The result was a remarkable improvement in American living standards. Similar gains were achieved in many other countries, too. As the twentieth century draws to a close—a century in which industrial enterprise has transformed the unimaginable into the mundane countless times—there is much discussion of the negative impacts of these changes on our daily lives. But the vastness of these gains, their scale and their inclusiveness, bear reflection. Ordinary people throughout the industrialized world who are now in their seventies and eighties have experienced a transformation in living conditions that is without precedent in recorded history. At no other time has there been even a remotely comparable phenomenon.

But sometime in the early 1970s the rate of productivity growth in the United States declined sharply, and for the last two decades the U.S. economy has been stuck in low gear. Labor productivity during this period grew at a rate of about 1.1 percent per year, compared with nearly 3 percent per year during much of the 1950s and the 1960s (see Figure 2.1). Multifactor productivity also declined sharply. Changes of this magnitude might not seem like much, but over long periods they matter a great deal. If productivity had continued to grow by 3 percent per year over the last two decades, the U.S. economy would now be 50 percent more productive than it actually is, and it is a safe bet that some of today's most pressing economic problems would be far easier to deal with, and perhaps not even visible at all.

Some might argue that the productivity performance of the 1950s and 1960s is an unfair yardstick to use, since this was a period when

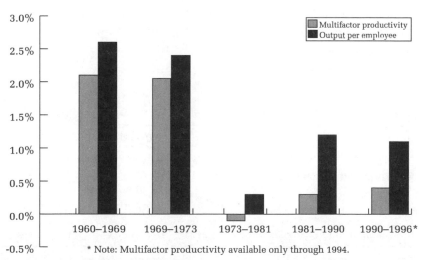

Figure 2.1 Two Measures of Productivity Growth: Nonfarm Business

Sources: Bureau of Labor Statistics, *Productivity and Costs*, released quarterly; *Multifactor Productivity*, occasional releases; both available on the World Wide Web at http://stats.bls.gov.

the economy was expanding unusually fast in order to satisfy the pent-up consumer demand that had been deferred first by the Great Depression and then by World War II. (Some of the gains during this period also arose from a rapid shift of labor out of low-productivity agricultural jobs—a card that had been more or less fully played by the 1960s.) But even if productivity growth during the past twenty-five years had only matched the previous century's *average* growth rate of 2.3 percent per year, instead of its actual 1.1 percent, American household incomes would still be about 35 percent higher than they are today—an increase of about $11,000 above the annual income of $32,000 of today's median household.

The causes of the productivity slowdown are still not well understood. Other advanced countries experienced something similar at around the same time, so the causes cannot have been peculiarly American. But the United States bears the dubious distinction of having had the lowest productivity growth of all the advanced industrial economies since then. More than anything else, it is this anemic productivity performance that accounts for the slow growth in the U.S. standard of living in recent years. Table 2.1 contrasts the economy's performance in the most recent decade (1984–94) with the higher-growth decade of the 1950s, and shows the impact of the productivity slowdown on wage growth. Another view of the close relationship between productivity growth and wage growth is presented in Figure 2.2, which compares the performance of several large industrialized nations in each domain. (The figure highlights how poorly the United States has done relative to the other countries during the last twenty-five years. Even so, the United States still has the most productive economy among this group.)

Table 2.1: U.S. Productivity and Wage Trends, 1950–60 and 1984–94

	1950–60	1984–94	
Average growth in output per hour (%/yr)	2.8	0.99	
Average growth in total compensation per FTE worker* (%/yr)	3.3	0.7	

	1950	1960	1984	1994
Total compensation per FTE worker*($1994)	14,487	20,645	29,015	31,070

*Total compensation per full-time equivalent worker consists of wage and salary income plus employer-provided fringe benefits.
Sources: Compensation data: Frank Levy, *Where Did All the Money Go? A Layman's Guide to Recent Trends in U.S. Living Standards,* Industrial Performance Center Working Paper, WP-96-008, MIT, July 1996; productivity data: U.S. Bureau of Labor Statistics.

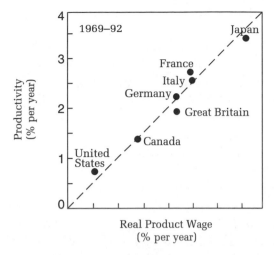

Figure 2.2 Changes in Productivity and the Real Product Wage, 1969–92

Source: Reprinted from Barry Bosworth and George L. Perry, "Productivity and Real Wages: Is There a Puzzle?" *Brookings Papers on Economic Activity*, 1994: 1, 332.

A lively debate on the accuracy of the U.S. productivity data is under way, with many asserting that the official statistics paint far too bleak a picture of the nation's productivity growth performance.[3] These productivity optimists argue that the method used to measure productivity is flawed. They complain that year-to-year increases in the nation's economic output—the numerator of the productivity ratio—are being systematically underestimated, which in turn creates a downward bias in the official figures on productivity trends. (A short note on the problem of productivity measurement is included as Appendix I of this book.)

Much of the argument centers on the difficulty of accounting fully for the economic benefits delivered to consumers by innovative new products and services, as well as improvements in the quality of existing products and services. An case in point is the ubiquitous automatic teller machine (ATM). Bank customers have derived great benefit from these machines since they were first introduced, yet the added convenience they deliver is not reflected in measured output.[4] A comprehensive accounting of innovation-driven quality and convenience gains from one year to the next is a heroic task that the productivity statisticians acknowledge is performed imperfectly. The productivity optimists point out that these measurement problems are especially acute in the service industries, which now account for the bulk of the nation's economic output, and that over long periods even a fairly small downward measurement bias would introduce a large cumulative error into the output statistics.

Some optimists go further, and assert that these measurement difficulties explain why the productivity figures have failed to pick up any evidence of a productivity rebound in the 1990s (see Figure 2.1). They claim that the absence of a rebound defies common sense, and that one only has to look at other recent trends in U.S. industry—the intensive downsizing and restructuring activity, the huge investments in new information technology, the dramatic improvements in the international competitiveness of U.S. firms, the surge in corporate profits, the combination of strong economic growth and low inflation, and so on—to see that there *must* have been a significant boost in productivity, whatever the statistics might say. Declared one leading Wall Street economist recently, "The numbers must be wrong; they must be understated. . . . There is no way we could have had the outstanding economic performance this country has had over the last couple of years if those numbers were remotely accurate."[5]

But this argument doesn't hold up very well on closer inspection. The problem of mismeasurement may well be serious, but it is not a new problem, so how could it suddenly have become so much more severe in the last few years? This would only be credible if those sources of productivity growth whose impacts are hardest to measure suddenly became much more important during this period. But there is little evidence that this is actually what happened.

Take the idea that the recent wave of corporate downsizing, whatever problems it may have created for laid-off workers, should at least have caused an improvement in productivity. In the first place, if there really was a gain from this source it is difficult to understand why it would not have been captured in the productivity statistics. But in fact it is more likely that no such improvement occurred. A 1994 survey of Fortune 500 companies by the American Management Association found that two thirds of the companies that had downsized between 1989 and 1994 did not achieve any productivity increases during the period of downsizing, and nearly a third of them reported that their productivity had actually declined.[6] Moreover, it is important to differentiate between the impact of downsizing on the productivity of individual firms and the impact on the economy as a whole. Even if all corporate downsizings yielded productivity gains for the firms that undertook them, the gains would only show up at the national level if (1) the employees whose jobs were eliminated had found new work in which they were at least as productive as before; or (2) they did not find new jobs at all (in which case their

labor would no longer be included in the denominator of the productivity ratio).

But neither condition seems to have held. Downsizing has not created new armies of unemployed workers; on the contrary, the unemployment rate has been falling steadily since the early 1990s. (The
ability of the U.S. economy to reabsorb laid-off employees into the
workforce quickly has been one of its great strengths.) On the other
hand, it isn't necessary to resort to the stereotype of laid-off auto
workers flipping hamburgers to recognize that the majority of downsized workers have not walked into higher-productivity jobs, either.[7]
Besides, we saw in the previous chapter that despite all of the publicity about downsizing, the recent rate of job displacement does not
seem to have been particularly high by historical standards, so one
would not expect to see an unusually large increase in productivity
from this source anyway, even if all the other requirements to produce one were in place.

What about the productivity gains associated with the remarkable
recent surge of investment in information technology—gains that the
official productivity figures almost certainly *do* understate? According to one estimate, spending on computers and peripheral equipment increased by an average of nearly 30 percent per year between
1990 and 1994—far outpacing all other types of spending. Shouldn't
such a large infusion of new investment have yielded a sizable boost
in productivity, regardless of what the statistics say? Not necessarily.
The latest wave of investment is not actually out of the ordinary.
Computer spending has been growing at a similar rate for the last
quarter of a century.[8] The argument that information technology has
been the cause of an unmeasured productivity surge in the 1990s
would therefore only make sense if there had been a sudden spurt in
the effectiveness with which the new technology was being used.
But is this really what has happened? To be sure, significant improvements have occurred (it would be astonishing if they had not).
But recent claims in the popular business press that the "productivity payoff" from information technology is finally here are surely
overdone.[9]

More to the point, for computers to have had a significant impact
on the nation's aggregate productivity performance, there would have
to have been enough of them to make a difference. Yet even today, despite the heavy spending, computers and peripherals still account
for less than 2 percent of the nation's net business capital stock.
Adding software, digital telecommunications equipment, and other

types of information technology might double this figure, but the total share of information technology in the economy is still quite small. According to one recent estimate, computers and peripherals added about 0.16 percentage points per year to the U.S. productivity growth rate between 1990 and 1994—*less,* in fact, than their contribution during the 1980s.[10]

The question of how well American industry is managing the risks and opportunities of information technology is an extremely important one to which we shall repeatedly return in this book. But much as industry marketers might like us to believe otherwise, the mere fact that spending on information technology reached unprecedented levels during the 1990s is not in itself proof that a pickup in U.S. productivity growth has occurred. As we shall see in chapter 11, there are indeed good reasons to be optimistic about the impact of information technology on productivity. But the case for optimism rests on developments that still lie largely in the future, rather than on existing evidence that we have somehow failed to detect.

To sum up, there are significant flaws in the method currently used to measure productivity growth. The official statistics almost certainly underestimate actual growth. The size of the measurement error is presently unknown, and could be considerable. But the uncertainty does not obscure the two most important facts about the nation's recent productivity performance: first, that productivity growth declined sharply in the early 1970s, to less than one-half the average growth rate during the previous century; and second, that there has been no significant improvement in the nation's productivity growth performance during the 1990s. In other words, the measurement uncertainties do not fundamentally alter the basic story told by Figure 2.1.

Trends in Living Standards

The productivity slowdown has had a predictably negative effect on American incomes, as both Figure 2.2 and Table 2.1 have already shown. But the story of what has been happening to U.S. living standards is more complicated than this. The economic experiences of individual Americans have varied considerably depending on the industry in which they work. Demographic factors such as age, educational background, gender, ethnicity, and geographical location are also important. As we shall see, these demographic variations are frequently shaped more by social choices than by economic ones. How well the nation produces—that is to say, productivity—determines how well we live on average. But much else affects how *differently* we live.

The best way to see what people in a particular demographic group have actually experienced is to follow the trend in their standard of living over time. Unfortunately, this is not what the majority of official government statistics actually do. Instead, they offer snapshots of a typical cross section of the population at different points in time. A good example of this sort of thing—and a good example of its pitfalls—is the report issued annually by the U.S. Bureau of Labor Statistics on the average hourly wages of American production and nonsupervisory workers. After correcting for inflation, this data series indicates that average wages in 1995 were 13.3 percent lower than they were in 1973. The obvious conclusion is that people are worse off today than they were twenty years ago. But there are several problems with this interpretation. One is that the number of women in this broad segment of the workforce increased much faster than the number of men during the past two decades. Since women were earning only 60–70 percent as much as men on average throughout this period, it would have been possible for the average wage of all workers to decline even if men's and women's wages were both increasing—simply because of the growing fraction of women in the workforce. The lesson is clear: year-to-year comparisons of the average earnings of all workers don't necessarily shed light on what individual workers are actually experiencing.

If one follows the earnings paths of different segments of the population over time, a mixed picture emerges. Some groups have slowly improved their position, others have lost ground, and still others are holding their own. Along some dimensions, income inequalities have declined. This is true, for example, of gender inequalities, as wage discrimination against women has become less pronounced. But the most striking trend has been the increase in the inequality of earnings between more and less educated workers.

The MIT economist Frank Levy has estimated the changes in average household income between 1979 and 1994 for four different types of two-parent families.[11] He found that families in which the husband was about forty years old in 1979 and had only a high school education saw essentially no increase in total household money income between 1979 and 1994 after adjusting for inflation. (Expressed in 1994 dollars, the average income for these families was about $48,000.) The husband's income actually fell by 16 percent during this period, despite the fact that he was presumably gaining skills and experience. The difference was made up by an increase in the wife's earnings—mainly the result of her spending more hours on paid work outside the home.

In contrast, families whose husbands were in the same age group but had a four-year college education experienced a 20 percent increase in total household money income between 1979 and 1994, from about $65,000 to $77,500 (in 1994 dollars). The biggest contribution to the increase came once again from the wife's earnings, which nearly doubled during this period (from $14,000 to $25,500). But in this case the husband's income increased too, though only by about 3 percent.

Younger families, in which the husband was about thirty years old in 1979, did somewhat better over this period on the whole. Once again, though, families with more educational qualifications again out-earned their less well educated counterparts by a widening margin.[12]

Levy's results thus confirm that economic conditions have increasingly been favoring those with higher educational qualifications, and that the earning power of men whose formal education stopped at high school has been deteriorating. The total household incomes realized by the families of these men held up only because their wives were working increasingly long hours outside the home. Obviously, the trend of wives contributing an increasing share of household earnings cannot continue indefinitely; about half of the women in this sample are already working close to full time. Moreover, the actual contribution of the second income earner to the family's standard of living is almost certainly overstated, because the official statistics do not account for the loss of unpaid housework and child care that occurs when the wife moves into the labor market (a loss that most often has to be offset by the purchase of commercial services).

For a different perspective on the growing education-earnings gap, we can compare the incomes of two-parent families in 1994 with their demographic counterparts in 1979. (This kind of comparison doesn't allow us to observe the earnings trajectories of particular groups of families, but it does capture general trends in the economy.) In 1979, thirty-year-old husbands with high school diplomas earned about $5,000 less than their college-educated counterparts, whereas in 1994 they earned about $11,000 less. (The difference is entirely due to the decline in the real earning power of the high school graduates; the earning power of college-educated husbands stayed about the same over this period.) When all other money income is included (mainly the wife's earnings), the gap between the high school and college-educated families rose from about $9,500 in 1979 to nearly $19,000 in 1994.[13]

The growing education-related earnings gap is an important contributor to what is becoming an increasingly unequal distribution of income across the American population. The U.S. Census Bureau recently reported that the income gap between the richest and poorest Americans is now greater than at any time since the end of World War II.[14] Figure 2.3 shows that the average income of the bottom fifth of American families (measured by income level) declined by about 17 percent between 1979 and 1993, while the average income of the top fifth increased by 18 percent. Keep in mind, though, that the income polarization trend shown by the figure is not just the product of changes in the workplace. Changes in the social structure of households have also played an important role. One such change is the rapid rise in the number of single-parent, female-headed families. On average, these families have very low incomes—many of the mothers are jobless, and even those with jobs find it hard to earn good incomes—and they are pulling the bottom of the family income distribution down. Another social change is the increasing tendency of the well-educated, highly skilled wives of well-educated, highly skilled men to enter the workforce, thus creating households with very high incomes. Figure 2.3 is therefore telling a larger story about income inequality in the United States than the fact that employers are prepared to pay relatively more for higher skills.

It is difficult to view these trends with equanimity. Yet the causes are complex and not fully understood, and the solutions are elusive. As already noted, social choices lying at least partly outside the economic realm have played a major role (the social acceptance of single-parent families, the acceptability of wives working outside the home). Moreover, even that part of the phenomenon that is attributable to the increasing divergence of individual earning power has complex roots and isn't solely a question of increasing returns to education. Indeed, even for workers in the same occupation and age group, and with the same amount of schooling, the gap between the highest and lowest paid has been widening.[15]

Several factors are thought to be contributing to the rise of earnings inequality. The growth of trade with less developed countries has forced some groups of low-skilled American workers into competition with large numbers of very low paid workers in these countries. In some parts of the United States, the wage and employment problems of native-born Americans at the low end of the pay scale have

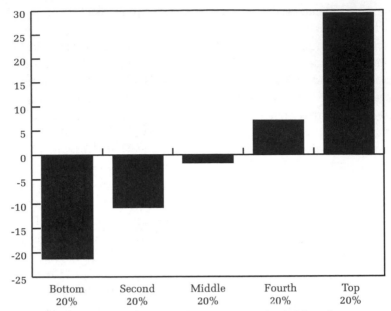

Figure 2.3 Changes in Real Incomes of Families with Children by Income Quantiles, 1978–80 to 1994–96

Source: Kathryn Larin and Elizabeth McNichol, "Pulling Apart: A State-by-State Analysis of Income Trends" (Washington, DC: Center on Budget and Policy Priorities, December 1997).

also been affected by the increased flow of low-skilled immigrant workers. The decline of the trade unions—which today claim only 10 percent of the private-sector workforce as members, down from 30 percent three decades ago—has also been a factor. Unions standardize pay rates among their members, and also induce nonunion firms to increase wages and benefits to avoid unionization. Another factor has been the decline in the real value of the minimum wage. Still another has been the slowdown in the growth of the supply of college graduates relative to less well educated entrants to the workforce. Finally, technological innovation in the workplace, especially growing computerization, is believed to be increasing the relative demand for more highly educated workers.

There is no consensus among the experts as to the relative importance of these factors. (One estimate, by the Harvard labor economist Richard Freeman, is shown in Table 2.2). Still less is there agreement on what, if anything, ought to be done to address the problem. An important part of any strategy is to provide better access to good education for everyone. (The biggest target of opportunity is the parlous state of much of the nation's primary and secondary public education system. Another very large target is the rising cost of a good college education, which is rapidly becoming prohibitively expensive even for many middle-income families.) Some analysts advocate additional, more interventionist measures, such as more social benefits and subsidized employment for the poor, increases in the minimum wage, targeted education subsidies, and more public-sector jobs, but others are strongly opposed to such measures.

Table 2.2: Estimated Causes of the Rise in U.S. Wage Inequality

	(%)
Changes in Labor Supply/Demand Due to World Economy	
Trade	
Immigration	} 15–20
Changes in Domestic Labor Supply	
Slower expansion of college	25
Changes in Wage-setting Institutions	
Decline in unionization	20
Decline in the real value of the minimum wage	5–10
Change in Labor Demand Due to Domestic Economy	
Technological change	25
Change in industry mix independent of technology/trade	5

Source: Richard B. Freeman, *When Earnings Diverge: Causes, Consequences and Cures for the New Inequality in the United States,* NPA Report 284, National Policy Association, Washington, DC, 1997.

Stronger productivity growth isn't, on its own, a solution to the problem of income inequality. In today's economy, a rising tide will not lift all boats. However, a more rapidly rising tide will certainly leave fewer boats stranded. What makes the problem of income inequality in America today especially troubling is the fact that so many of the working poor have been getting unambiguously poorer. In the worst case, a continuation of this trend would put the nation's democratic processes at risk. But even if that alarming scenario did not come to pass, a political backlash could well occur that would result in policies—trade protectionism, more corporate regulation, redistributive government spending and higher taxes to pay for it—that would make faster productivity growth even harder to achieve.

To summarize: over the last two decades the U.S. economy has delivered economic benefits to the American people that can best be described as mixed. Living standards have improved on the whole, but only slowly, and the rate of improvement seems if anything to have declined in recent years, despite claims of a productivity surge. Indeed, because much of the improvement has resulted from the movement of women into the workforce, a phenomenon that can only occur once, the rate of progress seems likely to decline further unless new sources of growth are tapped. Moreover, the benefits have been flowing disproportionately toward those with higher levels of education, leaving large numbers of semiskilled and unskilled workers and their families struggling, often unsuccessfully, to hold on to earlier gains.

It has been a lackluster performance: not the worst of times by any means, but not the best of times either. And to a working population sensing that the economy is on the threshold of rapid change, it is not a record to inspire much confidence. Such are the indifferent fruits of a quarter century of weak productivity growth.

Is Manufacturing the Exception?

One bright spot in the otherwise bleak productivity picture has been manufacturing. Productivity growth in manufacturing has far outpaced the economy's overall performance throughout the 1980s and 1990s. Indeed, as Figure 2.4 shows, the rate of manufacturing productivity growth has now pretty much returned to its pre-1973 level.

It is more than a little ironic that America's star productivity performer over the past decade should be the sector that has been most closely identified with economic decline. To compound the irony,

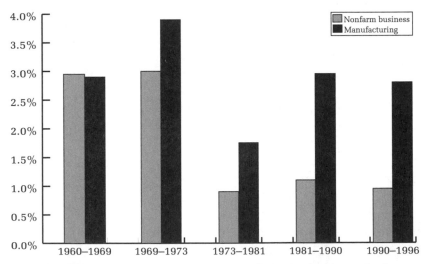

Figure 2.4 Average Annual Productivity Growth During Business Cycles (output per hour)

Source: Bureau of Labor Statistics, Productivity and Costs, released quarterly, available on the World Wide Web at http://stats.bls.gov.

these improvements in productivity, significant as they are, probably aren't the main cause of American manufacturing industry's improved international competitiveness. And in yet another twist, it is America's manufacturing workers who, despite their impressive productivity record, experienced perhaps the most adverse labor market conditions of any sector of the economy during this period.

Sorting out these apparent contradictions helps shed further light on the role played by productivity growth in the economy. Let's take them one by one.

First, in case there is any doubt that America's manufacturers have indeed become more competitive in international markets, we need only look at the export figures. Between 1987 and 1994, exports of durable manufactured goods increased at a robust 11 percent per year (compared with growth of industrial production of only 2.8 percent annually). Even more encouraging, the U.S. *share* of world manufacturing exports has also been rising. After a long period of decline, this increased from 14.1 percent to 17.4 percent between 1986 and 1992, and continued to increase subsequently.[16]

What accounts for the turnaround? Productivity improvements certainly played a role (as Table 2.3 shows, U.S. manufacturers actually widened their productivity lead over some other advanced economies during this period). But so too did the sharp decline in the value of the dollar against other leading international currencies. Over the course of a decade, the dollar's value fell 60 percent against the Japanese yen, from nearly 240 yen in 1985 to less than 100 in 1995. The dollar also fell 50 percent against the German mark over the same period. So which factor, productivity or the exchange-rate shift, was more important in strengthening American competitiveness? An exact answer would be difficult, but a simple calculation provides some useful clues.

Table 2.3: Labor Productivity in Manufacturing in OECD Countries

Value Added per Hour (U.S. = 100)							
	1960	1985	1995		1960	1985	1995
United States	100	100	100	Canada	69	84	70
Japan	19	69	73	Australia	51	57	52
West Germany	56	86	81	Netherlands	51	107	97
France	46	86	85	Sweden	50	87	90
Britain	45	60	70				

Source: D. Pilat, *Labor Productivity Levels in OECD Countries: Estimates for Manufacturing and Selected Service Sectors,* OECD Economics Working Paper 169, 1996.

Suppose a U.S. manufacturer was exporting a product for which the only required input was labor. The manufacturing cost of this hypothetical product in U.S. dollars would simply be equal to the wage rate divided by the productivity of labor, a ratio known as the unit labor cost:

Manufacturing cost (\$/unit) = $\dfrac{\text{wage rate (\$/hr)}}{\text{labor productivity (units/hr)}}$ = unit labor cost

The price at which the product could be sold abroad—let us say in Japan—would be:

Price (¥/unit) =
  unit labor cost (\$/unit) x (1 + profit rate) x exchange rate (¥/\$)

(These simple equations, incidentally, show why low-wage-cost countries don't dominate world trade. The industries in these countries also almost always have low productivity as well as low wages. The result is a unit labor cost that is as high or higher than those of the rich countries. And as economic development proceeds and productivity rises in the poor countries, real wages also tend to increase, so unit labor costs change much more slowly.)

Between 1986 and 1992, the export price of our hypothetical U.S. product would have declined at a rate of nearly 8 percent per year relative to the average price that manufacturers in the thirteen other leading industrial countries would have charged (assuming no change in profit margins). From the preceding equations, we can see that three factors could in principle have contributed to this result: faster productivity growth in the United States, faster wage growth elsewhere, and a decline in the exchange value of the dollar. It turns out that for this hypothetical example fully 75 percent of the relative price shift in favor of the U.S. product would have been the result of the falling dollar. (The widening U.S. advantage over Japan during this period would have been *entirely* due to the decline in the value of the dollar against the yen.)

For real products, of course, labor is just one of several cost components, and usually not the most important one. Still, U.S. manufacturers were concentrating heavily on cutting labor costs during this period, and the fact that even in this domain it was the volatile dollar rather than more aggressive downsizing efforts or tighter wage restraints that gave U.S. firms the bulk of their international cost advantage is a salutary reminder of the mutability of this advantage. As General Electric's chief executive Jack Welch observed, " . . . the U.S. must be ready to compete at 130 yen to the dollar. Until we are, we

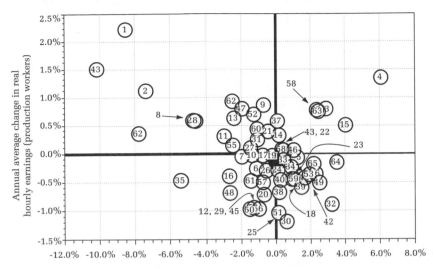

Figure 2.5 Trends in Manufacturing Employment and Real Wages, 1990–95

1 Aircraft	24 Handtools and cutlery	44 Newspapers
2 Aircraft parts	25 Household appliances	45 Ordinance
3 Automobiles	26 Household audio & video equip and	46 Paper and paperboard products
4 Automobiles—parts	recordings	47 Petroleum and coal products
5 Beverages	27 Iron and steel	48 Photographic equipment
6 Books and other published items	28 Leather and leather products	and supplies
7 Chemicals—agricultural	29 Logging and sawmills	49 Plastic products
8 Chemicals—industrial inorganic	30 Machinery—construction and related	50 Printed materials—n.e.c.
9 Chemicals—industrial organic	31 Machinery—farm and garden	51 Printing—commercial
10 Chemicals—other	32 Machinery—heating and cooling	52 Pulp and paper mill output
11 Clothing	33 Machinery—metalworking	53 Rubber products—n.e.c.
12 Communications equipment	34 Machinery—other industrial	54 Semiconductors
13 Computer and office equipment	35 Measuring and controlling	55 Shipbuilding
14 Dairy Products	instruments	56 Soaps, cosmetics and cleaners
15 Drugs	36 Meat and poultry products	57 Stone, clay, and glass products
16 Electric distribution equipment	37 Medical instruments and supplies	58 Sugar and confectionary products
17 Electrical equipment—n.e.c.*	38 Metal products—cans, forging and	59 Textiles—fabricated
18 Electronic components	stamping	60 Textiles—raw
(except semiconductors)	39 Metal products—heating, plumbing	61 Tires and inner tubes
19 Engines and turbines	and structures	62 Tobacco
20 Food products—n.e.c.	40 Metal products—n.e.c.	63 Toys, sporting goods, musical
21 Fruits and vegetables—preserved	41 Metal products—non-ferrous	instruments
22 Furniture	42 Miscellaneous manufactured products	64 Transportation products—n.e.c.
23 Grain mill and bakery products	43 Missiles—guided	65 Wood products, including millwork

*n.e.c. = not elsewhere counted.

delude ourselves if we think we are in control of our own fate."[17] When Welch made his comment the exchange rate was 105 yen, but the dollar has strengthened considerably since then (during the first half of 1997 it was trading in the 115–125 yen range).

The second apparent paradox of manufacturing performance is illustrated in Figure 2.5, which shows that even as manufacturing productivity and competitiveness have improved, employment and wages for production workers have been falling in many industries. From a manufacturing worker's point of view, the place to be on this chart is in the northeast quadrant: industries there are generating both wage growth and employment growth. But the figure shows that between 1990 and 1995 only a handful of industries were located in that quadrant, and that the great majority experienced either wage declines or net job loss or both. For the manufacturing sector as a whole, average wages and employment both declined slightly during this period.

Such results might seem to contradict the claim that productivity is "almost everything." If productivity really was almost everything, how could manufacturing wages have declined even as manufacturing productivity was growing briskly? And doesn't the decline in manufacturing employment confirm the worst fears about productivity growth—that it puts people out of work?

There isn't a very satisfactory answer to the first question. About the most that can be said is that the wage picture for manufacturing workers has at least become progressively less bad over the past two decades—in line with the trend in productivity performance.[18] As to why wages have failed to increase recently despite strong productivity growth, several of the factors mentioned previously as contributors to increasing earnings inequality may have played a role here, too, including the effect of low-cost overseas labor and the decline in the strength of the unions.

The answer to the second question—doesn't productivity growth inevitably put people out of work?—is a resounding no. The critical distinction here is between short-term, local effects and long-term, economywide impacts. In the short run, efforts to raise productivity may indeed result in significant local job losses. In the long run, both economic theory and the great weight of empirical evidence indicates that the opposite is true: productivity growth and job growth go hand in hand. During the last century, when, as we have seen, productivity increased more than tenfold, so too did the size of the U.S. labor force. The economy was finding ways to absorb vast numbers of new workers even as it was was generating spectacular advances in productivity. In fact, the productivity gains were essential to this accomplishment. By reducing costs and prices, and raising real wages and profits, their effect was to create higher real incomes, which raised the demand for goods and services, which in turn fueled the demand for new workers.

This period of growth was anything but tranquil, of course. Whole industries and occupations were wiped out in the course of it. But for every economic activity rendered obsolete, a newer, bigger, and more productive one grew up. For every job lost, more than one was gained—though often so remote in both function and location that the connections went unseen. A hundred years ago, one out of every two American workers was engaged in the task of feeding the American population and the majority of them worked on the farm. Today, although the total number of jobs related to food production and distribution is much larger, these account for only about one seventh of the employment base, and only about 4 percent of them are actually farming jobs. There are now as many lawyers, bankers, scientists, and accountants involved in bringing food to our tables as there are farmers.[19]

A similar cycle of productivity gains and job displacement unfolded decades later in manufacturing. Just as many farmworkers displaced by the agricultural productivity revolution migrated to the cities and found jobs in manufacturing, more recently many displaced manufacturing workers have found employment in the service sector. There is a quite widespread belief that the disappearance of large numbers of blue-collar jobs in manufacturing foreshadows the disappearance of manufacturing industry altogether. But it would be no more accurate to write off manufacturing today than it would have been to write off the American food industry a century ago, or for that matter to have concluded that because coachmen were a vanishing breed the transportation industry must be in decline, or that the disappearance of the telegraph operator must mean the end of the telecommunications sector. It is true that the U.S. manufacturing workforce has shrunk by 1 million workers since 1980, and at 18.5 million is now no bigger than it was in 1950. But since 1950 the nation's per capita expenditures on manufactured products have increased threefold in real terms, and even since 1980 have grown by nearly 30 percent—hardly a picture of a sector in decline. Indeed, despite all the talk about the United States becoming a "postindustrial" or service economy, for the last twenty-five years personal expenditures on durable manufactured goods have actually been increasing at a faster rate than expenditures on services, albeit from a smaller base.[20]

To be sure, almost all of the economy's net job creation during this period has come in services. But even in manufacturing attractive new jobs have been created, especially in more highly skilled and better-paying occupations like design, engineering, marketing, logistics management, and product development (these jobs are not included in Figure 2.5).

The word is getting around. In 1989, MIT introduced a new master's program in manufacturing engineering and management. The program has been highly successful, attracting some of the best management and engineering students at the institute and placing them in challenging and well-paid jobs in the manufacturing sector upon graduation. Similar programs have been introduced at other universities.

The recent pattern of employment in the manufacturing sector seems likely to persist for the foreseeable future: fewer but more highly skilled production jobs; new opportunities at the professional level; and a total workforce that might or might not be smaller but that certainly will be more productive and prosperous—not a bad prospect, especially in comparison with the doom-laden scenarios of just a few years ago. It is a measure of how far perceptions have evolved that many service firms are today looking at leading manufacturers with new interest, as paragons of renewal and competitiveness and as pioneers in managing the challenges of international competition, information technology, and globalization—challenges that have now, of course, spread to large parts of the service sector.

In Part II, we examine five cases of industrial renewal in closeup. In contrast to the top-down perspective of this chapter, we will focus on the patterns of behavior, the decisions, and the achievements of business enterprises and the individuals who work in them. In each case, we will ask three questions: Which factors have been most influential in bringing about recovery and renewal? What obstacles have prevented the lessons from these successes from being applied more broadly? And do these lessons, whatever they teach us about the past, also contain the key to achieving higher overall growth in the future?

PART II

*Five Routes
to Renewal*

CHAPTER 3

Something Borrowed, Something New: The Regeneration of the U.S. Automobile Industry

Throughout the 1980s, the U.S. motor vehicle industry was almost everyone's favorite example of the failure of American management. It was an easy target for the critics. Already by the beginning of the decade the stereotype of the arrogant and myopic American boss, out of touch with the customers and complacent about the competition, had become one of Detroit's best-known and least-admired products. And as the industry's woes deepened during the 1980s, the attempts of its leadership to shift the blame to others—the government, the unions, the Japanese, even its own customers—garnered less sympathy than scorn.

The facts were widely known. The American manufacturers had missed the turn in the market toward compact and subcompact cars during the 1970s. They had stuck to their historically profitable "family-sized" vehicles, stubbornly insisting that Americans did not want small cars and refusing to believe that the Japanese could progress beyond their reputation for making "tin cans on wheels." It was a spectacular misjudgment, and it opened the door to what later became a flood of competitively priced, high-quality Japanese imports in every segment of the U.S. market, eventually including high-end, luxury vehicles. As the decade wore on, Detroit's competitive weaknesses in quality, design, and the introduction of new technological features became increasingly evident.

Moreover, the Japanese seemed to have invented a distinct organizational alternative to the traditional American system for manufacturing automobiles. The so-called lean production system appeared different in almost every respect from the old mass production model that Henry Ford, Alfred Sloan, and their successors in Detroit had pursued over the decades to such great effect. And by the mid-1980s it was clear that the lean approach, originally developed for the particular circumstances of the Japanese domestic market, worked well in America, too. Irrefutable evidence on this score was provided by the so-called transplants—the automobile assembly factories that Japanese manufacturers had begun to establish in North America. Staffed with American workers, these Japanese-managed plants quickly surpassed the productivity and quality performance of the U.S. manufacturers' factories, and even approached the performance levels of their sister plants in Japan. A 1989 survey conducted by the MIT International Motor Vehicle Program revealed just how far the American industry had fallen behind. The survey showed that the average U.S. auto assembly plant was now only two thirds as efficient as its counterparts in Japan. In the face of such evidence, the attempts by Detroit's leaders to pin the blame for their plight on others seemed less and less credible. By the late 1980s, the U.S. auto industry was facing a stark choice: Catch up with the Japanese, or else.

The prognosis was not encouraging. As the new decade began, the three American automakers faced huge financial losses. General Motors alone lost an astounding $30 billion between 1990 and 1992, and the once unthinkable idea that the world's biggest automobile company might actually go under no longer seemed so far-fetched.

Today, the picture could hardly be more different. The fortunes of the American auto industry have taken a dramatic turn for the better. Perhaps most remarkable has been the resurrection of Chrysler. Chrysler, with its notoriously stodgy product line, had been the weakest of the Big Three during the 1980s, its most recognizable asset the blustery salesmanship of its chief executive, Lee Iacocca. But though Iacocca's forceful personality had helped the company through earlier crises, it could not solve Chrysler's fundamental problem: a lack of competitive products. Indeed, by 1991, Chrysler could no longer even claim to be a bona fide member of the Big Three, having fallen to fifth place in U.S. car sales, behind Honda and Toyota. Yet within three years, riding on a wave of innovative and attractive new vehicles, the company had increased its share of the U.S. market by 50 percent, and by the end of 1993 was reporting record earnings and the largest operating profits of the three American manufacturers. General Motors and Ford also announced respectable earnings that year, the first time in almost a decade that all three firms had been profitable. And after years of losing ground to the Japanese, the American industry finally began recapturing a significant share of the domestic market. Emblematic of the recovery was Detroit's domination of the "light truck" segment (which include minivans and sport utility vehicles), the product category that has accounted for essentially all of

(Bars show car sales; light truck sales shown in background area graph)

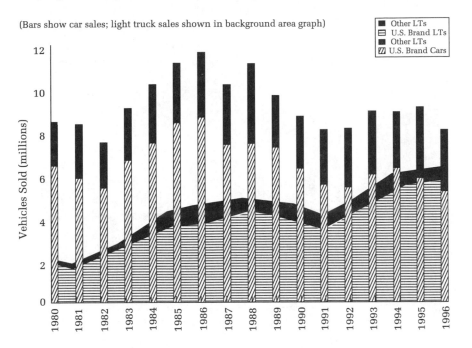

Figure 3.1 U.S. Car and Light Truck Sales by Brand Country, 1980–96

Source: Ward's Automotive Yearbook (various years).

the growth in the U.S. market since the early 1980s (see Figure 3.1). "Back on the Fast Track," proclaimed a celebratory cover story in *Time* at the end of 1993.[1]

Meanwhile, the leading Japanese carmakers were confronting the unpleasant and—for them—unfamiliar reality of falling sales and profits both at home and overseas. (Figure 3.2 compares the recent profit performance of the American and Japanese producers.) After a decade of high praise around the world, it was suddenly no longer uncommon to hear suggestions that Japanese managers might be losing their touch. A 1994 article in the *Wall Street Journal* bemoaned the dull styling and the sameness of the latest generation of Japanese cars. At about the same time, in a development that symbolized the changing competitive situation, Ford announced a plan to send three senior executives to help rescue Japan's financially troubled Mazda Motor Corporation, in which Ford is a major shareholder. (Two years later, Ford took overall control of the still-struggling Mazda, and a Ford employee was installed as president.)

What accounts for this unexpected reversal of fortunes? Partly it

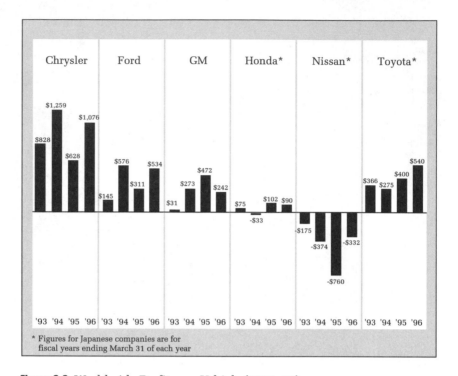

Figure 3.2 Worldwide Profits per Vehicle (1993–96)

Sources: Automotive News, 3 June 1996, p. 3; *Detroit Free Press,* 12 June 1997, p. 1.

was the result of macroeconomic forces that had nothing to do with the carmakers themselves. The vigorous economic recovery in the United States after 1992 helped spark Detroit's resurgence even as the Japanese carmakers were struggling with the worst recession to hit Japan in decades. Meanwhile, the sharp rise in the value of the yen had badly eroded the price competitiveness of Japan's exports of cars and parts, and was forcing the Japanese to move more and more of their production offshore. (In 1995, Honda became the first Japanese producer to build more cars overseas than in its Japanese factories.)

In contrast to these macroeconomic explanations, popular accounts of the turnaround in the industry have tended to dwell on the strategies and personalities of its top managers. The car industry, of course, has produced its fair share of larger-than-life characters, beginning with the towering figures of its earliest years—Henry Ford and Alfred P. Sloan among them. Later, such colorful individuals as the garrulous Mr. Iacocca of Ford and Chrysler, GM's imperious Roger Smith, and the flamboyant and risqué John Z. DeLorean all received wide coverage in the business and general press, with at least one of them—the unfortunate Mr. Smith—the subject of a very unflattering movie. The present generation of leaders in Detroit is understated by comparison; even so, their every move and utterance is minutely scrutinized by the business press for signs of competitive shifts.

But just as a purely macroeconomic perspective, focusing on things like business cycles and exchange-rate movements, misses much that is most interesting about recent developments in the industry, so too do accounts that concentrate exclusively on the personalities involved, on managerial triumph and defeat, on who is up and who is down. The real story is much richer and more complex than either of those interpretations allows. It is a story about how great business enterprises are shaped by and in turn shape the social, political, and competitive environment in which they operate. It is a story about what happens when industrial "best practice" crosses national borders, and about how it is often reinterpreted in the process. It is a story about how managerial aspiration is sometimes abetted, sometimes thwarted, but always constrained by the surrounding network of institutional and social practices. Above all, it is a story about the continuing evolution of vast systems of production, and about how even supposedly mature industries are capable of reinventing themselves.

It is this larger story of industrial renewal that is the subject of this chapter. As we shall see, one of the most striking changes of all has been the transformation of the car manufacturers into global enterprises. Today, all of the world's leading auto firms are producing in many countries around the world, sourcing parts and components from many more, and trying to sell their products almost everywhere. With the foreign content of U.S.-brand vehicles increasing, and Japanese "imports" now as likely to have been made in the United States as abroad, cars are losing their national identities faster than most consumers realize. For U.S. auto workers, however, the effects of globalization are more transparent. A decade ago, it was inexpensive, highly efficient Japanese production workers who seemed to pose the main threat to their livelihoods. Today, the threat comes from many countries, and from factory workers who are not unlikely to be working, directly or indirectly, for their own firm.

The Spread of Lean Production

Let's pick up this story in the mid-1980s. Already by then the extreme vulnerability of the American industry to foreign competition had been amply demonstrated. In one disastrous two-year period at

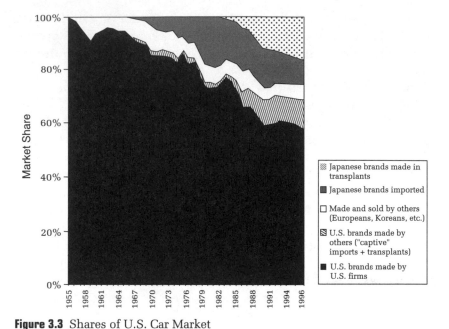

Figure 3.3 Shares of U.S. Car Market

Sources: Automotive News Market Data Book and *Ward's Automotive Yearbook* (various years).

the end of the 1970s, the share of imports in the U.S. automobile market, which had been gradually increasing throughout the decade, suddenly jumped from 18 percent to more than 28 percent. Following a brief respite the import share once again surged, and by 1987 nearly one in three of all new cars purchased in the United States were imports (see Figure 3.3).

The Japanese were by far the biggest factor in the wave of imports, accounting for more than 70 percent of foreign vehicles sold in the United States in 1987, and the remarkable rise of the Japanese car industry spawned a host of theories that sought to account for its success. Many turned out to be either only marginally relevant or simply wrong. But as time went on and a more detailed account of what the Japanese were really doing began to emerge, it became clear that their success did not stem from a "magic bullet" or a simple formula, but rather was rooted in a complex web of interdependent and mutually reinforcing organizational practices that pervaded the entire system of automobile production. The breadth and internal coherence of this set of practices led to its characterization as a distinct "system" in its own right—distinct, that is, from the prevailing approach to the organization of auto production in the United States (and, for that matter, in Europe). The MIT researcher John Krafcik coined the term "lean production" to describe this system, and a few years later the term—and the concepts for which it stood—gained wide attention with the publication of *The Machine That Changed the World,* the 1990 report of MIT's International Motor Vehicle Program.[2]

Why "lean"? Partly because the Japanese practitioners of this way of manufacturing required far fewer resources than their American counterparts—fewer people, less space, smaller inventories, less capital investment, and so on. But the lean production system in fact offered much more than just a reduction of waste. It also delivered higher-quality vehicles, an organizational capacity for continuous improvement, and fast, flexible responses to changes in the market.

The lean production approach was initially developed by the Toyota Motor Company in the years following World War II, and many in both Japan and the West still know it as the Toyota Production System.[3] At its core, the Toyota system is about paring down inventories—both finished product and material in process—nearly to zero. Some of the benefits of doing this are obvious. Smaller inventories mean lower costs; there is no need for expensive warehouse space to store materials, parts, and finished vehicles, and financial carrying costs are also much reduced. But the logic underlying Toyota's drive to eliminate inventory went far beyond those direct savings. Inventory is a buffer against things that go wrong. If a defective part is discovered in the middle of a production run, it can be discarded and another pulled out of inventory with scarcely any delay. If a machine breaks down, a buffer stock of what it normally produces can be worked down while repairs are conducted. As inventories are reduced, the system thus becomes more vulnerable to disruptions caused by equipment breakdowns or quality problems.

By relentlessly driving inventory down, Toyota was deliberately imposing increasingly high levels of stress on its system. But where others saw only the prospect of chaos, Toyota perceived a crucial benefit. Removing the safety net provided by inventory would quickly reveal the weak points in the process—the unreliable machine on which much else depended, a critical bottleneck in the flow of work, the badly performed welding process, and so on. And once identified, these problems could be quickly solved. Indeed, they would have to be, otherwise the entire factory would grind to a halt. Afterward the ratchet would be tightened again. Inventory would be further reduced, and new weak points would be discovered and eliminated. In this way, the overall performance of the system would be continuously improved. The effect was to impose a rigorous discipline on the manufacturing process. A high level of reliability and a high level of quality were an absolute necessity because the alternative was intolerable. Early detection of failure was therefore critical. Even more important was the prevention of failure in the first place.

When a businessman staring failure in the face brightly asserts that "we don't have problems, we have opportunities," it is easily dismissed as Panglossian nonsense. Yet that is precisely the idea behind the inventoryless production concept. Toyota's increasingly formidable car factories showed that this was not an idea to take lightly, although for a long time that is exactly what Toyota's counterparts in Detroit did. Their view of inventory was quite different, and was conditioned by a particular view of the benefits of economies of scale. To gain competitive advantage, you had to produce in very large volumes. Each step in the production process was therefore carried out on a very large scale. Huge machines dedicated to the production of high volumes of a single component or the execution of a single process were linked together in a vast, loosely coupled chain. To exploit the scale economies, the factories had to be kept running as close to full capacity as possible. Interruptions had to be avoided at all costs. To protect against the disruptive effects of strikes or equipment breakdowns or material shortages, buffers were built in at numerous points. Inventories accumulated everywhere—at the front end, at the back end, and in between the various stages of production. This was costly. But the costs were deemed to be outweighed by the benefits of being able to keep producing and hence fully exploit those all-important economies of scale.

But the direct costs of inventory were not the only disadvantage of this strategy. There were two others of which the American manufacturers were less well aware. The existence of all those buffer stocks practically guaranteed a lack of knowledge of what was really happening around the system at any given time. The lights in the factory may have been on, but the operators and their supervisors were mostly in the dark. A defective part might go undetected for weeks or even months while it sat in inventory before entering the next stage of the process. In the meantime, tens of thousands of identical parts with the same defect might have been produced, all of which would then have to be discarded. Second, and perhaps even more important, the heavily buffered system bred a tolerance of failure. Defects might not be welcome, but they could be accommodated. Perfection was not sought out because it wasn't needed.

As Columbia University professor Charles Sabel has pointed out, the central feature of inventoryless production compared with the standard mass production approach is that it generates a rich flow of precise and targeted information about what is happening everywhere throughout the production process. But it was not enough just to generate this information. Toyota also had to design an organization that could make prompt and effective use of it. And the company's production workers were a critical part of the solution. They were, quite literally, on the front line of the production system, and in principle could respond quicker than anyone else if problems arose there. But if this solution was to succeed in practice, the production workers would need the skills and knowledge that would enable them to recognize problems—in fact, preferably to anticipate them before they arose—and then to devise an effective course of action to deal with them. They would also need enough authority to be able to act without having first to jump through a time-wasting set of bureaucratic hoops. The most visible manifestation of the greater responsibility accorded these workers by Toyota—and certainly the most shocking to many Western managers—were the cords that were positioned above each workstation on the company's production line. By pulling the cord, any worker could stop the line if he—until very recently it was always a "he"—discovered a problem that could not be solved immediately.

All of this was quite alien to the Big Three. For decades, they had pursued a strategy that systematically bred initiative and knowledge out of the production workforce. This, too, had its own logic. Indeed, the strategy had been so successful that for a long time no one thought to question it. Early in the history of the industry a shortage of skilled workers and the high wages they commanded had led the architects of Detroit's manufacturing processes to divide up the work on the shop floor into very narrow, well-defined, and simple jobs that could be carried out by relatively unskilled workers with little training. To ensure that the work was done properly, lots of supervisors and "indirect" workers were also needed—quality checkers, repairmen, rework specialists, and the like. But for the chronically cyclical auto industry, this division of labor provided an important benefit. Large numbers of unskilled workers could be laid off during downturns without fear of losing knowledge valuable to the firm. In a curious echo of the principle of interchangeable parts, whose realization by Henry Ford at the turn of the century had made the mass production of automobiles possible, the workers themselves had now become interchangeable.

Toyota followed a different path. Amid the ruins of the postwar

Japanese economy, skilled labor was one of the few commodities not in short supply. The template for what today would be referred to as Toyota's human resource management strategy was laid down in the late 1940s in negotiations with the company's union. (The latter, a more radical and militant entity than it is today, incidentally drew indirect support for its effort to win concessions from Toyota from the American occupation authorities.) The resulting agreement—which set the pattern for labor relations throughout the Japanese auto industry—included several key guarantees for the employees. One was an assurance of lifetime employment. Another was pay scales that ramped up steeply with seniority. Compensation was also tied to company profitability through a bonus system. The effect was to promote a strong sense of mutual commitment and alignment. When workers hired on, the expectation was that they would stay. The seniority-based pay increases helped build loyalty. And the workers could easily see the connection between their own prospects and the fortunes of the company.

Toyota for its part grew to think of its workforce not, like Detroit, as a variable cost to be minimized, but rather as a fixed asset, whose value to the company would be progressively increased if the company kept investing in the development of its employees' knowledge and skills. The system of bonus payments also provided Toyota with an important source of flexibility. In the event of a downturn, the company could cut its costs by cutting bonuses without having to lay people off. The benefits of this scheme, subsequently widely adopted in Japan, were clearly seen during the severe recession of the early 1990s, which—despite a few well-publicized counterexamples—did not lead to wholesale abandonment of the lifetime employment principle.

So, in the very different context of Toyota' factories, giving line workers the opportunity to stop the line was not at all the radical step that it appeared to be in American eyes. And there was nothing unnatural about the idea that workers would look for ways to improve their own performance and that of their coworkers. The important thing was to provide them with the necessary tools. One such tool was statistical process control. The idea here was that as long as the manufacturing process kept running within an envelope of allowed operating conditions, the operator could have a high—and, in a statistical sense, precise—level of confidence that the products of the process, the materials or parts or systems, would meet their specifications. It was a way of "getting it right the first time," and in due course it largely replaced direct monitoring of finished product for quality.

Monitoring key process parameters, charting trends over time, and interpreting these trends as called for by statistical process control demands a certain sophistication on the part of those who practice the discipline, and Western visitors to Japanese factories were surprised to see production workers engaging in these tasks. In American car factories, checking for quality was a separate function, to be carried out by specialists, and it was many years before the idea took root that production workers trained in statistical techniques could be responsible for their own quality. When it did, the benefits matched those that Toyota had realized years before.

Another aspect of production that differentiated Toyota's system from the American approach concerned the organization of work on the factory floor. Whereas American factories were organized around individual workers and their narrowly defined tasks, the Japanese discovered that the more effective organizational unit was the work team. Each team was given the responsibility for dividing up the work in its area as it saw fit. The teams managed themselves, and so the need for at least one supervisory layer was eliminated. As in the American plants, each task was highly standardized. But each member of the team was expected to be able to do everyone else's job, and so typically could operate a range of machines. This was not just teamwork for its own sake. The kind of flexibility it provided was essential if plants operating without the security of buffer stocks were to be capable of responding rapidly to changes in demand or to unexpected developments on the shop floor. Nor was the idea of relatively autonomous teams restricted to the factory. The same decentralizing principle extended throughout Toyota's production system, including, as we shall soon see, its process for developing new cars.

To achieve a zero inventory production process, Toyota could not afford to stop at its own factories. Fully 70 percent of the parts and components that went into its cars were purchased from other companies. Its ability to run its factories smoothly with minimal inventories was therefore critically dependent on the supply of high-quality parts, delivered "just in time." So Toyota needed to pay as much attention to its suppliers' performance as to its own factories. The logic in both cases was the same: Push the system to its limits and the weak points will reveal themselves, eliminate them, then push some more.

Like its labor relations, Toyota's relations with its suppliers were characterized by mutual vulnerability: each was in a real sense a hostage to the other's performance. The suppliers were often almost totally dependent on Toyota for their business. Toyota for its part risked being shut down if one of its suppliers failed to deliver on its performance commitments. For this arrangement to have any chance of working, cooperation was essential, and both Toyota and its suppliers had to disclose a great deal of information about their operating practices. Once again, the contrast with Detroit could not have been plainer. There, the prevailing atmosphere was one of distrust and suspicion, and loyalty was rare on either side. The goal of the car companies was to extract the best (i.e., the lowest-cost) terms from their suppliers, while at the same time minimizing their own vulnerability to supplier incompetence or malfeasance.

While Toyota would routinely share detailed product and process information with its suppliers, and encouraged them to consult fully among themselves, the American firms provided as little information to their suppliers as possible, partly for fear that whatever they disclosed would be leaked to their own competitors, with whom the suppliers were typically also doing business. For their part, the suppliers discouraged customer interference in their operations, taking the position that "my plant is my business." It is difficult to quantify exactly what is lost in this kind of arm's-length transaction, but a simple counterexample, drawn from a "Japanese" setting, is suggestive. The supplier in this case realized that a part it had contracted to produce would never actually be seen by anyone looking at the finished vehicle. Yet the customer's blueprint specified that the part should be polished. The supplier, knowing how the part would be used, argued successfully that the polishing was unnecessary, and was able to eliminate this unnecessary step.[4]

Supply contracts in the United States were typically drawn up only for short periods, and manufacturers would often shift their orders to lower-cost suppliers at short notice. This meant that the suppliers had little incentive to invest their own funds in improving productivity. As they saw it, most of the benefits would probably have to be given up to their customers in the form of lower prices the next time the contract was put out to bid. Moreover, they might lose the business anyway, leaving them with no way of recouping their original investment.

In Japan, supplier switching was a much rarer event. One reason was the *keiretsu* structure of the Japanese industry, which linked the auto companies to many of their principal suppliers through equity holdings. But even without the constraints of joint ownership, the large investments that customer and supplier typically made in learning about each other tended to discourage switching. According to an official at the NUMMI assembly plant, Toyota's joint venture with General Motors in California, the factory would need two years to switch its rolled-steel supplier, because that was how long it would take a new supplier to develop a working understanding of the subtle interactions between NUMMI's stamping press and the chemical composition of the steel.

Toyota's subcontract pricing practices were designed to reward superior performance, again in contrast with the traditional American approach. The company needed its suppliers to meet constantly improving performance standards, and so periodically negotiated new target prices with them based on the historical rate of improvement in the industry. If a supplier exceeded its price target, the contract guaranteed that it could capture a share of the benefits.

Not everything about Toyota's supplier relations was sweetness and light. The suppliers were organized in a pyramidal structure, with Toyota, at the pinnacle of the pyramid, dealing directly only with a fairly small number of large suppliers in the first tier. These in turn subcontracted with a larger number of second-tier suppliers, who in turn dealt with a third tier, and so on. Many of the firms at the bottom of the pyramid were small, family-owned job shops. The mutually beneficial practices that pervaded the upper regions of the pyramid—long-term contracting, joint incentives for continuous improvement, lifetime employment for employees, and the like—usually did not extend to the bottom. There, wages and benefits were typically a good deal lower, with fewer guarantees that good performance would be rewarded. Some critics have suggested that the entire system was built on the backs of these small businesses at the bottom of the supply pyramid. That is an exaggeration. Nevertheless, it was, and remains, a system with two faces.

Toyota's system was adopted to varying degrees by all of the major Japanese car manufacturers, and accounts for much of their remarkable rise to global dominance during the 1980s. As their success grew, even the inward-looking leaders of America's car companies were forced to admit that it was not a fluke. Voices began to be heard urging change along Japanese lines. But the hierarchical, adversarial culture that had congealed around Detroit's business practices presented a huge obstacle. Resistance and denial were rampant, even when the superiority of Japanese performance was impossible to ignore. So it was that General Motors, still in the early 1980s the richest car company in the world, set out along a different path. Instead of trying to reform the workplace Toyota-style, GM embarked on an enormous program of investment in factory automation. Over the next few years the company spent tens of billions of dollars fitting out its factories with the latest high-technology manufacturing equipment—robots, automated guided vehicles for moving parts around, and so on. GM's program was widely interpreted as an attempt to deal with its fractious and unproductive workforce not by building skills, loyalty, and flexibility, but rather by cutting it back and reducing its influence.

What did GM achieve from all of this? Remarkably little. The company underestimated how difficult it would be to get the new technology to work at all, and some of its plants encountered serious start-up problems. But even after these were solved, GM discovered that its high-technology factories could not match the productivity performance of the much less technologically advanced Japanese transplants. Moreover, the company seemed unable to find a way to exploit the much-vaunted flexibility of its new technology. The new factories were operating in much the same way that their predecessors had—each one dedicated to the production of one or two models and styles. By the end of the decade, despite its colossal investment, GM's share of the domestic market had slipped by almost one third, from 50 percent to 34 percent, and with sales still declining the company found itself burdened with a large and costly surplus of production capacity. Many assembly-line workers had been laid off, but above them GM's vast, stifling management bureaucracy remained largely intact. Few could disagree with the verdict of one leading academic GM watcher: "one of the most remarkable failures in U.S. economic history."[5]

Chrysler, lacking GM's enormous capital reserves, did not attempt anything like the modernization program of its much bigger rival. For a long time, in fact, the company did very little to respond to the Japanese challenge. Of the Big Three, Ford was the first to attempt serious organizational reform along the lines of the Japanese model. Ford had been badly shaken in the early 1980s by one of the worst financial crises in its history. For a time its survival was in doubt. The company's leaders, instead of returning to business as usual, had used the crisis to mobilize support throughout the organization for far-reaching structural and cultural changes. Many of the specific ideas for change came from Mazda. After acquiring its sizable stake in the Japanese company in 1979, Ford assiduously studied its practices.

Unlike General Motors, Ford decided that its future depended on achieving greater employee involvement in decision making on the factory floor. The company negotiated new labor agreements with the United Auto Workers (UAW) Union. The contracts included profit-sharing provisions as well as guarantees of job and income security for its more senior workers. In collaboration with the union, it established a new Human Resources Center to offer training and retraining to its employees. At the plant level, committees jointly run by the company and the union were established to explore ways of improving operational effectiveness and employment security. And the company drastically scaled back its supplier base, and began to work much more closely on quality, training, and design with those that were left.

Ford's efforts soon began to bear fruit. By the second half of the 1980s, it had clearly established itself as the most efficient American producer, and indeed its manufacturing plants were performing at a level comparable to many Japanese factories (though not yet the best ones). But the competition was not standing still, and as the rest of the American industry began following Ford's lead in applying the techniques of lean production to their manufacturing plants, the Japanese firms were preparing the next phase of their assault on the lucrative American market. Not content with dominating the small car segment, they began moving upscale. Led by Honda, whose luxury Acura nameplate was introduced into the United States in 1986, all the major Japanese manufacturers began targeting the more profitable "high-end" market segments.

As the wave of attractive and price-competitive new Japanese cars rolled across the American market in the second half of the 1980s, it became evident that the Japanese manufacturers were raising the competition in the industry to a new plane. On top of their manufacturing cost and quality advantages, they had now developed an ability to introduce new models into the market at a rate that no Western company could match. Professor Kim Clark and his colleagues at the Harvard Business School estimated that a typical new car development project carried out in Japan during the mid-1980s required a third less time to complete and only about half the engineering manpower of its counterpart in the United States.[6] This meant that the Japanese firms were about eighteen months "closer" to their customers when they started a new development project. And when combined with their inherently more flexible production system, it also enabled them to field a wider range of models in the marketplace and to replace them twice as frequently as their American competitors.

The Limits of Lean

Armed with this formidable array of weapons, the Japanese continued to strengthen their position throughout the world, and especially in the United States. By 1991, the Japanese share of the U.S.
market had reached 30 percent (including transplant production).
The Japanese seemed unstoppable. Where would it end? Yet even as
Toyota and Honda and the others continued to rack up sales, there
were signs that the American manufacturers were finally beginning
to make significant inroads into the Japanese position. Ford, the most
persistent and dedicated of the American firms in its pursuit of lean
manufacturing, had gradually increased its share of the U.S. market
from 20 percent to 25 percent in the decade following its near collapse. The company received a welcome symbolic boost in 1992
when its popular Taurus displaced the Honda Accord as the nation's
best-selling car. In fact, Ford had five of the ten biggest selling cars in
America that year. (Even so, the company was not yet out of the
woods; its losses for the year approached half a billion dollars.)

Ford's successes could reasonably have been anticipated—the just
rewards of a decade of hard work. More surprising was Chrysler's
reemergence in the early 1990s. We shall return to this story shortly.
In the meantime, however, as the American position was improving,
strains were beginning to develop in the Japanese industry, and for
the first time there were suggestions that the famed Toyota system
might have reached the limits of its effectiveness. The booming Japanese economy (at least through 1991) and the declining appeal of blue-
collar jobs to Japanese high school graduates had contributed to an
increasingly acute labor shortage in the industry. The children of the
bubble economy, newly affluent and less inclined than their parents
to slog it out on the factory floor, were opting instead for more comfortable office jobs. Dismayed commentators pondered the meaning
of this for the country's future. Companies began looking for new
ways to attract and retain workers.

Some of the smaller suppliers, which had always had more difficulty than their bigger, brand-name customers in attracting employees, began importing blue-collar workers from Southeast Asia and
elsewhere. Worried managers wondered how the principles of the
decentralized workplace—of self-managed teams, worker responsibility for quality, and so on—could be adapted to workers who were
generally less well trained and often barely literate in Japanese. And
though the number of foreign workers was much smaller than in Ger-

many, say, or the United States, the social overtones of this practice nonetheless resonated widely in culturally homogeneous Japan.

The bigger firms began putting greater emphasis on making their factories more attractive both to current and to future workers. Returning from a visit to Toyota's newest assembly plant in southern Japan, MIT professor Charles Fine noted several such measures that had been taken there. Not only was the noise level far lower than the usual thunderous roar in such factories—Fine likened the sound of the stamping presses in the plant to that of "cannons being fired under a mountain of pillows"[7]—but the assembly line had been redesigned to make most of the jobs easier for women and older workers to perform. Japanese industry specialists began advocating the need for a "post-lean" system of production, which would strike a new balance between the traditional objective of customer satisfaction and the increasingly important goal of employee satisfaction.

Other features of the lean production system were also coming under stress. With hundreds of suppliers making several deliveries a day, severe traffic congestion around some factories was bringing supposedly "just-in-time" parts shipments to a standstill, with delivery trucks turning roads into parking lots. As one Japanese commentator put it, public thoroughfares were being transformed into private warehouses. The situation became so bad that the government began calling on companies to reduce the frequency of their deliveries in an attempt to ease the traffic problems.

An alternative strategy for dealing with both the congestion and the labor shortage was to shift production overseas. By the late 1980s, this had become an imperative for two other reasons: the ruinous effects of the rapidly strengthening yen, which was forcing up Japanese car prices in its export markets, and the gathering forces of protection in those markets. Both problems could be partly alleviated by locating new production capacity in those same markets. But this created other difficulties. With factories spread out across the world, the Japanese manufacturers obviously could not rely any longer on their traditional domestic suppliers for "just-in-time" deliveries. Sourcing too heavily from their domestic supply base would in any case be very costly (the effect of the strong yen) and would also fan the protectionist flames that the transplants were supposed to ward off. On the other hand, indigenous parts suppliers were unlikely to be able to match the quality levels of the Japanese supply industry, at least not without herculean training and acculturation efforts.

Then, in 1992, the recession set in at home. Like all recessions, this one exposed vulnerabilities that had been hidden during the boom years, and what had once been seen as key sources of competitive strength for Japanese carmakers suddenly started to look like weaknesses. Overwhelming the competition with rapid model turnovers and a dazzling variety of products may have been an effective way to build market share, but it was also very costly. Financing a constant stream of new development projects, no matter how well coordinated, is an expensive proposition. The sheer complexity of maintaining a rich product mix also carries a heavy cost burden. During the heady years of Japan's bubble economy in the late 1980s, these effects were partly obscured by the artificially low cost of capital, which overstimulated corporate investment across the board. But as Japanese asset and financial markets collapsed in the early 1990s, the cost of capital suddenly soared, and with it the real cost of developing new vehicles.

There were also signs that the Japanese auto companies might have misread their customers. In their move upmarket, they began equipping even rather ordinary cars with such sophisticated engineering features as four-wheel steering, traction control, all-wheel drive, and the like. These were impressive technical achievements, but to average buyers the performance enhancements they brought were often not worth the extra cost. Was this just an accident of timing? Were the Japanese carmakers simply unlucky that the arrival of many of these innovations coincided with the onset of the worldwide economic downturn in the late 1980s? Or had their great success caused them to forget what had made them so successful in the first place? Was the over-engineering problem symptomatic of a broader tendency to stop paying attention to their customers?

Enter Neon

As these doubts swirled around the Japanese car industry, Detroit was converting many of its own vast army of doubters into believers. Some of the strongest new believers were Chrysler's shareholders. This long-suffering group saw the value of its stock rise more than fivefold between January 1992 and the end of 1993, the best performance of any stock in the Standard and Poor's 500. From 1991 to 1994, the company increased its market share by 50 percent, while simultaneously becoming the most profitable American producer, a distinction that it continues to enjoy.

What accounted for Chrysler's success? Many factors contributed, including a vigorous cost-cutting program, increased production efficiency at its manufacturing plants, and a chastened and more pragmatic United Auto Workers Union. But the most important thing was that for the first time in years Chrysler had begun making cars that people wanted to buy, and to do so, moreover, at a time when demand for new cars in the United States was starting to pick up strongly. After twelve years during which it developed only one new car platform, starting in the early 1990s the company introduced five in a period of twenty-four months. The new models included the stylish mid-range LH series, the first to embody Chrysler's innovative "cab-forward" design, and the Neon, a low-cost subcompact car expected to have a several thousand dollar price advantage over its Japanese rivals. The affable-chic announcement of its arrival ("Hi Neon!" said the advertisements) was the occasion for much hand-wringing in Japan. Dubbed "the Japanese car killer" in Japan's press, Neon was clearly a highly competitive American product in a segment of the U.S. market that many thought had been permanently ceded to the Japanese.

How did Chrysler achieve these surprising results? Developing a new car is an extremely large and complex task. A single project can cost billions of dollars, take several years to complete, and typically involves thousands of people, including electrical and mechanical engineers, stylists, marketing specialists, manufacturing experts, and purchasing agents. Coordinating all of these people and functional areas so that everything is completed on schedule and efficiently; ensuring that the end product is responsive to customer needs; preserving space for creativity so that the product stands out from the crowd: all of this adds up to one of the toughest management assignments in the industry.

It was a task at which Chrysler and the rest of the Big Three had not shone for years. Coordination typically meant passing on the job from one department to the next—"throwing it over the wall." Styling was separate from engineering and marketing was estranged from both. The state of relations between the departments was summed up by a GM engineer's assessment of his own company's marketing department: "GM has a total lack of knowledge when it comes to its customer. If the marketing guy is big and fat and smokes cigars, you can bet the car will have a tilt wheel and a huge ashtray. It won't matter if the car is targeted at women who don't smoke, the marketing guy will only think of himself."[8] Manufacturing was typically brought in at the end, and if, as was very often the case, the design posed insoluble manufacturing problems, it was simply tossed back over the wall to be reworked, with attendant delays and disruptions.

Imaginative design withered in such conditions. Every now and again there would be an efflorescence of interesting design ideas. But mostly the process resembled the way things usually work in Hollywood's big film studios, where layer after layer of people are to be found whose only apparent role is to say no. The products of such a process, whether cars or movies, almost always have a look-alike feel to them, and the most talented people tend to become fed up and leave. Hollywood still has no serious external competition, and neither did Detroit when it began to develop these habits. But when things changed and the automakers failed to notice, they found themselves in serious trouble.

For Chrysler, the trouble had nearly been fatal. Much smaller than either GM or Ford, Chrysler had always been the most vulnerable of the three to economic downturns. The two oil price shocks of the 1970s, the ensuing recessions, and the rise of Japanese imports had driven the company nearly into bankruptcy in 1980. CEO Lee Iacocca was a highly visible pitchman for his company's cars and later for his own autobiography. He enjoyed better luck with the latter, which became his publisher's biggest-selling book of the decade. But with the notable exception of its pioneering minivan product line, success eluded Chrysler. And though it never again came quite as close to the brink until the 1990–91 recession, it continued to lose ground throughout the 1980s, unable, despite Iacocca's boosterism, to shed its image as a dull, low-quality plodder.

There were occasional attempts to spice up the product line. In 1987, the company acquired the exotic Italian sports carmaker Lamborghini as part of a major diversification program that also included the purchase of American Motors Corporation (from Renault), three rental car companies, a defense contractor, and a manufacturer of corporate jets. On the whole these investments performed with little distinction, and a number were subsequently resold (including Lamborghini). Later, even Iacocca admitted that they had been a distraction, diverting resources and management attention from the central task of strengthening Chrysler's core business.

But Chrysler did extract something of value from these acquisitions. When the company bought American Motors in 1987, the latter had already begun development work on the Jeep Grand Cherokee, a major remodeling of its successful Jeep Cherokee line. To minimize disruptions, Chrysler decided to leave the Grand Cherokee development team intact and keep it separate from the rest of its engineering organization. The results compared very favorably with anything it had been able to accomplish previously with its own, strongly functional development organization, in which each department, separately financed, had performed one step in the sequence.

With this experience in hand, and further fortified by the results of an intensive two-year benchmarking study of Honda, the leader among the Japanese in deploying cross-functional product development teams, Chrysler embarked on a fundamental reorganization of its own product development process. Taking the concept of product team autonomy much further than either Ford or GM, the company eventually created five autonomous "platform teams," each devoted to a different product line (small cars, large cars, minivans, Jeeps, and trucks). Each team consisted of all of the people needed to design and produce a new car, including manufacturing, purchasing, finance and marketing professionals, hourly manufacturing workers, and even representatives of key outside suppliers, as well as engineering and design staff. The new structure broke down the traditional departmental barriers that had plagued Chrysler for years. Indeed, save for a few specialist units, the functional departments were done away with entirely.

Hardly any bureaucracy has since been allowed to remain above the platform teams, either. Each team is presided over by a top executive, giving it a voice at the highest levels of the corporation. The teams receive precise instructions from the top regarding key vehicle specifications—engine power, weight, fuel economy, and so on—as well as the total budgets for the projects. Once these specifications are set, however, the teams are free to work out how to meet them, with little or no interference from senior management. In return for this increased authority, the platform teams are also held accountable for their performance. And since the members of the team are judged by the overall success of the vehicle, rather than their particular piece of it, they are more inclined to find ways to cooperate with each other.

Developing a new car involves a dense and intricate web of negotiations between different constituencies. The stylist may demand a particular set of contours as an attention-getter, or to preserve the design "theme" of the car. But can door panels with the desired shape be stamped out in the manufacturing plant without wasting too much steel? Can a hinge be designed that will allow the doors to swing properly? Will the door panels offer enough impact resistance to satisfy the safety standards? If each of these issues is dealt with separately and sequentially, between people with strong departmental affiliations whose main motivation is not to lose an argument to another department, an enormous amount of time will be wasted in futile wrangling. The platform team approach finesses this. And because representatives of all of the functional areas are involved early on in making key design decisions and trade-offs, the risk of costly last-minute changes is much reduced. The early involvement of manufacturing has been particularly important. So, too, has the participation of the suppliers. As Chrysler president Bob Lutz has pointed out, "If you don't get the cost down on the 70% of the vehicle that you buy outside, what you do in the assembly plant is almost irrelevant."[9]

Under its traditional parts procurement strategy, Chrysler's engineers would design the part, send out the drawings, and wait for the lowest-cost bid. The company would reopen the bidding every year or so to try to drive down prices further. Today, that process has been reversed. Chrysler uses "target pricing" to determine component prices, working backwards from the price that it thinks consumers will pay for a finished vehicle to figure out how much it can afford to pay for individual parts. The goal is not always to find the lowest-cost source of supply, because a part that costs more may lead to savings elsewhere, for example, in ease of assembly. Chrysler's purchasing agents are aware of these possibilities because they are in constant touch with the engineers and designers on the platform team. The company chooses one or two key suppliers for each component early on, and asks them to design it themselves. Because the suppliers are allowed to use their own knowledge in the design, and because many engineering tasks can be performed simultaneously rather than sequentially this way, lower costs and shorter lead times usually result. And because parts are typically sourced for the life of the product, and the contracts provide the suppliers with financial incentives to find cost savings over time, supplier performance keeps improving. The company and its suppliers no longer look upon their relationships as a zero-sum game. According to Chrysler's procurement chief, Tom Stallkamp, supplier-generated ideas were saving Chrysler $1.7 billion per year by 1995.[10]

These were the innovations that lay behind Chrysler's flurry of new product introductions in the early 1990s. Neon has been one of the most impressive launches yet, with a reported total development cost of about $1.3 billion (compared with an average of $5 billion for new platform developments at Ford and GM), and a lead time from product concept approval to the start of production of just thirty-one months—comparable to the best Japanese performance. Indeed, in key respects, Neon is better. Nissan's president noted recently that "[w]here we would have five parts to make up a component, the Neon has three. Where we would use five bolts, the Neon body-side was designed so cleverly it only needs three bolts."[11] Such disclosures were big news in Japan. Returning from a short visit to Tokyo, my Industrial Performance Center colleague Professor Suzanne Berger reported hearing more about Neon in a week there than she had ever heard in the United States. Still, Neon's launch wasn't trouble-free. Quality problems—Chrysler's old nemesis—forced a recall, delaying consumer acceptance of the new car.

A Different Kind of Car, A Different Kind of Company

Neon was conceived as Chrysler's bid to recapture the small car market from the Japanese. But by the time it was introduced, the small car with the best reputation in America was not an import at all. It was General Motor's Saturn. The still-unfolding story of Saturn has aroused intense interest. This is not surprising, for the scenario is irresistible: the giant GM, crippled by a devastating and possibly terminal disease, hatches a new offspring on which it lavishes loving attention—perhaps the last chance for the old dinosaur to revive its fading bloodline. Against all the odds, the vigorous young upstart tosses away the old rulebook, reinvents the business of making and selling cars, jolts the Japanese, and quickly builds an almost cultish devotion and loyalty among customers and dealers.

A stirring tale, to be sure, but also one that demonstrates the enormous difficulty of changing huge corporate organizations from the inside. In fact, GM's decision a decade ago to establish Saturn as a separate corporation was a deliberate attempt to get around this problem. The Saturn manufacturing plant and corporate headquarters were located at Spring Hill, a tiny rural community in the rolling hills of Tennessee, and the company was set up so as to be as independent of the rest of GM as possible, with its own development, manufacturing, marketing, and distribution operations. The much-maligned Roger Smith, GM's chief executive at the time, in this case cannot fairly be accused of lacking either vision or audacity. At the outset, few outside Saturn expected the new venture to be able to compete successfully against the Japanese in the small car segment, while those on the inside recognized that nothing less than a revolution in GM's traditional practices would be needed to bring this about.

The heart of the Saturn organization is an experiment in labor-management cooperation that is unprecedented in the modern history of U.S. industrial relations. At every level of the corporation, from the president on down, the local United Auto Workers Union is a full partner of management in decision making. The union, in effect, is co-managing the business. The company is run by teams. Everybody in the organization is a member of at least one of them. Decisions are made by consensus (defined to occur when the team is 70 percent comfortable with the decision and 100 percent committed to its implementation). On the shop floor, self-managed work teams are responsible for their own scheduling, budgeting, hiring, and training. Everyone, including production workers, is on salary. Everyone spends at least 5 percent of his or her working hours in classroom training. There are no time clocks, no privileged parking spaces, no private dining rooms. To increase flexibility, the number of job classifications has been reduced to a minimum; indeed, all production workers are assigned to a single class. Visitors to the plant find it impossible to distinguish between managers and union members. They work side by side, make decisions together, and wear the same clothes (no ties). The blurring of roles between management and labor is not quite complete, but when the distinction reappears it sometimes does so in unexpected ways, such as the occasion when the Saturn employees wore wore black armbands in protest at what they saw as a weakening of management's commitment to quality.[12]

How successful has the Saturn experiment been? The answer depends on who is judging. As a business venture in its own right, Saturn has had some remarkable achievements: by 1994 the best customer satisfaction rating of any American car, and the best of *all* basic small cars, domestic or imported. Saturn dealers are currently tied with Toyota's luxury Lexus distributorships for first place in customer satisfaction. Their trademark no-dicker, no-hassle sales technique has made the rest of the industry sit up and take notice. And today, just a few years after its launch, the Saturn nameplate is synonymous with high quality and dedicated service.

But GM's shareholders have yet to earn a significant return on the $5 billion the company has invested in Saturn since its formation. Financially, at least, Saturn has not been all that "lean." Moreover, if the company is to have a decent chance of making healthy profits, new production capacity will have to be added and the product line extended upmarket to retain the relatively youthful Saturn customer base as it ages and begins shopping for roomier cars. But as Saturn has emerged as a direct competitor for scarce capital resources, there have been rumbles of opposition elsewhere in the GM organization, where resentment has long simmered over the special treatment accorded the newcomer. Some of GM's big car divisions have also worried that a move upmarket by Saturn would mainly serve to cannibalize their own markets, something that already seems to have happened to Chevrolet in the small car segment.

The other main criterion for judging Saturn is its effectiveness as a prototype for change in the rest of GM. Here, again, the evidence is mixed. GM officials, still in the midst of a prolonged struggle to cut costs and transform old and inefficient ways of doing things, speak of "Saturnizing" the corporation. But progress to date has been quite slow. Many GM employees remain skeptical about Saturn, arguing that the real reason for its success is the billions that have been spent on it. With that kind of money, they suggest, anyone else would have succeeded, too.

Another big obstacle to Saturnization is the national UAW organization. More conservative than the Spring Hill local, the UAW headquarters remains suspicious of many of Saturn's shop-floor innovations. The union leadership has said that this is not a model that it wants to see replicated. Its dislike of Saturn was made quite clear during the 1992 strike against GM, when it deliberately tried to shut Saturn down by targeting strike action at the plant's UAW suppliers—an area of extreme vulnerability at Spring Hill given the plant's heavy reliance on "just-in-time" deliveries. (The national UAW organization had pushed hard to maximize the participation of UAW shops when Saturn's suppliers were first being selected.)

So, all in all, despite the division's remarkable achievements, the jury is still out on Saturn, both as a business venture in its own right and as a catalyst for change. As time goes on, Saturn and the rest of GM will surely come to look more alike. But whose traits will dominate? Will Saturn become just another GM car division? Or will the rest of the corporation be made over in Saturn's image?

The answer to this question became a bit clearer recently, when GM decided to go ahead with a larger Saturn model. The new car will be a modified version of one of GM's European products. But to the disappointment of the Saturn workforce, the car won't be made at the Spring Hill factory. Under heavy pressure from the national UAW, GM elected instead to assemble it in Delaware, at a plant that was facing closure. For its part, the UAW agreed to GM's plan to cut production costs by outsourcing a much larger percentage of the new car's components to non-UAW factories, many of them in Canada and Mexico. Clearly, both GM and the UAW had larger fish to fry in reaching this agreement. But it remains to be seen whether the labor-management comity at Spring Hill will survive these developments, and indeed whether Saturn's famously loyal American customers will be willing transfer their affections to an "international" car that no longer has any connections to Spring Hill.

The Outlook

Over the past decade the American car industry has made major strides in the fundamentals of manufacturing performance. When researchers for the MIT International Motor Vehicle Program recently repeated the worldwide survey of automobile assembly plants they had first conducted in the late 1980s, they discovered that Japan's big lead in productivity had eroded in the intervening five years (see Table 3.1). Indeed, though the Japanese industry as a whole remains the world's most efficient, there is no longer much difference between the leading factories in the United States and in Japan: the best Big Three plant in America requires about fourteen hours of production labor to assemble a car, compared with about twelve hours at the best Japanese plant (and thirteen hours for the leading Japanese transplant in North America). As Table 3.2 shows, the gap is closing in quality performance, too.

Table 3.1: Automobile Assembly Plant Productivity (hours per vehicle)

	1989	1994
Japanese-owned plants in Japan	15.6	14.7
Japanese-owned plants in North America	22.6	18.2
Big Three plants in North America	24.1	20.0
European plants	37.8	26.5
Plants in emerging economies	34.4	29.6

Source: John Paul MacDuffie and Fritz Pils, Wharton School, cited in *Automotive News,* 4 March 1996, p. 1.

Table 3.2: Automobile Assembly Plant Quality
(Owner-reported defects per 100 vehicles in the first three months of use)

	1989	1994
Japanese-owned plants in Japan	63	55
Japanese-owned plants in North America	68	56
Big Three plants in North America	86	63
European plants	91	61

Source: John Paul MacDuffie and Fritz Pils, Wharton School, based on data from Initial Quality Survey of J. D. Power & Associates, cited in *Automotive News,* 4 March 1996, p. 1.

Yet the Japanese carmakers continue to lead in key aspects of manufacturing practice, and after several difficult years the Japanese industry is showing signs of recovery. Although some smaller producers have been seriously and probably irreversibly weakened by the recent recession and the yen's rapid rise, the bigger firms, particularly Toyota and Honda, have emerged leaner and stronger than ever. With several competitive models in the pipeline, they are preparing a new assault on the U.S. light truck market—long the most profitable segment for the American automakers. Moreover, the exchange rate has recently been shifting in favor of the Japanese firms. In the seventeen months after reaching its peak in April 1995, the yen lost nearly 30 percent of its value against the dollar, a decline estimated to have reduced the cost in dollars of bringing a Japanese-built car to the American market by nearly 25 percent—enough to wipe out all of the hard-won gains in production efficiency achieved by the American carmakers over the previous several years.[13] Since then, the yen has fallen still further against the dollar.

The nature of competition in the industry is likely to change considerably in the coming decade. All the world's leading car firms have signed on, more or less, to the model of manufacturing pioneered by Toyota, and as lean production techniques take root around the world and high quality becomes the *sine qua non* of doing business everywhere, new frontiers of competition will open up:

Internationalization: The fastest growth in car demand is occurring in the emerging economies of Latin America and, especially, Asia, where most of the world's population lives and where a burgeoning middle class has money to spend. Japanese, European, and American carmakers are all focusing heavily on these potentially huge new markets even as many of the host governments attempt to build up indigenous car industries. (GM's near-term goal is to have half of its production capacity located outside the United States.)[14] In Asia, the Japanese producers dominate the competition, with a market share of 90 percent in some countries. Although all three U.S. firms have begun to invest heavily in new production capacity in the region, they have much ground to make up.

All the leading carmakers are moving to establish integrated global production networks. Many see opportunities to realize new manufacturing efficiencies and cut product development costs by organizing around global product platforms using common systems and components. Others are electing to forego some of these scale economies in favor of serving the particular needs of local markets. Whatever their configuration, these new production networks will pose unprecedented problems of coordination.

New Technologies: A typical luxury car today contains about $3,000 worth of electronics (compared with a steel content of less than $1,000). One leading industry executive described the modern automobile, only half jokingly, as a "computer on wheels." The use of electronics has been growing by 12 percent per year recently, and new applications are continually being introduced, many in support of greater safety. Antilock braking systems are now standard on many cars, and electronic traction control is becoming increasingly widespread. A new generation of "intelligent vehicle" technologies is under development, including computer navigation (already available in fairly primitive versions), real-time traffic information, collision avoidance radar, intelligent cruise control, and night-vision systems. In the materials field, advances in composites and aluminum processing are opening up new possibilities to use these lighter-weight alternatives to steel. Further out on the horizon is the prospect of alternatives to the conventional internal combustion engine itself. Investment in the development of all-electric vehicles is now substantial, and there are also promising new developments in hybrid systems combining combustion or turbine engines with electric motors. Many of the best technological ideas come from outside the car industry, and the ability to identify, select, and exploit these external advances will become an increasingly important source of competitive advantage for the carmakers.

Environmental Impact Minimization: Environmental regulations affecting recycling, fuel economy, and exhaust emissions will continue to have a major influence on the technical direction of the industry. Today, about 75 percent of an automobile by weight is recycled, and this figure is likely to increase as policymakers seek to mitigate environmental impacts and address resource conservation concerns. The German government recently introduced a requirement for carmakers to take full responsibility for disposing of their vehicles at the end of their useful life. This will likely promote design changes making recycling easier. The German government has also imposed stricter controls on automobile emissions than in most other countries. The historical pattern of countries around the world eventually ratcheting up their regulations to follow the environmental pacesetters is likely to persist. Thus, although manufacturers often complain about the imposition of more stringent requirements, some firms will exploit the stimulus created by new regulation to gain competitive advantage both at home and in markets around the world.

New Product Development: All the leading firms are trying to speed up the process of developing new cars. New computer technologies for rapid prototyping, electronic simulation, and integrated design and manufacturing will yield major time savings. Some firms already claim to have cut the time it takes to bring a new car from conceptual design to market to about eighteen months—less than half the current industry average.

Customer Service: As differences between manufacturers in product quality and reliability diminish, firms will increasingly compete with each other to make the process of buying a new car a more efficient and more satisfying experience for the customer. Electronic communications systems linking dealers to assemblers and suppliers will make it possible for customers to order cars with customized features and take delivery within a few days, rendering today's sprawling lots full of new cars obsolete. Ford's chairman Alex Trotman recently predicted that "the great battleground between successful and unsuccessful manufacturers will be the process of selling, financing, maturing, servicing, warranting, and very importantly, disposing of a vehicle bought from a manufacturer."[15]

   A final possibility should also be mentioned. For almost the entire history of the automobile industry, Ford, GM, Toyota, and the other big assemblers have dominated the value chains to which they belong. Upstream, they have dominated the parts and components suppliers. Downstream, they have dominated the distribution channels, and in a fundamental sense they have dominated the end users too. It is the car companies who have decided what products should be produced; it is they who have determined which new ideas should be introduced to the marketplace, and on what schedule. In the future, however, these value chains may become a good deal more decentralized. The most innovative ideas are increasingly likely to come from elsewhere—from electronic component suppliers, from dealers, from financial service providers, and so on. And as advances in information technology make it possible to couple systems of production more closely to customer needs, the customers themselves will come to play more of a role as partners in the product development process. How will the car companies deal with these shifts? Will they seek to preserve their traditionally dominant position in the value chain? Or will they encourage or at least acquiesce in the emergence of "flatter" structures? For the U.S. car companies, the coming challenge to the traditional vertical structure of the industry could turn out to be as destabilizing and invigorating as the competitive struggle with their Japanese rivals has been over the past decade.

The U.S. motor vehicle industry recently celebrated its one hundredth birthday, and from afar it seems as slow-moving as most centenarians—sluggish demand growth, a declining domestic employment base, and a cast of leading firms that hasn't changed in decades. But when viewed in closeup, as we have done here, the industry presents a very different aspect. Technologies, production methods, markets, and products are all in rapid flux. It is a picture that in many ways more closely resembles an emerging industry than the stereotype of an aging sector whose best days are behind it.

CHAPTER 4

Salvation from Outside: The Triumph of Electric Steel

There is a paradigmatic quality to the story told in the previous chapter. An American industry grows smug and fat on its own success, gets caught unaware by more efficient, innovative, and quality-conscious Japanese competitors, and is almost driven out of business, but scrambles back, unashamedly borrowing the Japanese business practices that had earlier almost destroyed it.

It might be thought that the U.S. steel industry also fits this pattern. Like the auto industry, it too suffered catastrophic reverses in the 1970s and 1980s, and now it too is enjoying a kind of renaissance. But there is no parallel here to the rejuvenation of Detroit's Big Three. Big Steel—the oligopoly that dominated the American industry for much of the century—is in improving but still delicate health, its ranks decimated by plant closures and bankruptcies, and its survivors, firms like Bethlehem Steel and U.S. Steel, plagued by high overhead costs and a massive, multi-billion-dollar legacy of unfunded pension and benefit obligations to tens of thousands of retirees. The recovery in the steel industry has been led instead by outsiders, a new group of much smaller, highly entrepreneurial American firms with names like Nucor, Oregon Steel, Chaparral, North Star, and Birmingham Steel. And their core innovation—a transformation of the traditional approach to steelmaking that in many ways is more radical than the shift to lean production in the auto industry—was not borrowed from the Japanese or from anybody else. On the contrary, it was developed independently in the United States, albeit with the help of foreign technology.

The smaller, highly competitive American firms have been taking market share away from Big Steel and foreign producers alike. Under pressure from the newcomers, the big American mills have improved their performance greatly, even managing to turn a profit in the latest recovery. But in a further twist, Big Steel's chances of renewal may actually have been harmed by its earlier attempts to emulate its Japanese rivals: at a critical point the big U.S. firms looked overseas for inspiration when they should have been looking in their own backyard.

Why did a group of upstart American companies emerge out of nowhere to make the running in the steel industry, when nothing of the sort ever seemed likely in the auto sector until now? How did the entrepreneurial capital and managerial talent required to pull off such a feat find its way into this most unglamorous and seemingly moribund of industries? Steel, after all, is the very antithesis of the high-growth industries normally associated with successful start-ups: steel consumption in the United States has been either stagnant or declining for two decades, with engineered plastics and other new materials encroaching on key segments of the market; steel imports have been rising; highly competitive new sources of supply are coming on line in low-labor cost countries like South Korea, Taiwan, and Brazil; and prices have been depressed by a global surplus of production capacity, the result of decades of intervention by governments to prop up their domestic industries. Not exactly hospitable terrain for entrepreneurs, one might think.

The answer to these questions lies in a series of technological innovations that turned the traditional scale economies in the industry upside down. The key innovation was the development of electric arc furnaces that could produce molten steel from recycled scrap metal, an abundant commodity in mature industrial economies like the United States. In a traditional "integrated" steel mill (so called because all of the principal stages of steelmaking are incorporated in the plant), the primary feedstock is iron ore. The ore is first smelted with coke in a giant blast furnace to produce pig iron. In the next stage, the impure pig iron is refined in a second large furnace, where it is converted to molten steel. Then, in the downstream part of the mill, the steel is cooled, rolled to the required shape, and further treated to produce the desired combination of strength, corrosion resistance, and finish.

The new electric furnaces simplified the steelmaking process. As shown in Figure 4.1, in the new kind of mill the entire front end of traditional steel plants was eliminated, including the expensive ore-smelting stage, as well as the ore-handling facilities and the big ovens needed to convert metallurgical coal to coke. Moreover, the new electric mills could be built economically at one tenth the scale of the big integrated plants. These developments meant that a company could

construct a competitive new steel "minimill" with an initial investment of, say, $50–$100 million—not exactly pocket change, to be
sure, but a small fraction of the billions of dollars needed to build a
brand-new integrated plant.

Besides being cheaper to build, the minimills were simpler and
less costly to operate. Their product range was narrower and less
complicated, and this allowed them to achieve efficient production
at lower output levels. They were also much more flexible. Unlike integrated plants, they did not have to be located where there was easy
access to iron ore and coal supplies; also, because of their modest
scale they did not need to be close to large markets, for either scrap
supplies or end-use products. They could therefore be sited where
markets were still quite small but growing fast (often in the South and
West), where electric-power supplies were cheap, and where unionization was less likely (most minimill entrepreneurs have been im-
placably opposed to unionization, fearing the higher labor costs,
inflexible work rules, and antagonistic labor relations that helped to
bring down Big Steel). The inherent flexibility of minimill technology
also made it possible to achieve more rapid product changeovers
(within their relatively narrow product range) than in the more complex integrated mills.

Like many other cases of industrial innovation, however, the story
of the American minimills is as much about organizational change as
it is about new technology. What distinguished the successful minimills both from the traditional integrated firms and from other, less
efficient minimills was their skill in combining the new technology
with equally far-reaching ideas about business strategy, organizational
structure, and the management of people. Building on the solid foundation provided by a carefully selected, well-trained, and highly motivated workforce, the real accomplishment of the minimill
entrepreneurs was to invent an entirely different business model for
steelmaking. In a sense, it is they, rather than their older rivals, that
deserve to be called "integrated."

During the last decade, the minimills have continued their assault
on Big Steel's crumbling citadel. By the mid-1990s, their share of domestic steel production was approaching 40 percent. But even this
figure understates their influence. The ideas and ways of doing business of these firms have spread throughout the industry. Many of the
innovations first introduced by the minimills have now been adopted
by the surviving integrated firms. Under intense market pressure
these firms have been modernizing their mills, reorganizing their operations, and achieving significant performance improvements of

(a) Traditional Steel Mill

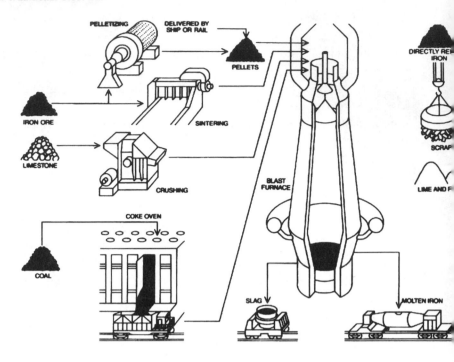

(b) Minimill

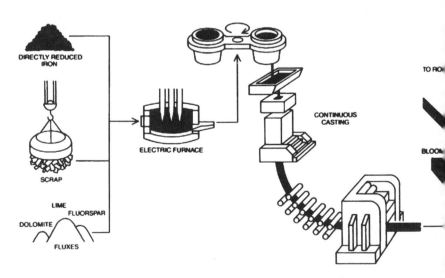

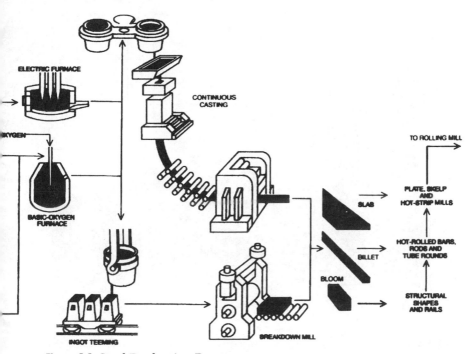

Figure 4.1 Steel Production Processes

Source: Jack Robert Miller, "Steel Minimills," *Scientific American* (May 1984): 34–35.

their own. The most widely used measure of efficiency in the industry is labor productivity. At the leading integrated mills, it now takes an average of less than 3 man-hours to produce a ton of steel. This is still far behind the 0.5 man-hour per ton performance of the best minimills; nevertheless, it is a vast improvement over past practice. Taken as a whole, the productivity of the U.S. steel industry—in which the integrated mills still account for about two thirds of total capacity—has doubled in the last ten years (see Figure 4.2). As a result of these gains, the American industry is today the most efficient in the world (see Figure 4.3).

The minimill firms continue to evolve. They started out by supplying small, regional markets with low-grade products. Today, they are building much bigger plants, serving national (and in some cases even international) markets, and moving increasingly into the high-quality product areas once thought to be the exclusive preserve of Big Steel. And as the scale and scope of their operations increase, the largest of these enterprises are now approaching the integrated firms in size, if not in style and culture. At this point, in fact, the term "minimill" has itself become a bit of a misnomer. A better term would

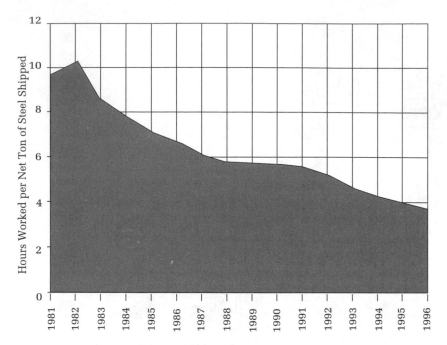

Figure 4.2 Hours Worked per Net Ton Shipped, U.S. Steel Industry, 1981–96

Source: American Iron and Steel Institute (various years).

be "electric mill," but we shall bow to convention here and stick to the more familiar label in the rest of this chapter.

How the minimills managed to rise "phoenixlike"[1] from the ashes of the American steel industry is an intriguing and remarkable story in its own right. But the story also contains broader lessons for American industry. Among them:

- new sources of capital *can* flow into a basic industry like steel and earn a healthy return. The leading minimills have even managed to remain profitable during recessions, in sharp contrast to their integrated rivals;
- major technological innovations with transforming potential can occur in old-line, "mature" industries as well as in new ones;
- successful commercial exploitation of major technological innovations often requires parallel organizational innovations of comparable magnitude.

In hindsight the triumph of the minimills might seem to have been preordained, but at the outset their success was not at all assured. Big Steel, even in its debilitated state, could have crushed the interlopers early on with a flick of its tail. Had the minimill entrepreneurs not

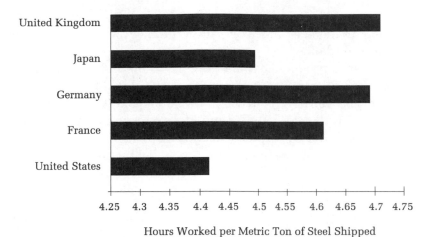

Figure 4.3 Hours Worked per Metric Ton of Steel Shipped, U.S. Steel Industry, Selected Countries, 1995

Source: Paine Webber, cited in the *New York Times*, 16 April 1996, D1.

been willing to bet their careers and their companies, and had the integrated mills not been so obstinate in their refusal to take the newcomers seriously, the outcome would probably have been quite different. Even as things were, the minimills faced rough going. Since the U.S. steel market was not expanding, the only growth path available was to lure customers away from the suppliers they were already used to—the toughest, most elemental kind of industrial competition, especially in a commodity market like steel, where even a cent or two on the price per pound can be the difference between success and failure. There is nothing easy about the steel business. Kenneth Iverson, chairman of Nucor, the largest and most successful of the minimills, was once asked how he could sleep at night. "I sleep like a baby," replied Iverson. "I wake up every ninety minutes and cry."

The immediate cause of Iverson's insomnia was the start-up troubles just then plaguing Nucor's innovative new mill at Crawfordsville, Indiana. The events that led up to those sleepless nights are a microcosm of how the minimills have been changing the face of the American steel industry, and of the big risks they have taken along the way.

For some fifteen years before Nucor started building the Crawfordsville plant, its minimill operations had been growing steadily and profitably. But by the mid-1980s, the company was running up against a wall. The product markets that it had been supplying were becoming saturated and the company's future growth was in danger of being choked off.

Steel comes in all shapes and sizes, and the industry produces thousands of different products, ranging from the humble concrete reinforcing bar ("rebar"), produced in megaton quantities, to elite specialty products like the stainless and tool steel families, produced in small volumes at high cost for specialized applications. Table 4.1 illustrates the wide range of prices commanded by these products in the marketplace.

Table 4.1: Steel Prices, by Product

Product Type	$/Ton
High-speed tool steel (M-42 grade, 1" round)	11,600–17,700
316 grade uncoiled stainless plate	3,100–3,240
Premium rail	560–637
Hot-rolled sheet	525
Wire rod (low carbon)	350
Rebar	290–310

Source: American Metal Market, 7 June 1996, p. 6.

The minimills' initial foray into the steel market had been with the lowest-grade steels. This was not a matter of choice. Because of the impurities in the scrap charged to their electric furnaces, the minimills could only produce products like rebar and wire rod, where the quality of the steel is less important. Over time, by constantly tinkering with processes and technologies (for example, by learning better how to weed out scrap laden with too many "tramp" materials), they found ways to make progressively higher-quality products like construction beams, higher-quality bars, and rails. Thanks to their lower capital and operating costs, the minimills had all but driven the integrated producers out of many of these so-called long product markets by the mid-1980s. But the big prize still lay out of reach: the market for "flat-rolled" products, made from thin plate and even thinner sheet steel. The flat-rolled market, which accounts for over 50 percent of all steel sold in the United States, includes products like steel decking, plates used to make ship hulls, equipment casings, and, at the high-quality end, the coated sheet steels used for the outside panels of cars, vans, and household appliances like washing machines, where excellent surface finish is essential.

Unfortunately for the minimills, economies of scale still favored the big integrated mills in these markets. In the big mills, flat-rolled products are produced by driving thick slabs of steel through massive rolling mills. Up-to-date integrated mills use continuous casters to produce these thick, "semifinished" slabs directly from molten steel. The big American steel companies had lagged well behind the Europeans and Japanese in adopting continuous-casting technology, but by the mid-1980s many of their plants had been retrofitted with the new casters. The heart of a continuous caster is a water-cooled mold that is open at both ends. Molten steel is poured into the top of the mold, and a strand of hot metal 8–10 inches thick and several feet wide is continuously extruded from the bottom. As the steel emerges from the caster, it is cut into slabs 100 feet long or more. The slabs are then cooled and transported to a rolling mill, where they are reheated until red-hot and forced through a long train of rolling machines. The rolling mills crush the slabs into sheets as thin as one tenth of an inch. The scale of the hot-rolling operation is vast. Each machine weighs thousands of tons, and a typical rolling mill is up to half a mile long. After hot-rolling, the steel is often then subjected to a sequence of additional processing, shaping, and finishing stages, including cold-rolling, annealing, and coating.

For minimills to use this kind of technology to make sheet steel did not make sense. The economies of scale worked to their disadvantage. To be cost-competitive, a new casting and rolling facility would have to produce as much as 3 million tons of steel per year and would cost $2 billion to build. That was too big a risk for even the most ambitious minimill. It would also mean sacrificing the benefits of small scale and flexibility that the electric arc furnaces could provide. In effect, it would mean challenging Big Steel on its home turf.

But there was a way around this problem. If molten steel could be cast not into thick slabs but directly into thin sheet, there would no longer be any need for the giant hot-rolling mills, the most expensive part of a steel plant. Direct sheet casting turns out to be an extremely difficult technical problem that no one has yet been able to solve. But even if you could only go partway, and cast the steel into thinner slabs, there was still much to be gained. Part of the long train of rolling machines could be eliminated. So, too, could the costly and energy-intensive intermediate reheat furnaces. And a mill with a continuous thin-slab caster could be built economically on a smaller scale than a conventional integrated plant—a particularly attractive feature for the minimills.

Several groups were working on the development of thin-slab casters in the mid-1980s, but Nucor was the first to introduce such a

caster into a full-scale plant—the new mill at Crawfordsville. It selected a technology developed by SMS Schloemann-Sieman AG, a
leading German machinery firm. The SMS caster converts molten
steel from the electric furnace into a slab 1.5–2 inches thick, compared with the 8–10-inch slabs produced in conventional continuous
casters. The thin slab is sheared into 150-foot-long sections that are
fed directly into a hot-rolling mill, where they are crushed into sheet
steel one tenth of an inch thick. At a mere three football fields long,
the rolling mill is a midget by the standards of Big Steel. The plant
produces 800,000 tons of hot-rolled steel a year, compared with the
multi-million-ton behemoths in the integrated sector.

The story of how Nucor chose the SMS process and went on to
build the Crawfordsville plant in record time has been vividly told by
Richard Preston in his splendid book, *American Steel.*[2] As Preston
succinctly observes, there were two good reasons for Nucor *not* to
proceed with the Crawfordsville project. In the first place, the new
technology might fail. In the second place, it might succeed. The risks
of failure were formidable. Nucor estimated that the plant would cost
about a quarter of a billion dollars—almost equal to the entire net
worth of the company at the time. Moreover, SMS had so far only
demonstrated its innovative casting technology on a pilot scale.
Nucor had no way of knowing for sure how well it would operate in
a full-scale plant. There was a big question mark about the reliability
of the process. Nucor had calculated that a commercial plant would
have to operate at least 96 percent of the time to be economical. (Because steel flows continuously through the plant, high reliability was
crucial; a breakdown in the caster would immediately bring the entire plant to a standstill.) Could the new process achieve this level of
performance? There were also uncertainties about whether the mill
could consistently achieve the quality levels required for flat-rolled
products.

And what if it worked? SMS, which still owned the technology
and was eager to sell it widely, would quickly find new buyers, and
within a short time Nucor would be faced with a bevy of Crawfordsville clones and competitors. At best the company could only
expect a two- or three-year window before losing its first-mover advantage. (Nucor actually widened the window a bit by mounting a
crash construction program at Crawfordsville, designing the plant
even as it was being built, erecting structures in parallel instead of in
sequence, and so on. This saved time, but it also entailed additional
risks, especially for a mill like Crawfordsville that was the first of its
kind.)

There were other risks, too. If the Crawfordsville project succeeded, the predictable rush to adopt the new technology would also
create a strong new demand for scrap, which would in turn drive up
its price, and the economics of the project were very sensitive to the
price of scrap. There was also the strong possibility that a better
process, capable of producing still thinner slabs, would soon come
along. Several firms were working on this, including SMS itself. And
somewhere out in the future was the steelmakers' holy grail—direct
casting into thin sheet.

Why was Nucor willing to take such risks at Crawfordsville? Because the alternative—doing nothing—was in many ways even
riskier. There was little growth potential left for Nucor's primary
products, steel bars, and now that the integrated companies were no
longer much of a factor in this market, the main competition was
coming from other minimills—tough, aggressive competitors like
Nucor itself—so profit margins were likely to shrink. Another alternative might have been to diversify into other businesses, but Nucor
never seriously considered this. As Iverson later explained, "We do
two things really well. We build plants efficiently, and we run them
economically. We know the steel industry. We don't want to buy
banks, and we don't want to buy oil companies."[3] This last comment
was a not-so-subtle dig at Iverson's Big Steel rivals, whose earlier efforts to diversify into other industries had mostly ended in failure.

Despite all the risks, Iverson's assault on the flat-rolled market paid
off handsomely. The start-up problems at Crawfordsville were soon
resolved, and within a year the mill was running flat out and turning
a profit. At $500 per ton of annual capacity, its capital cost was not
even a quarter of the cost of a new integrated plant. The mill required
less than 0.8 man-hours to produce a ton of hot-rolled product,[4] and
its operating costs were lower than those of the world's best integrated mill.[5] Nucor's managers claim that they can now make steel for
less than it costs low-wage Asian producers merely to *ship* it to the
United States—the implication being that the latter could pay their
workers nothing at all and still be uncompetitive in the U.S. market.
The company has gone on to build two more flat-rolling mills in
Arkansas and South Carolina.[6] Partly on the strength of its surge into
the flat-rolled market, Nucor's share price increased fivefold between
1988 and 1997.

Encouraged by Nucor's success, several other minimills have now
entered the flat-rolled market with their own thin-slab casters. (Their
ranks include Steel Dynamics, Inc., a new venture formed by Keith
Busse, the general manager of the Crawfordsville project, who left

Nucor in 1993 after a rival moved ahead in the race to succeed Iverson.) The minimills are thus poised to make further inroads into the integrated firms' shrinking market share. According to some industry projections, they will be supplying nearly half of the flat-rolled market within a few years.

What explains the rise of the minimills? Five interrelated characteristics of these companies stand out most strongly in a comparison with the integrated firms:
- their attitudes toward risk
- their decentralized organizational structures
- their compensation systems
- their hiring and training practices
- their culture of continuous improvement

Risk Taking: The appetite for risk of leaders like Nucor's Iverson has clearly been central to the minimills' success. But risk taking has not just been confined to the upper reaches of these firms. Similar attitudes have been cultivated throughout. When asked to define the most important organizational differences between minimills and integrated producers, Gordon Forward, chief executive officer of Chaparral Steel, put the risk-taking culture of the minimills at the top of the list. "You can't wait until it's obvious," said Forward. "By then, everyone is doing it."[7] Forward contrasted this with what he saw as the integrated firms' preoccupation with avoiding mistakes. Iverson of Nucor stresses that even good managers make bad decisions nearly half the time. Trying to prevent mistakes by punishing them is therefore worse than useless because it risks killing all initiative. People must be allowed to make mistakes. The important thing, according to Iverson, is to avoid making the same mistake more than once.

Decentralization and Compression of the Hierarchy: The founders of the minimills were highly conscious of the influence of organizational structure on the behavior of their employees, and fought with missionary zeal against the proliferation of unnecessary layers of management. "We strongly believe that the best companies have the fewest layers of management," says Iverson. "The fewer a company has, the better it communicates with employees and the better it makes rapid and effective decisions."[8] At Nucor, with 6600 employees and annual sales of nearly $4 billion, the company's famously spartan North Carolina headquarters houses only about twenty-five staff overall, including clerical and secretarial workers, and there are just four management layers between the CEO and the production workers. (In a typical integrated firm, there are as many as a dozen.) Differences in status are minimized. The "corporate dining room" is a lunch counter across the street. Says Iverson: "We all have the same group insurance program, holidays, and vacations. We all wear the same color hard hat (green). We have no company cars, company airplanes, company boats, executive dining rooms, assigned parking places, hunting lodges or fishing lodges, and everyone travels economy class. We think it is very important to destroy that hierarchy of privilege that is so prevalent and pervasive in many corporations in the United States."[9]

Lean structures like Nucor's can only work if everyone at each level is given as much responsibility as they can handle. Teams of production workers are organized into self-managed, autonomous units. The production crews install new equipment, do their own maintenance, write up operating manuals and safety regulations, and design training programs for new hires. Often they also function as part of the sales force. Further up the organization, plant managers are given broad autonomy to achieve the financial targets set by corporate headquarters. At Nucor, each of the seventeen plants is responsible for managing its own business. Plant managers set their own production quotas, procure their own raw materials, and interact with their own customers. Explains Iverson, "We don't do much here at [headquarters]. . . . Except the cash! We handle the cash!"[10]

Compensation: Compensation systems are in some ways the glue that holds these decentralized organizations together. They are structured to promote employee initiative, emphasize the link between pay and performance, and align the interests of employees, managers, and stockholders. Employee stock ownership plans (ESOPs) are common. Base compensation is typically below the industry average, but is supplemented by large, performance-related bonuses. At Nucor, a regular steelworker might make $40,000 a year, a foreman $70,000.[11]

Nucor attaches much importance to its incentive programs. Hourly employees earn up to 70 percent of their total annual compensation from production-oriented incentives. In any given week, it is not unusual for an average worker's bonus to exceed 150 percent of base pay. These bonuses are based on group rather than individual performance so as to promote teamwork. But they are also linked to the achievement of specific objectives. Nucor professes not to be enthusiastic about quarterly profit-sharing programs for its regular workers because the link between reward and individual effort is less obvious than when the results show up in the weekly paycheck. For managerial employees, though, profitability is the critical performance measure. Nucor's plant managers can earn up to 40 percent of their total annual compensation through bonuses based on their plant's return on assets. And because they have authority over almost every aspect of their plants except capital investment decisions, they too see a clear link between their success in keeping overhead down and productivity up and their compensation.

Compensation systems do not always work according to plan. Oregon Steel, owned 100 percent by its employees after a management buyout in the early 1980s, made a success of buying up outdated mills, refurbishing them, introducing more flexible labor practices, and achieving big productivity gains. The company went public in 1988, making millionaires out of nearly one hundred of its steelworkers. Company rules required workers who wanted to cash in most of their stock to leave. Many did. Turnover soared, and valuable talent was lost.[12]

Hiring and Training: The minimills have placed great emphasis on careful hiring. With twenty or thirty applicants for every new slot, these companies can afford to be selective. At Nucor, all applicants for positions above the level of front-line foreman are interviewed by the chairman. At Chaparral, it is typical for applicants to be interviewed five times before they are hired. As Chaparral's Gordon Forward observed, "[i]f there is only one man-hour in a ton of steel, we need to make sure it is a very good one."[13] For production and maintenance workers, prior steelmaking experience has not been a prerequisite, but positive attitudes have been highly valued; the minimills have typically looked for self-reliant people who are willing to work hard and to learn. Twenty years ago, when Chaparral built its first mill at a greenfield site in South Texas, many of its initial workers were recruited from the local farm country. This tradition has continued; Indiana farmworkers make up a sizable fraction of the workforce at Nucor's Crawfordsville plant. But as plants become increasingly automated, the threshold of skills for new hires is ramping up. Gordon Forward reports that knowledge of mathematics and computers is becoming increasingly important, even for line workers. The importance of additional training is also emphasized. At Chaparral, 85 percent of the workforce is involved in some form of continuing education. North Star Steel president Robert Garvey recently commented that "[t]he technology is passing line workers by so rapidly that you've got to provide a mechanism for people to go out and gain the necessary skills."[14]

Benchmarking and Continuous Improvement: The minimills have made a specialty of entering markets with lower-grade products, using their cost advantage to push aside the bigger but weaker integrated producers, and then building on their experience to drive their costs down further, and to develop and introduce higher-quality steels. The minimills' brisk growth has been an important advantage in this respect, giving them the opportunity to incorporate the latest technical advances in the next generation of plants. The integrated firms, with shrinking markets, have not been building new plants, and so have been restricted to a strategy of retrofitting their existing mills. This has typically been very costly. Because the different parts of these huge plants are tightly coupled to each other, an innovation in one area often requires making expensive compensatory changes throughout the rest of the plant.

But having the advantage of newer and more flexible capital stock is only part of the story. The leading minimills have also been distinguished by a culture of continuous improvement. They have benchmarked themselves against the leading practitioners in the industry since long before that term entered into common use. Another hallmark of the minimills has been an openness to new ideas and a willingness to try them out on their own plants. In fact, these firms have generally avoided investing in separate research and development facilities at all. Instead, they have used their factories and those of their suppliers as de facto laboratories to adapt and perfect the new techniques. So, while the basic architecture of the minimill process provided inherent advantages over their integrated rivals, the minimills achieved many additional gains from a continuous stream of small improvements in important process parameters like energy efficiency, rolling speed and thickness, roller wear and tear, furnace and caster lifetimes, and the like.

This accounting of the minimills' competitive advantages is heavily slanted toward organizational factors. That might seem odd in light of the importance of technological innovation in giving these firms their start. But the fact is that all companies in the industry, minimills and integrated firms alike, have had relatively equal access to new technological developments, and having a proprietary position in technology has not been a particularly important source of competitive advantage. From this perspective, then, the emphasis on organizational factors is less surprising. James Todd, now-retired chairman of Birmingham Steel, has gone further. His company made a success of acquiring antiquated mills and converting them into competitive, profitable businesses. According to Todd, "we have come to believe that success is *solely* dependent on internal management and labor policies" (emphasis added).[15]

Making Steel: Some International Comparisons

What role has government policy played in the rise of the American minimills? The short answer is not much. The same also turns out to be true of other countries where the minimills have made substantial inroads. In fact, a comparison of the world's steel industries reveals a kind of pattern: where governments have stood aside, minimills have managed to establish themselves as the low-cost producers in the industry, and where governments have actively supported the traditional steelmakers, as in much of Europe, minimills have found it more difficult to break into the market.

To what purpose has this government support been directed? In the advanced industrialized economies, the main objective of steel policy in recent years has been to deal with the problem of overcapacity—a problem that itself stems partly from earlier government subsidies and bailouts. Steel communities everywhere have been devastated by production cutbacks, plant closures, and job losses, and the pressure on governments to protect what remains of their domestic industries has been intense. Policies have varied from country to country. In the United States, the government began to impose restrictions on steel imports in the late 1960s, and trade limitations of one kind or another (mostly "voluntary" quotas on imports from specific countries, but more recently also large import tariffs) have been in effect almost ever since. Arguments about the true impact of these restrictions have flared up periodically over the years. Have they provided the American producers with the profit margins needed to modernize their plants, or was their main effect to delay the closure of inefficient capacity? Have the benefits to the steel industry been outweighed by the adverse impacts on steel consumers and their customers, who have had to pay more for their steel? For every steelworker's job that was saved, how many were lost in downstream industries whose products became less competitive?

This debate has been almost exclusively concerned with the impact on the traditional steel producers. Both sides would probably agree that the consequences for the minimills have been secondary. Certainly, those firms were not the intended beneficiaries of the trade measures. Some may in fact have benefited from the higher domestic prices caused by import quotas. In other cases, the opposite was true; for example, the integrated firms' ability to persuade the government to negotiate particularly stringent restrictions on the flat-rolled products where they specialized probably shifted imports toward the lower-end product markets where the minimills were most active. But the net effect of all this was quite small.

The independent analysts Donald Barnett and Robert Crandall concluded a few years ago that the minimills have been neither much helped nor much hindered by the U.S. government. Most minimills seem to see things the same way. They have generally taken the position that the government's efforts to protect the integrated sector have been more of a nuisance than anything else. And they have been dismissive of the import controls, portraying them as just another attempt by the integrated firms to stave off their day of reckoning.[16] A typical voice is that of Robert Garvey: "Instead of dealing with economics and doing it on the basis of technology and the fundamentals . . . [the integrateds] are looking to legislation and protection. And that's very short-term oriented. . . . They're going to get a huge return in the short term, but in the long term maybe it will keep them around for 10 years as opposed to five. But nothing is going to change the technology and the fundamental economics. They are being victimized to a large part by decisions they made a long time ago."[17]

In Japan, the expansion of the electric mills has tracked the American experience, as Figure 4.4 shows. For the last decade, a small group of independent Japanese minimills have been locked in fierce competition with giant integrated firms like NKK and Nippon Steel, the world's biggest steelmaker. Like their American counterparts, the Japanese minimills began with low-quality structural steels, moved gradually into higher-quality products, and are now entering the market for sheet steels. Today, minimills account for about a third of all steel sales in Japan, and thanks to their more efficient processes they are substantially undercutting the integrated mills in a wide range of product markets. (The minimills' cost advantage is particularly noteworthy given that firms like Nippon Steel and NKK operate integrated mills that are a good deal more modern and technologically advanced than the corresponding U.S. plants.)

The parallels between Japan and the United States go further, and Tokyo Steel, the leading Japanese minimill and an industry maverick, is often referred to as the Nucor of Japan (a label that its fiercely in-

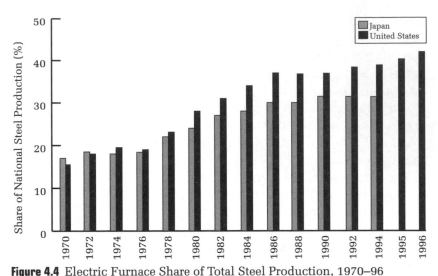

Figure 4.4 Electric Furnace Share of Total Steel Production, 1970–96

Sources: American Iron and Steel Institute; International Iron and Steel Institute; OECD.

dependent and iconoclastic president, Masanari Iketani, reportedly is not fond of). And as in the United States, the emergence of the Japanese minimills has coincided with stagnation in the integrated sector. The output of Japan's Big Steel firms declined during the 1980s, and their attempts to diversify into new industries were mostly unsuccessful. Nippon Steel's efforts included forays into silicon wafer production, notebook computers, and even a theme park in southern Japan, intended to compete with the hugely successful Tokyo Disneyland. None proved profitable.

To be sure, during most of the period when the minimills were establishing themselves, the plight of the Japanese integrated producers was not nearly as serious as that of their American counterparts. Indeed, in the late 1980s they profited from an unexpected surge in demand as the domestic construction sector boomed. Moreover, the Japanese integrated firms could hardly be considered hidebound organizations. The five biggest of them—Nippon, NKK, Kawasaki, Kobe, and Sumitomo—operate many of the world's most modern steel mills, and have long been the technological leaders in the industry. Their commitment to quality and continuous improvement has also been much admired in the West. And unlike their American counterparts, they did not shun minimill technology early on; most of them in fact have minimills as subsidiaries or affiliated companies. Nevertheless, the basic cost structure of integrated steelmaking in Japan has made these firms very vulnerable to competitive Asian neighbors like Taiwan's China Steel and Posco, a huge South Korean producer with world-class facilities and a highly educated and effi-cient workforce that earns about a third the wage of its Japanese coun-terparts.

During the first half of this decade, the combined effects of the do-mestic recession and the strengthening yen made things much worse for the integrated Japanese firms. And as big customers like Toyota and Nissan have increasingly moved their own factories offshore, the Japanese steelmakers are no longer as well positioned to offset their premium prices with "just-in-time" delivery. One leading American minimill executive remarked to me recently that he thinks the prospects for survival of the big Japanese integrated mills are quite poor.

The crisis arrived much earlier for the steel industry in Europe, and for years many European governments tried to prop up their large, failing, and often nationalized integrated firms in a variety of ways. Import controls were one such approach, but there were also lavish subsidies and, eventually, an elaborate system of Community-wide production quotas, policed by the European Commission, that was tantamount to the creation of a steel cartel. In contrast to the ac-tions of the U.S. and Japanese governments, European steel policies were sometimes intentionally designed to shelter the integrated pro-ducers from the encroachments of low-cost domestic minimills. Even where this was not the case, the practical effect of government poli-cies was to create higher de facto barriers to minimill entry.

Not surprisingly, the minimill sector has grown more slowly there. Production quotas were finally abandoned in 1988, and attempts to wean Europe's integrated producers from their rich diet of state aid have gradually been gaining ground. Even so, the long history of sub-sidies and handouts has left as its legacy a severe and continuing overcapacity crisis in Western Europe. And the penetration of the minimills there still lags well behind North America and Japan.[18] There are still essentially no flat-rolled-product minimills in Europe of the type pioneered by Nucor at Crawfordsville, despite the fact that the leading suppliers of thin-slab continuous-casting technology are themselves European.[19]

The Outlook

Like factional divisions after a political revolution has run its course, many of the old distinctions between minimills and inte-grated firms are now fading. The leading minimills are evolving into large, increasingly complex enterprises, while the surviving members of the Big Steel clan are aggressively "restructuring," which often means deintegrating. Nucor, once too small to be noticed by the likes of Bethlehem Steel and U.S. Steel, is now the nation's fourth or fifth-largest steel producer and may soon become the largest.[20] The minimills continue to infiltrate higher-grade product markets that until recently were out of reach. Some are also integrating backwards, developing high-quality iron feedstocks as alternatives to scrap for their electric furnaces.

For their part, the integrated firms have been shutting down inefficient old blast furnaces and steelmaking facilities and buying cheaper semifinished steel from the minimills to process in their rolling mills. U.S. Steel and Bethlehem, the two biggest integrated producers, are themselves now building electric furnaces, and U.S. Steel has even entered into a partnership with Nucor to develop a new steelmaking process using iron carbide as the feedstock.[21] Dofasco, a Canadian integrated firm, has built a minimill in Kentucky in a joint venture with fellow Canadian Co-Steel, a minimill firm, and LTV is building a nonunion minimill in Alabama.[22]

Even as the old distinctions in size and strategy fade, cultural differences between the integrated and minimill firms persist, despite efforts by many integrated producers to create more decentralized and entrepreneurial organizations. Eventually, though, these differences too will probably fade. The founding leaders of the minimills will depart, and the hard-driving, improvisational, and irreverent attitudes with which they infused their firms may prove difficult to sustain. For their part, the integrateds will continue their attempts at organizational transformation. Those that fail will surely not survive. But those that succeed will most likely beat a strategic retreat into product and process niches where they retain a comparative advantage. In the longer run, as the intermingling of products and process technologies runs its course, the generic distinction between minimills and integrated mills may disappear entirely. The prospect is for "competitive specialization," in which the identity of individual firms will be based on the particular position they occupy in increasingly fragmented product markets. All this will take time, however, and in the meantime the minimills will continue to be the industry's pacesetters. Here are some examples of what can be expected:

New Products and Markets:

The leading minimills will continue to seek out more specialized and more profitable markets, using their skills in process innovation as a platform for developing new products. For example,

Chaparral Steel, having recently developed a new process for efficiently producing lightweight steel beams, now has a product that can compete with pressed particle board joists in the residential construction industry. Chaparral is working with a mobile home builder to develop all-steel frame homes. These promise to be stronger, more resistant to pests (important in hot climates), and, most significant, much cheaper to transport than traditional mobile homes. The frames are sized so that they can be stacked in standard shipping containers and assembled on site. Chaparral sees great potential for this product in the developing world, and is involved in a joint venture in Mexico, where there is a huge demand for low-income housing.

In parallel, Nucor and others will try to establish footholds at the higher end of the flat-rolled market. So far, they have concentrated on lower-priced sheet products like oil drums, decking, and siding. But if experience is any guide, they will gradually move up-market. In the long run, a prime target is the high-quality coated sheet steel used for the outside panels of motor vehicles and home appliances. The integrated companies that currently serve these markets dismiss the minimills' prospects here. They point out that Nucor's thin-slab casting process cannot today produce steel with the necessary quality and surface finish, adding that their customers' technical requirements are becoming increasingly demanding. But the integrated mills have been wrong before, and the possibility that the minimills will eventually solve these problems cannot be ruled out.

Indeed, Nucor is setting its sights higher still. The company has begun producing 409-grade stainless, used primarily in automotive exhaust systems. This product currently sells for about $1,600 per ton, compared with $525 for basic hot-rolled sheet steel.

As the minimills continue their drive into higher-quality product markets, they will exchange one kind of competitor for another. The leading U.S. stainless manufacturer is the Big Steel spin-off Allegheny Ludlum, today among the most profitable steel companies in America, and one of the most consistently successful over the past decade. There will also be growing pressure from alternative materials. The auto companies, the industry's biggest customers, are under pressure to find lightweight alternatives to steel in order to improve fuel efficiency and comply with environmental requirements. Jack Smith, CEO of General Motors, the world's biggest steel buyer, warned recently that materials like aluminum, plastic, carbon fiber, and other composite materials are looking increasingly attractive as their costs come down.[23] Environmental issues will also figure more prominently in the steel industry itself. With an eye firmly on the times, one leading minimill executive has taken to describing his firm as "a recycling company that happens to make steel."

Alternative Sources of Raw Materials:

The minimills are moving to relieve the upward pressure on scrap prices by making greater use of processed iron ore in their electric furnaces. Companies like North Star Steel and Oregon Steel are developing innovative processes to convert iron ore into suitable scrap substitutes. Nucor recently completed a plant in Trinidad to convert Brazilian iron ore into iron carbide—like the Crawfordsville minimill, the first plant of its kind in the world. The granular carbide product is shipped to Nucor's American minimills, where it is combined with scrap. Finding substitutes for scrap is becoming increasingly important now that the minimills are moving into flat-rolled products. Producing sheet steel in electric furnace mills requires high-quality scrap feedstock with few residuals—material that is expensive and in chronically short supply. As one industry specialist observed, Nucor is having to become more integrated in order to move up the product scale.[24] Successful operation of the Trinidad plant will give Nucor a new source of advantage in its competition with the integrated producers.

New Channels:

As long as the minimills were producing commodity products, where price was the main differentiator, they paid relatively little attention to marketing. Instead, they relied heavily on so-called service centers, which purchase steel from different producers across a region, warehouse it, perform light fabrication tasks on it, and then resell it to end users. As the minimills move into higher value-added products, however, direct interactions with end users are becoming more important. Gordon Forward illustrated the point in a recent conversation. After trying without much success to describe the company's new lightweight beam product to a prospective customer, a Texas stadium builder, the Chaparral sales representative finally gave him a small sample to hold. According to Forward, "the light went on," and the customer was able to see the value of the product for his business. Other new products have recently been developed in response to direct customer requests, a significant departure from the minimills' traditional way of doing business.

The complexion of American steel today is quite different from what it was even a short while ago. In large part thanks to the entrepreneurial exertions of the minimills, steel is a dynamic and competitive industry, if not a booming one. Productivity continues to grow at a healthy rate, and for the better performers there are decent wages and profits to be had.

But there is another side to the story. In an industry where output grows only slowly, the inescapable result of rapid productivity growth is job loss. Over the past twenty-five years employment in the steel industry has declined by more than two thirds, from over half a million in the early 1970s to less than 140,000 today. The entire steel industry now employs fewer people than does McDonald's. The fundamentals of this situation are not about to change. Even a prolonged period of economic growth will not reverse it. Today, the steel industry accounts for only 0.5 percent of the nation's total output, compared with 2.4 percent thirty years ago, and demand for steel will continue to grow more slowly than the economy as a whole, as it has for at least the last quarter of a century. Productivity gains will continue, so at best employment will grow even more slowly, and more likely will shrink.

Thus American steel, which swept magisterially into the twentieth century as the "mother of industry," will slip quietly into the next with a much-diminished hold on the nation's attention. Yet neither will it be the dinosaur of latterday myth. The most likely state of steel at the millennium? A compact, modern, dynamic industry, like many others. One in a crowd.

CHAPTER 5

Doom, Gloom, and Boom: The Comeback of the American Semiconductor Industry

Nearly an entire continent separates Pennsylvania's Lehigh Valley from the Santa Clara Valley in Northern California. For much of the 1970s and 1980s, the distance between them seemed larger still. Journeying from one to the other was almost like traveling through time. It was a voyage between eras: the iron age and the age of silicon; one decaying, grim, in terminal decline; the other confident, full of promise, its face to the world the sleek glass-and-steel structures that sprawled across the rich agricultural region now known as Silicon Valley.

Then, suddenly, the great divide seemed to close. Shockingly, Silicon Valley, the headquarters of the American semiconductor industry, discovered that, like steel, it too was in a fight for survival. Imports of semiconductor chips from Japan, of which there had been only a trickle until the late 1970s, turned into a flood. By 1986, the industry's main trade group was reporting that Japan had moved past the United States to become the world's largest producer of chips. Within two more years, the Japanese share of the world market would reach 50 percent.

The financial and psychological impacts on the U.S. industry were devastating. Considered practically unassailable just a few years earlier, the American manufacturers seemed in danger of being completely overrun by the aggressively priced, high-quality Japanese products. Dynamic random access memory chips, or DRAMs (pronounced "dee-rams"), were the largest and most important segment of the market, and here the American defeat was almost total. DRAMs had been invented by Intel in 1971, and for some years afterwards had been exclusively made in the United States. Yet by 1986 most of the leading American "merchant" firms (those who sell their products to other customers) had announced their withdrawal from the DRAM business. The Japanese share of the world DRAM market rose above 80 percent. In the United States, only IBM and AT&T, which at that time made DRAM chips exclusively for their own use, remained as major producers. In other important semiconductor markets, too, the U.S. position was quickly eroding. By 1988, five of the world's six biggest semiconductor manufacturers were Japanese. And Japanese firms were also beginning to dominate the supply of a broad range of highly specialized capital equipment, materials, and services essential to the manufacture of semiconductors.

In parallel with their sweeping market victories the Japanese were acquiring substantial equity positions in U.S. semiconductor companies. In one such action, Fujitsu in 1987 launched a bid for Fairchild Semiconductor. By then in poor health, Fairchild was nonetheless one of the oldest and most admired firms in Silicon Valley, the legendary incubator of many of the industry's most important firms, including Intel, National Semiconductor, and Advanced Micro Devices. Fujitsu was prevented by the Pentagon from completing the Fairchild purchase on national security grounds, but the attempt nevertheless symbolized the seismic shift in the balance of power in the industry toward the Japanese.

To Americans already worried about the nation's declining competitiveness, these events seemed to be the last straw. Semiconductors occupied a place at the heart of high-technology industry, the supposed core of America's comparative advantage in future global industrial competition. The decline of older industries like textiles and steel was regrettable, of course, and was certainly devastating to those who depended on them for their livelihood, but by the mid-1980s many had come to believe that the time of these industries had passed. The spread of manufacturing know-how and the lowering of trade barriers seemed to have put American producers of commodity products at an irreversible disadvantage relative to their low-wage counterparts in the developing world. Even the loss of radio and television manufacturing during the 1970s could be rationalized in this way.

But semiconductors were different. Semiconductors were the fundamental building blocks of advanced industrial societies, touching almost every aspect of modern life. They were the critical components of computers, telecommunications systems, factory automation, and a vast range of consumer products. They provided the means of controlling still other products, including machine tools, automobiles, and aircraft. As the Japanese liked to say, they were the rice of industry.

Semiconductors were also crucial to the functioning of modern weaponry. As the cold war entered its final stages, America's enormous military strength depended more and more on its ability to maintain a qualitative edge in advanced weapons systems. What would it mean if the semiconductors that enabled these systems to operate were no longer made in the United States? Military leaders began worrying about the risk of wartime interruptions of critical materiel.

As the rise of the Japanese semiconductor industry continued during the 1980s, analysts in the United States vied with each other to paint the most alarming scenarios. In 1987, a task force of the Defense Science Board, an advisory body to the secretary of defense, reached a stark conclusion: "U.S. defense will soon depend on foreign sources for state-of-the-art technology in semiconductors. The Task Force views this as an unacceptable situation."[1] The CIA weighed in with a similarly gloomy assessment. "We believe the U.S. semiconductor industry is at a crucial turning point in its history. It fundamentally cannot compete in its present form."[2]

A report published by the National Research Council that same year warned of the "dire effects" on the U.S. economy of dependence on Japanese semiconductors. It predicted that the ability of Japan to withhold chips from American users would put the Japanese in a position to "impede the U.S. ability to compete in almost any area of manufacturing."[3]

The National Advisory Committee on Semiconductors, established by Congress in 1988 to develop a national semiconductor strategy, was particularly worried about the decline of the semiconductor manufacturing equipment sector:

> [A] scenario believed possible by many observers in industry and government foresees the withering away of the U.S. semiconductor materials and equipment industry in the face of cyclical downturns in U.S. semiconductor production and increased Japanese competition. In this scenario, the fate of the U.S. semiconductor industry—and, by extension, U.S. downstream industries—would soon be in the hands of mostly Asian suppliers. In the scenario's denouement, Asia dominates the U.S. downstream electronics industry and ultimately the global electronics landscape. . . . U.S. industry has already lost control of its own destiny, and as a result U.S. economic strength and national security are at risk.[4]

Many in Japan also expected the rout to continue. A 1990 survey of the world's semiconductor and computer industries prepared by the Nomura Research Institute concluded that it would be impossible for Americans to compete with Japan's "oligopolistic dominance," and that in these industries, "the basic trend since the start of the 1980s—market share gains by Japanese companies, market share losses by American companies—will likely continue in the 1990s."[5]

The American semiconductor crisis inspired much soul-searching about what had gone wrong. As the gloom deepened, an initially reluctant Reagan administration was eventually persuaded to sacrifice some of its free market scruples in favor of a more interventionist policy in support of the industry. Behind this shift lay a widespread conviction that the rise of the Japanese chipmakers had been greatly helped by the Japanese government, particularly the powerful Ministry of International Trade and Industry (MITI). A watershed event for America's industrial policy advocates was Japan's VLSI project, a consortium of five leading Japanese electronics companies organized by MITI in the late 1970s to establish advanced semiconductor development and manufacturing capabilities in Japan. MITI provided the consortium with interest-free loans and ensured that major domestic buyers of chips would give preference to Japanese producers. By all accounts the VLSI (very large scale integrated) consortium was a great success, and was widely regarded as a model for government intervention in high-technology industry. (It would later become clear that the VLSI project was actually not a representative example of government-funded joint ventures in Japan, and that the majority of these initiatives were far less successful.)

An early result of the new U.S. policy was the negotiation of an important semiconductor trade agreement with the Japanese, completed in 1986 (a follow-on agreement was negotiated five years later). The agreement was intended to provide American and third-party producers with relief against Japanese "dumping" (i.e., selling semiconductors overseas at prices below the fair market value in Japan). It also established a framework for opening up the Japanese domestic market to foreign suppliers. At home, the government committed additional funds for research and development on advanced product and manufacturing technologies. A centerpiece of these efforts was the formation in 1987 of SEMATECH, a new public-private R&D partnership funded 50 percent by the government.

While welcoming these developments, many advocates believed they did not go nearly far enough, and there were urgent calls for more radical measures, such as the creation of a government-financed high-technology investment corporation, and even the formation of a "European-American *keiretsu*" to take on the Japanese. Neither the

Reagan nor the Bush administrations were very receptive to most of these ideas. (A skeptical Reagan administration official is alleged to have said of the American industry, "if our guys can't hack it, we ought to let 'em go.")[6] But the election of President Clinton in 1992 promised a more sympathetic climate.[7] The new president had stressed the importance of high-technology industry as a source of "good jobs at good wages" in his campaign, and went on to appoint several officials with strong industrial policy credentials to senior positions in his administration.

Yet already by 1992 there were unmistakable signs that the competitive balance in the industry was shifting once again. In that year, the United States regained its former position as the world's largest producer of semiconductors. And just six years after having being forced out of the DRAM market by the Japanese, Intel emerged as the world's biggest and most profitable semiconductor manufacturer, largely on the strength of its dominant position as a supplier of microprocessors for the booming personal computer market, which was dominated by American firms like Compaq, Apple, and IBM. Motorola and Texas Instruments also reported major gains, joining Intel among the world's top six semiconductor producers. (Table 5.1 lists the top ten producers in 1996.) Among other American successes, Applied Materials, another Silicon Valley firm, became the world's largest supplier of semiconductor manufacturing equipment. Overall, the U.S. semiconductor industry achieved levels of profitability not seen since the mid-1980s, and its 1992 stock price performance was the strongest of all seventeen industry groups tracked by Dow Jones.[8]

Table 5.1: Leading Semiconductor Producers
(ranked by worldwide merchant sales), 1996

Company	Country	1996 Worldwide Merchant Semiconductor Sales ($ billions)
Intel Corp.	United States	17.8
NEC	Japan	9.2
Hitachi	Japan	7.1
Toshiba	Japan	7.0
Texas Instruments	United States	6.7
Motorola	United States	6.5
Samsung	South Korea	5.8
IBM	United States	5.1
SGS-Thomson	European Union	3.6
Mitsubishi	Japan	3.6

Source: Integrated Circuit Engineering Corporation.

With the economic recovery in full swing, 1993 was an even better year for the American manufacturers. Once-struggling companies like National Semiconductor, Advanced Micro Devices, and Analog Devices all reported a return to profitability. And a host of smaller companies like Altera, LSI Logic, Xilinx, and Cypress Semiconductor continued to report strong growth. The U.S. share of the rapidly growing world market climbed to 43 percent, up from a low of 37 percent four years earlier. And with new semiconductor production also coming on line in Korea and Taiwan, the Japanese began to lose ground. Between 1988, when it had peaked, and 1993, the Japanese share of the world semiconductor market slid from 51 percent to 42 percent. The turnaround in the semiconductor equipment industry was even more striking. After edging out the Americans for the first time in 1990, the Japanese share of the world market declined to 33.8 percent in 1994, while the American share rose to 52.7 percent.[9, 10]

It was a startling reversal, that left many in the United States who had feared the worst wondering what exactly had happened. The changed situation was nicely captured in a graph published in 1994 by the Washington-based Council on Competitiveness, reproduced here in Figure 5.1. As the graph shows, predictions made just a few years earlier of continuing U.S. decline and Japanese ascendance are seen to be spectacularly at odds with actual outcomes. The good news for the American industry has continued. Global demand for semiconductors has risen by leaps and bounds (32 percent growth in 1994, another 42 percent in 1995), and U.S. chipmakers have continued to perform strongly in the world market. Worldwide sales declined somewhat in 1996, but the U.S. share surged further, to 46 percent—the highest level since 1985 (when the global market was less than a sixth as large). On Wall Street, enthusiastic investors drove equity prices in the industry to extraordinary heights. (By mid-1997, the shares of leading firms like Intel and Applied Materials were trading at prices several times higher than their levels just a year or so earlier.)

What *did* happen? Did the problems identified in the 1980s really disappear? If so, how? Or are the fundamental weaknesses of the U.S. semiconductor industry still there, temporarily hidden, perhaps, by the effects of the business cycle? Or was the original diagnosis mistaken all along? Were the predictions of continuing U.S. decline based on a faulty assessment of the industry's strengths and weaknesses?

A large part of the answer is that those predicting the demise of the U.S. semiconductor industry simply failed to anticipate the speed and direction of technological and market changes, and underesti-

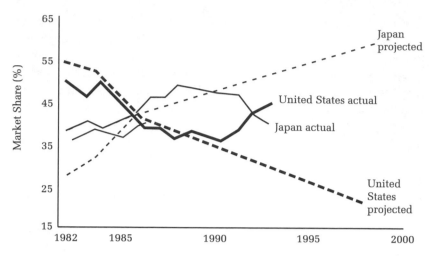

Figure 5.1 Projected and Actual U.S. and Japanese Market Share of the Global Semiconductor Industry, 1982–2000

Source: Council on Competitiveness, *Challenges* (July 1994):3.

mated the ability of American firms to respond. They assumed that the future would look much like the present, and their view of the future was strongly influenced by the prevailing view in Japan. Both turned out to be more wrong than right, but the difference was that in the tightly coordinated Japanese industry there was little room for different visions, whereas American semiconductor firms were less constrained by the orthodoxies of industry planners. Ironically, in an industry that was supposed to prove the case for government-orchestrated industrial coordination, the events of the last few years have instead demonstrated the collective benefits of individual firms acting independently in their own self-interest.

To gain further insight into the great forces that have been transforming the industry, we must first make a brief descent into the microscopic world of the chipmakers.

A World in Miniature

As I began to write this book, the United States was celebrating the twenty-fifth anniversary of the first Apollo moon landing. The television and the newspapers were full of pictures and commentary. The prevailing tone was one of awe, tinged with nostalgia for a seemingly vanished age, a simpler time when the nation's leaders could set heroic goals and then summon up the vast resources needed to achieve them. To some, in fact, the interrupted program of moon landings was a bittersweet triumph; Apollo, in this view, was the pinnacle of the nation's technological achievement, a feat not yet surpassed, and one that perhaps never will be.

But to a young engineer reading about it all, the accounts perhaps inspired wonder of a different kind—wonder about how far our technological society has come in the past quarter of a century. For even as the historic journey into space was interrupted, scientists had embarked on another, equally awesome journey—a great voyage into the interior of matter, where distances are measured not in millions of miles but in millionths of an inch, a voyage that is revealing the fundamental structure of the material that surrounds us, and indeed the very matter of which we ourselves are made. Already this journey has brought forth a cornucopia of extraordinary new tools for measuring and manipulating the behavior of matter at the atomic level—the tools that lie at the heart of the microelectronics revolution.

A passing remark about Apollo's on-board computer helps to bring home the point. To today's computer-savvy generation, the machine that guided Apollo 11 to the moon will seem almost unimaginably primitive. Weighing in at 65 pounds, NASA's finest crawled through its paces at the rate of one calculation every 11.7 microseconds. With an erasable memory—equivalent to today's RAM—of about 33,000 bits, and a fixed (read only) memory of 600,000 bits, its ponderous bulk hid a tiny store of data.[11] Compare this with the not particularly supercharged notebook computer on which this chapter is being written, weighing just a few pounds but nearly 1,000 times faster than the Apollo machine, with 20 million bits of RAM and a billion bits of storage capacity in the hard drive.

The story behind these astonishing gains in computational performance is, of course, a story about the continuing miniaturization of electronic circuitry. For designers of integrated circuits—devices that combine two or more transistors on a silicon base—miniaturization provides three crucial advantages. The smaller a transistor, the faster it can be switched on or off. Making transistors smaller also means that more of them can be packed onto a silicon surface; this reduces the distance that electrical signals must travel between transistors, again increasing the speed of the device. And squeezing more transistors onto the silicon also reduces manufacturing costs, since the cost of each processing step can be spread over more units.

The rapid pace of miniaturization was anticipated three decades ago by the semiconductor industry pioneer Gordon Moore, the cofounder and chairman of Intel. Moore, who at the time was director of research at Fairchild, suggested that the number of transistors that

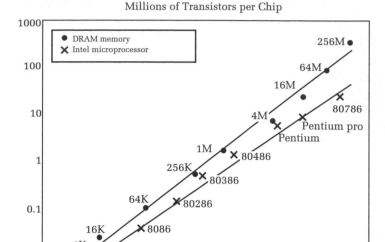

Figure 5.2 Moore's Law

Source: Science, vol. 274, 13 December 1996, p. 1834.

can be fabricated on a microchip would continue to double every eighteen months or so, an exponential growth rate that has in fact been maintained more or less ever since (see Figure 5.2). The compounding relation stated in "Moore's Law" yields numbers worth savoring. In the four decades since the first integrated circuit was produced, the number of transistors that can be fabricated on a silicon chip has increased by a factor of 100 *million*.[12] Every three years the processing power and memory capacity of silicon chips have increased fourfold, while the cost per chip has stayed roughly constant. Today's memory chips can store 16 million bits (16 MB) of information—the equivalent of 500 pages of typed text. And the same frenetic pace of miniaturization will continue for at least a while longer. Within about ten years, the capacity of the most advanced memory chips is expected to increase to 4 billion bits (4 gigabits)—enough to store the equivalent of nearly two complete sets of *Encyclopaedia Britannica* on a single DRAM chip.[13]

    Each reduction in the scale of silicon circuitry has brought new challenges. On today's most advanced chips, the characteristic feature size is now about a third of a micron—about 1/300 of the thickness of a single strand of human hair. Put another way, with a circuitry dimension this small, a complete roadmap of Manhattan could be etched on the head of a pin.

Reliably imprinting circuits comprised of millions of sub-micron-scale features on the surface of silicon wafers is as demanding a manufacturing task as has ever been undertaken. With a feature size so small, even a tiny speck of dust would be enough to ruin a chip, so manufacturers have been driven to attain heroic heights of industrial hygiene. Most of today's integrated circuits are produced in so-called Class 1 clean rooms, in which each cubic foot of air is permitted to contain no more than one foreign particle larger than 0.5 microns. By comparison, a human being typically sheds 15,000 to 20,000 such particles every minute, even when resting.[14]

The heart of the process for manufacturing integrated circuits is photolithography, the technique used to print the electronic circuitry onto the thin, circular silicon wafers. The wafers themselves, previously exposed to ultra-pure oxygen in a furnace to produce a highly uniform surface layer of silicon dioxide, are coated with photoresist—a light-sensitive film that gives the wafer the characteristics of photographic paper. Intense light is then projected through a quartz template (or "mask") onto the surface of the wafer via a series of reducing lenses. The wafer is thus exposed to the circuitry pattern that has previously been printed onto the mask. The machine that aligns the wafer with the mask and projects the light onto the wafer surface is called a "stepper," because it prints only a small area of the surface at a time; after each area is patterned, the machine moves, or "steps," to the next. The areas exposed to the light are etched away chemically, the surface carefully cleaned, and the tiny valleys then implanted with materials which control the conductivity of the transistors. Other circuit devices—resistors, capacitors, conductors—are fabricated in a similar way.

The various operations—oxidation, masking, etching, cleaning, and implantation—are repeated many times, and up to thirty successive layers may be patterned onto a single chip. Some two hundred separate steps are required to make today's 16 MB memory chips.[15] Even the most stringent quality control cannot eliminate variability from the manufacturing process, and some of the components imprinted on the silicon will inevitably be bad. If the number of defects is too large, the chip must be thrown away—an expensive, wasteful procedure. The proportion of defective components thus places a practical limit on the size of the chip.[16]

To improve the economics of the process, the diameter of the silicon wafers has steadily increased over the years. The number of chips that can be made from a single wafer is proportional to its area, and therefore increases in proportion to the square of the wafer diameter. Today's state-of-the-art manufacturing plants (or "fabs") work with wafers that are 8 inches in diameter. The wafers are sliced into individual chips using a diamond saw, and each 8-inch wafer can yield over two hundred chips. Every chip is tested at several different stages of the process with highly sophisticated computer-controlled electrical test systems. Those that are not discarded are fitted with contact leads to which tiny wires are attached. The chip assembly is then treated with a protective plastic coating, and tested once again prior to shipment.

To achieve its miniaturization goals, the semiconductor industry has perfected a long series of ingenious innovations in circuit design and manufacturing techniques. Further innovations are on the drawing board, and industry planners project a series of important advances in semiconductor performance over the next decade. There are, to be sure, some major uncertainties. One concerns the longevity of photolithography itself. The problem is that the sharpness of the images projected onto the wafer surface is degraded by light diffraction phenomena, and as the individual features get smaller and approach the wavelength of the light itself, the consequences of this degradation grow more severe. Steppers have shifted from visible- to shorter-wavelength ultraviolet light to achieve finer optical resolution, and today can fashion features that are only 0.35 micron wide. But eventually—though perhaps not until the line width has shrunk to 0.1 micron, small enough to make 4-gigabit memory chips—optical lithography will reach its physical limit, and new circuit-printing technologies will be needed. X-ray lithography and electron-beam lithography may eventually be candidates, though each has formidable technical hurdles to overcome.

Another major uncertainty is cost. Until now, the increasing cost of the capital equipment used in wafer fabs has always been more than offset by the increasing packing density of the transistors on the wafer surface, and the cost per function (i.e., per bit of memory storage or per switch in a logic circuit) has continued to decline at an annual rate of 25 to 30 percent. But the cost curve may soon bottom out. The half-micron fabs coming on line today are costing $1 billion or more, and the cost of the next generation of fabs is expected to reach $2 billion. With less time between product generations—today's new fabs will become obsolete in as little as three years—capital equipment depreciation costs are rising even more rapidly. At this rate, the cost per function may eventually begin to rise. How markets would react to such an unfamiliar situation is unclear.

Notwithstanding such uncertainties, the Semiconductor Industry Association, the industry's leading trade group, has laid out a detailed "technology roadmap." The roadmap, reproduced here in Figure 5.3, specifies the key manufacturing milestones that the industry has set as targets for the next decade. It directs attention to the future technological developments that its authors believe will be necessary for U.S. manufacturers to remain competitive.

For companies struggling to find their bearings in this fast-moving and intensely competitive industry, the roadmap provides valuable guidance and perhaps even some comfort. But its orderly appearance belies the tumultuous realities of the semiconductor industry. The precise cartography of the mapmakers stands in odd counterpoint to the immensely unpredictable consequences of their labors. How will our society harness the vast power unleashed by the availability of inexpensive, high-performance integrated circuits? The possibilities

	1992	1995	1998	2001	2004	2007
Feature Size	0.5	0.35	0.25	.18	.12	.10
Gates/chip	300K	800K	2M	5M	10M	20M
Bits/chip • DRAM • SRAM	 16M 4M	 64M 16M	 256M 64M	 1G 256M	 4G 1G	 16G 4G
Wafer processing cost ($/cm²)	$4.00	$3.90	$3.80	$3.70	$3.60	$3.50
Chip size (mm²) • Logic/microprocessor • DRAM	 250 132	 400 200	 600 320	 800 500	 1000 700	 1250 1000
Wafer diameter (mm)	200	200	200–400	200–400	200–400	200–400
Defect density (defects/cm²)	0.1	0.05	0.03	0.01	0.004	0.002
# of interconnect levels (logic)	3	4–5	5	5–6	6	6–7
Maximum power (W/die) • High performance • Portable	 10 3	 15 4	 30 4	 40 4	 40–120 4	 40–200 4
Power supply voltage (V) • Desktop • Portable	 5 3.3	 3.3 2.2	 2.2 2.2	 2.2 1.5	 1.5 1.5	 1.5 1.5
# of I/Os	500	750	1500	2000	3500	5000
Performance (MHz) • Off chip • On chip	 60 120	 100 200	 175 350	 250 500	 350 700	 500 1000

Figure 5.3 The Semiconductor Industry Roadmap, 1992–2007

Source: Semiconductor Industry Association.

are almost unlimited. What will the systems that exploit these chips look like? Which will prove to be the most important?

Already the range of applications of integrated circuits covers almost every aspect of business life, and a growing fraction of home life, too. In neither case has the record of prediction been very encouraging. The industry's history of getting it wrong goes back at least as far as the famous forecast attributed to IBM founder Thomas J. Watson, Sr., in the late 1940s—ludicrous in hindsight but no doubt reasonable at the time—that the company's first electronic computer was capable of solving all of the important scientific problems in the world, and that general purpose computers would never be used in large numbers by IBM's customers.[17] This particular Watsonian tradition remains alive and well; certainly very few forecasters in the 1970s and 1980s came close to anticipating today's semiconductor marketplace. (Watson, by the way, was in good company. In 1956, the eminent computer scientist Howard Aiken stated that "if it should ever turn out that the basic logics of a machine designed for the numerical solution of differential equations coincide with the logics of a machine intended to make bills for a department store, I would regard this as the most amazing coincidence that I have ever encountered."[18] Even Gordon Moore's foresight has been less than perfect. In the 1970s, he rejected a proposal that Intel build home computers based on an early microprocessor. "I personally didn't see anything useful in it," he said later, "so we never gave it another thought.")[19]

In an industry that is evolving so rapidly and unpredictably there is a premium on speed and responsiveness, on the skills needed to divine previously unsuspected market opportunities, translate them rapidly into workable designs, and bring the designs quickly to commercialization. This is true not only of the system builders who integrate chips into new products but also of the chipmakers themselves. Indeed, as it becomes possible to fabricate more and more functions onto a single chip, the distinction between semiconductors and "systems" is blurring; increasingly, the chip *is* the system.

The interplay between these two facets of the semiconductor industry, between the steady march of miniaturization foreseen by Moore's Law and the unpredictability of applications markets, between the mastery of micron-scale manufacturing and the ability to develop innovative and often highly specialized designs, is one of the keys to understanding the competitive dynamics of the industry. Both kinds of skills are essential. But at different times and in different segments of the market, one may command a higher premium than the

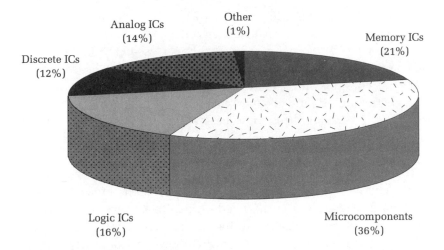

Figure 5.4 World Semiconductor Market by Product, 1997 Estimate

Source: World Semiconductor Trade Statistics Mid-Year Forecast (1997), cited in "Global Semiconductor Market Should Grow 4.6% in 1997; Growth Rates of 20% or More Forecast for 1998, 1999, and 2000," Semiconductor Industry Association Press Release, 12 May 1997.

other. And when the balance between them shifts, so too do the characteristics of the winners and losers. We will return to this point later in the chapter.

Figure 5.4 shows the main categories of semiconductor products currently sold on the world market. The second-largest category (until recently, the largest) is memory products, of which DRAMs are the most important type, with nearly two thirds of the total memory market. A much smaller but rapidly growing product type is high-speed flash memory. Unlike DRAMs, flash memory chips retain data when the power is turned off. A promising application is to substitute for the bulky hard disks that are presently the main form of permanent storage for personal computers, as this would greatly enhance computer portability. Other possible applications of flash memory products include a wide range of noncomputer portable devices for which permanent memory has until now been impractical.

The largest category of semiconductor products today is microcomponents, which combine memory and logic and are sometimes referred to as "computers on a chip." The most important product in this class is the microprocessor—the key component in most computers. (In 1997, for the first time, microprocessor sales exceeded DRAM sales.) Microcontrollers are another important product. These combine basic microprocessors with memory and are used as embedded controllers in a huge range of products, from home appliances like microwave ovens to automobiles.

Another rapidly growing microcomponent segment is the digital signal processor (DSP). DSP chips are high-speed circuits designed to carry out complex mathematical computations, for which they are much better suited (and cheaper) than general purpose microprocessors. They are widely used to process voice and image data in order to improve sound and picture quality in products like fax machines, modems, mobile phones, and answering machines.

To understand the semiconductor market it is useful to make a distinction between commodity products, produced in large volumes to a standard design, and customized chips. In practice, this is really more of a continuous spectrum than a sharp division. For example, the largest class of logic chips, application specific integrated circuits (or ASICs), range from fully customized products designed from scratch for a single customer to fairly generic programmable logic devices, which are sometimes customized by users themselves in the field.

The general trend in the industry is toward increasing product differentiation and specialization. Even the DRAM, often thought of as the archetypal commodity product, is becoming increasingly specialized. There are nearly one thousand varieties of the latest generation of 16 MB DRAMs on the market today, including increasingly important specialty products like video RAMs, designed to store high-resolution video graphics images. One consequence of the trend

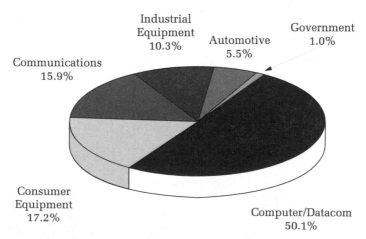

Figure 5.5 Worldwide Merchant Semiconductor Consumption (1996)

Source: Standard and Poor's Industry Survey: Semiconductors, 31 July 1997, p. 6.

toward increasing specialization of integrated circuits is that the average "design content" of chips is growing. This in turn is one of the reasons why the value of semiconductor sales as a percentage of total electronic equipment sales is also rising. The principal end-use markets for semiconductors are shown in Figure 5.5.

Explaining the Comeback

As the U.S. industry's comeback has continued during the 1990s, three theories have been advanced to explain it:
1. The turnaround is largely an illusion, the artifact of exchange-rate fluctuations and lagged macroeconomic cycles in the United States and Japan. The fundamentals remain essentially unchanged, and the rise of Japan's semiconductor industry will resume when the Japanese economy recovers.
2. The recovery in the United States is real, and mainly the result of the government's interventions on behalf of the industry.
3. The U.S. industry's problems during the 1980s were largely of its own making, and the more recent turnaround is also mainly the fruit of its own labors.
Let's consider each of these arguments in turn.

The "Comeback" Is a Macroeconomic Artifact: There is no doubt that business cycles have a big effect on who is up and who is down in the semiconductor industry. The United States and Japan are by far the largest semiconductor markets in the world, between them accounting for nearly two thirds of global demand. More than half of all Japanese-made chips are still consumed in Japan, and half of U.S. production is purchased by American users.[20] So, when aggregate demand dips in one country but not the other, the industry in the former appears to be losing ground, even though it may not have slipped at all in the fundamentals of performance. The deep recession that hit Japan in the early 1990s did not really take hold until the American recession had ended, and is only now beginning to lift, lagging the U.S. recovery by several years. This accounts for at least some of the Japanese industry's recent loss of global market share. If, instead of its actual behavior, Japanese demand had mirrored that in the United States, where the downturn came earlier, was less severe, and didn't last as long, Japan's loss of global market share between 1988 and 1993 would have been less than 5 percentage points, compared with the actual 9-point loss. (And had Japanese domestic demand continued to grow between 1988 and 1993 at the same, supercharged rate as it did during the mid-1980s, the Japanese share of the world market would have *increased* from 51 percent to 60 percent, other things being equal.)

The impact of these staggered cycles has been even more pronounced in the semiconductor manufacturing equipment sector. Like all capital equipment industries, the chipmaking equipment industry is particularly sensitive to macroeconomic fluctuations. When profits are squeezed during a recession, one of the first things to be cut is the allocation of funds for new capital investment. Conversely, new investment typically surges during recoveries, as firms hasten to get rid of obsolete equipment that they could not afford to retire during the preceding recession. Cyclically induced swings of 50 percent per year in the demand for new capital equipment are not uncommon. Because of this, even more caution is needed in interpreting sudden changes in market share in the semiconductor equipment industry.

Fluctuations in currency exchange rates have further muddied these waters. Between 1985 and 1988, the value of the dollar against the Japanese yen fell nearly 50 percent. During the first half of the 1980s, when the dollar was overvalued against the yen, American-made semiconductors and the electronics goods that contained them were priced too high relative to the Japanese competition, and this was one of the reasons for the rapid American loss of market share during this period. But the decline in the U.S. market share persisted during the second half of the decade, well after the devaluation of the dollar had begun (see Figure 5.1). This added to the alarm in the American semiconductor industry. By rights, the steep fall in the dollar's value should have helped the international competitiveness of the industry. Its seeming failure to do so was taken as further evidence that the U.S. industry was in deep trouble.

It turns out, however, that the erosion of the U.S. position after 1985 was exaggerated by a quirk in the way market shares are calculated. To understand why, keep in mind that there are two ways to compute market share. One approach bases the calculation on physical quantities: each country's share of the world market in a given year is computed by dividing the physical amount produced by that country's firms by the total world production in that year. For a commodity—like wheat or oil—where one unit of production is very much like any other, this makes perfect sense. But for industries where products vary widely in performance and price, simply adding up the total physical output—the total number of units produced, or the total tonnage—will not do (except in the pathologically unlikely circumstance that every producer produces exactly the same mix of product types in exactly the same proportions).

In the semiconductor industry, where a basic microprocessor used for controlling, say, a washing machine might today cost a few dollars, whereas the sophisticated microprocessor chip in a personal computer costs a hundred times as much, measuring shares of output based solely on the total *number* of chips produced mixes apples and oranges and risks introducing serious distortions. To avoid this, market shares are computed using a *revenue* measure of output. The U.S. market share in a given year is defined as the worldwide sales revenues reported by U.S. firms divided by the total sales revenues earned by all semiconductor-producing countries. To make the computation, each country's revenues are first converted into a common currency using the average currency exchange rates for the period.

As long as exchange rates remain relatively stable, everything is fine. But if they fluctuate rapidly, revenue-based market share calculations can under certain circumstances introduce a significant source of error. This turns out to be exactly what happened in the semiconductor industry after 1985. The rapid devaluation of the dollar against the yen had the effect of artificially inflating the Japanese market share, and correspondingly deflating the U.S. share. A rough estimate suggests that the swing to the Japanese during 1985–87, a critical period for the shaping of U.S. perceptions and policy, may have been exaggerated by as much as 5 percent.

To sum up, both the decline of the U.S. semiconductor industry during the 1980s and its more recent recovery have been exaggerated by factors that had nothing at all to do with real shifts in industry performance. The Japanese were not as strong as they seemed in the 1980s, and they are not as weak as they seem today.

But although the vagaries of macroeconomic cycles and the currency markets have *amplified* the swings back and forth across the Pacific, they do not explain them away entirely. The gap between expectation and reality in Figure 5.1 is too big for that. The U.S. position in semiconductors clearly *has* improved relative to the Japanese in recent years. The question remains. Why?

Industrial Policy Saves the Day: Was government policy responsible for the turnaround? Did the combination of a more muscular trade policy and increased government funding for R&D at home stem the Japanese tide? One of those who thinks so is the American writer James Fallows (now editor-in-chief of *U.S. News & World Report*), whose studies of the dynamic East Asian economies have led him to advocate the need for stronger intervention by Washington in support of U.S. industry. In his 1994 book *Looking at the Sun,* Fallows flatly concludes that government intervention is what made the difference in semiconductors.[21]

But the evidence for this is decidedly mixed. Let's begin with the 1986 trade pact. The agreement established a floor price below which Japanese producers were not supposed to sell chips outside Japan. It also sought to make trade fairer in the Japanese market. A side agreement called for the foreign (in practice mostly American) share of the Japanese market to increase to 20 percent by 1991 (though the Japanese vehemently insisted afterwards that they had never viewed this as an enforceable commitment).

In the months following the agreement, it became clear that the American negotiators had scored an embarrassing own goal. Acting under MITI guidance, the Japanese chipmakers responded to the antidumping provisions by forming a tacit cartel and restricting supply—not at all what the American negotiators had intended. Within months, moreover, users of memory chips in the United States and elsewhere bid up the price of these chips to double the pre-agreement level. And although the U.S. government had hoped that the agreement would persuade American DRAM producers to return to the market, hardly any did, so the price increase simply meant windfall profits for the Japanese, who promptly reinvested them in even more advanced manufacturing capacity. There were also reports of American computer makers being forced to fly across the Pacific to plead with the Japanese for supplies of scarce memory chips without which their own factories would be brought to a halt. Some even suggested that they would have to move their manufacturing operations offshore to improve their access to Japanese chips. The memory chip shortages and price hikes soon dissipated as new production capacity came on line in Japan and elsewhere, but all in all it was not an auspicious beginning.

Nor, at first, did the 1986 trade pact give the U.S. industry increased access to the Japanese semiconductor market. Before the agreement was signed, the foreign share of the Japanese market had been about 9 percent. In the immediate aftermath, it actually shrank slightly. Over time, though, the foreign share crept up, and by early 1996 it had reached 30 percent (of which the American firms accounted for about three quarters).[22] There is no doubt that the first trade agreement, its 1991 successor (which also called for a 20 percent foreign share), and the years of arguing and cajoling, threats, and occasional sanctions levied by the U.S. government, did indeed help to pry open the Japanese market. Even in Japan this is widely acknowledged.

Some of the growth in the U.S. share might have occurred anyway, of course, even without pressure from Washington, though how much is anybody's guess. But let us give the American negotiators the benefit of the doubt and assume that the entire gain in Japan was attributable to U.S. trade policy. Could this account for the dramatic competitive reversal shown in Figure 5.1? No. A simple calculation shows that at most the effects of this policy could have increased the U.S. share of the *global* market by about 3.5 percent (and correspondingly reduced the Japanese share by the same amount), only a small fraction of the actual U.S. gain (shown in Figure 5.1) relative to the expectations of just a few years ago.

What about SEMATECH, the other main pillar of U.S. semiconductor policy? SEMATECH (the name is an abbreviation of its formal title, the Semiconductor Manufacturing Technology Institute) was formed in 1987, shortly after most U.S. merchant firms had been unceremoniously bundled out of the DRAM market by the Japanese. With Japanese industry and government preparing to target the manufacturing equipment sector, fears were running high that the United States was about to lose its semiconductor manufacturing base altogether. The new semiconductor consortium was given a five-year mandate, and received about $100 million per year from the Defense Advanced Research Projects Agency (DARPA) and roughly the same amount from its fourteen original industrial members (now reduced to ten). Though the government was paying almost half the bill, a key provision of the partnership was that industry would take the lead in setting its goals and managing its operations.

The new initiative got off to a rocky start. Some participants argued that the consortium should develop and produce new commercial memory devices. Others advocated a more limited role as a developer of generic manufacturing technologies. Longtime rivalries and clashing egos made agreement more difficult. The situation improved when the semiconductor pioneer Robert Noyce, a highly respected figure in the industry, was persuaded to become CEO. Soon afterwards, the idea that SEMATECH should become a commercial-scale producer of DRAMs was abandoned in favor of the more modest goal of strengthening the semiconductor industry's supply base. There was to be a particular focus on the equipment manufacturers and the materials suppliers (not themselves members of the consortium). Thus SEMATECH sponsored the development of next-generation processes and tools, and developed a range of standards for equipment safety, cleanliness, reliability, and systems integration. It also established common qualification procedures for new equipment. Previously, every U.S. semiconductor manufacturer had set its own requirements for accepting a new piece of equipment, and having to satisfy each of them separately was an expensive and time-consuming process. Being qualified simultaneously by all of the companies significantly reduced the business risks facing the equipment manufacturers, many of whom were quite small and lacked deep capital resources.

But SEMATECH's most valuable contribution has been to establish strong working relationships between the semiconductor manufacturers and their suppliers. As one industry analyst explained, the semiconductor firms used to treat their equipment vendors as if they were used-car salesmen: "a chip maker would pit two equipment vendors against each other. So they'd get the prices down, but there was no incentive to produce reliable equipment."[23] SEMATECH's contribution was to provide a forum for engineers from both sides to sit across the table and have substantive technical discussions about future needs. The equipment makers are unanimous that SEMATECH has enabled them to gain a much better understanding of these needs. Conversely, the manufacturers have been able to obtain detailed knowledge of the capabilities of new manufacturing tools while they are still under development, which removes much of the guesswork from equipment purchases and eliminates much of the time and cost required to get the new equipment operational.

Since completing its first five years of work, SEMATECH has broadened its scope. Whereas the earlier focus was on building up the industry's supply base, the new plan calls for an emphasis on the application to semiconductor factories of advanced software technologies such as simulation, modeling, and computer-integrated manufacturing. But in recognition of both the stringent fiscal climate in Washington and its own newfound prosperity, the consortium also announced that it would cease relying on federal funds by 1997.[24]

Has the SEMATECH experiment worked? Judged on its own terms, the answer is surely yes. SEMATECH's interventions undoubtedly did help the U.S. equipment supply industry at a critical juncture, and the consortium has almost certainly had a positive impact on the manufacturing performance of its members. The latter report that they are buying more U.S.-made manufacturing equipment than they expected, and that the costs of purchasing, operating, and maintaining this equipment, as well as the time taken to install it, have been reduced thanks to SEMATECH's efforts.

There is lingering disgruntlement among those outside the SEMATECH club about the uneven distribution of these benefits. T. J. Rogers, CEO of Cypress Semiconductor, has been a persistent and vocal critic of the consortium, arguing at different times that its membership fee structure is unfair to smaller firms, that it has used public funds to discriminate against U.S. semiconductor producers that are not members, and that it has favored bigger, older equipment makers over smaller, innovative newcomers that want to compete with them. SEMATECH has responded to some of these criticisms while shrugging off others. Rogers is surely correct that the consortium has tilted the playing field within the U.S. industry somewhat, but a persuasive argument can be made that its impact on the industry as a whole has been positive.

But was SEMATECH a major cause of the competitive turnaround in the semiconductor industry? The case is inherently difficult to prove either way. Perhaps the best we can do is listen to those who should be the consortium's strongest advocates—its member firms and its leadership. Did the members increase their market share as a result of SEMATECH's efforts? Reporters for *Science* magazine who posed that question to the membership discovered that none of the firms they contacted were willing to make such a claim.[25] What many of them *are* willing to say is that the returns from their investments in SEMATECH have been very handsome. A few years ago, a leading Intel official estimated that his company would ultimately realize $200–$300 million in savings in the form of improved yields and production efficiencies from its annual SEMATECH investment of about $17 million.[26] Even given the government's one-for-one matching of corporate commitments, this is an impressive return. On the other hand, SEMATECH is clearly just one of many contributors to the success of Intel, a company with annual sales now exceeding $20 billion and total spending on research and development of $1.8 billion per year. The current SEMATECH chief executive, Bill Spencer, a courtly, soft-spoken man whose skillful leadership of the consortium following Noyce's untimely death in 1990 has drawn widespread praise in the industry, makes no extravagant claims on its behalf. When asked, he prefers to dwell on the specific technical and organizational contributions that SEMATECH has made, pointing out that any aggregate impact on the industry's market share would be very hard to measure.

On balance, it seems fair to conclude that SEMATECH played a modest role in the semiconductor industry's turnaround (though probably a larger one in the recovery in the equipment industry). President Bill Clinton recently called SEMATECH "a model for federal consortiums funded to advance other critical technologies."[27] Intentional or not, the president's endorsement of the SEMATECH model was simultaneously an acknowledgment of the limits of federal technology policy as an instrument of industrial rejuvenation.

The Comeback Was Self-engineered: Since the revival of the American semiconductor industry can't be explained by macroeconomic influences or by government intervention alone, we must consider two other possibilities: either the U.S. firms, by dint of their own efforts, were able to regain their former leadership, or the Japanese, perhaps through overconfidence or strategic misjudgment, squandered theirs. Neither possibility was anticipated as recently as a few years ago. Indeed, the mainstream view in the United States at the time positively ruled them out. That pessimistic assessment rested on two powerful arguments: first, that the U.S. industry, fragmented both vertically and horizontally, was structurally unstable and too weak to compete head-to-head with the huge, diversified, vertically integrated firms that dominated the Japanese industry; and second, that the Japanese industry was receiving a wide range of vital inputs from its government (preferential access to low-cost capital, funding for research and development, help in licensing foreign technology, import controls, export assistance, and so on) whereas the U.S. industry was largely bereft of such support, so that even if its firms *were* on a par with the Japanese in efficiency and quality, they were being forced to compete with one hand tied behind their backs.

The argument about government support was familiar from other industries, but the structural critique was a radical one. It challenged the conventional wisdom about the benefits of entrepreneurial activity. Indeed, it asserted that what many understood to be the essence of Silicon Valley—the constant creation of new ventures, the ceaseless traffic of engineers changing companies in restless pursuit of more exciting, more remunerative work—was precisely what was leading to its demise. Though all this entrepreneurial activity might give American firms the edge in innovation, it was also creating an industry with a lack of staying power. The phenomenon of large firms suffering defections of key individuals and even entire product groups was undermining the very companies that were most able to deal with the huge Japanese firms.

In the crucial area of manufacturing, which demanded dedication to quality and the relentless pursuit of incremental improvement over long periods, the small U.S. firms were at a fundamental disadvantage, or so the argument went. They lacked expertise, and they lacked access to the increasingly large sums of money needed to build new fabrication facilities. The critique portrayed the dark side of American venture capitalism: start-up ventures, innovative at first, quickly making their owners millionaires, but then languishing, unable or unwilling to raise the capital to fund the next, costly new product development project; small firms, cash-strapped during industry downturns, having to forego investments and forced to license their technology (often to foreign competitors) to keep profits up.

All of this was contrasted with Japanese giants like NEC, Fujitsu, Toshiba, and Hitachi. These firms, it was pointed out, were consuming a good deal of their output internally, for their consumer products, automated machinery, computers, and the like. The downstream divisions constantly pushed their semiconductor affiliates to provide them with the most advanced chips so as to keep their products competitive. The upstream linkages to manufacturing equipment divisions gave the semiconductor makers a head start in introducing the latest production technology. (There were reports—never confirmed—that the newest equipment developed in Japan was being withheld from American chipmakers until the Japanese had had time to exploit their lead.) And because of their tremendous financial resources, the vertically integrated Japanese firms could weather the cycles much better than the American firms. They could finance their rapidly growing capital requirements for research and development and capacity expansion. They could afford to take the long view. As the MIT Commission on Industrial Productivity put it in *Made in America,* "the contest was between small, single-product, inexperienced, underfinanced American start-ups and the heavyweights of Japanese industry. David did not defeat Goliath."[28]

Several years on, though, David is still in the ring, scoring points at a brisk rate. In view of this, how well do the preceding arguments hold up? For one answer, we can turn to the industry analyst Charles Ferguson, one of the most influential voices in the great semiconductor policy debate of the 1980s. Ferguson, a bright, intense young man, had been at MIT during the work of the Productivity Commission, and, though still working on his doctoral dissertation, had had a strong influence on the commission's thinking. His views reached full bloom in two widely quoted articles published by the *Harvard Business Review* in 1988 and 1990. Entitled "From the People Who

Brought You Voodoo Economics" (a reference to the Reagan administration, with whose reluctance to intervene on behalf of the semiconductor industry the author took sharp exception) and "Computers
and the Coming of the U.S. Keiretsu," Ferguson's articles left his readers in no doubt that the only way for "David" to avoid an otherwise
certain fate was to evolve, rapidly, into a kind of Goliath itself. He ex-
coriated the "chronic entrepreneurialism" of Silicon Valley (a term
first introduced by Robert Reich, later to be President Clinton's labor
secretary), and insisted that the chaotic, fragmented American electronics industry would be overwhelmed by the Japanese without the
firm direction and coordination that could only be provided by a
combination of large, vertically integrated companies (like AT&T and
IBM) and the government. "Without imminent changes," warned Ferguson, "U.S. and European vendors of information systems hardware
risk becoming subordinate research, prototyping, and distribution
arms for the Japanese industry's vertically integrated industrial complexes."[29] Such arguments commanded much attention on the Washington stage during the late 1980s.

But Ferguson's views, like the industry itself, would soon undergo
a radical metamorphosis. Within three years he had published a book
(with co-author Charles Morris) embracing the Silicon Valley model
that he had earlier so scathingly indicted, and explaining how it was
that ponderous, sclerotic IBM had lost control of the computer market to a swarm of smaller, aggressive, entrepreneurial *American* companies. Ferguson himself provided only a terse acknowledgment of
his change of mind. "The earlier case for pessimism [about the U.S.
electronics industry]," stated a note at the end of his 1993 book, "has
been superseded." But no explanation was really needed. The juxta-
position of IBM's highly visible decline with the soaring fortunes of
Intel, merchant producer *extraordinaire,* had made the previous case
for vertical integration (and with it a good part of the argument for
why the Japanese would inevitably win the semiconductor wars) simply unsustainable.

The contrasting fortunes of IBM and Intel are intimately linked to
their strategies toward the personal computer—the single most important new application of semiconductor technology of the past
decade. IBM had rather reluctantly entered the PC market in the early
1980s by arranging with Intel, then still a relatively small Silicon Valley chipmaker, to supply its machine's microprocessor, and separately with Microsoft, smaller still, to provide the operating software.
(Microsoft did not actually have a commercial operating system at the
time, and the story goes that Bill Gates, having sealed the deal with

IBM, promptly rushed out to buy one from another small software company.)

A good indication that the mainframe-centered IBM didn't take the PC market very seriously was its failure to secure the rights to Intel's chip and Microsoft's software. It was a fateful omission, and the two small companies pounced on the opportunity they had been given. They made their technology available to the many firms that were seeking to enter the PC market with "clones" of IBM's machine, and Intel's microprocessors and the Microsoft operating software quickly became the primary standard for what was to be by far the most important segment of the entire computer industry. (According to one estimate, four out of every five dollars spent on information technology now goes to PCs.)[30] By 1996, more than 80 percent of the 250 million personal computers in use around the world were based on the Intel-Microsoft standard, and these two firms had become the richest and most powerful firms in the industry.

Having given away control of the PC architecture, IBM quickly lost any chance of dominating the personal computer market in the way it had previously dominated the market for mainframes, and today, with about 8 percent of the world PC market, the company is just another player in this intensely competitive industry.

The spectacular growth of the PC market could not have occurred without the rapid gains that were being made in semiconductor performance. As a vertically integrated manufacturer, with one of the world's largest semiconductor businesses in house, IBM might have been expected to have an inside track on these developments. Yet the company either failed to see or chose to ignore the transforming potential of the new technology. For the mainframe-dominated IBM, the PC was a distraction, or worse, a direct threat. In this sense, being vertically integrated did not help; indeed, it probably hurt. Nor did IBM's semiconductor division gain any decisive strategic or financial advantage from its links to the company's vast downstream operations, as the proponents of vertical integration had earlier predicted. In fact, IBM's chipmaking operations fared no better than most other American semiconductor manufacturers.

Further evidence of the limits of vertical integration was to come from Japan itself. During the 1970s and 1980s the semiconductor units of integrated electronics giants like Fujitsu, NEC, and Toshiba had benefited from the large, captive markets provided by their downstream consumer electronics and mainframe computer divisions. They developed outstanding capabilities in high-volume manufacturing of high-quality products. But their strategies were so

dominated by the needs of their downstream units that when demand for mainframes and consumer electronics products faltered,
the chipmakers were poorly prepared to respond. Compounding the
problem was that the computer divisions of the Japanese firms, in-
sular and protected in their home markets, had held on to their mainframe focus long after the rapid growth of the workstation and
personal computer segments in the United States had persuaded even
IBM of the need to change. So, while the Japanese chipmakers were
focusing on commodity memory chips for mainframes, their American competitors were shifting over to a range of new, more profitable
products for PCs, including microprocessors, graphics accelerators,
math coprocessors, and disk-drive controllers.[31] The Japanese remain
a formidable force in the world semiconductor industry, and will regain momentum as their economy recovers. But, as is often the case,
their earlier successes turned out to contain the seeds of later weakness.

The travails of Japan's chipmakers also eroded the reputation of
MITI, whose earlier successes in orchestrating the semiconductor industry's development had had such a powerful influence on America's industrial policy lobby. This time MITI's touch proved less sure.
Convinced of the strategic importance of DRAMs, MITI continued to
promote Japanese investment in DRAM manufacturing capacity into
the late 1980s. Its policies helped create a capacity surplus in Japan
that drove down DRAM prices to unprofitable levels. Profitability
was further eroded by aggressive price cutting by Korean and Tai-
wanese producers, new entrants in the DRAM sector who, like the
Japanese themselves several years before, were very willing to use
price reductions and relentless investment as competitive weapons to
win market share. The rapid emergence of the Koreans, especially,
was almost as much of a shock to the Japanese as Japan's own rise had
been to the Americans a decade earlier. In 1992, Samsung, the leading Korean firm, shouldered past its Japanese rivals to become the
world's largest supplier of DRAMs. And it was the Koreans, not the
Japanese, who were first to introduce 16 MB DRAMs. According to
the head of the memory division of Oki Electric Industry Company,
one of Japan's largest memory chip producers, "Korean manufacturers have already replaced Japanese makers as the main producers of
memory chips. . . . From now on, that kind of competition is over for
Japan."[32] Yet Japan's diversification into new product areas has proceeded slowly, and even today the leading Japanese semiconductor
manufacturers remain heavily dependent on memory chips for sales
and profits.

At the end of the 1980s, little of this was foreseen in the United States. Indeed, influential American voices, citing the example of Japan, were urging the government to rebuild the American merchant DRAM sector. DRAMs, asserted these advocates, were the "process driver" for the entire electronics industry, a key link in the high-technology food chain. Since DRAM makers were in the vanguard of efforts to squeeze more transistors onto silicon wafers, the DRAM sector would drive the manufacturing innovations necessary to maintain the competitiveness of the entire semiconductor industry. If the United States dropped out of DRAMs, the process equipment industry—another key link in the food chain—would soon wither away, and then so would other segments of the semiconductor industry that depended on it, and, ultimately, the downstream products that depended on *them*. (The same kind of argument was used to make the case for federal support of the process equipment industry, too. Once again the idea of a critical link in the food chain was invoked, only this time the logic ran in reverse. Unless the U.S. equipment industry was shored up, the Japanese would use their increasingly dominant position to restrict sales of advanced semiconductor manufacturing equipment to U.S. companies, and thereby gain dominance of the semiconductor industry itself. The argument was circular: you had to be strong in manufacturing equipment in order to be strong in semiconductors. But unless you were strong in semiconductors—and DRAMs in particular—you couldn't be strong in manufacturing equipment.)

In retrospect, it is fortunate that the U.S. government did not heed the advice to try to rebuild the American DRAM sector. A possible DRAM capacity surplus in the United States was avoided, and American producers were left free to focus on more profitable market segments. (Soon afterwards, in 1989, an industry-only consortium to revive DRAM manufacturing was formed, but with DRAMs by then in cheap and plentiful supply, the consortium, U.S. Memories, soon collapsed.)

The aftermath of the DRAM episode left the technology food chain argument looking more than a little threadbare. The food chain is an appealing metaphor, easily understood even by nonparticipants in this most esoteric of industries. But as a guide for action, it is problematic. Since everything in the chain is at least indirectly connected to everything else, nothing can be overlooked. Everything is important by definition. It is but a short step to concluding, as one industry leader did not long ago, that "the nation or continent that aspires to be internationally independent and competitive in the information technology sector must command the *entire* electronic 'food chain,' from semiconductors to end-products" (emphasis added).[33] In other words, to be strong, you have to be in control of every stage of production, because the food chain—like a physical chain—is only as strong as its weakest link. And it is the government's responsibility to lend a hand wherever needed to achieve this end.

But even the less promiscuous version of the argument, in which the imperative is to secure the "strategic" link in the chain—the one stage that controls the rest—poses a serious practical problem. The difficulty is not that there is no such thing as a critical link in the chain. On the contrary, at any given time there usually *is* at least one stage in any value chain that yields higher-than-average profits, or that delivers strategic control of another important stage. In fact, DRAM manufacturing probably did once meet this criterion. The problem is rather that in the fast-moving electronics industry, where product cycles are measured in months, and where entirely new markets open up with extraordinary speed, the identity of the critical link (or links) is constantly changing. Keeping track is difficult enough for firms that are active participants in the industry. For government agencies, with less knowledge of the marketplace and subject to the unwieldy and politicized oversight of Congress, it is more difficult still. Government-led strategies to "keep control of the food chain," requiring coordination and consensus among many players, are very unlikely to succeed. And getting there too late, or hanging on to an outdated strategy for too long, is no better than not getting there at all.

The real story behind the resurgence of the American semiconductor industry has less to do with industrywide coordination than with the successes of individual firms in mastering the fundamentals of efficient, high-quality manufacturing operations, and in creating and exploiting new market opportunities for themselves. A particularly important chapter of this story has been written by a single company, Intel, whose annual sales—anchored by its phenomenally successful microprocessor business line—now account for a third of the revenues of the entire U.S. industry. Significantly, Intel's achievements over the last decade have stemmed in large part from its willingness to do what American companies in general have been sharply criticized for failing to do: the company has built up its design and manufacturing capabilities in order to preserve its technology leadership, and has plowed its profits back into a massive program of new investment. Between 1991 and 1996, Intel spent $13 billion in capital additions, outpacing even its biggest rivals by a wide margin.[34] Being the first to bring new manufacturing processes into commercial operation has not only given Intel a head start in new product markets but also enabled it to begin marching down the manufacturing learning curve sooner, learning how to reduce defect rates and improve plant yields before its competitors have even entered the fray. As a result, Intel's plants have earned the highest profits in the industry, which the company has in turn used to outspend its competitors in the race to build the next generation of fabs, making it even harder for them to catch up the next time around.

The rise of Intel is a remarkable development. It should not, however, obscure the broader phenomenon of the entire U.S. merchant industry exploiting a fundamental shift in the competitive structure of the computer sector—still the biggest market for semiconductor producers. In a sense, the prophets of doom were right to focus on industry structure as the source of competitive advantage for chipmakers. The problem was that their interpretation of events was almost exactly contrary to what was really happening. While they were preaching the virtues of vertical integration, the industry was beginning to move in the opposite direction. The "old" computer industry had indeed been dominated by vertically integrated firms. Companies like NCR, Wang, DEC, Data General, NEC, and IBM supplied complete systems—the chips, the computer platforms, the systems software, and the applications software—and typically controlled their own distribution channels, too.

The components of these systems were not interchangeable: one company's operating system software wouldn't run on another company's hardware; computer architectures were "closed." This was the context in which IBM came to dominate the mainframe market and later DEC the minicomputer market. But even as these firms were savoring their triumphs, the structural pillars on which their success was based were crumbling. The computer world began to gravitate toward the PC, and as it did so, the basic structure of the marketplace was shifting from vertical to horizontal competition. This was the larger significance of IBM's decision to outsource the microprocessor from Intel and the operating system from Microsoft. As Figure 5.6 shows, the industry was *de*integrating. Each horizontal segment of the market came to be dominated by a different group of firms, many of which had little presence in other segments. Indeed, for a time in the mid-1990s the fastest-growing firm in the American computer industry was Packard Bell, a company that was competing *only* in the distribution segment of the industry.

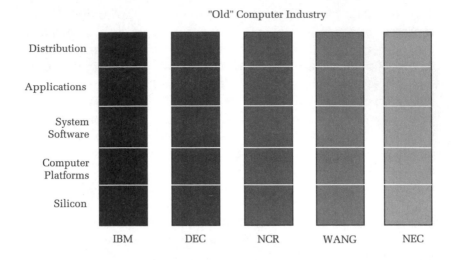

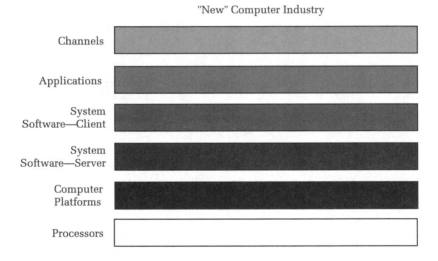

Figure 5.6 Computer Industry Deintegration

Source: Craig R. Barrett, "Life in the Fast Lane, Electronics: The Biggest, Fastest Growing Game in Town," MIT Seminar, 10 May 1995.

In the "new" computer industry, the horizontal segments are connected not by proprietary links between different divisions of the same corporation, but rather by industrywide standards—specifications prescribing the technical characteristics of the interfaces.[35] Much of the competition within each segment is about who will set the standards. In this environment, being first to market with a proprietary new product is particularly important, not only for the temporary monopoly profits that it brings, but because the first mover has more chance of being able to set the standard for the entire industry. The art, of course, is to disclose enough about the technology to allow others the opportunity to approximate it (since purchasers generally do not like to be beholden to a single supplier), but not so much that the competitive advantage deriving from proprietary control of the technology is lost.

The critical competitive weapons in this kind of environment are design skills, speed in converting new designs into manufactured products, and the flexibility to identify and respond to new market opportunities. Compared with the semiconductor divisions of vertically integrated firms, the U.S. merchant producers have been better positioned to adapt to this new form of competition. Even as the storm clouds were gathering over the U.S. industry in the mid-1980s, not only Intel but other big American merchant firms like Motorola and Texas Instruments began to upgrade their manufacturing skills while using their strengths in design to establish and defend proprietary product positions, and before long they too began to reap the benefits. So did National Semiconductor, whose successes with proprietary communications and networking chips helped return this once-struggling company to profitability.[36]

The new marketplace has also worked to the advantage of smaller merchant suppliers whose main strengths are in design. Many highly specialized niche producers have emerged over the past few years: Zilog in ASICs, Maxim and Linear Technology in analog circuits, Altera in field programmable gate arrays, and Cirrus Logic in multimedia chips, for example. Some of these firms do not actually own or operate fabs at all, but contract with other manufacturers to produce their designs. At the other end of the spectrum, even IBM's semiconductor group has begun to place more emphasis on design relative to process development.[37]

Overall, a key competitive advantage for U.S. firms has been their ability to respond quickly to technological and market changes by developing complex, innovative products that play to their strengths in design. An important contributing factor has been the increased willingness of U.S. courts to provide legal protection for chip design and related intellectual property rights. Companies have consequently become more aggressive about exercising those rights. By one estimate, royalty income from patents and other licensing arrangements has accounted for more than 40 percent of Texas Instruments' operating profits in recent years.[38]

The Outlook

Since 1959 the world market for semiconductors has grown at an average rate of 17 percent per year. Growth was even more rapid during the first half of the 1990s (see Figure 5.7), and, despite a downturn in 1996, industry forecasters are projecting a roughly 20 percent annual growth rate through the rest of the decade.[39] At that rate, global industry revenues in the year 2000 will approach $250 billion, up from $138 billion in 1997 and $50 billion in 1990. If the long-term trend continues (and few forecasters expect anything less) a further doubling of worldwide sales will occur before the year 2005. One of the few safe predictions about an industry that is growing as fast as this is that ten years from now its markets, product mix, and competitive structure will all be much different from today.

In the near term, some of the most important new markets are clear. There will be continued rapid growth in demand for chips that link personal computers into local and wide area networks, and for data communications products more generally, both wireless and fixed-

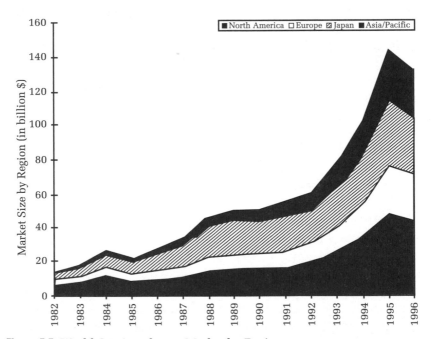

Figure 5.7 World Semiconductor Market by Region

Source: Semiconductor Industry Association (1997)

link. Also, a wide range of new consumer electronics products is appearing, including digital videodisk systems, digital cameras and camcorders, home videophones, and handheld pen computers. These are based on advanced technologies like image processing, character recognition, three-dimensional graphics, and voice recognition and synthesis that will require large numbers of sophisticated new semiconductor chips.

The extremely rapid growth of the Internet—and especially the graphics-intensive World Wide Web—will fuel additional demand for chips. There is much current debate about which kinds of devices ("appliances," in the current vernacular) will plug into the Internet most successfully. High performance personal computers? Stripped-down computer terminals dedicated to Internet browsing? Set-top boxes that add Internet-browsing capability to conventional televisions? Smart phones? Wireless digital notepads? It is probable that all of these, and more, will be developed and introduced commercially. Eventually, the market may stabilize around a few of them. But under almost any scenario the likelihood is that large new markets for memory, microprocessors, and other semiconductor products will open up.

In the longer run, as the advancing frontier of miniaturization yields up inexpensive chips able to perform hitherto-unimaginable feats of memory and computation, integrated circuits will become ubiquitous, their potential applications almost as varied as everyday life itself. Digital books that roam the world's information highways to update themselves; machines with vision, hearing, and speech. It seems fair to say that nobody, not even the most farsighted entrepreneur or engineer, could plausibly claim today to be able to define the possibilities, let alone predict which of them will emerge and in what manifestations.

What does this imply for the sources of competitive advantage in the industry? According to one view, the increasing specialization of semiconductor applications will lead to a more pronounced division of labor in the industry, with much of the value being captured by companies specializing in innovative, quick-response design.[40] For such companies, manufacturing skills will be less critical, and so-called fabless chip producers, contracting out for manufacturing services with commodity facilities, will become an increasingly important presence. (Fabless suppliers already account for about 7 percent of the U.S. market, up from 3 percent in 1988, and the largest of them, Cirrus Logic, now ranks among the top ten U.S. merchant producers; meanwhile, the number of dedicated wafer "foundries," providing contract manufacturing services to chip designers, is also growing.)[41]

Others, including Intel CEO Andrew Grove, dispute this view, arguing that for many key kinds of chips, design and manufacturing are too closely connected for this kind of separation to make sense. Says Grove, " . . . just as you cannot build Formula One racing cars with stock parts, you cannot develop high-performance microprocessors with generic semiconductor [processing] technologies. You have to tune the microarchitecture of an advanced architecture to the underlying silicon technology and the silicon technology to the microarchitecture to get the maximum performance."[42]

In fact, both views are probably right. There will be ample room in the marketplace for a wide variety of firms, from boutiquelike fabless custom-chip designers to high-volume producers whose competitive advantage hinges on their ability to exploit manufacturing know-how and scale economies. The solution to the problem of industrial structure will emerge from individual firms learning how best to exploit the complex interactions between the different stages in the production chain—between device design, manufacturing, upstream manufacturing equipment design, downstream system architecture, and the customer base itself. New and different organizational solutions will continually be found. Commercial and strategic alliances will form and dissolve. Firms will integrate and deintegrate. The proper goal of public policy should be not to shape the outcome, but to create the conditions under which a truly adaptive structure can thrive.

With its diversified portfolio of firms, and with strengths at each stage of the production chain, the U.S. semiconductor industry now seems well positioned to compete successfully in the world market over the next several years. If there is a cloud on the horizon, it is more distant. Who will replenish the reservoir of fundamental science and technology that will drive the industry's growth in the longer run? At a seminar at the MIT Industrial Performance Center, SEMATECH's Bill Spencer remarked on the transformation of the great industrial research laboratories that spawned the most important technological breakthroughs in the industry over the last forty years—AT&T's Murray Hill Laboratories, Xerox PARC, IBM's Yorktown Laboratory, the RCA Laboratories, and a few others. Most have been redirected away from the fundamental research that produced these breakthroughs toward activities with a shorter-term commercial payoff. Some have been dismantled altogether. Long-term corporate research relevant to semiconductors has largely disappeared. Not long ago, in a speech to an industry trade group in the heart of Silicon Valley, Gordon Moore described the semiconductor industry as "a monstrous and efficient machine to exploit the evolving technology."[43] But who, wondered Moore, will feed the monster?

CHAPTER 6

The Deregulation Solution: Competition Comes to the Power Industry

Economists pride themselves on their hardheadedness. Rarely do they expect to be appreciated or even much understood by the general public, and rarely are they disappointed. It is nonetheless true that at least one theoretical insight from the economic discipline has seized the popular imagination and influenced political discourse around the world like few other policy ideas over the past two decades. When it comes to setting prices, allocating economic resources, or otherwise directing the flow of commercial activity, the man in the street would agree with the professional economist: government bureaucrats run a distant second to markets.

Beginning with President Jimmy Carter's deregulation initiatives in the late 1970s, American administrations of both political parties have been committed to the idea that expanding the domain of market competition will lead to lower prices and improved service to consumers. In terms of the sheer numbers of people directly affected, the deregulation movement has been comparable to the growth of international competition as a force for change in U.S. industry over the last fifteen years, as government controls have been rolled back from vast reaches of the economy, including the natural gas and oil industries, the airlines, the railroads, trucking, the banking sector, and telecommunications. The latest sector to undergo deregulation—and one of the biggest, with annual revenues larger than those of the airlines, railroads, and long-distance telecommunications combined—is electric power.

This is the story of how deregulation is transforming the American electric-power industry. It is also the story of how three very different firms have been negotiating the transition. The story is still unfolding, and it is still too early to say how it will end. There is no standard blueprint for deregulating an industry, and for electric power, as for its predecessors, the rules are being written even as the process rolls along. Implementation is lengthy, immensely complicated, and, often, intensely political. At each stage there are losers as well as winners, and though the ultimate goal is to reduce the reach of government, the process of deregulation paradoxically often seems to draw government even more deeply into the industry's affairs. How companies have responded to the crises and opportunities presented by deregulation is one of the keys to understanding recent developments in American industrial performance.

Like many of its predecessors, the electric-power industry's encounter with deregulation began in the Carter administration. But the real roots of the process go back another hundred years, to the dawn of the age of electricity itself, and the first commercial power plant, built by Thomas Edison in 1882 in a lower Manhattan warehouse to light a nearby block of offices. Edison's famous Pearl Street plant set the pattern that the supply of electricity would be vertically integrated, that the generation, transmission, and distribution of electricity would all be carried out by the same enterprise. (Edison's firm actually provided the light bulbs, too.) For the next century, most of the electricity supply industry would be organized along these lines.

The other great organizational principle that would shape the industry emerged soon afterwards. After an early period of intense competition among private power producers like Edison and George Westinghouse, it began to be apparent that the supply of electricity was a "natural" monopoly—that is, that a single enterprise could provide electrical service more efficiently than competing suppliers. The challenge for public policymakers was to invent a scheme that would avoid the waste and inefficiency of competing electricity suppliers, each erecting utility poles and running their own line into every house, while at the same time protecting customers from the price gouging and second-rate performance to which unregulated private monopolists are prone. The solution was to grant power companies monopoly franchises within well-defined service territories, while regulating the prices that the companies could charge for their services. A new "regulatory compact" began to take shape, according to which power companies would be allowed by the regulator to recover their costs, including a reasonable return on investor capital, in return for providing reliable service to all customers within their franchise territories.

Thus the American electric-power industry came to be dominated by vertically integrated monopoly franchises, owned by private investors, and subject to government regulation of price and financial performance. Regulatory authority over the industry was shared by the states and the federal government, in a sometimes uneasy partnership. State utility commissions were responsible for the bulk of the regulation, while transactions that crossed state boundaries were supervised by the federal government. The federal role grew over the years, as the transmission network linked utilities together ever more tightly and as inter-utility transactions became more common. (The distinction between "transmission" and "distribution" is not very precise, and is mainly a matter of the distances involved; transmission lines cover longer distances, and to reduce energy losses operate at higher voltages than the distribution network.)

Regulated private franchise monopolies are not the only answer to the natural monopoly problem, and most other countries in fact opted for a different solution. They put ownership of their electric-power industries directly into the hands of the state. (Indeed, even in the United States, publicly owned entities—municipal utilities, federal power agencies, and electric cooperatives—operate about 20 percent of the electric-power system.) In many of these countries, governments are now moving to privatize their utilities and liberalize their electric-power markets. The United Kingdom, Chile, Australia, and New Zealand are among the countries where market liberalization is furthest advanced.

Curiously, the first significant move toward deregulation in the United States came about as a result of attempts by the federal government during the 1970s to become even more involved in industry decision making. President Carter's efforts to craft a national energy strategy included new legislation designed to nudge the electric-utility sector into line with the administration's energy conservation and efficiency goals. Enacted in 1978, the Public Utilities Regulatory Policy Act of 1978 (known as PURPA) included a provision that obligated the utilities to purchase electricity from operators of small power plants relying on renewable resources like hydroelectricity and windpower as well as from cogeneration plants.[1] The intent was to overcome what the legislation's sponsors believed to be foot-dragging by utilities (often abetted, in this view, by state regulatory commissions) in introducing more efficient and environmentally benign generating technologies. The scheme worked at least as well as its proponents had expected, if not better. Within a decade, many so-called PURPA plants had come on line.

But the legislation had another result that its architects had not anticipated. Though there was nothing competitive about PURPA—the utilities were mandated to buy the power, at prices that were administratively determined (and often very favorable to the new suppliers)—the effect of the legislation was to create a new class of independent, nonintegrated power producers, and for the first time the idea that there might be an alternative to the traditional model of vertically integrated, regulated monopolies began to take root. More precisely, there began to be serious discussion of the possibility of at least limited market competition in power generation, if not transmission and distribution, whose status as a classic natural monopoly still seemed inviolable.

Debate on these matters was much influenced by a parallel rethinking of the nature of economies of scale in the industry. For decades, the conventional view had been that bigger was better in electricity generation; and indeed, the utilities had been steadily reducing their costs for years by building ever larger power stations. But by the 1980s, evidence was mounting that the returns to increasing scale had been exhausted. One reason was the utilities' unhappy encounter with nuclear power. By mid-decade, the distressed balance sheets of utilities struggling with runaway nuclear construction costs had joined the looming cooling towers at Three Mile Island as the most familiar symbols of this troubled technology. In parallel, important gains in the efficiency of gas turbines (many of them the product of innovations in aircraft engine technology), coupled with low natural gas prices and the environmental advantages of this clean-burning fuel, had made gas-fired power plants the technology of choice for new generating capacity. Instead of the multi-billion-dollar investment needed to build a 1200-megawatt nuclear station, the price of entry into the power-generating business was now a much more digestible $100–$150 million for a compact gas turbine plant of 200 megawatts or less. Given this, the idea of true market competition among rival generators of electricity no longer seemed unthinkable.

Predictably, most utilities at first resisted the idea vociferously. They insisted that in order to discharge their legal obligation to supply all of their retail customers reliably and economically, they had to have complete control over all of the stages of supply and delivery, including the generating plants. Being forced to rely on independent producers who had no such obligation to serve, who were not fully integrated into their systems, and who, it was implied, would lack the utilities' own dedication to quality operation, would inevitably degrade the quality of service they could provide to their customers.

But the excellent operating performance achieved by the nonutility producers soon neutralized one of the utilities' chief objections. The force of their arguments was further muted by the willingness of the independent producers to assume many of the financial risks of building and operating power plants—risks which under the old system of rate-of-return regulation had effectively been borne by the utilities' customers—while at the same time allowing their units to be subject to the operational control of the utilities.

The momentum for further deregulation continued to build, and throughout the 1980s a succession of initiatives at both the state and federal levels liberalized restrictions on the entry of nonutility generators and expanded the role of market competition in setting the price of "bulk" or wholesale power supplies. A number of utilities began to conduct auctions, open to all comers, in which they awarded long-term bulk power purchase contracts to the low-price bidder. Some state regulatory commissions began to insist that the utilities in their jurisdictions use competitive bidding as the mechanism for deciding who should build new generating capacity.

Even so, it wasn't until 1992 that one of the main barriers blocking the entry of nonutility generating companies was removed. The problem concerned the access of these companies to the transmission grid. Very often, the power from a new generating unit cannot reach its intended market without flowing along transmission lines owned by at least one and possibly several intermediate utilities. And these utilities have not always been inclined to make their lines available to the newcomers (especially if they were interested in selling power into the same market themselves).[2] Nonutility generators also worried that they would have to pay exorbitant tolls for the right to use the grid.

The Energy Policy Act of 1992 gave federal regulators the authority to order intermediate utilities to make their transmission lines available to *all* prospective users, including nonutility generators. As subsequently interpreted by the regulators, the legislation in effect barred the utilities from favoring their own generating plants in allocating their transmission resources, and required them to "wheel" power for others at a price comparable to what they would charge themselves to use the same lines.[3]

The new legislation also removed most of the other remaining obstacles to the entry of new firms into the power generation business. In particular, it amended a sixty-year-old statute that effectively prevented utilities from building and operating new power plants outside their service territories. PURPA had partially removed these restrictions fourteen years earlier, but its exemptions applied only to cogeneration and small renewable technologies. The Energy Policy Act went much further. Henceforth, a utility could in principle build a new power plant of any description outside its service territory and sell the power to any other utility that was prepared to buy it. The act also made it easier for other kinds of companies to get into the power generation business. Thus, for example, electric-power equipment manufacturers like General Electric, which had been forced to divest its holdings in electric utilities decades ago, are today reentering the generation business as owner-operators of commercial power plants. (Another significant provision of the act was to remove many of the restrictions preventing U.S. companies, utilities or otherwise, from building and operating power plants overseas.)

With the passage of the 1992 act, the old world of vertically integrated utilities was rapidly fading away. Some utilities announced that they were no longer in the business of building power plants. Many others—perhaps the majority—had every intention of following suit, even if they did not say so publicly. Between 1990 and 1994, nonutility generators accounted for more than half of all new capacity additions.

But in one critical respect things had not yet changed. Retail customers were still obliged to buy all their electricity from their local utility, even though that utility might be generating less and less of the power itself. Unlike long-distance telephone service after deregulation, retail electricity customers did not have the option to purchase kilowatt hours from their generator of choice. Each local utility continued to "bundle" transmission and distribution services and kilowatt hours into a single package for its retail customers, while nonutility generators were only permitted to wholesale their power—that is, to sell it to utilities.

The next step on the road to deregulation would mean giving retail customers the right to purchase kilowatt hours from whomever they wanted, and letting independent generators and others—importantly including other utilities—sell directly to end users. In effect, utilities would be required to unbundle transmission, distribution, and generation services, and retail customers would be given direct access to the transmission grid to arrange their own electricity supplies. But this step—"retail wheeling," in the jargon of the industry—was more controversial than any that had preceded it, because it precipitated the explosive question of what to do about the expensive power plants—including many nuclear plants—that the utilities had built under the old system of regulation and that had not yet been fully paid for.

Given the choice, customers would bypass these plants and buy electricity from the cheapest alternative source. But who, then, would pay for the unamortized portion of the unused plants? Would the investors in these plants be left with the bill? Or would the customers still have to bear the cost? By the mid-1990s, the problem presented by these "stranded investments" was looming as a major roadblock on the path to deregulation. We will return to this problem shortly, but first let us look once again at the events that led up to the present situation, this time from the perspective of some of the companies that responded to the opportunities the new laws and regulations were creating.

When Jacek Makowski resigned as CEO of the Cabot Corporation's Boston-based Distrigas subsidiary in the early 1970s to start his own energy firm, utility deregulation was not yet on the horizon. Makowski started a consulting practice that built on his extensive knowledge of the gas industry. Soon, perhaps realizing that he would never become rich on a consultant's salary, he and his partners set about acquiring a variety of gas-related assets, including a depleted gas field, which was turned into a gas-storage facility, and a cryogenic tanker, which became the basis for a new liquefied gas transportation venture. Another Makowski project at around this time was a small hydroelectric development in the old mill town of Lawrence, Massachusetts, that would eventually bear the distinction of being the first generating unit to be designated as a PURPA plant.

Begun in 1976, the Lawrence hydroelectric project was unusual in more ways than one. Small-scale hydro plants had been a common sight in the early days of the electric-power industry, but most had long since fallen into disuse as cheaper alternatives became available, and many had been abandoned. In Lawrence, Makowski and his partners saw an opportunity to redevelop an old site and sell the 15 megawatts of power to the local utility, which, like most utilities in the Northeast at the time, was trying to reduce its heavy dependence on oil following the massive price increases engineered by the OPEC cartel. Even so, the Lawrence project was an unlikely venture. As one researcher put it later, "in 1976 small-scale hydroelectric projects were still new; the partners had neither assets nor credibility as power producers; and the utilities and the state and federal regulatory

agencies were unaccustomed to dealing with private developers."[4]
But Makowski and his partners persevered, at considerable financial
risk to themselves.

The project was actually arranged before the passage of PURPA,
but the new legislation made it much more attractive to its developers. Though a long-term power sales contract had already been negotiated, PURPA in effect required the utility to agree to new terms.
As a "qualifying facility" under PURPA, the Lawrence project had the
right to sell its power at a price equal to the cost that the utility
would otherwise incur to produce the power in house. This was a
very good arrangement for Makowski, since the utility's alternative
was to use fuel oil, and after the second OPEC price shock in 1979,
the utility's fuel cost had risen well above the price it had previously
agreed to pay for Makowski's power. The Lawrence project, quite literally, was in the right place at the right time. As a Makowski aide
would put it much later, the plant "minted money," at least for a
while.

Later, after the world oil market cooled off, the Lawrence plant
was sold. But the J. Makowski Company went on to develop several
larger power plants in the Northeast, each one selling its electricity to
local utilities under long-term contract, and some also selling steam
to neighboring industrial customers. All of these plants used natural
gas as fuel, and took advantage of the extensive network of natural gas
subsidiaries and pipelines that Makowski was developing in parallel.
By the early 1990s, Makowski's gas operations were supplying 10
percent of the natural gas to the Northeast, and the company also had
five power plants producing a total of 1400 megawatts in operation or
under construction, making it one of the largest independent power
operators in the region.

A central feature of Makowski's growth strategy was its innovative
use of joint ventures and consortia. This was actually a necessity.
The company's equity reserves were small for the very capital-
intensive power business, and it had no construction and operating
experience to speak of. But with the help of a wide range of partners,
many of them much bigger than itself, this small, privately owned
firm, able to move rapidly to take advantage of changing conditions
and willing to take considerable financial risks, parlayed its deep
knowledge of natural gas markets into a substantial power generation
business. Along the way, it achieved several other significant firsts in
the industry, including the first large "non-PURPA" independent
power plant to be built anywhere in the country, the first new inter-

state gas pipeline to be built in the Northeast since the 1950s, and the first nonutility power plant to rely on a long-term contract for liquefied natural gas from Algeria. By the time the company was sold to a competitor in 1994, for a sum reported to be in the $250–$300 million range, Jacek Makowski was a wealthy man.

The company that bought Makowski's firm, U.S. Generating Company, had entered the independent power market much later than its new acquisition, but had quickly established itself as one of the foremost nonutility generators in the country. Formed in 1989 as a partnership of the big Californian utility Pacific Gas & Electric (PG&E) and Bechtel, the international engineering and construction group, and drawing on the formidable financial and technical resources of its two parents, U.S. Generating Company by mid-1997 had seventeen plants in operation or under construction in eight states.

With corporate headquarters across the street from each other in San Francisco, the relationship between Pacific Gas & Electric and Bechtel stretches back over many years. PG&E, one of the nation's largest investor-owned utilities, serves 4.4 million customers in northern and central California, and over the years Bechtel has helped it design and build many of its power plants. Bechtel, known around the world for its large-scale engineering and construction projects, is also recognized as a skillful and influential player at the intersection of international politics, technology, and finance, a reputation that was not diminished in the 1980s by the appointment of several of its alumni to high positions in the Reagan administration, including Secretary of State George Shultz and Secretary of Defense Caspar Weinberger.

The two main architects of the independent power joint venture were Bechtel's Cordell Hull and Mason Willrich, president and CEO of PG&E Enterprises, the affiliate that the utility had formed to pursue unregulated businesses. For PG&E, the joint venture offered a chance to earn higher returns for its investors by applying its expertise in building and operating power plants to a business with no regulatory ceiling on profits. Bechtel likewise saw an attractive investment opportunity, but also a potentially important new source of revenue for its core power plant construction business. This had recently been hit hard by the worldwide downturn in nuclear construction and by the dearth of construction activity of all kinds in the domestic utility sector. An independent power venture promised a new, captive market for Bechtel's power plant builders.

Willrich and Hull recruited Joseph Kearney, a young executive from Coastal Corporation, to lead the new joint venture. Their decision to bring in an outsider reflected a shared conviction that independent power was indeed a new kind of enterprise, one for which business as usual, as both organizations had understood it, would not suffice. From the outset, Kearney's ambitious goal was to build a national electric-power company. He had to act quickly, for the new venture was already a late entrant into the field. Almost a full decade had passed since Makowski had secured the first PURPA plant qualification, and since then more than a hundred new independent generating companies had been formed. Many of these were "one plant wonders," local entrepreneurs who happened to own a key resource—an attractive site, or an inexpensive fuel source. But others were serious competitors, with the depth and breadth of resources to remain in the market for the long haul.

To capture a significant share of the new market, Kearney had to create an aggressive, entrepreneurial organization, and in its first years the firm was dominated by a "development" culture, in which success was measured by the ability to strike deals with a wide array of players: owners of prospective plant sites, industrial users of steam, fuel suppliers, and, most important, utilities willing to sign long-term power purchase contracts—the meat and potatoes of the independent power business, without which lenders were not willing to finance new projects. It was a culture quite alien to the staid, sleepy traditions of the electric utility industry.

As Kearney saw it, the ability to manage customer price risk effectively would differentiate the most successful competitors from the rest of the independent power industry. By this he meant taking on the various kinds of business risk associated with a new power plant project and properly apportioning them among the different project participants. To the traditional regulated electric utility industry, the concept of risk management was itself novel. Most risks were eventually borne by the ratepayers in one way or another, unless they were the result of utility actions deemed imprudent by the regulators, in which case the utility's investors were also required to foot part of the bill. In a true market, however, customers ought to be able to choose how much of the risk they are willing to bear.

In pricing its product in the new wholesale market, therefore, an independent generator would need explicitly to consider the uncertain trajectory of fuel prices over the thirty-year life of the project, the risk of delays in permitting and construction, the risk of interest-rate fluctuations, technological risks (the independent generators were leading the way in introducing a variety of new technologies), and the uncertain needs of its utility customer. A successful project would be one in which these risks were allocated among the project participants—the fuel supplier, the equipment manufacturer, the lenders, and the developer and its equity partners, and, ultimately, the capital markets—in a way that best matched the ability of the participants to accommodate them.

But while Kearney emphasized dealmaking and risk management in the early years, he also made several important strategic choices with an eye toward the long-term development of the organization. He positioned U.S. Generating Company as a genuine partner of its utility customers—still an unorthodox marketing strategy in an industry in which most firms had got their start by using laws to force reluctant utilities to do business with them. He also pushed the firm to play a proactive role in environmental protection efforts. At times this strategy created internal frictions, but U.S. Gen gained a reputation as a community-minded, responsible neighbor and a reasonable interlocutor in regulatory proceedings. Among other benefits, this helped it to build the first new coal-fueled power plant in New Jersey in more than a quarter of a century.

Soon, as several of U.S. Gen's development projects began to come to fruition, the focus shifted toward plant construction and operations. A key challenge for Kearney was to create a culture that would promote rigorous stewardship of the firm's expensive power plant assets, while at the same time preserving the freewheeling, dealmaking culture that was essential to the company's rapid growth. As one of the company's senior executives put it, "We have to make room for both the hunters and the farmers." Another challenge was to create a structure that would promote learning and realize scale economies across the company's far-flung network of power plants—the sine qua non of being a national power company—while simultaneously ensuring that each plant was run essentially as an autonomous business unit, with the ability to respond quickly and creatively to local market developments affecting its profitability.

In many other industries such management challenges are the norm, but at the time they were quite new to the electric-power industry. Kearney and his colleagues were in effect inventing a new business model for power generation as they went along.

Then, within a very short time, another wave of change swept across the industry, forcing the company to confront an entirely new set of challenges. By 1994, the pace of deregulation was accelerating. The passage of the Energy Policy Act and the prospect of "retail wheeling" were opening up the industry to competition much faster than almost anyone had anticipated. For U.S. Gen, virtually everything was in flux. Its competitors, its customers, and the products they were demanding were all changing rapidly.

No longer was the company only competing against other independent power producers. As the transmission grid opened up, more and more utilities began selling their own unused generating capacity in the wholesale power market, often at aggressively low prices. Suddenly, the universe of competitors had grown to encompass a large portion of the utility industry itself. Almost overnight, in each region of the country in which it was operating, U.S. Generating Company had to contend with a new batch of utility rivals. Many of these had a much larger regional presence than U.S. Gen itself, and some were also its customers. A number of these firms were still hamstrung by outdated business practices. But others, seeing the deregulatory writing on the wall and committed to staying in the generation business, had been working hard to transform themselves into formidable competitors.

Meanwhile, the wholesale power market was also rapidly evolving. Customers were no longer willing to sign long-term contracts for large blocks of power. Increasingly, they were requesting smaller amounts of power, for shorter periods, and with more conditions attached. Increasingly, too, they were looking to their wholesale suppliers for flexibility, as a way of protecting themselves against their own increasingly unpredictable retail markets. In short, the wholesale market was becoming more sophisticated and demanding at just the time that competition was intensifying on the supply side. And overshadowing all of this was the prospect of retail wheeling and direct retail customer access to the transmission grid. As U.S. Gen's utility customers started to face the prospect of having to compete to supply their formerly captive customer base, they began putting pressure on U.S. Gen to reduce its electricity prices. All around the country cost-conscious utilities were seeking to renegotiate and even terminate power purchase contracts they had previously signed with nonutility generators. Some independents slid into bankruptcy—victims, in a sense, of the competitive forces they themselves had helped to unleash a decade earlier.

The situation demanded a rapid response from U.S. Generating Company. Its big new utility rivals could mix and match power supplies from multiple sources, enabling them to offer a broad range of flexible supply options. To compete effectively, U.S. Gen would have to quickly gain control of enough generating capacity to do the same. Since it obviously could not do this everywhere, it would have to target particular regions. And even in regions where it already had a significant presence, the only way to obtain the requisite base of capacity would be to acquire existing generating assets, or to enter into alliances with other generators that would allow it to aggregate their production with its own.

By late 1996, a promising opportunity was developing in New England, where U.S. Gen already had its biggest concentration of power plants. The region's second-largest utility, New England Electric System (NEES), announced a plan to divest its generating assets as part of an agreement with the Massachusetts state government and others under which it would be allowed to recover all of its stranded investment from customers.

The decision to become a transmission and distribution company only was a very difficult step for NEES, whose power-generating activities had been at the core of its mission for ninety years. But the company had been contemplating such a step for some time, and in fact was one of the first U.S. electric utilities to acknowledge publicly that it didn't necessarily have to remain vertically integrated in order to be profitable.

Indeed, NEES has long been regarded as one of the most innovative utilities in the country. Twenty years ago, the company was dangerously dependent on oil for 80 percent of its electricity production (only two other American utilities were more dependent on oil at the time). Its farsighted strategy for reducing this exposure (today the company is only 10 percent dependent on oil) included pioneering initiatives in new energy development and energy conservation. It was a leader in developing small-scale, alternative energy resources such as windmills, solid waste, and low-head hydroelectric projects (NEES was the customer for J. Makowski's inaugural PURPA project in Lawrence). It was also one of the first utilities to embrace the then-heretical idea that by deliberately working to slow the growth of electricity demand, it would benefit both its customers and its shareholders, and was the first American utility to create a "chauffagist" subsidiary—a business dedicated to reducing the energy needs of its clients. These programs also helped the company to gain a national reputation for responsible environmental stewardship.

In August 1997, NEES announced that it was selling its eighteen nonnuclear generating plants to U.S. Generating Company. It is clear that both companies are on the verge of radical change. As NEES's chief executive officer John Rowe observed, "the [divestiture] decision will change the very nature of our business." U.S. Generating Company will more than double in size and may soon become the largest generator of electricity in the New England region as a result of its acquisition. As one of U.S. Gen's senior managers put it recently, "we're going to have to reinvent ourselves again"—the third time in the company's short life that it has had to do so.[5]

In its fundamentals, this story of constant change and reinvention is no different from the experiences of any number of companies in a wide range of industries. But it is a story that until recently was largely unknown to the electric-power sector. All this is now changing. Multiply the intertwined experiences of New England Electric, U.S. Generating Company, and Makowski many times over, and you have some idea of the energy and creativity now pouring into an industry that for a long time lacked much of either. During the last several years, for example, more than 350 power-marketing firms have entered the industry, offering to package electricity from multiple suppliers for resale to customers. Though currently limited to serving wholesale buyers, many hope eventually to enter the much bigger retail market—at $210 billion per year, about the size of the U.S. market for new automobiles. In 1997, this group of firms overtook traditional investor-owned utilities and federal agencies to become the largest source of wholesale power.[6] It is a strikingly diverse collection of firms. Some, like Jacek Makowski fifteen years earlier, are independent entrepreneurs. Others are natural gas marketers or pipeline operators. Still others are commodity traders, some of them affiliated with Wall Street investment banks. And many utilities have also formed power-marketing affiliates. Many of these new businesses will likely fade from view. Nevertheless, it is difficult to believe that the majority of electricity consumers will not be well served by all this activity in the long run.

In the short run, though, much is uncertain. The immediate issue concerns the future of retail competition. Will the transmission and distribution grid indeed be opened up so that anyone will be allowed to sell electricity and related services to anyone else? If so, how, and on what timetable? Jurisdiction over this issue for the moment lies mainly with the states. California and the northeastern states, with the nation's highest electricity costs (see Table 6.1), have been making the early running.

Table 6.1: Average Electricity Rates for All Customers, by State, 1996

	Rate (cents/kilowatt-hour)		Rate (cents/kilowatt-hour)
Hawaii	12.1	**U.S. Average**	**6.9**
New Hampshire	11.7	Tennessee	5.2
New York	11.2	Montana	5.0
Rhode Island	10.5	Oregon	4.8
Connecticut	10.5	Wyoming	4.3
New Jersey	10.5	Kentucky	4.1
Massachusetts	10.2	Washington	4.2
Alaska	10.2	Idaho	4.0
California	9.3		

Source: Energy Information Agency, *Electric Power Annual, 1996,* Vol. I, August 1997, p.42.

The strongest pressure for direct customer access to generation services is arising where the gap between retail and wholesale power rates is greatest. As the deregulation of wholesale markets proceeds, the price of bulk power supplies is increasingly being set by market forces. And where substantial surplus generating capacity exists—as is the case in most parts of the country—it is the operating cost of the marginal unused unit that determines the wholesale price, at least in the short run. Retail prices, on the other hand, are based on the utility's historical or "embedded" costs. These are determined by past capacity investment decisions, many of which were made during the 1970s, when oil and gas prices were very high and projected to go higher still. This was the climate in which utilities and their regulators agreed that expensive new nuclear and coal projects should go forward. Under the rules of the regulatory compact, ratepayers are now paying for those judgments, and if nothing changes, they will continue to do so until the investments are fully amortized. And there is the rub. No one disagrees that these investments are uneconomic in today's environment. The question is who should pay for the sunk costs.

The utilities are caught in an exquisite dilemma. They would dearly love to avoid shifting the burden of these sunk costs to their investors. But they also recognize that high retail prices increase the likelihood that they will lose control of their customer base altogether. To many utilities, the prospect of a free-for-all, with customers fleeing, uncontrolled, to cheaper suppliers, may be even more disturbing than a "managed" transition scenario that would call for their shareholders to take sizable but predictable losses. A new federal rule allows utilities a transition period during which they can potentially recover the cost of investments that have been stranded by *wholesale* competition, but the bigger question concerns competition at the retail level, where the federal government, as we saw, lacks jurisdiction.

Expert opinion on the stranded cost issue is divided. Alfred Kahn, doyen of America's regulatory economists and a powerful advocate of competition in regulated industries, argues that utility shareholders should not be penalized by *ex post facto* deregulation decisions. According to Kahn, who presided over airline deregulation as chairman of President Carter's Civil Aeronautics Board and also served as chairman of the New York State Public Service Commission, "regulators made promises to investors, and government has a moral obligation to honor them."[7] But others disagree, arguing that compensatory investors for stranded investment would be both "inefficient and inequitable,"[8] would delay the coming of competition, and would "give the greatest rewards to those utilities which had the poorest foresight."[9] Still others advocate drawing a distinction between uneconomic investments that utilities made voluntarily, and those that they were forced to make, such as the high-cost, long-term power purchase contracts with cogenerators and small renewable developers that some were obliged to sign under PURPA.

The stakes are very large. For some utilities, the difference between the value of future revenues under current regulatory pricing rules and the future revenue stream if they were forced to sell their power in a competitive retail market is larger than the total value of shareholder equity. Competition at the retail level would therefore drive these companies into bankruptcy. On the West Coast, Edison International (parent of Southern California Edison) is estimated to have $12.4 billion in stranded costs alone, more than 150 percent of the value of its market capitalization.[10] One recent study conservatively estimated the stranded cost problem for the American industry as a whole as somewhere between $69 billion and $99 billion, or between 38 percent and 54 percent of total utility shareholder equity.[11]

Direct access to transmission service raises other issues, too. Will large customers use their greater clout in the marketplace to lock up the cheapest power supplies, leaving small businesses and residential customers to fight over the high-cost sources (and to pay the overhead costs of operating the system besides)? What will happen to the lifeline rates and other special discounts provided to low-income and elderly customers today? What about the conservation and clean energy programs that environmental activist groups have pressured the utilities to adopt? (There is a certain irony in the spectacle of these groups, which have long regarded the utilities with deep suspicion, now joining with them to oppose deregulation proposals intended to erode the utilities' privileged position in the marketplace.) As Professor Paul Joskow of MIT has observed, the debate about retail competition

> has also become a debate about how we conceptualize the role of private utilities in our society . . . private utilities in the United States have also traditionally taken on a quasi-public role in providing various services and supporting various social programs that firms in competitive markets would not ordinarily find attractive. . . . Some opponents of retail wheeling want to maintain the utility as an entity that has a "public service obligation fulfilled with private sector efficiency." Many proponents of retail wheeling see it as an opportunity to get utilities out of the "taxation by regulation" business and focus their attention on producing electricity as a commodity as cheaply as they can.[12]

In California, after a protracted and closely watched debate, the state assembly enacted a new law in 1996 that will soon open up the retail market to competition. On 1 January 1998, all individual customers in the state will be free to purchase electricity from a source of their own choosing. The law further provides for an immediate reduction of 10 percent in the rates for residential and small business customers who continue to purchase service from their utility, and another 10 percent reduction by 2002. At the same time, the utilities will be allowed to recover 100 percent of their stranded investments through a surcharge that all customers will have to pay.[13]

On the other side of the country, several New England states are closely following California's lead. In Massachusetts, the Department of Public Utilities has played a less intrusive rule, laying out general guidelines while leaving the principal stakeholders to work out the details; but there, too, customer choice is scheduled to be introduced in 1998.

The pace of deregulation is likely to accelerate. Though state governments are presently the main arbiters, neither physical flows of power nor transactions in the marketplace respect state boundaries. If some states opt for full deregulation of the retail market, it is unlikely that others will have much success in keeping it out. This is one reason why the debate on retail wheeling in California is being so closely watched around the country.

The prospect of deregulation has stimulated a flurry of utility mergers, as firms seek to prepare for retail competition by pooling resources and cutting costs. New entrants are also appearing. Enron, the nation's largest natural gas marketer and also the leading wholesale power marketer, recently acquired Oregon's Portland General Electric, giving it direct access to retail electricity markets for the first time.[14] Several other big electric utility/gas company mergers have followed.

One effect of the growing competition will be to sweep away the big electricity price differences between neighboring utilities and between one region and another that were a standard feature of the regulation era. Hundreds of billions of dollars of existing assets in this most capital-intensive of industries are likely to change hands, as firms that are best able to optimize asset performance and deliver lower rates acquire ownership from weaker rivals. Further asset transfers will be induced by the progressive unbundling of generation, transmission, distribution, and related services, with firms assessing their strengths and weaknesses and deciding which phase of the industry to concentrate on. Big new national and international generating companies are likely to emerge in this process.

As regulatory uncertainties continue at home, new investment opportunities are opening up overseas. The Energy Policy Act of 1992 removed long-standing restrictions on U.S. corporate ownership of overseas utility operations. With demand for electricity growing at 10 percent per year or more in some parts of Asia and Latin America, and barriers to private ownership of power plants coming down around the world, the electricity supply industry is quickly becoming a global business, with large and growing international flows of capital, technology, and managerial know-how. Many American independent generators and utility affiliates are seeking out investment opportunities in countries where deregulation is further along than in the United States. Some are doing so with the explicit intention of preparing themselves for the eventual opening of the domestic market.

The Outlook

In the short run, the uncertain progress of deregulation will continue to dominate the American electric-power industry. In the longer term, technological innovation may change the face of the industry even more radically. Two broad trends can already be discerned.

Distributed Generation: The reversal of the historic trend toward ever larger central station power plants, which began during the 1980s, will continue. For the time being, conditions in the industry will favor the construction of relatively compact, fossil-fueled generators with capacity on the order of a couple of hundred megawatts or less. In parallel, advances in fuel-cell, solar photovoltaic, and microturbine technology are improving the relative economics of self-generation by certain classes of businesses and homeowners. The prospects for distributed generation will be further improved by the availability of cost-effective, small-scale electricity-storage devices. These are still some way off, but advances in battery technology, as well as the development of compact flywheels using a new generation of strong, lightweight composite materials, may eventually bring decentralized storage within reach. For the foreseeable future, the deployment of user-scale electricity generation and storage technologies in the United States will be concentrated in relatively remote locations, where the costs of delivering central station power are highest (though the opportunities may be greater in developing countries with more primitive transmission networks). But although the primacy of central station generation is not in serious doubt, in the long run the character of the electricity network will likely evolve toward a mix of large central power stations and a much greater number of small, dispersed generators, raising new issues of network coordination and control.

Intelligent Power Networks: As the costs of information processing and communication continue to decline, the electricity network will spawn an increasingly rich flow of associated information. Eventually, pricing information will become available in real time at every location on the grid, with local prices reflecting local supply and demand conditions, including the availability of scarce transmission and distribution resources, and possibly also the environmental costs of operating different generating units. Central and distributed generators, distributed storage devices, and intelligent appliances in homes and businesses will all be linked together by information networks. Appliances as well as generators will be programmed to switch on and off in response to local price fluctuations. As market information multiplies, retail customers with the appropriate metering will be able to choose from a proliferation of supply options. Supply packages will be tailored to match customer preferences for electricity quality, with prices reflecting different levels of interruptibility in service.

Customers will also have the option to pay a premium for guarantees of long-term price stability, with others preferring lower but more volatile prices. Independent power aggregators and retailers will emerge to serve these markets. Information about patterns of electricity use will become more complete as microelectronic control of heating, refrigeration, lighting, and electrical appliances grows more pervasive and increasingly precise. "Smart" homes and offices will create a treasure trove of market data for electricity service providers. The effect of all this will be to improve greatly the efficiency with which the industry's physical assets—the generating capacity and the transmission and distribution system—are used.

Already the prospect of growing overlap between the electricity and information networks has generated interest in synergies between the different kinds of providers. Telephone and cable companies are exploring opportunities to use electric utility rights of way to lay new fiber networks and install switching in distribution substations. Utilities, some of which have already built fiber networks for their internal communication needs, are beginning to consider a dual role as electricity and telecommunications providers.

The search for synergies has pitfalls. Although the sharing of rights of way is a well-established practice in the infrastructure industries, the joint packaging of electricity and information services may lure power companies into unfamiliar and inhospitable territory. In the information sector, the boundaries between infrastructure and "content" are fluid and ill-defined, and it is not difficult to imagine electricity companies intently pursuing infrastructure synergies, only to find themselves on the wrong side of the line.

All this is obviously speculative. But what is not in doubt is that the electric-power industry—like the semiconductor industry although for quite different reasons—will be vastly different in almost every respect ten years from now. Increased competition, massive asset transfers, structural deintegration, technological innovation, and political intervention will make for a tumultuous, even chaotic decade. Much of the action will remain invisible to the average electric consumer. Paradoxically, however, the firms most likely to thrive amid all the turbulence will be those that are most effective in finding new ways to deliver value to the huge consumer base.

CHAPTER 7

Creating New Industries: Systems Competition and the Emerging Age of Wireless

The patterns of recovery traced out in the last four chapters make it clear that there has been no standard template for America's industrial renewal. Each industry's experience has been quite different. This chapter fills in yet another part of the mosaic: the creation of new industries. It tells the story of one such industry, wireless communications. Led by cellular telephony, wireless is today the fastest-growing segment of the rapidly expanding global telecommunications sector.

The pace of growth is extraordinary, as Figure 7.1 shows. As recently as the early 1980s, cellular telephony still could not claim to be a recognized industry. Yet by the end of the decade there were 10 million cellular phone users worldwide. That population is projected to rise to 200 million by the year 1999.[1] This is equivalent to the addition of more than 60,000 new subscribers each day. American firms have figured prominently in the development of this new industry, among them Motorola—today the world's leading supplier of cellular phones, pagers, and two-way radios.

The rapid advance of miniaturization predicted by Moore's Law has helped fuel the wireless industry's spectacular growth. Already 5-ounce phones are commonplace, and today's leading-edge products, 3-ounce phones tiny enough to be worn as pendants, will no doubt soon seem hopelessly dated. In due course, portable wireless devices—handheld or even smaller—will send and receive electronic mail, data, and eventually even video transmissions as well as voice. Industry leaders describe a (not entirely reassuring) future in which everyone will have access to the full capabilities of the global telephone network and the Internet wherever they are: whether at home in a remote village, in a car stuck in downtown traffic, or in a jet streaking over the open ocean. Local wireless networks will span of-

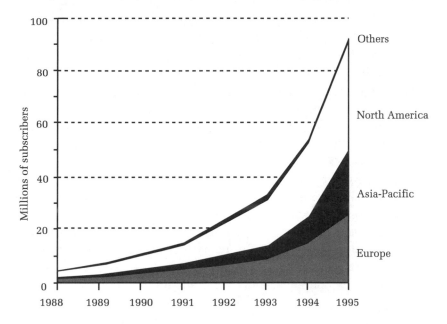

Figure 7.1 Worldwide Cellular Market Growth, 1988–95

Source: Jorma Ollila, "Telecommunications: Accepting the Challenge of Growth," MIT seminar, 8 March 1996.

fice complexes and university campuses, linking the highly evolved descendants of today's desktop computers—"virtual" whiteboards, handheld digital assistants, and the like—into cooperative computing environments. In the home, wireless technologies are already being developed to control lighting, heating, sound, and security systems, even garden sprinklers. And wireless communication is also finding many new applications in industry, enabling transportation companies, for example, to pinpoint the location and track the condition of cargo shipments anywhere in the world. (A short introduction to the main categories of wireless service is provided in Appendix II.)

The invention of new products and services, and the development of new industries around them, has long been one of the core strengths of the American economy, and was an important cause of the overwhelming superiority of American industry in the years following World War II. America's advantages in innovation during that period rested on four pillars: a domestic market that was vastly larger than anyone else's; a scientific and technological establishment that, unlike those in much of the rest of the world, had actually been strengthened by the war, in part by the influx of thousands of immigrant scientists from Europe and elsewhere; a workforce that was second to none in its education and skill levels; and a relatively abundant supply of investment capital. All of this enabled American industries to innovate, to exploit economies of scale, and to move down the learning curve faster than anyone else. In many fields, in fact, American firms were not really competing with foreign rivals at all. By the time serious competition emerged elsewhere, the American firms had frequently moved on to newer, more profitable products and markets.

In time, as the economies of Europe and Japan grew in size and sophistication, America's intrinsic advantages as a creator of new industries faded. Its confidence in its innovative abilities was further shaken during the 1980s as Japanese firms gained control of numerous high-technology markets, in many cases successfully exploiting discoveries that had been made in the United States. But even at the height of the Japanese ascendancy, the belief that America enjoyed unique advantages as a home for innovation never completely disappeared. And more recently, with the rise to dominance of American firms in software, biotechnology, Internet services, and a host of other new and emerging industries, much of the old confidence has returned.

Accounts of America's successes in these new industries typically stress the role of its nurseries of innovation: its deep, sophisticated venture capital markets; its system of industrially connected, high-quality research universities; and an entrepreneurial culture that encourages risk takers and rewards them handsomely when they succeed.

The story of cellular telephony and the rest of the wireless industry in the United States conforms to this picture in many respects. Emblematic is the career of the Seattle billionaire Craig McCaw, whose company, McCaw Cellular, founded in his university dorm room in the early 1980s and aggressively financed with risk capital, grew to be the nation's largest cellular service provider before being purchased by AT&T for $12 billion in 1994.

But there is also much about the story of wireless that departs from the standard view of how industries are created. The rise of cellular and the rest of the wireless industry reminds us that it is not only in dorm rooms and garages that new industries are hatched, and that size, too, has its advantages. On the equipment side of the cellular sector, the world's most successful suppliers—Motorola and AT&T (now Lucent Technologies) in the United States, Telefon AB L. M. Ericsson of Sweden, and Finland's Nokia—were already large, well-established companies with decades of relevant experience on which to draw when they launched their cellular businesses. From the outset, cellular was a large-scale, highly complex endeavor, demanding a depth and breadth of technical and financial resources that did not favor the entry of small or start-up ventures. The interesting question here is what differentiated the large firms that succeeded from others that might also have developed strong cellular businesses. How did these successful firms reconcile the need for scale with the role of risk-taking entrepreneur? Where did they find the flexibility to deal with the enormous uncertainties that are typical of the early stages of any industry, when even the most basic characteristics of products and markets have yet to be defined?

In another departure from the standard view of innovation, the cellular industry was global at birth, and suppliers needed a global perspective from the very beginning. The first commercial cellular networks appeared almost simultaneously in Japan, Europe, and the United States during the early 1980s. Subsequently, the most rapid market penetration occurred in Scandinavia and Australia (see Figure 7.2). And today some of the most advanced cellular technology is being introduced first not in the United States, nor in other advanced industrialized countries, but rather in the developing world, where huge numbers of people currently have no telephone service at all and for whom cellular networks—which take only a few months to install—are an attractive alternative to the costly, time-consuming process of building a landline infrastructure. Service providers in countries like China, Thailand, Malaysia, and India are leapfrogging over the wireline stage, as well as the first generations of cellular technology, and ordering the newest cellular equipment ahead even of European and American operators.[2] Equipment suppliers ignore these markets at their peril. As a practical matter, therefore, the scale of resources necessary to compete globally has been a prerequisite for success in the cellular industry since its inception.

Third, the rise of wireless reminds us that governments often play a more complex, multifaceted role in the development of new industries, especially in their early stages, than the stereotype of unshackled private entrepreneurialism would suggest. To be sure, deregulation has been a major stimulus to wireless development around the world. Jorma Ollila, Nokia's chief executive officer, points out that it has been a great boon to his company. In the old era, close working relationships between regulated telecoms companies and their preferred national equipment suppliers—which often stretched back over a century—made it very difficult for even the most innov-

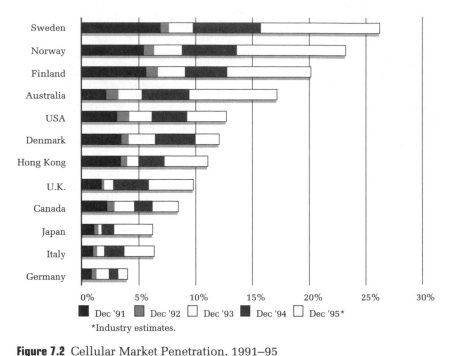

Figure 7.2 Cellular Market Penetration, 1991–95

Source: Jorma Ollila, "Telecommunications: Accepting the Challenge of Growth," MIT
seminar, 8 March 1996.

ative outside suppliers to break in. Now, however, with many countries deregulating, suppliers with relatively tiny home markets like
Finland are no longer operating at a crippling disadvantage.

Conversely, in countries where the pace of deregulation has been
slower, wireless industry development has often also lagged. The
French and German governments have been relatively slow to open
up their telecommunication markets to competition, and it is surely
no coincidence that Alcatel Alsthom of France and Siemens A.G. of
Germany, Europe's largest telecom equipment manufacturers, have
been absent from the top ranks of cellular suppliers. In Japan, too,
deregulation has been slow in coming (not until 1994, for example,
were individual Japanese consumers permitted to own portable
phones), and Japan's giant electronics and communications concerns
have also notably failed to establish a commanding presence in the
global cellular market.

But governments have also played important *proactive* roles in
wireless, in financing research and development, in equipment procurement, in allocating radio frequencies, and in helping to set technical standards for the industry. Indeed, the arcane domain of

standards has turned out to be one of the most intensely contested arenas of cellular competition, with both governments and companies jockeying for advantage in standard-setting forums around the world. As we shall see, the standard-setting process offers a valuable window on the role of government in the creation of new industries. First, though, it is useful to review some of the basic concepts of wireless technology, with a particular focus on cellular telephony.

At its core, cellular is a hybrid, a synthesis of two of the twentieth century's most successful technologies: radio communications and the telephone. The idea of combining the two dates back at least eighty years. As early as 1915, when radios were still primarily being used for naval communications, the American Telephone and Telegraph Company foresaw a different future for the radio telephone. "The results of long-distance tests," said AT&T's chief engineer, John Carty, "show clearly that the function of the wireless telephone is primarily to reach inaccessible places where wires cannot be strung. It will act mainly as an extension of the wire system and a feeder to it."[3]

The radio spectrum is a limited natural resource, and a basic thrust in the development of radio technology is to maximize the number of transmissions that can be crammed into a given frequency "bandwidth." In virtually all countries, the spectrum is controlled by public authorities. These authorities allocate the spectrum to different uses, such as commercial broadcasting, military telecommunications, two-way radio communications systems for police and fire departments, and taxi fleet dispatching.

The basic concepts of cellular systems, which promised much more efficient use of the radio spectrum than anything that had gone before, were laid out at AT&T's Bell Laboratories in the late 1940s. But many technical and institutional problems had to be solved before a commercial cellular industry could be seriously contemplated. One important hurdle was the allocation of the necessary frequencies. In the United States this entailed reallocating a portion of the spectrum that had previously been assigned to television broadcasters. After much delay, the Federal Communications Commission (FCC) finally took this step in 1970. Even so, another thirteen years would pass before the nation's first commercial cellular network began operating in the Chicago area.

The key innovation that differentiated cellular from previous forms of mobile telephony was its solution to the problem of spectrum scarcity. Earlier mobile systems had used a single, high-powered transmitter, which typically covered an area extending 50 or 100 kilometers from the transmission tower. Mobile callers were connected through the tower, or "base station," to the landline telephone system. Each caller was assigned a frequency channel—a narrow portion of bandwith—and any given channel could only be used by one caller at a time. This severely restricted the volume of call traffic. The mobile service offered by the Bell System in New York during the 1970s, for example, could only support twelve simultaneous conversations across the entire metropolitan area; the next would-be caller was blocked.[4]

The cellular idea was to divide the service area into much smaller zones, or "cells," each with its own low-power base station. Each caller within a cell would be connected through that cell's base station to the cellular system switch. The switch would then route the call either to a conventional telephone on the landline network or to another mobile user in a different cell. A given frequency could only be used by one caller at a time within a cell, but the same frequency could simultaneously be used by other callers in different cells. (To avoid interference problems, the same frequency couldn't be used in immediately adjacent cells.) By reusing the frequency spectrum in this way, cellular systems could support a far higher density of users than before. Moreover, as the number of users in each cell reached its limit, the cell could simply be divided into smaller cells, each with its own base station. Thus the capacity of the overall system could be continually increased.

Restricting the range of the radio transmissions in this way produced another important benefit. It reduced the power requirements of the telephone handsets, which in turn opened up the possibility of introducing small, handheld, battery-powered units.

A critical problem that cellular engineers had to solve was "handoff": a mobile user with a call in progress has to be able to continue the call without interruption as he crosses into a different cell. As the user approaches the cell boundary, a central control system must first decide which of the adjacent cells the call should be handed off to, and at what instant. An idle frequency channel in the newly chosen cell must then be assigned to the call, and the caller's phone instructed (via the original base station) as to the new frequency to which the call will be shifted. The frequency shift and the shift to the new base station must then be executed without the caller experiencing any interruption.

Another key problem that had to be solved was how to keep track of where subscribers are. When a traveling ("roaming") user turns on a phone to make or receive a call, the phone must first register its location with the nearest base station, which then sends the information on to the local switching center. This in turn identifies the user's home location, checks with the home switching center that the user is in good standing, and requests and receives the user's service profile. When all this has been completed, a call can be made and received as if the user were in her home service area.

From this brief description we can see that a cellular system has four major components: the phones themselves; the base stations; a base station controller, which manages the hand-off between different base stations; and a mobile switching center, which connects mobile users to one another and to the landline network. These components are arranged in what can loosely be thought of as two parallel networks: the transport network, along which the subscribers' calls actually flow; and an intelligent network that controls the performance of the transport network, that keeps track of where subscribers are, and that also carries out monitoring and billing functions.

The complex architecture of cellular networks encompasses a wide range of technologies, and much of the technological challenge lies in finding the best way to combine them. Since many of the component technologies are themselves evolving rapidly, the optimization task entails juggling advances on several technological fronts at once. It is a bit like trying to complete a jigsaw puzzle with pieces whose shapes are constantly changing. These system interdependencies help to explain why all of the leading cellular manufacturers have developed all of the main components of cellular networks. They also account for the prominent role that system integration skills have played in cellular competition.

As demand for cellular service has grown, the search for more efficient ways to use the radio spectrum has remained at the top of the technical agenda, and is driving the transition from analog to digital cellular systems. At first (and even today in many markets, including the United States), cellular networks used analog transmissions, a well-established technology that is also the basis for conventional radio and telephone communications. In analog systems, the voice signal is encoded into continuous variations on a carrier frequency using the technique of frequency modulation (FM). The modulated signal is decoded by the receiver at the other end.

The digital alternative involves first translating the voice signal into a stream of binary information (1's and 0's), then modulating the digital signal onto a carrier frequency. After transmission, the digital signal is converted back to an analog waveform.

Digital technology is more parsimonious in its use of the spectrum than analog. Digitized messages can be broken up, regrouped, and stored in ways which make it possible to use the same frequency channel for several concurrent transmissions. The spectral efficiency can be further improved with the aid of sophisticated data compression techniques that allow the same information to be represented in fewer bits.[5] In addition, interference between digitally transmitted conversations in neighboring cells can generally be reduced, facilitating reuse of the spectrum (as well as improving voice quality).

Digital systems have other advantages, too. They operate at lower power, allowing phones to be smaller and lighter and base stations more compact, and they can be readily adapted to transmit fax images, E-mail messages, and other kinds of data, as well as voice.

The industry is now in the midst of the transition from analog to digital, and the major uncertainty centers on which digital scheme will prove most effective. The main alternatives are known as Time Division Multiple Access (TDMA) and Code Division Multiple Access (CDMA).

The TDMA scheme takes advantage of the fact that a cellular radio channel can transmit information at a much higher rate than the information contained in human speech. As a result, a human voice need not be transmitted continuously. It may be broken into segments which can be sent at staggered intervals and reconstructed at the other end without the listener perceiving any interruption. The intervals between segments of one call are used to transmit segments of other calls, thus enabling the same frequency channel to be used for several calls simultaneously.

The other major digital scheme, CDMA, uses the whole of the available spectrum, rather than a particular channel. The basic idea is that the call is made to hop continuously from one carrier frequency to another over the entire spectrum bandwith. Each call is assigned its own "spreading code," the unique pattern of frequency hopping that will be used for that call. The codes are generated pseudo-randomly, and so are hard for an outsider to break (the technology was originally developed by the military to frustrate eavesdropping), but the sender and receiver of each call are preprogrammed to be able to interpret that call's code. Thus, after the code is selected at the beginning of the transmission, the receiver is able to follow the sender as the message shifts frequencies. Since each call uses a different code, the chance that two simultaneous calls will end up using the same frequency at the same time is small; moreover, even if this happens, the calls coincide for only a fraction of a second and the resulting interference is barely noticeable to the human ear. For similar reasons, interference between calls in adjacent cells is also less of a problem.

CDMA currently looks to have the edge over TDMA in the battle to pack more calls into the available spectrum. CDMA networks also have lower power requirements. This is likely to mean both smaller handsets and fewer base stations. But TDMA is the older and better understood of the two schemes, and to date has been the digital technology of choice in most countries.[6] Meanwhile, the commercialization of CDMA has fallen behind schedule, and at the end of 1996 the only working commercial networks of significant scale were in Hong Kong and South Korea.

Government Policy and the Analog-to-Digital Transition

The transition from analog to digital has occurred at different rates and has followed different paths in the United States, Europe, and Japan. Governments have been actively involved in each case, seeking to balance the sometimes conflicting interests of service providers, equipment manufacturers, and the public, and the different outcomes in the three regions partly reflect the different goals and methods of the government policymakers. The digital transition thus offers a fascinating glimpse of alternative government strategies in action—a sort of natural laboratory for technology policy.

On the whole, the U.S. government has been less inclined to intervene in the process than its European and Japanese counterparts, and this has created an environment that has been more conducive to private innovation. European policies, partly motivated by the goal of achieving continentwide interoperability, have been more interventionist, and one result has been that digital technology has penetrated the market more rapidly there. Japanese policy, perhaps the least flexible of the three, has arguably also been the least effective to date.

In the first phase of cellular development, which began in the early 1980s, analog was the technology of choice in all three regions. The second stage has involved a mixture of analog and first-generation digital networks. And the third phase—not yet fully implemented anywhere—will be dominated by more advanced digital systems with improved spectrum efficiency, and added functionality (e.g., fax and data transmission and Internet access, as well as voice). (In the United States this third generation of systems, which uses a different part of the radio spectrum, is called PCS, an abbreviation of Personal Communications Services.)[7] (see Table 7.1)

Table 7.1: Three Generations of Cellular Standards*

	First Generation (Analog)	Second Generation (Analog/Digital)	Third Generation (Digital)
United States	AMPS	N-AMPS (an.) D-AMPS (dig.) E-TDMA (dig.) CDMA (dig.) GSM (dig.)	D-AMPS (PCS) CDMA (PCS)
Europe	TACS (U.K.) NMT (Scandinavia)	GSM (dig.)	DCS-1800 (GSM)
Japan	NTT J-TACS	PDC (dig.)	PHS

*The three generations aren't contemporaneous in the three regions.
Source: R. Sakhuja, "Air Interface Standards for Digital Mobile Cellular Systems in the U.S., Europe, and Japan," S. M. Thesis, Department of Electrical Engineering and Computer Science, Massachusetts Institute of Technology, 1995.

The transition to digital technology has been taking place against a background of continuing deregulation of the telephone sector. Local cellular markets in all three areas have been partially opened to competition, in the expectation that this would improve the cost and quality of service. But policymakers and service providers recognized that users would not take kindly to competition if it created fragmented markets and restrictions on service. The value of a cellular phone to an individual user increases with the size of the population with whom the user can communicate, and users also want to be able to use their phones in as many locations as possible. The advent of multiple service providers was a potential threat to this, and created a pressing need for compatibility standards.

This in turn raised several tough questions for government policymakers. How should such standards be set? Should they be imposed by government fiat? Or should they be permitted to emerge de facto from a contest in the marketplace (much as the Microsoft-Intel standard for personal computers did)? Or should the government play an intermediate role, providing background support and legitimation to a cooperative, consensus process among competing firms? Also, *when* should standards be set? Acting too early would risk locking the industry into an obsolete technology; but waiting too long would create confusion in the marketplace, discouraging investment and perhaps penalizing domestic cellular manufacturers in interna-

tional competition. And how ought the demands of earlier generations of equipment to be balanced against the potential for future
technological advance? Understandably, neither current subscribers
nor service providers would want to be left holding obsolete equipment. But how could this be prevented without also inhibiting the introduction of newer, more advanced services?

Policymakers in Europe, the United States, and Japan have dealt
with these questions in different ways:

Europe: Cellular in Europe began as a patchwork of incompatible
national analog networks, and only recently have subscribers been
able to use their phones in different countries. The proposal to establish a single, pan-European standard was initially made by the
Scandinavian countries, who had already deployed the world's first
international cellular network in the Nordic area. The goal of continentwide interoperability was embraced by service operators in other
European countries as well as by the European Commission, which
saw both political and economic benefits in the idea. National governments welcomed it, too, though with varying degrees of enthusiasm. In 1984 it was decided that the new European standard, called
GSM (Groupe Speciale Mobile), should be based on digital technology. This was the first adoption of a digital scheme anywhere in the
world, and the standard setters hoped that the selection of a technically advanced standard would give the European equipment manufacturers a competitive edge both in the European market and
overseas, as well as providing consumers with superior service. Three
years later, following a series of competitive tests, a version of TDMA
was chosen for the new digital standard. (The CDMA option was considered to be insufficiently mature at the time.) The first GSM networks began operating in Europe in 1991, and the European
Commission has mandated that GSM will be the only cellular service
available in the Union by the end of the century.

Being the first to adopt digital technology does seem to have paid
off for Europe's cellular equipment manufacturers, especially Scandinavia's Ericsson and Nokia. There are about ten times more digital
phones in Europe than in the United States, and between 70 and 80
percent of the European GSM market is held by European manufacturers. (Motorola is the only non-European supplier with a significant
market share.) GSM is also selling well overseas. Many developing
countries without a well-established analog infrastructure are opting
to go directly to digital networks, and already more than eighty countries have chosen GSM equipment.[8] And the early installation of dig-

ital networks in Europe has given European wireless service providers and phone manufacturers a head start in offering the next generation of specialized information services—for example, smart digital cellular phones with built-in Internet browsers.

United States: In contrast to the early European hotchpotch, AT&T's complete dominance of the U.S. telecommunications market through the mid-1980s ensured that the first generation of American cellular networks all used the AT&T-developed AMPS analog standard. But since the breakup of AT&T in 1984, the Federal Communications Commission has sought to rely as far as possible on the market to determine which technologies will best meet subscriber needs. Service providers have been given broad latitude to choose among competing systems, and no single standard has emerged.[9]

Partly to protect their existing investments, the service providers have imposed some general technical requirements. In 1988, their trade organization mandated that all digital telephones should be "dual mode" to ensure backward compatibility with analog systems (i.e., the phones would have to support analog as well as digital service). This had the effect of making digital handsets 20–30 percent more costly than analog phones.

The net result has been that digital technology has been slower to make inroads in the United States than in Europe. A voluntary digital standard based on TDMA technology was selected in 1988, and was introduced commercially in 1992. The new standard, called D-AMPS, was designed to be compatible with the analog infrastructure and therefore to make the analog-to-digital transition easier. Even so, many service providers have chosen not to make the transition just yet, opting instead to deal with short-run capacity problems by upgrading their analog networks. Some conversion to digital technology is occurring, but widespread adoption is not likely to take place until the full-scale deployment of higher-frequency PCS networks, just now beginning.[10] These will almost certainly be all-digital, but in keeping with previous market-oriented policies, PCS operators are free to use any technical standard they wish.

Though the transition to digital in the United States has been slower than in Europe, one consequence has been to broaden the range of digital options that are available to service providers. CDMA technology has now advanced to the point that it is a credible alternative to both the American and European variants of TDMA, and in fact appears to be the technology of choice for many PCS networks.[11] Other American PCS operators plan to use the GSM standard.

The stage is thus set for a worldwide competition between TDMA and CDMA technologies. American manufacturers currently have the CDMA field largely to themselves, while the leading American and European suppliers each claim strong positions in TDMA, with the Europeans particularly well placed in GSM, the leading TDMA variant and the digital standard with by far the largest share of the global market. If CDMA overcomes GSM's lead and emerges as the standard of choice not only in the United States but in the rest of the world outside Europe, European manufacturers may be left at a disadvantage, and the merits of the more liberal American approach to standard setting will seem in hindsight to be greater. But any standard, once entrenched, is difficult to dislodge, and for the moment, the European strategy of adopting a single, technology-forcing standard early appears to be paying off.

Japan: In neither of those scenarios are the Japanese equipment manufacturers likely to enjoy a comparative advantage. Technology decisions for both the first (analog) and second (digital) generations of cellular services in Japan were dominated by NTT, the national telecommunications giant, and by the Ministry of Posts and Telecommunications.[12] As in Europe, the Japanese authorities selected a single, digital standard for the second generation of services, and, also like the Europeans, the Japanese opted for a TDMA scheme. Japan lagged the Europeans and Americans in its choice of TDMA by two or three years, and so in principle could have directly adopted either GSM or the American D-AMPS standard. (Indeed, by this time CDMA was also a more plausible candidate.) In the end, the Japanese decided to develop their own TDMA standard, called Personal Digital Cellular (PDC), a decision that seems to have been driven mainly by considerations of technological sovereignty and industrial competitiveness. But the PDC standard has not been adopted anywhere outside Japan, and is not likely to be in the future, since it offers no significant advantage over either GSM or D-AMPS.

Moreover, because NTT maintains such tight control over the PDC standard, other Japanese cellular carriers have developed their own, customized services, which has raised the cost of total service to the customer, and some have sought to introduce other digital standards from overseas in an attempt to preserve their competitive independence from NTT. The Japanese equipment manufacturers, though dominant in their home market, have not done well in overseas competition. They have had only modest success in the U.S. D-AMPS market, and hardly any at all in GSM markets in Europe or elsewhere.

Indeed, only recently have big manufacturers like Matsushita, Sony, and NEC begun selling GSM phones. With a head start of several years, their leading GSM rivals, Nokia, Ericsson, and Motorola, will be hard to catch. Nor are the Japanese firms likely to be well positioned if the advantage shifts to CDMA systems in the future. Though the problems that Japanese firms have had in international cellular markets are not purely the result of the country's standards policies, it is clear that these policies have not been much help, and may actually have hurt.

One bright spot for Japan is its Personal Handyphone System (PHS). This is a low-cost digital phone service that is proving to be immensely popular, especially among young Japanese consumers. It is a low-range, low-mobility service suitable for pedestrians in high-usage areas rather than occupants of fast-moving vehicles. The reduced mobility requirement means that the base stations and switches are much simpler than for conventional cellular systems, which partly accounts for the substantially lower cost. Unlike its counterparts in other countries, the Ministry of Posts and Telecommunications promoted the goal of a low-cost system that could bring affordable service to the masses (the target was to bring the cost down to a quarter of that of regular cellular service), and the result has been to open up an entirely new market niche for mobile communications. Services based on the PHS system are now being tested or implemented in eighteen other countries, and since there are no foreign firms competing successfully in the Japanese PHS market, the Japanese manufacturers are obviously very well positioned to exploit this interest.[13]

For the world's cellular equipment manufacturers, the different standards policies pursued by governments in the United States, Europe, and Japan have added an extra layer of complexity to an already complex and volatile business environment. The global progress of the cellular industry has encompassed many different streams of products, markets, and technologies—streams that periodically swell and shrink, branch out and recombine, and sometimes break off into isolated, short-lived eddies. At any given moment it is unclear which of these will grow and which will fade. Companies naturally try to channel the flow in the direction that is most favorable to them, but their abilities to do this are limited; in such volatile markets surprises are inevitable, and firms must remain open to new possibilities and new directions. Even the largest of them can't afford to immerse themselves in every stream, but nor can they risk not staying in the swim.

It is an extremely difficult balancing act. Firms must single-mindedly build competitive advantage through scale economies in manufacturing, marketing, and distribution, while simultaneously staying flexible enough to exploit new technical and market developments that might destroy those same, hard-earned competitive assets. To gain insight into how firms have balanced these competing requirements, let's consider the experiences of Motorola, by many measures the world's most successful supplier of cellular equipment over the past decade.[14]

Cellular Development at Motorola

For much of decade between 1985 and 1995, Motorola's General Systems unit, which includes both cellular phone manufacturing (the "subscriber" division) and the cellular infrastructure group, grew more rapidly than any other business in this fast-growing company.[15] In 1996, General Systems accounted for 40 percent of Motorola's total sales, and the company today is the second-largest manufacturer of cellular infrastructure equipment and the world's leading producer of cellular telephones (see Figure 7.3).

It wasn't always so. In the mid-1980s, Motorola seriously considered pulling out of the nascent cellular phone business altogether. Plagued by quality problems—defect rates on its phones were reported to be ten to twenty times higher than their Japanese competitors—the company's share of the domestic market was falling rapidly.

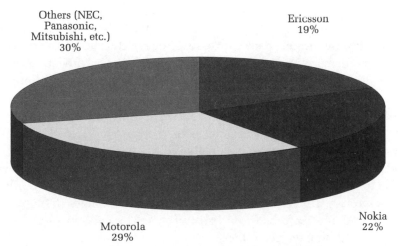

Figure 7.3 Cellular Phone Market Share (in units), First Quarter 1997

Source: Donaldson, Lufkin & Jenrette, cited in *Wall Street Journal*, 9 July 1997, A4.

In one disastrous month the cellular business unit actually reported a negative shipment rate; more phones were returned with faults than were shipped. Moreover, its main product, a derivative of the company's line of two-way mobile radios, was complex and too expensive. "We had the wrong product," acknowledged a senior Motorola official afterwards. To many both inside and outside the company, cellular seemed destined to go the way of the company's color television unit, abandoned in the mid-1970s under pressure from low-cost, high-quality Japanese imports, as well as its DRAM semiconductor operation, which was about to meet the same fate.

A few years later the company's cellular infrastructure group underwent a crisis of its own, as competition intensified and key customers began switching to other suppliers. Symptomatic was the 1990 decision by GTE, the nation's second-largest cellular operator, to replace its Motorola gear with equipment from archrival AT&T.

How did Motorola rebound from these potentially fatal setbacks? In the end, the best answer is probably the most straightforward one. By concentrating intensively on the fundamentals of its business, on cost, quality, and technical leadership, the company learned to deliver better products to the marketplace sooner than its rivals. But as we shall see, this superior performance in turn derived from a combination of organizational flexibility and internal discipline rarely found in such a large firm—a combination which, when coupled with Motorola's global reach, gave the company a set of organizational capabilities that was well adapted to the particular demands of this emerging industry.

For Motorola's subscriber (phone-manufacturing) unit, a critical turning point came in 1984. The company's cellular chief, Ed Staiano, then coming under heavy pressure either to move the phone-manufacturing operation offshore or to abandon it altogether, challenged his staff to rethink the entire manufacturing process from the ground up. In a powerful speech that cellular veterans could clearly recall a decade later, Staiano pleaded with the company for one last chance. If Motorola couldn't compete with the Japanese in cellular phones, he argued, its more established businesses like land mobile radio and pagers would sooner or later meet the same fate. It was time to draw the line. Survival was possible, he insisted, but only if the company was willing to make fundamental changes in the way it developed and manufactured its products. The cellular phone division would pioneer this effort.

Cellular, still at that time a fairly small business, was a limited gamble for the company, and the unit won a reprieve. (Years later, a senior Motorola official speculated that had it been much bigger the financial risk might have been prohibitive.) Staiano and his colleagues then set in train a series of innovations that culminated in the introduction of a breakthrough product eighteen months later. At that time the cellular market was still dominated by bulky "mobiles," intended for use in vehicles. The new phone, half the size of anything else then available, offered true portability for the first time. "We were doing portable while everyone else was still doing mobile," recalled one Motorola engineer. The new phone was also much simpler to manufacture than its predecessors. The part count was reduced threefold, and in parallel the manufacturing process was completely redesigned. The result was to cut the manufacturing cycle time from forty days to eight hours.

The new product was an immediate success, and Motorola's cellular phone sales began to pick up. The company gained additional breathing space when the Commerce Department ruled in Motorola's favor on dumping charges it had brought against Japanese cellular telephone exporters. But neither its own product leadership nor the protection provided by the Commerce ruling offered more than a few months' respite. Competitive products soon came crowding onto the market. Motorola had to find a way to institutionalize the changes that had made the initial success possible.

A major step was the initiation of the company's famed 6-Sigma quality program. Launched in 1987, the new program set out a series of very ambitious quality goals for the entire company. (These were later extended to the company's suppliers.) The resulting improvements in quality, while not quite achieving the original goals, were nevertheless extremely impressive, and helped to make Motorola one of the world's most closely studied companies. Much has been written about the 6-Sigma program, though the company's head of quality, Dick Buetow, insists that there is nothing complicated or mysterious about it. What it all boils down to, said Buetow in a 1993 interview, is a simple formula: "First map the process. Then fix the defects."

An important but often overlooked feature of the 6-Sigma program was that it created, at a time of extremely rapid growth and diversification, a universal goal and a language that everyone in the company could understand. It helped hold the company together even as the company's senior management was preaching the virtues of decentralization and employee "empowerment." In fact, Motorola has gone further than most large companies in practicing this philosophy, according much importance and internal visibility to its training programs and the contributions of its many autonomous problem-solving teams.[16] But at the same time the goals and principles of the quality program helped to harness the energies of an increasingly diverse and physically dispersed workforce. As Buetow pointed out, "You can go into any Motorola plant around the world and see the same charts."

Company principals increased the awareness of quality through well-publicized actions that quickly became part of company folklore. Every board meeting would start with a review of progress toward the quality goal, and only later would financial matters be taken up. And longtime chairman Robert Galvin made a practice of leaving operational meetings once the discussion of quality issues had been concluded. In keeping with the company's emphasis on decentralization, the "how" of quality was typically left to work groups and teams to figure out. But no one was in any doubt as to the "what." "We are the most dictatorial participative company in the world," explained Buetow.

This ability to strike a balance between decentralization and strong direction from the top helped Motorola to retain some of the flexibility and nimbleness of a small company while exploiting the advantages of its formidable size. The company's achievements in this regard are probably best known in the operational domain—in quality improvement, as just noted, and more recently in reducing cycle times. But Motorola also sought, and to a significant extent achieved, the same kind of balance in the strategic arena. George Fisher, Motorola's CEO until 1993, described it this way:

> You need a strategic intent—but within that context, you have to be totally opportunistic and aware. . . . Bob Galvin would always say, "You can't know what's around the next corner, so construct an organization that is able to adapt. But you have to have a framework, or you get too distracted and diversified. You keep your eye on the road."[17]

Galvin himself has pointed out that there have been many occasions during the company's history when it has been surprised by an unexpected turn in the market or a new technological development. He suggests that what has differentiated Motorola from its competitors has been its schooling in surprise, its capacity to recognize the unexpected for what it is and then change course quickly.

As the cellular industry continues its transition from analog to digital technology, one of the biggest unknowns, as we have seen, concerns the relative advantages of GSM, CDMA, and the other digital alternatives. But this is only the latest in a long stream of uncertainties with which cellular firms have had to contend. For a long time it was unclear how quickly the analog-to-digital transition would proceed. Part of the uncertainty centered on the rate of improvement of analog technology. Continuing improvements in the efficiency with which analog systems used the spectrum created a moving target for the digital competition. There was also uncertainty about the speed with which the entire market for cellular would develop, and with it the need for more efficient use of the existing spectrum. This was compounded by uncertainty about the willingness of various regulatory authorities to allocate additional spectrum, and hence to relieve market pressure in that way. And the divergent approaches to standard setting in the three regulatory arenas of Europe, North America, and Japan only added to the volatility of the situation.

For Motorola and its rivals in the cellular industry, all of these uncertainties have complicated the resolution of three fundamental strategic issues: (1) which areas of the world they should compete in; (2) which technical standards they should adopt; and (3) which of the components of cellular systems they should manufacture in house.

On the first question, Motorola appears never to have seriously considered holding back from any market. As one company executive put it during an interview: "If we don't compete everywhere, we'll create profit sanctuaries [for our competitors], and then they'll kill us. We even sold infrastructure in Sweden, to take on Ericsson." Another motivation was to use international competition to sharpen the company's technical and marketing skills. When Europe became the first part of the world to adopt a digital standard, Motorola moved quickly to establish a presence there in the new technology. It has since built on this experience to become a significant supplier of GSM equipment worldwide.[18]

For similar reasons, Motorola waged an epic battle during the late 1980s to gain access to the Japanese cellular market. Japan was a tougher nut to crack, in large part because of obstacles thrown up by the Japanese government. But eventually Motorola succeeded there, too, skillfully mobilizing the support of Washington in its fight (and in the process earning a reputation as perhaps the nation's most effective corporate practitioner of international technopolitics). Its calculation was straightforward. It couldn't afford *not* to compete in the huge Japanese market. It couldn't afford to give its Japanese competitors a profit sanctuary there; and it couldn't afford not to be exposed to Japan's demanding customers. As a high-level internal memorandum put it, "Japan is a marketplace where excellence in implementation, on-time delivery, full customer support, timely introduction of products, and competitive pricing can be nothing less than consistently perfect."[19] In 1993, the first customer for Motorola's new "Supercell" base station was a Japanese firm. Today, 80 percent of the infrastructure group's revenues come from overseas markets.

The strategy of competing everywhere has committed Motorola to developing technology to support all three leading digital standards—TDMA, CDMA, and GSM. But there are some technical domains in which the company has been less willing to compete. A continuing problem has been its relative lack of expertise in building complex cellular switches. Unlike its two biggest rivals, AT&T and Ericsson, switching technology was not one of Motorola's core strengths. For the two big telephone equipment manufacturers, the switch was the natural point of entry into the cellular business, and both companies used their formidable knowledge of switching technology as a base from which to move out into the rest of the cellular system.

But Motorola's starting point was different. Historically a radio company, the key technological asset it brought to the cellular business was its deep knowledge, accumulated over many decades, of how to use the radio spectrum efficiently. Moreover, unlike its competitors, who had initially thought in terms of mobile (i.e., vehicle-mounted) telephones, Motorola was committed from the outset to the development of the portable, handheld instruments that have become the hallmark of the industry, and its strength in semiconductor design and manufacturing was an important factor in the race to produce ever more compact, lightweight telephones. These capabilities helped establish Motorola as the leader in the handset segment, and also contributed to the company's leadership in the radio area of the cellular infrastructure business. In switching, however, Motorola was playing catch-up almost from the start.

The company had in fact originally intended only to be a supplier of cellular radios to what was then still the Bell System monopoly, expecting AT&T to produce its own switches. But the adoption of new federal regulations promoting competition in local cellular markets in 1982, and the breakup of AT&T two years later, transformed the structure of the market, and Motorola began competing fiercely with AT&T to supply complete working cellular systems—including the switches—to local cellular operators.[20]

The new emphasis on supplying integrated systems to a wide range of customers impelled Motorola to develop a very different approach to sales and marketing from the one it had started out with. (This was one of the reasons why, at around this time, the whole cellular operation was moved out of the Land Mobile Radio division, where it had grown up, into a new stand-alone unit, General Systems.) Furthermore, the systems themselves were rapidly becoming more complex, posing a new set of technical challenges. To design a new base station now entailed writing as much as a million lines of code—a far larger software development task than Motorola had been used to. Even more problematic was its relative inexperience in switching, where the software development demands were even greater.

Toward the end of the 1980s, the company decided that it would no longer try to be a major vendor of cellular switches. This was a controversial decision within the company, since it would clearly give AT&T and Ericsson an advantage in many markets. But the reality was that the resources needed to become a world-class supplier of cellular switches were too large, even for Motorola. The size and complexity of these devices was now such that an investment of billions of dollars would be required—and this at a time when Motorola's cellular telephone-manufacturing operation and its booming semiconductor unit were both also demanding multi-billion-dollar capital infusions to keep pace with rapid market growth.

Even before taking this decision, Motorola had sought to protect its position by developing partnerships with specialized switch manufacturers, including the Canadian firm Northern Telecom. But these alliances have not been completely satisfactory, and to reduce its exposure Motorola has simultaneously pushed for the adoption of "open" system architectures, which allow any vendor's switch to work with any other vendor's base station. The trend in the industry is, in fact, in this direction. (The European standard-setting authorities have championed it strongly, and many network operators want the flexibility to mix and match system components.) Even so, Motorola officials privately acknowledge that switching may be a continuing source of vulnerability for the company.

For the rest of Motorola's cellular infrastructure group, already committed to selling base station equipment under each of the three main international standards, the open architecture policy meant that an even wider array of product offerings would have to be developed. Customers, moreover, have been demanding more versatile systems. In the early days, when most cellular networks were still small, network operators sometimes replaced their entire infrastructure when a new generation of technology became available. But as systems have become larger and more complex, this is no longer practical. Operators, mindful of the still-unfolding competition among analog and digital technologies, want equipment that can operate in a variety of transmission modes and that can be reconfigured to exploit future technical advances as they come along.[21]

Paradoxically, as customers have come to put more emphasis on flexibility, Motorola's own product development organization has become more formal. Early on, the infrastructure group had handled each customer's needs in an ad hoc fashion. But as the number of customers and the menu of technological options expanded, the costs of customization—of engineering overhead, of extra inventory, and so on—were rapidly becoming unmanageable. No longer could product development be treated as a collection of "issues" dealt with in separate, loosely coordinated conversations with customers. The company realized that it needed a more systematic approach to product development, which maximized component commonality, software reusability, and a more formal project structure.

But as the cellular business has become more mature and the product development process more structured, the trap of unimaginativeness and conformism looms larger. In a recent speech at the MIT Industrial Performance Center, Robert Galvin reflected on the importance of creativity to his company:

> Our objective is to make our organization about five times more creative per person than we are today. . . . Then we match that to a purposeful expectation that we will accomplish a far higher level of achievement of anticipating and committing to our customers' needs. It is one thing to perform to the stated expectation; it is another thing to anticipate and then to have committed in such a timely fashion that no one is ever in a market before, and, as a matter of fact, we should be creating industries. Our company has created about six industries in the last 60 years, and when you create an industry you have the opportunity to dominate that industry. So we have a declared intention that we are going to become masters of the art of anticipation and commitment . . . just as we have organized so that quality is a dominant, driving force in our company.

Competition is intensifying in the industry. Nokia, Ericsson, and other firms are encroaching on Motorola's share of the phone market even as retailers are increasingly resorting to phone giveaways in order to tempt customers to sign up for more lucrative cellular service. As phones (and pagers) evolve into commodities and consumers overtake business users as the principal purchasers, consumer marketing and product differentiation based on brand identity and styling are likely to become more important.[22] Motorola's wireless divisions, which have historically thought of themselves as technological pioneers, will have another big adjustment to make. In a sense, the company is coming full circle, returning to a consumer business for the first time since its unceremonious retreat from radio and TV manufacturing two decades ago at the hands of the Japanese.

The lessons to be drawn from Motorola's cellular successes and emerging challenges are in many ways unique to that company. Had we focused on one of its leading rivals—Lucent, say, or Ericsson, or Nokia—a different set of issues would have been highlighted, reflecting the particular history and circumstances of that company.[23,24] But some of the lessons from the Motorola case are quite general. Perhaps most important, no single factor, no "silver bullet," accounted for its success. Dedication to quality, product leadership, global reach, strategic and organizational flexibility, and a management style that encouraged initiative at every level; all of these played a part. Moreover, these diverse organizational capabilities could not have developed without the conscious efforts of the leadership of the company—including, for much of this period, Robert Galvin himself, a master at the art of knowing when to lead his employees, when to goad them (albeit always civilly), and when to sit back and watch.

Throughout much of 1996 and 1997, Wall Street and the business press judged Motorola harshly, as a series of unexpected problems arose in several key business areas, including semiconductors and cellular telephones. The company was variously criticized for making bad strategic decisions (its handheld wireless "personal communicator" products, Envoy and Marco, had to be discontinued because of lack of demand); lack of coordination among business units; and slow product introductions, especially in the new PCS markets, where it was widely perceived to have fallen behind rivals like Nokia. But even though a recovery is not assured, it seems unwise to write off a firm that over the decades has repeatedly demonstrated an ability to find the wherewithal for organizational renewal.

The Outlook

The world foreseen by the wireless visionaries—a world in which everyone will be able to transfer all forms of information quickly and economically to anyone else over a global web of seamlessly connected wireless and wireline networks—remains a distant prospect. Today, the wireless industry is best understood as a collection of distinct services, each focusing on a different class of data. The boundaries between these service categories are ill-defined, however, and are likely to migrate around in the coming years as both service providers and manufacturers compete to stake out the most favorable terrain. Consider the following examples:

- *Personal Communications Services (PCS):* In the United States the number of PCS networks will grow rapidly over the next few years. PCS operators will be competing not only with each other to provide new kinds of wireless service such as fax and Internet access but also with pagers and with older analog networks for traditional cellular customers. For their part, many of the existing service providers will convert from analog to digital in an effort to increase capacity, broaden their service offerings, and so compete more effectively with PCS.

- *Cordless phones:* The first generation of cordless phones came with their own private base stations. Their range was typically less than 100 meters, and they couldn't be used anywhere else. The latest cordless phones are being designed to operate in larger networks. Private cordless phone owners will be able to use their phones in office environments equipped with cordless PBXs, and in some countries will also have access to the base stations of public "telepoint" service—a kind of short-range wireless payphone service available in high-traffic public places like shopping districts or airports, particularly in the Pacific Rim. Cordless service will thus begin to look more like cellular. Meanwhile, as cell sizes continue to shrink, cellular will acquire more of the characteristics of short-range telepoint and cordless service; cellular phones are already becoming available that can double as desk phone extensions.

- *Pagers:* An older technology that many predicted would be driven into obsolescence by cellular, pagers have on the contrary been gaining in popularity recently. The newest paging services offer two-way paging, and also provide text and voice messaging and specialized information services like stock market updates and sports scores. As time goes on, pagers seem likely to evolve into something approximating wireless "personal digital assistants" (PDAs), sophisticated handheld devices which previously had been considered as a separate segment of the market and which have had a rather disappointing track record until now. This in turn may bring paging service providers into competition with advanced digital cellular operators, who are also eyeing these new markets. (Indeed, the smart digital cellular phones now becoming available in Europe have many of the attributes of a wireless PDA.) Meanwhile, in developing countries like China, where only one in a hundred people own a telephone, pagers are becoming an inexpensive alternative to telephone service, cellular as well as landline.

- *Private mobile radio:* Private land mobile radio networks, traditionally providers of two-way radio and dispatching services to fleets of police cars, taxis, and the like, are now seeking to use the valuable spectrum resources they control to build new cellular-like networks for consumer and business communications markets.

- *Wireless cable:* Some cable television operators are expected to try to put their fiber-optic and coaxial cable systems to work as the spines of alternative "wireless cable" networks.[25] Most cable systems have formidable call-carrying capacity, and wireless calls can be routed through them just as they are today routed though the landline telephone network. Some PCS operators are now beginning to develop alliances with cable companies that may eventually enable them to offer an alternative to conventional wireline service. Alternatively, by adding base stations using the same air interface standard as the local cellular carrier, cable companies will in principle be able to offer cellular customers a compatible, alternative wireless service.

Against this background of continually shifting product market boundaries, a debate with potentially even more far-reaching implications for the industry is beginning to take shape over the basic architecture of wireless networks. The fundamental issue has to do with where the "intelligence" in these networks will be located—a question that is becoming increasingly important as the phones, pagers, and other wireless terminals are taking on a wider range of functions. In one vision, more and more of the intelligence will be placed in the network itself. An AT&T engineer has described this conception:

> The smarter a device must be, the greater the risk that its complexity will baffle the user. . . . One way to simplify the operation of handheld wireless gadgets and make them more user-friendly is to place some of the intelligence needed to accomplish useful tasks in the network. Our vision of PCS is that it will deliver the right service to the right location and device without any intervention by the caller or the subscriber. . . . The smart network, knowing your service preferences and whereabouts at all times, could direct the communication, whether a fax, e-mail, page, whatever, to the appropriate device and location, depending on where you are, and the type of call it is.[26]

An alternative approach would put more of the intelligence in the terminal, for example, in a "smart card" carried by the user. The user could plug the card into any phone that was equipped with a card reader, whomever it belonged to. The card would register the user's presence with the network, and all calls (or just those specifically requested by the user) would be directed to that phone.

The point here is not to debate the pros and cons of these alternatives, or to try to predict which service category or which particular provider will gain the upper hand in future wireless competition. The key point is rather that there is no end in sight to the uncertainty and instability that have characterized the cellular industry since its inception. This is something new. In the conventional model of industrial development, the turbulence surrounding the birth and early stages of development of new industries eventually dissipates as markets, products, and production methods become better defined. And as this transition takes place, the ingredients of competitive success also change. As the industry matures, the need for creativity and nimbleness and a willingness to challenge the status quo—the upstart instinct—gives way to the need for the capability to produce on a large scale at low cost and high quality.

But in the case of cellular, these phase transitions do not seem to have applied. Cellular was a large-scale enterprise essentially from birth, and quality, scale, and global reach were requirements from the very start. On the other hand, "stability," in the form of well-defined product markets, is still nowhere on the horizon. For the foreseeable future, the ability to manage uncertainty will remain a critical ingredient of success. The most successful firms in this industry will be those that combine a mastery of scale and the learning curve with an almost unnatural willingness to walk away from those hard-won assets if that is what the market calls for—the capacity, in other words, to turn on a dime.

PART III:

Best Practice
Revisited

CHAPTER 8

Three Forces of Industrial Change: Innovation, Globalization, and Deregulation

On the preceding evidence, there are as many explanations for America's industrial renewal as there are industries themselves. Each of our five case studies tells a different story. In the case of automobiles, the regeneration came from within, a rebuilding of Detroit's decaying organizational structures in the face of intense competitive pressures from Japan. In the steel industry, it was the outsiders, the upstart American minimills, that led the way. In the electric-power sector, deregulation has allowed the entry of new, entrepreneurial firms, and seems likely to drive out many old, inefficient ones. The fortunes of the semiconductor industry were reversed thanks in part to the American merchant firms' ability to respond more quickly than their vertically integrated rivals to extremely rapid changes in markets and technology, together with their success in overcoming earlier deficiencies in manufacturing performance. And as all of this was going on, new industries like cellular wireless, barely in existence a decade earlier, were emerging as major players on the industrial scene. In *Anna Karenina,* Leo Tolstoy famously observed that "all happy families are alike, (while) each unhappy family is unhappy in its own way." The story of America's recent industrial revival would seem to teach the opposite lesson.

But what about the leading firms in these industries? Do *they* have anything in common? Are there certain fundamental patterns of thought or practice associated with successful performance that transcend industry boundaries? At first blush, the idea that such firms would have anything in common seems even less likely than that entire industries would. What could such vastly different firms as Intel, Nucor, and Chrysler, to take just three successful companies we encountered in the preceding chapters, have in common aside from the fact of their success itself? Even within the same industry, the most successful firms often seem to be pursuing quite different strategies. Clearly, there is room for more than one model of success. Still, the question remains: Do the case studies point toward any general lessons for firms striving to succeed in today's economy?

Despite the diversity of the case studies, two broad trends do stand out. First, in each of the five industries, the traditional distinction between manufacturing and services is becoming less and less well defined; one manifestation is the growing pervasiveness of "service-enhanced" products. Second, almost all of the firms we encountered in the previous chapters were grappling with extraordinary instabilities in their environment; for these firms, clarity of purpose and function has been replaced by ambiguity. Let us briefly examine the origins of these two important trends.

The Rise of Service-Enhanced Manufacturing

The distinction between manufacturing and services has actually always been rather artificial. Many important activities carried out by manufacturing firms—marketing, distribution, engineering, design, maintenance, accounting, and so on—would be counted as services if they were supplied externally, by firms engaged exclusively in these activities (as, indeed, they are in many cases). For most manufacturers, in fact, these service inputs, whether internally or externally produced, account for a large fraction of overall production costs.

On the output side, too, the distinction between manufacturing and services is blurring. Traditionally, the essential difference between a service and a manufactured product has been that the former cannot be stored and therefore must be produced where it is consumed. (Janitorial services are an example). But in many fields this distinction is becoming less and less clear-cut. Think of the services that used to be provided by bank tellers but now are available from automatic teller machines. Or think of the preparation of income tax returns, where prepackaged software running on home computers is replacing some of the advice that used to be dispensed by local tax accountants. As the ability to store services like this makes it possible to produce them at a central location, far from the point of consumption, they take on many of the attributes of manufactured products.

Conversely, while "manufacturing" has traditionally meant the production of tangible objects, for today's customers the value of manufactured products increasingly hinges on intangible attributes—

speedy delivery, convenience of use, style, brand identity, reliability—that, were they not embodied in the product, would be thought of as services. Our case studies included many examples. Take the car industry, where firms are beginning to augment their traditional emphasis on product cost and quality with a new focus on making the purchase of a new car a more efficient and satisfying experience for the customer. In the semiconductor industry, we observed a growing emphasis on innovative, quick-response design, as integrated circuits become increasingly ubiquitous and integrated into daily life. Or recall the manufacturers of wireless communications devices, whose success is so dependent on their ability to divine the most desirable package of information services for consumers whose preferences in this area are still nascent.

The trend toward service-enhanced products has roots on both the demand side and the supply side of manufacturing markets. On the demand side, increasingly sophisticated and well-educated consumers are seeking out products with these characteristics, while on the supply side the new technologies of customization and quick response are bringing such products within reach of vast numbers of consumers at reasonable cost.

Even the emergence of "green" consumerism can be understood in these terms. In a wide range of product markets, consumers now seek assurances that their purchases are not contributing to environmental degradation. The product guarantees provided by manufacturers are a type of service. Thus, for example, clothing manufacturers like Patagonia affix labels to their garments telling consumers of their use of natural fabrics and environmentally benign processing techniques. And office equipment manufacturers like Xerox provide disposal services for copier waste products and guarantees to repossess and recycle old equipment.

The trend toward service-enhanced manufacturing extends to the industrial goods sector, too. Think, for example, of the machine-tool industry, the archetypal manufacturing business. Machine-tool manufacturers today sell not just hardware but integrated systems, consisting of the tools themselves, electronic controls, information systems, software packages, reliability guarantees, and operating and maintenance support. (It is not unusual for such firms to second their employees to their customers' factories for a year or more at a time to help operate and maintain their products.) They see themselves as providing "processes" and selling "solutions," rather than as selling hardware.

In a wide range of markets, then, it is the ability to bundle together a tangible good with an array of intangible services in order to produce the most desirable product that is becoming one of the most important keys to success in manufacturing competition. Information technology is playing a critical role in this integration, and it is a measure of its influence that the traditional distinctions between "high-tech" and "low-tech" industries are also fast disappearing. The productive use of information and knowledge is becoming the basis for success in *all* industries. In this sense, there is little difference between a "new media" company like the one that delivers a customized newssheet to my computer each morning and a hundred-year-old company like Levi Strauss that today can electronically measure an individual customer in one of its flagship stores, send the measurements over the Internet to one of its sewing sites, and deliver a custom-cut pair of blue jeans within a week or so.

Ambiguity as a Constant

The second broad trend revealed by the case studies is the rising level of volatility in the external environment of many firms. Unpredictability is hardly a new phenomenon in economic life, of course. One could even say that it is the lifeblood of business. Where there is risk, there is usually also opportunity. But the firms in our industries have recently been forced to confront uncertainties on an unusual scale. The case studies showed that three separate developments—deregulation, rapid technological change, and globalization—have combined to produce unusually volatile business conditions for a wide range of firms.

Deregulation: The lifting of government controls on prices and market entry across a wide range of industries is exposing many firms to new competitors for the first time. Industry boundaries that had stood unchanged for decades are rapidly dissolving as firms are allowed to discover new outlets and markets for their skills. Recall our study of the electric-power sector, where deregulation is attracting new entrants from several other industries, and may eventually erode the traditional distinction between the electricity and gas industries altogether. Or think of telephony, where the former regional Bell monopolies must now compete with long-distance carriers, cable companies, and possibly even wireless firms to provide local service, and where in the longer run the distinctions between wireline and wireless networks may disappear completely. The same phenomenon is occurring in other industries, including the financial sector, where traditional geographical restrictions on bank operations are being dismantled, and long-standing regulatory boundaries between banking, insurance, and brokerage are also eroding.

Technological Innovation: The boundary-disrupting effects of deregulation are being reinforced by technological innovation. Our cellular industry case study described the emerging competition for telecommunications markets between traditional wireline service, various forms of cellular wireless, and satellite technologies. (Inexpensive long-distance phone service over the Internet is another recent entry.) The competition between the personal computer and television industries to deliver Internet services to the home is a further case in point. On a larger scale, the use of digital techniques for storing and transmitting sound, images and data is rapidly breaking down the traditional boundaries between the computer, consumer electronics, telecommunications, entertainment, and media industries. Broadcast media are moving from the air waves to fiber-optic lines, while personal communications are moving from the wires to the air waves. Firms from each sector are jockeying for position simultaneously in "pipe," "platform," and "content."

Other industries are also being affected. Banks are nervously seeking to protect their flanks against the emergence of new competitors from the information industries offering innovative electronic banking services. Stand-alone management consulting firms like McKinsey find themselves competing with the consulting arms of accounting firms like Arthur Anderson and big manufacturers like IBM, while Anderson's computer services professionals compete with IBM in the market for software and related services. Professor James Brian Quinn of Dartmouth has gone so far as to suggest that information technology and other new service technologies (for communications, transportation, materials handling and storage, and health care) have "virtually destroyed the boundaries of all industries."[1]

Technological advances are contributing to business volatility in other ways, too. Some technological sectors are characterized by increasing returns to scale, and are susceptible to "tipping"—the phenomenon in which a supplier is able to convert a small initial lead into a large, lasting one by using its customer base to establish a de facto technology standard that becomes increasingly difficult to dislodge. (Think of Microsoft and Intel in the PC sector.) Elsewhere, rapid prototyping and simulation technologies are helping to bring about dramatic reductions in product development costs and cycle times, increasing what MIT professor Charles Fine calls the "clock-speed" of economic activity.

Other technologies are making it possible for firms to pay ever closer attention to the vagaries of consumer tastes, and to manage a far richer, less predictable product mix than ever before. Point-of-sale data systems provide nearly instant information to manufacturers about changes in consumer demand, while flexible manufacturing technologies coupled with computerized inventory control systems make it possible to produce a continuous stream of customized products not much more expensively than if all were identical. As production systems become increasingly responsive to market shifts, and as markets themselves become more segmented and specialized, the old adage that the customer is king is taking on new meaning; increasingly, consumers are finding themselves in the driving seat, able to call forth customized products and services from systems of production that until recently were more accustomed to performing repetitive, routine tasks according to well-rehearsed rules and procedures. Now the work of production organizations is no longer predictable, and the specialization and standardization that were characteristic of the old business bureaucracies are having to give way to more fluid, flexible arrangements.

Globalization: The growth of world trade and global economic integration is the third important source of economic unpredictability. High-speed communications, computerized trading, and relaxations on international capital flows are shortening the reaction time of investors to the latest economic news around the world and increasing the volatility of the world's capital markets. And in the "real" economy, new competitors can quickly emerge on the scene from almost anywhere, even as established multinationals, capable of coordinating production chains across vast distances, move their operations in and out of different countries at unprecedented speed in response to exchange rates fluctuations and local policy shifts. Paradoxically, closer global economic integration seems only to have brought greater volatility in the international division of labor.

For many firms, the effect of all this has been to create an environment of essentially continuous change, in which not even the most fundamental questions of strategy and identity remain settled for long. Which markets to compete in? What products to make?

Which competitors to watch? Where to produce? How to organize? Firms must constantly ask these questions because the answers are continually changing.

The presence of all this uncertainty also helps us to understand the larger questions with which this book began, the three interlocking puzzles of how well American industry is doing, how well the American people are doing, and how well the American people *think* they are doing. Two implications are fairly obvious. A third is less so, but may in the long run be the most important of all.

The first obvious outcome of heightened volatility is to complicate the task of taking stock: when everything is changing rapidly, it is more difficult to measure how well firms, industries, and individuals are actually doing. As we saw in chapter 2, uncertainty pervades even some of the most basic indicators of economic performance, including year-to-year changes in output and wages.

The second consequence is that rapid economic change tends to makes people nervous. When firms find it impossible to say with much confidence what they will be doing and where they will be doing it even just a few years into the future, the people they employ will naturally be more inclined to worry about their own circumstances.

But beyond these complications and anxieties, there is another consequence of economic uncertainty that may threaten the nation's well-being in a more fundamental way. The problem concerns investment. Other things being equal, investment by individuals and enterprises is more likely to be forthcoming when economic conditions are stable and predictable, and will conversely be inhibited at times of uncertainty. It is well known that instabilities and uncertainties in demand have the effect of shortening business planning horizons.

During the past decade or so, our economic institutions have in fact become much more sophisticated about measuring and managing economic risk. Capital market innovations like portfolio insurance, currency swaps, trading in financial derivatives, and other volatility hedges have now become commonplace. Insurance markets have proliferated. New techniques for quantifying and controlling the physical risks of economic activity to health, safety, and the environment have also been introduced. Still, the question remains: Is the uncertainty and volatility of the new economy contributing to a shortfall of investment, a shortfall that may in turn be largely responsible for what we identified at the beginning of this book as America's biggest industrial problem today, the problem of weak productivity growth? If so, what special measures might be needed to deal with this? These issues are the subject of Part IV.

First, though, let us revisit the evidence presented in the previous chapters, and look more closely at how individual firms have been adapting to these economic uncertainties so far. What general lessons, if any, do the most successful firms of the past decade teach us about how to thrive under such conditions? This is the subject of the next four chapters.

CHAPTER 9

Fads and Fashions and Nuts and Bolts

Over the last several years a great tide of books filled with detailed blueprints for improving national and corporate competitiveness has washed through the nation's bookstores. Many different tools and techniques have been advocated, among them teaming, benchmarking, time-based competition, outsourcing, strategic partnering, reengineering, concurrent engineering, listening to the voice of the customer, agile manufacturing, the learning organization, the virtual corporation, and many more. Keeping up with the latest trends, and sorting through them to find the insights and prescriptions most germane to their own situation, could easily have been a full-time occupation for America's business practitioners, and no doubt was for some.

But what difference has it all made? Is it here that the essential difference between the best of firms and the rest can be found? Or does the real secret lie elsewhere? Are the tools and techniques laid out in the management literature better understood as fashions, modish behaviors that are tried on and discarded like the Parisian spring collections, and as inconsequential in the end?

A recent article in *The Economist* crisply put the debunkers' case:

The average management fad, like the average love-affair, goes through a fairly predictable cycle from infatuation to disillusionment. First, a management guru comes up with an idea, coins a buzz-word, and sweet-talks the press. Next, one or two big companies, threatened with bankruptcy or desperate to seem with-it, give the idea a go. Stories are published about sensational results, the corporate world clamors for advice, and the guru forms a million-dollar consultancy. Finally, some business-school professor produces an authoritative report arguing that the fad is a fraud; the press discovers a raft of sensational failures; and the guru, muttering that he was misunderstood, comes up with another idea.[1]

It is easy enough to burlesque some of the more obviously marginal manifestos on the business bookshelf—the twelve-step programs, the personal growth agendas, and the other paraphernalia of the self-help movement. But not all of the contenders are so easily dismissed. Some have gained large followings among both practitioners and business theorists. A few can truly be said to advocate systemic change in business organizations, leaving no corner of the enterprise untouched. In this last category we find the two most influential American business reform movements of the last decade: total quality management (TQM) and business process reengineering.

The first to arrive on the scene was TQM, a comprehensive system of management practices based on the fundamental premise that quality is defined by and should be driven by the customer. Though its roots date back more than seventy years, to the legendary Bell Labs statistician Walter Shewhart, the TQM movement did not achieve prominence in the United States until the 1980s, when high-quality, low-cost Japanese imports were sweeping across the American economy. Humbled by the experience, many American companies started to pay serious attention to the quality techniques used by Japanese companies. They were further encouraged by the impressive revivals of American firms like Ford, Xerox, and Motorola, whose leaders took every opportunity to link their business successes to their own quality initiatives.

The reengineering movement took shape a few years later, in the early 1990s, and was a response to a somewhat different set of challenges. But as with TQM, its proponents advocated a comprehensive program of changes in organization and management practice.

Each of these reform movements has caught the imagination of a remarkably wide audience. Each has occupied the time and energies of vast numbers of people. If these are indeed mere fads, a great many firms have been willing to expend enormous resources on keeping up with them. But as we shall see in the following pages, they are not fads—if by this we mean behavior without content. Each embodies useful, even powerful ideas, with much relevance to the present circumstances of many companies. Each can claim triumphs—firms with greatly improved performance whose managers fervently believe that one or other of these approaches is the cause of their success.

As we shall also see, however, each also has serious limitations,

and there have been too many examples of failure and disappointment for either of them to be considered the panacea that their more
messianic advocates have claimed. Let's look in more detail at what
each of them has achieved.

The Quality Story

The story of how the quality movement reentered the United States
has an almost biblical cadence: a tiny group of octogenarian prophets,
without honor in their own land, wandering in exile for decades before returning triumphant, at the head of mighty armies of low-cost,
high-quality Japanese products. Then these stubborn visionaries, each
with his own band of faithful disciples, begin the huge task of converting America's corporate masses. Stern and unyielding in their insistence on total commitment to quality principles, they preach the
virtues of sacrifice and the need for struggle without end, promising
rewards both psychic and material in return. A new priesthood of
consultants and corporate directors of quality rises up, dedicated to
studying and interpreting the sometimes obscure texts of the patriarchs. The language of quality sweeps across American industry.
More American firms step forward to join Ford, Xerox, and Motorola
as exemplars of the quality creed. A new national quality award con-
secrates the movement. Within a decade, the quest for quality becomes the country's new business orthodoxy.

It is an irresistible story, made all the more intriguing by the anom-
alies and ironies that spice it. At a time when "change" was already
becoming the corporate mantra, firms were gravitating toward an ideology with intellectual roots in the 1920s. At a time when industry
stood accused of seeking only quick, tangible financial gain, it was
embracing an activity with no bottom line to speak of, merely a goal
of continuous improvement. At a time when firms were being advised to be flexible above all, they were willingly submitting to a
strict, all-enveloping regimen of quality management practices and
procedures. Even the advanced age of the movement's leading figures
seemed at odds with America's youth-oriented business culture, in
which leaders twenty years their junior were routinely superannu-
ated.

But by the end of the 1980s, the converts vastly outnumbered the
doubters. When the Malcolm Baldrige National Quality Award program (named after a former secretary of commerce) was launched in
1988, interested firms submitted hundreds of thousands of requests
for the application materials. Though only a small fraction of them

formally applied for the award, many more used the Baldrige materials to conduct self-audits and to guide their internal quality improvement efforts. A 1992 Conference Board survey of large American corporations estimated that more than 80 percent of them had a quality management program in place, and that a third of the rest were planning to introduce one soon.[2] Many of these companies also began pressing their suppliers to adopt quality programs of their own.[3]

But now there are clear signs that the quality tide is ebbing. A bellwether is the Baldrige program itself, which reports a significant decline in the number of applications, down from a peak of 106 in 1991 to only 29 in 1996.[4] To be sure, there are other possible explanations. Perhaps the principles embodied in the program have by now been internalized by the majority of firms; certainly even a casual look around the home strongly suggests that the quality of American-made products ranging from cars to cookers has, in fact, improved significantly over the past decade. Another possible cause is the proliferation of competing quality programs. Instead of applying for the Baldrige, smaller firms with a mainly regional market presence may be opting instead to participate in the growing number of quality award programs at the state and local level. And some export-oriented firms have declared a preference for obtaining certification under the ISO 9000 international quality standards program. (Many companies in Europe and elsewhere are beginning to require ISO 9000 certification of their suppliers.)

Curt Reimann, director of the Baldrige program at the National Institute of Standards and Technology, insists that the decline in the number of Baldrige applicants is not an indicator of overall interest in quality programs. But other evidence suggests that firms are, in fact, having second thoughts about TQM. A survey of five hundred American manufacturing and service companies by the Arthur D. Little consultancy found that only a third felt that their TQM programs were having a significant impact on their competitiveness.[5] Other studies have also concluded that many quality programs are not delivering on their promise.[6]

What accounts for the second thoughts about quality? A likely cause is that many companies embarked on TQM with unrealistic expectations about what it would do for them, and then became discouraged when it failed to produce results right away. The spectacle of troubled firms flitting from one improvement scheme to another in the hope of finding a panacea is unfortunately all too common. Such firms are often encouraged by overzealous consultants promising large gains at no cost (except, of course, their own fees). TQM is surely no different in this regard. Indeed, it may be particularly susceptible to the problem because, as the quality patriarchs repeatedly stress, it *is* a demanding discipline that cannot quickly be mastered by even the best companies. As one Japanese quality expert put it, there is a lot of "sweating work" involved—the hard, painstaking work of codifying and standardizing work processes, collecting and analyzing data, and implementing education and training programs.[7] Without this sweating work, even the most stirring declarations of dedication to quality and total customer satisfaction by the CEO will not amount to very much.

A second problem is that firms may be confusing means with ends. "At Motorola, TQM is how we do things," says Dick Buetow, the company's director of quality. "At other companies, where it isn't sticking, they think of it as something you do in addition to what you do in your business." This is a critical distinction; what Buetow is saying in effect is that quality has to enter the corporate bloodstream. But behind this lies another very important distinction: the fact that *as a business goal,* quality is inherently contingent. No one likes defective equipment or shoddy service. But beyond a certain point customers may be indifferent to improvements in reliability or increased functionality and unwilling to pay extra for them. In many markets, high quality is a condition of entry—a threshold to be overcome—but it is not a differentiating feature; the competition revolves around other factors. A company's need to absorb quality principles does not necessarily mean that it should always produce the highest-quality products or services of which it is capable. Companies that fail to make this distinction will often be disappointed.

Another cause of disappointment lies in the failure of many companies to grasp fully what needs to be done to implement TQM, despite having the best of intentions. Quality experts frequently criticize American firms for their piecemeal approach to TQM, for failing to understand the need for companywide, systemic change. This criticism first arose in the early 1980s when companies across the United States began to experiment with "quality circles." The ineffectiveness of most of those early experiments could be traced to a lack of management commitment and involvement; it was clear that even the most heroic efforts on the shop floor would come to naught in the absence of leadership from the top.

That particular lesson was absorbed, but the underlying critique of piecemeal American approaches to quality has persisted. Today, a principal focus of criticism from the quality gurus is American managers' continuing preference for "management by objective." These managers set the right goals, say the quality experts, but don't pay enough attention to the detailed planning and implementation needed to achieve them. Reportedly, this is true even of the firms that achieve the highest scores in the Baldrige evaluation.[8] According to one of the Baldrige examiners, senior American managers simply do not see the task of developing and deploying detailed processes and methods as the kind of thing they should be spending their time on.

This "hands-off" attitude is compared unfavorably with the approach typically taken in Japanese companies. There, much emphasis is placed on *Hoshin Kanri,* a term that has been translated into English, rather uninformatively, as "policy management." This is the formal, detailed planning process by which a firm's top-level goals are cascaded down through the organization to the level of small work teams and even individuals. It involves developing a complex hierarchy of subgoals and specifying the means for accomplishing them at every level of the organization. It is typical for Japanese corporate presidents to be intimately involved in developing and improving the *Hoshin Kanri* system, and in monitoring progress toward the goals at each level.

At the Industrial Performance Center we compared a group of American and Japanese companies that are at the pinnacle of quality achievement in the two countries—the quality elite, so to speak. The American firms had all recently won a Baldrige Award, while the Japanese firms were recent recipients of the Deming Prize—since the 1950s the premier form of recognition for quality accomplishment in Japan. Even in this exalted company, the more systematic and methodological character of Japanese TQM practices was apparent, as was the contrast between the senior Japanese executives' nuts and bolts orientation and the broad brush approach of their American counterparts. The latter devoted much energy to articulating the vision and broad philosophical principles and goals of TQM and to communicating them throughout the company. The Japanese Deming Prize winners hardly mentioned this role at all, but told elaborate stories demonstrating how intimately their senior executives were involved in the details of the *Hoshin Kanri* process.[9]

Joseph Juran, who, along with the late W. Edwards Deming, is generally credited with introducing quality management ideas into Japan after World War II, has sharply criticized American CEOs for delegating the responsibility for quality action plans to middle managers, a responsibility he regards as fundamentally nondelegable. "They thought they could make the right speeches, establish broad goals, and leave everything else to subordinates. . . . They didn't realize that fixing quality meant fixing whole companies, a task that can't be delegated."[10] Juran's criticism is no doubt on target. Yet a preoccupation with the details can sometimes cause companies to lose sight of the forest for the trees. One of the most notorious examples is Florida Power and Light, the first American firm to receive Japan's prestigious Deming Prize, in 1989. The utility's triumph was short-lived. Its quality control bureaucracy swelled to embarrassing proportions, while real gains in performance were hard to detect. Employees who in the first flush of enthusiasm had dedicated themselves to the pursuit of total quality later admitted that now they were only going through the motions. Within a year, most of the company's quality staff were gone.

The company's CEO, James Broadhead (who was not closely associated with the quality program to begin with), argues that its extensive preparation for the Deming Prize actually contributed to the problem, because of the excessive emphasis placed on process and structured reporting. This is, in fact, a common complaint about TQM programs. An overemphasis on the mechanics of the process breeds frustration and resentment among employees, who never reach the point of applying their own creativity to the solution of quality problems, thus depriving the company of the true benefits of TQM.

The swing of the pendulum at Florida Power and Light may have been extreme, but its experience points to a managerial dilemma that may be at the root of the problem that many companies are having with TQM. On the one hand, it is clear that in large, complex business enterprises philosophy, vision, and the communication of goals will only go so far in the absence of detailed management systems to implement them. On the other hand, detailed and highly prescriptive management systems, while very effective for dealing with the problems for which they were devised, also risk breeding organizational rigidities that limit the ability of companies to deal with new situations.

One other probable cause of the diminishing enthusiasm for quality management also deserves mention. This is that, in a sort of fratricide of the fads, it ran afoul of the next great wave of managerial activism: reengineering. Indeed, though similar enough in some respects, TQM and reengineering are radical opposites in others. Whereas TQM is a long-term process, a system designed to deliver continuous improvement over extended periods, reengineering proceeds in short, sharp bursts, its field commanders mindful of their general's crisp standing order: "Don't automate, obliterate."[11] Whereas design and execution are intentionally not distinguished in TQM, they are deliberately separated in reengineering. Whereas TQM seeks to align the organization by implementing detailed processes and procedures, the language of reengineering emphasizes disruption and revolutionary change. Amid the swirling chaos of reengineering, the painstaking "sweating work" of TQM is even more difficult to sustain.

Reengineering

Like many influential ideas, the concept at the core of the reengineering movement is simple: Instead of structuring a business enterprise around narrowly defined functions and tasks, it is better to organize around integrated business *processes,* sequences, or agglomerations of tasks, which in combination deliver something of value to the customer—the sequence of tasks that culminates in an automobile company unveiling a new car to its consuming public, for example, or that enables a bank customer to cash a check. Even the ostensibly simple operation of cashing a check in fact involves a complex series of steps involving many different people and functions. And the basic argument of the reengineers is that in enterprises that are organized along traditional, functional lines, the economic benefits of specialization, of dividing work up into narrow, differentiated tasks, have come to be greatly outweighed by the costs of coordination and integration.

These traditional organizations are fragmented, inflexible, and inefficient. A great deal of time and effort is wasted in handing off work from one function or department to another; errors proliferate, and the mechanisms that are created to correct the errors add redundancy and waste to the system. Much of what is done has no purpose other than to satisfy some internal organizational requirement that has no value to the customer. Tasks are divided into such narrow slices that they have no meaning for the front-line workers who must carry them out, and who therefore become bored and alienated. No one feels responsible for the final product.

The sort of thing that can happen when organizations become excessively fragmented is illustrated by the following description of the process for ordering new service from a local telephone company:

> The current systems have evolved through add-ons over the years. We first had a manual, serial process that handed off service orders from the business office to the assignment center to installation . . . then we

mechanized some of it in the business office and sent the mechanized information to the assignment center. Then another piece would be mechanized and sent on. We ended up with very complicated interfaces between the mechanized systems, with a lot of leakage of orders that did not flow through the system due to slightly incorrect information, errors, or mismatch. . . . So we would build another group of people to handle the exceptions . . . and as new services came on, we added more people to correct the problems that the system couldn't handle. Now, only 40% of our new orders and transfer requests flow through the system. With almost 5 million new orders and transfers a year, that's a lot of problems, and that negatively affects customer service. . . . That's where we are today. . . .[12]

The only way to overcome such problems, say the advocates of reengineering, is to rethink the division of labor in the enterprise from scratch, to start from a clean slate. And the way to do this is to make a cognitive shift from thinking about the organization as a set of functions to thinking about it as a collection of business processes—flows of work that cut across functional divisions. Each process must be redesigned from the ground up. All unnecessary stages and inputs must be eliminated, and only those elements that directly add value to the customer should be preserved. Everything else in the enterprise must then be redesigned to support these streamlined processes: the physical layout; the content and classification of jobs; the skills and training that are required for those jobs; the information systems; and so on.

The appearance in 1993 of the book *Reengineering the Corporation* by the management consultants Michael Hammer and James Champy propelled these ideas (and the authors) to the forefront of the management debate.[13] The book, which remained on the *New York Times* bestseller list for more than six months and has sold millions of copies worldwide, is notable for the vigor with which its authors argue their case for revolutionary organizational change. Nothing less than a radical redesign of business processes will do. A recurring metaphor is the "clean sheet of paper" with which companies should start their reengineering projects. *Everything* must be rethought, even the people. "In effect, a new process requires new people," says Hammer. "They may have the same Social Security numbers and inhabit the same bodies, but make no mistake about it: These are new people."[14]

Why did these ideas, which already by the early 1990s were no longer very new, achieve such prominence at that particular moment? The answer has two parts. Across a wide range of industries, customer-driven pressures for greater product variety and higher levels of service were giving decisive competitive advantage to the most nimble and responsive enterprises, and companies everywhere, especially big ones, were anxiously seeking a formula for organizational flexibility and agility. At the same time, there were signs that the enormous corporate investment in information technology over the previous decade might actually be starting to pay off. In particular, the rapid penetration of distributed computing systems that had begun in earnest in the late 1980s—networked PCs and workstations, client-server architectures, and the like—was bringing within reach the organizational theorists' nirvana of information instantly available to everyone in the enterprise who needed to know. The old, hierarchical organizational structures, with multiple layers of middle managers whose main function was to pass information up and down the chain of command, were rapidly becoming obsolete. Information technology, properly deployed, could help firms simultaneously become lean and flexible.

So the framework for change laid out in *Reengineering the Corporation* fell on receptive ears. It promised leanness and flexibility, and it provided a roadmap for making the most of information technology, and American industry was ready for the message. By 1994, 83 percent of America's largest industrial corporations reported having reengineered their workplaces.[15] Like TQM before it, but quicker, reengineering had attained the rare status of a business concept that almost everyone felt was too important to ignore.

It is still too early to have a comprehensive picture of what all this has wrought. Reengineering experts cite many examples of companies whose performance has been greatly enhanced, including Bell Atlantic, Federal Express, and Frito-Lay, and many more companies also report significant efficiency gains. Michael Hammer claims that reengineering has succeeded "beyond my wildest imagination," and that three out of four reengineering efforts work.[16]

But other evidence is less encouraging. Mutual Benefit Life, the insurance company whose success in reengineering its process for handling insurance applications was prominently cited in an influential early article on the subject,[17] was declared insolvent and taken over by state regulators not long after the article's publication. That is only one story, but other more systematic surveys point in a similar direction. A detailed analysis of twenty reengineering projects by the McKinsey consultancy revealed that while many had achieved sizable efficiency improvements in individual processes, only a small fraction had delivered significant benefits to the bottom line of the business unit as a whole.[18] Even one of the authors of the original reengineering manifesto admits that it has not been an unqualified success. "Reengineering is in trouble," announced James Champy in his sequel to the earlier book.[19]

The newer literature on reengineering is indeed replete with case studies of reengineering projects that have not succeeded. Many of the explanations echo almost word for word the earlier diagnoses of stalled TQM programs: a lack of strong leadership from top management; too much delegation to people who lack the authority to push through major changes; failures of communication; an insufficiently radical perspective; approaches that are too narrow and superficial, that fail to penetrate to the core of the organization.

Perhaps the audience really is to blame; perhaps Michael Hammer is correct in claiming that "a lot of people embark on reengineering but don't go anywhere because of failures of intellect or courage."[20] But a bigger problem may be the troublesome paradox that lies at the heart of the reengineering project itself. On the one hand, reengineering is predicated on enabling and empowering employees. As James Champy put it, "we need their hearts and minds because we're asking them to be more accountable—we're giving them more authority."[21] On the other hand, reengineering is also virtually synonymous with dislocation and job loss; for many companies, indeed, it has provided the methodology of downsizing. This is a divide that is not easily bridged.

Advocates of reengineering argue vigorously that it is *not* the same as downsizing. "Downsizing managers insist on misrepresenting their activities as reengineering," complains Hammer, but reengineering "is about rethinking work, not about eliminating jobs." Even though it might not be "about" eliminating jobs, however, more often than not it has had that result. And employees who perceive their jobs to be in jeopardy will be inclined to see Hammer's point as a distinction without a difference. They will not be reassured by stories such as the one told by one manager to Champy: "We don't really know how to do reengineering in our company; so what we do is, we regularly downsize the company and leave it to the three people who are left to figure out how to do their work differently."[22]

In an interview with the *Wall Street Journal* two years after *Reengineering the Corporation* was published, the two authors confessed to having been taken aback by the effectiveness of the resistance to reengineering, especially from middle managers. But since one of the principal objectives of reengineering is to eliminate many managerial functions, it is difficult to understand why they should have been surprised by this. In any case, the problem of reconciling the need for employees' "hearts and minds" with the imperative of eliminating tasks remains acute. Champy now seems resigned to a two-stage process, in which any vestige of a distinction between reengineering and downsizing seems to have disappeared: "We're brutalizing the workforce right now during this transitional period. If we're going to get what we need, the brutalization has to stop. I think it will when we dramatically downsize and learn to do much more with less. Then we can settle into the new social contract with our people and be more stable."[23]

But what exactly is this new social contract? The two authors refer generally to the need for employers to invest in the development of their employees, in return for which the latter will presumably give their all to the company. Hammer writes elsewhere of the need to build trust between employer and employee. (The operative metaphor here, a bit oddly, is drawn from the world of physics: "Trust is the 'strong force' that binds the atoms of the team.") Yet Hammer's view of the new employment relation evidently has little room for traditional notions of loyalty: "In the old corporation, what I needed to guarantee my future was hard work and loyalty. Those aren't worth John Nance Garner's bucket of warm spit any more. . . . You have to continually update, train and develop yourself so that you're ready for tomorrow's jobs. If you do that, I'm going to run after you because you're the kind of person I need."[24] Adds Champy: "What I'll tell my kids is: Have a profession, don't ever have a dependency on a single company, and measure your success by growth in skills and knowledge and what you have in the bank."[25] Evidently there is less to the battle for the hearts and minds of employees than meets the eye. The hearts, it would seem, are not to be contested after all.

CHAPTER 10

Putting People First

On 11 December 1995, a huge fire swept through a mill complex in the heart of the old Massachusetts industrial city of Lawrence. The factory was owned by Malden Mills, one of the very few textile firms still operating successfully in New England, most having long since fled to the South and overseas in search of low-wage labor. The destruction directly threatened fourteen hundred jobs at the mill, a cruel blow to a community already reeling from the loss of many of its traditional manufacturing jobs. A thousand more jobs at other company plants were also threatened. But on the morning after the fire, the owner of Malden Mills, Aaron Feuerstein, promised his employees that their jobs were secure, that the company would rebuild the ruined plant, and that it would continue to provide them with full paychecks and medical benefits through the Christmas season.

The fire and its aftermath generated widespread publicity. Feuerstein's actions were warmly praised, and he himself was portrayed in near-heroic terms in many press accounts. A few months later, a welder at the plant, in a not atypical sentiment, declared of Feuerstein, " . . . with what he's doing with Malden Mills, it's an honor to work in this place."[1] This was something quite different from the stories of reengineering that had been filling the business news up to then. Local politicians, more accustomed to standing by helplessly as employers downsized, outsourced, or otherwise moved out of town, rushed to Feuerstein's side to announce supplementary assistance measures, and to bask for a change in the reflected goodwill.

In the midst of all this, a few commentators noted wryly that one of the most remarkable things about the events at Malden Mills was how unremarkable the company's actions might have seemed in an earlier era. The acclaim for Feuerstein was a measure of just how rare a species the community-minded firm, loyal to its employees and committed to the welfare of their families, had become.

Indeed, by reminding everyone of the virtues of corporate loyalty, the Lawrence fire seemed also to underscore the dangers of its erosion, not only for employees and their community but also for corporate performance. For Malden Mills, besides being an enlightened employer, was a flourishing company. Feuerstein, a man obviously dedicated to improving the welfare of his employees, was also a prospering businessman. His company had thrived even as it had embraced—indeed, perhaps *because* it had embraced—an old-fashioned bargain: in return for the boss's guarantees of job security and decent (actually above-average) wages and benefits, the employees had dedicated themselves to serving the firm loyally, and to working hard and cooperatively to produce high-quality products. As Feuerstein put it, "We consider this community and its workers to be our greatest asset in supplying the quality and performance our products require."[2]

Not *all* of Malden Mills' successes could be attributed to this unwritten social contract, of course. Technological innovation and sound business strategy had also played an important role. The company had invented the wool-like Polartec and Polarfleece synthetic fabrics in the early 1980s, and its ownership of these brands had given it a highly profitable niche in the market for upscale outdoor apparel for more than a decade. This proprietary position in technology had helped Feuerstein to bankroll his convictions as an enlightened employer. On the other hand, those same convictions had been a factor in the company's development of these innovative fabrics in the first place. Feuerstein's faith in his workforce had been amply rewarded when production engineers and line workers at the Lawrence factory, working largely on their own initiative, had come up with the basic technical concepts for the new product line. Feuerstein had returned the favor with his decision to build the new production plant in Lawrence, despite its relatively high labor costs. He had determined that this was feasible because, unusually, the profitability of the new fabrics would not be dictated by low labor costs. But this same feature also made it a particularly attractive investment to someone with Feuerstein's strong sense of obligation to his workforce.

In any case, it was impossible not to be struck by the contrast between the latest manifestation of Feuerstein's convictions following the Lawrence fire and the general climate of anxiety and indignation over the downsizing actions of many large American employers (see

Table 10.1). "Corporate Killers," screamed the headline of a February 1996 *Newsweek* cover story about several very well paid CEOs ("Hit Men") who had recently presided over big layoffs. Other critics lambasted investors for "rewarding" companies announcing major reductions in workforce with higher stock prices. Still others painted unflattering portraits of rootless American multinationals prowling the globe in search of profits while paying scant heed to their domestic employees. Against this tense background, the case of Malden Mills seemed to provide an arresting counterpoint: a powerful reminder of what was being sacrificed along with the traditional social contract, not only by the employees and their communities, but also by the firms themselves.

Table 10.1A: Largest U.S. Layoff Announcements, 1997

Company	Job Losses	Company	Job Losses
Kodak	16,000	Levi Strauss	6,400
Boeing	12,000	Singer	6,000
Woolworth	9,200	Fruit of the Loom	4,800
Citicorp	9,000	Whirlpool	4,700
International Paper	9,000	Stanley Works	4,500

Sources: Challenger, Gray & Christmas, Inc., cited in *Wall Street Journal*, 13 November 1997, A2; *Wall Street Journal*, 5 December 1997, B2; *Wall Street Journal*, 17 December 1997, A4; *Wall Street Journal*, 18 December 1997, A3.

Table 10.1B: Largest U.S. Layoff Announcements: January 1993–January 1996

Company	Month Announced	Job Losses
IBM	July 1993	63,000
Sears	January 1993	50,000
AT&T	January 1996	40,000
Boeing	February 1993	28,000
Digital Equipment	May 1994	20,000

Source: Challenger, Gray & Christmas, cited in *Time* magazine, 15 January 1996, p. 45.

It is easy to exaggerate the role played by this social contract in American industrial history. Not everyone remembers the good old days fondly. Corporate loyalty may have been a two-way street, but access to it was restricted. Even at the height of American industry's postwar dominance, most blue-collar and hourly employees did not enjoy the same level of job security as the white-collar workforce, and were more likely to be laid off during economic downturns. And the loyal corporate soldier, a type made familiar by studies such as William Whyte's well-known (and highly critical) work, *The Organization Man* (1956), was almost always a managerial employee.

But Feuerstein's version of the social contract is both more inclusive and more comprehensive. It extends beyond employment security guarantees to encompass better training, fuller employee participation, work teams, incentive pay schemes, and other measures that are repeatedly cited by academics, consultants, labor representatives, and managers themselves as key contributors to improved all-around performance.

Notwithstanding the hyperbole and thick layers of jargon that so often surround these claims, the story is certainly a credible one: well-trained, well-motivated workers, broadly responsible and cooperating with each other and with management, will produce better outcomes for both their firms and themselves than an unskilled workforce, operating within narrow, strictly enforced job categories, and subject to military-style command and control management, with little scope for creativity and initiative. Especially where markets are changing rapidly, where product quality commands a premium, and where complex technologies dominate the production process, it is surely self-evident that firms should need motivated, skilled, engaged, adaptable workers at every level. "Putting people first"—just another cliché in the wrong hands perhaps, but in the right ones surely a winning competitive strategy.

But what is the evidence that it actually works? Do these human resource practices really result in improved productivity and improved financial performance? Certainly the experience of Malden Mills and other companies we have already encountered in this book seems to lend weight to this view. Yet the possibility remains that the strong performance of these firms is mainly attributable to other factors, and that their adoption of these human resource practices has been more a result than a cause of their success. Beyond these anecdotal accounts, is there any hard evidence that demonstrates conclusively the performance benefits of putting people first? Moreover, even if such evidence exists, *how* exactly should people be put first?

Table 10.2 includes some of the progressive management practices with which firms have been experimenting. It is a long list. Which of these practices are most effective? Is training and development more useful than job redesign? Are employee involvement programs more or less effective than incentive compensation schemes? Which form of incentive compensation works best? How does profit sharing compare with gain sharing (i.e., tying wages to some measure of group output other than profits)? Do either of them work better than employment stock ownership plans (ESOPs)? Than "pay for knowledge" schemes? Should firms do all of these things? What if they only do some of them?

Table 10.2: Progressive Human Resource Practices

1. Recruiting and Selection
   - careful screening
   - orientation
2. Training and Development
   - quality training
   - customer visits
   - cross-training
   - interpersonal skill development
   - statistical process control training
3. Incentive Compensation
   - profit sharing
   - gain sharing
   - ESOPs
   - "pay for knowledge"
4. Participation
   - quality circles
   - self-managed work teams
   - employee suggestion systems
   - quality of work life programs
   - labor-management problem-solving committees
   - TQM programs
   - labor represented on board of directors
5. Job Design
   - job autonomy
   - variety of tasks
   - job rotation
   - reduced job classifications
   - 360° performance appraisals
   - fewer management layers + increased span of control
   - absorption of supervisory and quality tasks
6. Communication
   - financial/business information sharing with employees
   - social gatherings
7. Employment Security

Despite all the attention that these various policies and practices have received in the popular business press, there have been surprisingly few careful evaluations of their actual impact on performance. Partly this is because of the formidable measurement problems that are involved. With so many different approaches, it is difficult to separate out the effect of any single one. Moreover, even in their entirety human resource policies are only one of many instruments used by managers to try to improve the performance of their firms. Isolating the impacts of human resource management practices from those of, say, procurement strategies or capital investment policies is no easy task. And the job becomes all the more difficult if it is the financial performance of the entire firm that is to be evaluated rather than the operating performance of a single production site, because then a still larger number of factors must be disentangled.

Fortunately, a small body of research—most of it of recent origin—is now beginning to shed light on these questions. The preliminary evidence from this work points toward several interesting conclusions:

- the impact on performance of any single human resource management practice is generally quite small;
- combinations of *internally consistent* practices appear to act synergistically, producing overall impacts that are larger than the sum of the individual contributions;
- the more "progressive" these clusters of practices are, the more performance seems to improve;
- relatively few firms are fully committed to progressive human resource practices.

Let's review the evidence for each point in turn.

Many people, if asked to name an "innovative" work practice, would probably think first of "pay for performance" plans. Most workers have traditionally been paid on the basis of the amount of time they spend on the job. Today, the practice of giving employees a stake in the financial well-being of their company through measures such as profit sharing or ESOPs is increasingly widespread. Does tying compensation to performance outcomes yield better results? A few years ago, Princeton University professor Alan Blinder (later to serve a term as vice chairman of America's Federal Reserve Bank) organized a conference to consider this question. Published in 1990, the papers from this conference provide perhaps the best assessment of the evidence to date.[3] As Blinder noted at the time, while the advantages of incentive compensation might seem obvious, what is obvious is not always true. Sure enough, the evidence presented produced a few surprises. Although the data on profit sharing does indeed suggest that it raised productivity, the effect is fairly weak, and it is unclear whether the productivity dividend is large enough to pay for the profit-based supplements to wages. ESOPs, much in favor recently, seem not to have had much effect at all, and there is not enough evidence on gain sharing to support a conclusion either way.

A review of the evidence on alternative worker participation schemes at the same conference came to similarly hedged conclusions. While participation usually leads to productivity improvements, the effect is often small and sometimes statistically insignificant. A bigger contribution is more likely if the form of participation allows workers to make substantive decisions about their work tasks on a day-to-day basis, as distinct from "consultative" arrangements in which workers make suggestions to management in off-line problem-solving groups. But there is insufficient evidence to resolve the question of which particular participation mechanisms raise productivity the most, aside from a fairly definitive *negative* finding concerning the effect of giving labor a seat on the board of directors.

The most interesting insight from the conference was that the productivity impact of most incentive compensation schemes is likely to be enhanced if meaningful forms of worker participation are also in place, suggesting that there are important synergies between different human resource policies. As we shall see below, other researchers have found evidence of similar synergies.

At the most basic level, the proposition that different human resource policies are mutually reinforcing is nothing more than common sense. It seems unarguable that people will contribute most effectively to the performance of their firms if: (a) they are motivated to do so; (b) they have the necessary skills; and (c) they have opportunities to use those skills. If any one of these conditions is absent, performance will likely fall short of its potential. So human resource strategies that address all three of these criteria simultaneously should produce larger gains than would be predicted by simply summing the individual impacts of each one operating in isolation.

A closer look reveals the links between different human resource policies even more clearly. Take, for instance, a firm that is considering spending more money on screening job applicants and training the new hirees. Those investments should yield a higher return the longer the employees stay with the firm. Longer tenures will in turn be more likely if working conditions are attractive and if there are good prospects for internal promotion. The returns to screening and training investments will also be greater the more opportunities there are for the now more qualified employees to participate in decision making. The employees will in turn be more inclined to participate if they know that performance improvements resulting from their suggestions will not cause them to lose their own jobs. Worker participation is also likely to be more effective if the employees can expect to be compensated for their efforts. A good incentive compensation scheme in turn requires a performance appraisal process that is (and is perceived to be) fair and effective at recognizing strong employee performance. And if employees have confidence in the performance appraisal process, this will make them more likely to stay with the firm, thereby increasing the returns to training investments. And on it goes. In other words, recruiting and training programs, employee participation, pledges of employment security, incentive compensation, internal promotion systems, and good working conditions are all linked in a kind of virtuous circle. Conversely, the effectiveness of any one of these things will be reduced by the absence of the others.

This at least is the theory. But does it square with the facts? A growing body of research, much of it funded by the Alfred P. Sloan Foundation as part of a larger program of studies on American industrial competitiveness, suggests that it does.[4] Some of the first hard evidence confirming the internal logic of human resource policies has come from the steel industry. A team of researchers associated with the Center on the Steel Industry at Carnegie Mellon University and the University of Pittsburgh studied the effects of different human resource management practices on the productivity of American integrated steel plants.[5] No two of these plants are identical, so to minimize the problem of comparing apples and oranges the researchers focused exclusively on a single type of steel-finishing operation (confidentiality restrictions prevented them from disclosing which one). It turns out that fifty-one plants across the United States use this process. The researchers were able to visit forty-two of them, and discovered wide variations in the types of human resource policies that were being employed. They wanted to know whether the lines with more "progressive" policies were also performing better.

The chosen measure of performance was line "uptime"—the number of hours each year that the line is actually in operation. (An important goal of the plant operators is to maximize the output of these lines, which means running them as much of the time as possible.) After controlling for other factors that might degrade line performance—aging machinery, for example, or lower levels of quality in the steel being treated in the finishing operation—the research team was able to isolate the effects of the human resource policies. The results were quite striking. Taken on their own, individual measures such as work teams, quality circles, and incentive pay schemes seemed not to have much effect on performance. But when several of these measures were present, the overall impact was quite significant. Moreover, as predicted, the combined effect was greater than the sum of its parts. The evidence is thus consistent with the idea that the individual practices are mutually reinforcing, that is, that they operate as *systems*.

In all, the researchers found four dominant types of systems at the finishing lines they were studying. At one end of the spectrum were the lines that employed "traditional" or Tayloristic policies: minimal training beyond what workers were able to pick up on the job; strict work rules and narrow job responsibilities; minimal worker involvement in decision making; little labor-management communication; and incentive pay based on output quantity rather than quality. At the other end of the spectrum were the lines employing the most innovative practices—sometimes referred to as "high performance work systems." These had implemented progressive policies in all of the seven broad categories listed in Table 10.2. For example, the firms typically spent more than a year selecting, orienting, and training new employees before they actually began work on the line. Contacts between workers and managers were frequent and substantive and included the sharing of financial information. There was formal and informal training in production skills and team-based problem solving. All employees were paid salaries, with the salary level based on skills. There was also a "multi-attribute" gain-sharing pay plan. And the employees were given employment security guarantees. As Table 10.3 shows, the two other types of human resource systems occupied intermediate positions between these two extremes.

Table 10.3: Human Resource Management Systems in the U.S. Steel Industry

Specific Practices	Traditional System	Communication System	High Teamwork System	High Performance System
Multi-attribute incentive pay	NO	NO	YES	YES
Very extensive screening	NO	NO	NO	YES
Job assignment flexibility	NO	NO	SOMETIMES	YES
High worker participation in teams	NO	NO	YES	YES
Some teamwork practice	NO	YES	YES	YES
Employment security pledge	NO	SOMETIMES	SOMETIMES	YES
Regular off-site skills training	NO	NO	YES	YES
Information sharing and/or regular meetings with workers	NO	YES	YES	YES

Source: Kathryn Shaw, presentation at the Fourth Annual Sloan Industry Studies Conference, Pittsburgh, 17 April 1995.

What effect did these different approaches to human resource management have on performance? Some of the results are shown in Figure 10.1. Productivity was significantly higher at the lines with high performance work systems than at any of the other plants, whereas the "traditional" lines had the worst performance. (The research team

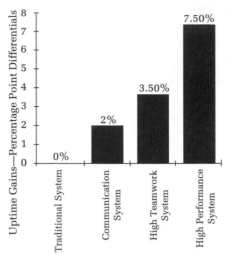

Figure 10.1 Relative Uptime Performance of Human Resource Systems in Steel-Finishing Processes

Source: Kathryn Shaw, presentation at the Fourth Annual Sloan Industry Studies Conference, Pittsburgh, 17 April 1995.

also measured quality outcomes and found that quality was also higher at the plants with the new work systems.)[6] A difference of 7 percentage points in uptime between the best and the worst-performing plants might not seem like much, but in the fiercely competitive steel industry, with its notoriously narrow profit margins, even small improvements in operating performance can go a long way.[7]

Implementing high performance work systems is not cost-free, of course, and an important question that the study did not resolve is whether the added costs of recruiting, training, performance bonuses, and so on exceeded the savings associated with the higher uptime. A perception that the cost-benefit balance is unfavorable might explain why so many of the lines had not adopted high performance work systems at the time the study was conducted.

Several other recent studies have provided additional evidence of the benefits of progressive human resource policies, including one survey of thirty American steel minimills,[8] and another of sixty-two automotive assembly plants around the world conducted by John Paul MacDuffie of the Wharton School.[9] The latter, a comprehensive study covering a large fraction of the world's nonluxury car production capacity conducted under the auspices of MIT's International Motor Vehicle Program, puts flesh on the bones of the "lean" production model that the MIT group helped to popularize a few years ago. (MacDuffie himself, then still a graduate student at MIT, was a member of the group at the time.) In his new research, MacDuffie finds hard statistical evidence that "bundles" of progressive human resource practices are associated with higher assembly plant productivity (fewer assembly hours per vehicle produced) and improved quality (based on surveys of new car buyers). MacDuffie's results also show that the benefit of these progressive human resource management policies is greatest when they are accompanied by manufacturing policies that deliberately seek to minimize inventories everywhere throughout the production process—the essence of the lean production approach, as discussed in more detail in chapter 3.

This research thus provides quantitative confirmation of the observation first made at Toyota's famous "just-in-time" assembly plants years earlier: that in order to take full advantage of low-inventory production systems, you have to have knowledgeable front-line workers with the skills, motivation, and the authority to solve problems on the line as they arise. More generally, MacDuffie's finding of "complementarities" between human resource practices and manufacturing policies is consistent with evidence that will be presented in chapter 12 suggesting that one of the most important attributes of the leading companies has been their success in aligning a broad range of corporate policies, practices, and strategies.

The similarity of the findings from the steel mills and automobile assembly plants regarding the mutually reinforcing nature of human resource policies is striking. But the results weren't completely convergent. While many of the same policies were observed in each case, the "high performance bundles" identified by the different research teams are not identical. Conceivably, this is merely an artifact of divergent research methodologies: the observed differences may have stemmed from differences in the way the researchers went about their research, and may be more apparent than real. But there is another possible explanation. Perhaps the details of the package matter less than the fundamental management philosophy lying behind it.[10] The critical issue may not be the effectiveness of any particular policy or group of policies, but rather the strength of the underlying management commitment to seeking greater worker participation. Or perhaps what really matters is even more fundamental, something that the quantitative models of the human resource researchers will probably never be able to capture very well: the presence of a high level of trust in relations between management and employees. As 3M CEO Livio DeSimone said of his firm recently, "Senior management's primary role is to create an internal environment in which people understand

and value our way of operating. . . . Our job is one of creation and de-struction—supporting individual initiative while breaking down bu-reaucracy and cynicism. It all depends on developing a personal trust relationship between those at the top and those at lower levels."[11]

Some of the research previously described does in fact support this more fundamental interpretation of the statistical results. At the end of a day-long interview, the plant manager at a steel-finishing line that had experienced one of the biggest transformations in both human resource policies and performance grew concerned that his in-terviewers might have been overlooking what he viewed as the main driving force for the turnaround at his plant. "Paramount in the whole thing," insisted this manager, "is that we began to establish trust."[12]

And as another steel plant manager acknowledged, creating trust where it has never previously existed, or after it has recently broken down, is one of the most difficult of all social tasks: "It's just difficult to change attitudes in old plants with a history of tension and mis-trust. We now share financial information with workers, but some workers still believe that there are two sets of books."[13]

In the absence of trust, even the most comprehensive package of human resource policies may not make much difference. The intro-duction of such policies may, of course, be instrumental in helping to build trust. But no more important, perhaps, than policies that are largely symbolic—the elimination of privileged parking spaces and executive cafeterias, for example, or the introduction of a uniform dress code for managers and workers. From a purely functional point of view, such measures seem superfluous; not harmful, of course, but not really relevant either. But when it comes to the creation of trust, symbolism can carry real weight.

If what matters is trust, actions that undermine it may have nega-tive consequences that are difficult to contain. Again, there is sup-porting evidence from the steel-finishing lines. Acknowledged one interviewee:

> At the end of a slow period, we forced all the workers who hadn't al-ready scheduled their vacations to take the week off. . . . This was a mis-take. It destroyed the cooperative spirit that had been building up around here. It's taking a long time to rebuild that spirit. . . . It would have been better to shut the line down and have the workers do more maintenance or training.[14]

And at another plant that was trying to introduce a "pay for knowl-edge" incentive plan which depended on necessarily subjective performance appraisals: "Once we said we were going to lay off workers after the equipment failure, the union really started dragging its feet on working out our pay-for-knowledge system. We still don't have it implemented yet."[15]

The layoffs in these examples were localized and did not last long—small perturbations compared with the restructuring programs now rolling across American industry. But their residue of shattered trust hints at the magnitude of the obstacles to the implementation of "high performance work systems," obstacles that may turn out to be one of the most damaging legacies of downsizing.

In fact, the best available evidence indicates that only a relatively small proportion of firms across all industries are implementing progressive human resource policies on a large scale. My MIT colleague Paul Osterman recently collected data on almost seven hundred large private-sector "establishments" (i.e., business locations), each with at least fifty employees. He looked specifically at four of the employee participation and job design practices listed in Table 10.2: self-managed teams, job rotation, quality circles, and TQM. He found that although nearly 80 percent of the establishments were experimenting with one or other of these practices, a much smaller percentage were using them on a substantial scale (see Table 10.4). Though the data are not definitive on this score, it seems certain that less than one third of them (and very likely much less) were broadly implementing policies in all of the seven broad categories listed in Table 10.2. Other evidence is consistent with this picture: the majority of American firms have adopted innovative work practices of one form or another, but only a small percentage have introduced a comprehensive system of these practices.[16]

Table 10.4: The Extent of Use of Innovative Work Practices*

Establishments using at least one practice on any scale	78%
Establishments using at least one practice affecting at least 50% of core employees†	64%
Establishments using at least two practices affecting at least 50% of core employees†	35%

*Practices included in the survey were: self-directed work teams, job rotation, quality circles, and TQM.

†Core employees are defined as "the largest group of non-supervisory, non-managerial workers at this location who are directly involved in making the product or service" at the location.

Source: Paul Osterman, "How Common Is Workplace Transformation and Who Adopts It?", *Industrial and Labor Relations Review,* vol. 47, no. 2 (January 1994): 173–88.

If trust is what matters, if "high performance" organizations must also be "high commitment" organizations, it is not terribly surprising that these practices should not have diffused more widely across industry. The problem may simply have been the absence, in the great majority of firms, of the kind of stable and secure working environment in which trust and commitment can thrive.

It is possible to take an optimistic view of the current situation. The present round of restructuring will be completed in due course, and memories of the turbulence and insecurity that accompanied it will eventually fade. At that point it might then be possible to reconstruct something like the old bargain with those workers who have not been marginalized. Firms that had once provided stable, secure employment would do so again for the workers who remained, and this in turn would provide the foundation for building a flexible, high performance organization.

The problem with this scenario is that it presumes an eventual return to market stability that for many firms may never occur. As we have already seen, relatively few firms today can predict with much confidence what their markets, products, and competitors are going to look like even a few years into the future. And for most of them this uncertainty is unlikely to be dispelled any time soon. For these firms, volatility has become endemic. To survive, they must above all stay flexible. Stability, once an objective, is now a risk—too much of it is a dangerous thing. The old bargain that was implicitly offered by the majority of employers to at least some of their employees—do your job, be loyal, and we'll take care of you—is no longer on the table, and may never be recreated. Even if they wanted to, firms facing rapidly changing markets, swift and unpredictable technological obsolescence, huge fluctuations in exchange rates, and omnidirectional global competition probably cannot offer the kind of employment security that much of the American workforce took for granted until recently.

To be sure, even in this more contingent scenario there will always be exceptions—firms like Malden Mills that are driven by a conviction that guaranteeing work for their employees is both the right thing to do and good business strategy, and able, through good fortune or their own ingenuity, to act on this conviction. Some other firms, enjoying sustained success in the marketplace, will be able to offer employment security as a collateral benefit, a by-product of their success. And a few industries may remain relatively insulated from the volatility that pervades so many others. But the great majority of firms are unlikely to fall into any of these categories. For them, the relatively stable market conditions that may once have made it possible to provide at least some of their employees with a secure working environment have for all practical purposes gone for good. These firms are more likely to see their salvation in maximizing employment flexibility.

The fundamental question posed by the evidence in this chapter is whether such flexibility is a Faustian bargain. Will employees who know that their firm regards them as "contingent" be prepared to make the wholehearted commitment of effort and initiative that the firm needs in order to succeed? Is it reasonable for firms to expect such a commitment if they cannot reciprocate in kind? Will the firms themselves be prepared to invest the necessary funds in recruiting and training employees to whom they are unwilling or unable to make a long-term commitment and who have no particular sense of loyalty to them? We shall return to these questions in chapter 14.

In the next chapter we turn from considering one business strategy, "high performance work systems," with demonstrable performance benefits but relatively few practitioners, to another strategy, large-scale investment in information technology, with few measured benefits but very widespread implementation.

CHAPTER 11

Information Technology: Doing IT Right

Revolutions come in many guises. Some are blindingly fast—sudden, shocking upheavals. Others unfold slowly and quietly, barely noticeable above the clamor of daily life. Still others are old news before they begin, their virtues and vices noisily debated far in advance of their arrival. So it has been with the information revolution—the subject of countless prognostications, polemics, and exhortations stretching back over more than four decades.

Much of the excitement has focused on the computer's transformation of business enterprise. Yet until very recently it was difficult to find hard evidence that "the biggest technological revolution men have known" (to quote one famous assessment of thirty years ago) had actually made much difference to overall business performance.[1] Indeed, through the end of the 1980s there was no sign that the huge investments in computers and software and new telecommunications systems—more than $1 trillion worth in the United States during the 1980s alone, according to one estimate—had led to either higher corporate profits or higher business productivity. As the MIT economist Robert Solow remarked, "You can see computers everywhere but in the productivity statistics." To some this was a genuine puzzle, the "productivity paradox" of information technology, while for others it merely confirmed the suspicion that the vaunted information revolution had been greatly oversold.

Solow made his much-quoted observation in the late 1980s, but a skeptic could almost as easily make it today. Heavy investment in information technology has continued in the intervening years. Today, it accounts for more than 40 percent of total business expenditures on capital equipment.[2] Yet recent productivity performance shows little sign of improving, and remains far weaker than what it was before the productivity slowdown of the early 1970s—hardly the stuff of which revolutions are made.

How could such a pervasive and promising technological advance have had so little apparent impact? There are several plausible explanations. One—intuitively appealing to anyone who has struggled with a stream of incomprehensible error messages on the computer monitor—is that technological change has proceeded at a pace that has spawned complexity, unreliability, and high costs in roughly equal measure with benefits. Perhaps Moore's Law, the rule of thumb that states that semiconductor transistor density will double every eighteen months, has a dark side to match the cornucopia of new possibilities it has opened up. New computer models becoming obsolete after a year; the constant need to upgrade systems; the complexity of designing software providing "backward compatibility" with multiple previous generations of hardware and applications; the difficulty of maintaining interoperability in networks whose components are constantly changing: all of this has added greatly to the costs of owning and maintaining computers, now estimated at approximately $10,000 per year for a typical networked desktop machine. Perhaps the technology has been changing too fast for the users' good.[3]

A very different interpretation of Solow's epigram (though almost certainly not the one he intended) is that it is more of an indictment of the way productivity is measured than it is of the true value of information technology.

No one, least of all those directly involved, would deny that productivity measurement is a very inexact science. (A short description of what is involved is included in Appendix I.) But is the productivity paradox of information technology really just a problem of mismeasurement? This is a tougher case to make, since it depends on showing not only that there are weaknesses in the measurement process, but that there is a systematic downward bias that is uniquely associated with the measured outputs of information technology.

The case has been made. It hinges on the argument that the contribution of information technology is disproportionately weighted toward just those kinds of output—increased quality, increased speed and responsiveness, greater convenience, greater variety, and so on— that conventional productivity measurement schemes have greatest difficulty in capturing. Measuring the growth in output, the numerator in the productivity ratio, is most straightforward when the output is a simple, tangible commodity—tons of raw steel, bushels of wheat, and so on. It becomes more complicated when intangibles are also involved, like quality and service. In principle, output measurements should reflect these factors, too. Improvements in quality and service should increase the market value of the product, and the higher value, in turn, should be factored into measures of output growth. In practice, however, the measurement process does this ineffectively. Improvements in quality and service aren't always reflected in higher market prices (the measure of value that the statisticians use); moreover, even when they are, their effect is often difficult to separate out from other contributors to price movements.

The problem is that it is just those sorts of improvements that new information technologies are best able to deliver. Think, for example, of the convenience of twenty-four-hour banking provided by automatic teller machines; or the added convenience of mobile telephones and electronic voice-mail systems; or the benefit of knowing that your local apparel retailer will never be out of your size for more than a day or two; or the value of instantaneously transmitting your medical scan to the world's leading specialist thousands of miles away. Quantifying the value of such benefits is not at all straightforward, especially when, as is usually the case, it is not possible to link them to specific price movements. There are thousands upon thousands of examples like this, and many of them go unreported in the official tabulations of output.

So the basic argument is that information technologies tend to increase the value of products and services by increasing their information content in ways that are difficult to quantify and that are therefore likely to be underreported. And as these technologies become more pervasive in the economy, the downward bias in estimates of productivity growth is getting bigger.

The belief that the measurements increasingly understate true output is shared by no less a figure than Federal Reserve Board chairman Alan Greenspan. "The proliferation of cutting-edge technologies is making it especially difficult to measure how well or poorly our economy is performing overall," said Greenspan recently. It is therefore "reasonable to conjecture that our productivity and output have been growing faster than our existing data imply."[4]

Well before Greenspan's pronouncement, MIT professor Erik Brynjolfsson and his students had attempted to estimate the aggregate impacts of information technology using a different approach. By studying the relationship between a firm's overall sales and its level of spending on information systems in a sample of more than 360 large Fortune 500 manufacturers and service companies, they found evidence suggesting that computers have been making disproportionately large contributions to output and growth relative to other kinds of investment.[5]

Findings like these led to a flurry of articles in the business press announcing that the payoff from the information revolution was finally here.[6] These reports cited, as supporting evidence, an apparent surge in U.S. productivity growth during the early 1990s. But a more careful analysis revealed that this growth spurt was no greater than the usual acceleration that takes place in the early stages of an economic recovery, and, sure enough, it soon petered out. Before disappointment could set in, however, the dramatic emergence of the Internet as a general purpose communications tool sparked a new wave of optimism, opening up whole new vistas of revolutionary possibilities for both businesses and home users, and creating a level of excitement not seen since the birth of the personal computer era fifteen years earlier. Once again the business press was filled with sightings of the long-awaited productivity payoff from information technology. A 1997 *BusinessWeek* editorial reflected the optimistic mood:

> In 1995, corporate spending on information technology skyrocketed. The big surprise was that investment in computers and software rose to account for an amazing three-quarters of the increase in all business investment. The Internet captured Corporate America's attention. Networking finally united all the systems, and voilà! Productivity began to take off.[7]

Others were not ready to concede that the so-called productivity paradox was over, though, and as of mid-1997 the official productivity statistics certainly lent no support to this view. But whether or not, to paraphrase Mark Twain, reports of its death are premature, the paradox itself also needs to be placed in a larger historical context. For the truth is that although information technologies have already begun to transform a vast range of industrial and commercial operations, we are still almost certainly only at the early stages of learning how to exploit their capabilities. The economic historian Paul David of Stanford University has drawn instructive parallels between the computer and another "general purpose engine" from an earlier era, the electric dynamo.[8] David points out that the availability of electric power eventually utterly transformed factories, homes, and offices, but that the transition from the old technological regime to the new took several decades. Indeed, during the early stages of electrification there was actually a slowdown in the rate of aggregate productivity growth in both the United States and the United Kingdom, the two leading industrialized nations of the day, and another forty years would pass before positive effects on the rate of growth began to be visible.

Why did it take so long? The simplest answer is that so many other things had to change before the full potential of the new technology could be realized. Physical systems that had been designed and built in the pre-dynamo era—factories, transportation systems, office buildings, and so on—couldn't be swept away overnight. Nor could the organizational routines—the ways of doing things—that were associated with them. This would have been true even if full knowledge of how to use the new technology had been instantly available. But in practice it took decades to develop and refine the countless other innovations, organizational as well as technical, that were needed to take full advantage of electric power, and to build up the necessary reservoir of skills within the population. In short, the new technology took so long to absorb and assimilate precisely *because* its implications were so revolutionary.

The same will surely be true of computers and communications technologies. Just as inexpensive electricity radically transformed the physical layout and flows of materials in factories, transportation systems, and homes, so information technologies will radically transform the way businesses collect, process, interpret, and distribute information—in other words, the way the work gets done. (The reengineering movement will almost certainly be seen in retrospect as a primitive step in this direction.) Think, for example, of the physical design of office space, which will have to change to accommodate the new styles of work made possible by the new technology. Some changes are already beginning to be evident: layouts that promote group work; space that can be rapidly reconfigured to match the rapid reconfiguration of project teams; shared offices to exploit the growth of telecommuting and the ability to spend more time in the field that laptops, E-mail, and wireless communications make possible. And just as the availability of electricity opened up wholly new frontiers of economic activity, so too will information technologies make possible the delivery of hitherto unimagined products and services.

But all of this will take time. The raw technological gains—the advances in processing power and communications capacity and so on—are in many respects the easy part. It is the *other* changes, the complementary innovations that are needed to embody these advances within working economic systems, that very often demand much larger investments of financial capital and human effort. Consider just a few examples:

- Advances in information technology are creating new opportunities to improve the performance of the construction industry (historically one of the poorest performers from a productivity standpoint). New three-dimensional modeling techniques, for example, allow architectural drawings to be linked electronically to a database containing the specifications and current costs of building materials. But taking full advantage of this technology requires close coordination of the many independent entities that typically participate in a construction project, including the traditionally separate domains of design and construction. This is the hard part. As a leading construction industry executive pointed out at a recent conference at the MIT Industrial Performance Center, it will require a complete departure from the arm's-length, hierarchical, and legalistic practices that have traditionally dominated the industry.

- Information technologies are also revolutionizing process control in many manufacturing industries. Without advanced process controls it would have been impossible, for example, to develop and commercialize the process for thin-slab continuous casting of steel—an innovation that, as we saw in chapter 4, has helped to transform the steel industry. But as chapter 4 also showed, it was not until the introduction of the electric arc furnace into steel mills that the business case for thin-slab casting became truly compelling. Together, these two innovations changed the scale economies of producing flat-rolled steel products in a way that neither one could have done on its own. Moreover, it took the emergence of a new group of steelmaking entrepreneurs, with radically different ideas about organization, strategy, and the management of people, to bring electric arc furnace technology into the mainstream of the industry. In this case, as in so many others, the introduction of new information technologies was just one link in a complex chain of interlocking innovations.

- Advances in bar-code technology and electronic communication are changing the flow of goods, services, and information between retail distributors and their suppliers. Bar codes now enable large retailers like Wal-Mart to match their floor stock more closely with changing consumer demands. Electronic communication links between retailers and their suppliers facilitate automatic reordering, and make it possible for manufacturers to produce on demand, in much shorter production runs. Warehousing needs can be greatly reduced, even as the probability of "stock-outs"—customers demanding products that are not in stock—is also diminished. But taking full advantage of these technological developments requires much closer coordination between retailers and their suppliers, with joint production planning, collaboration on product design, and innovations such as suppliers holding their inventory in retailers' shelf space.[9]

These few examples help to make the point that the economy as a whole will take time to shift to the new technological regime. In the end, "revolutionary" is probably not too strong a word to describe the impact that these technologies will have on business organization and practice; but at this stage the most interesting and important question is not whether the revolution has arrived, but rather what are the possible forms that it might take, and what choices are available today that might influence the outcome. Do these technologies force firms and their managers to act in particular ways? Is there only one way to do IT right? Or do firms have choices? If so, what are the main alternatives?

To answer these questions, let us examine three features of business organization that many think are especially susceptible to the influences of information technology: the skills of the workforce; organizational structure; and firm size. Much has been written about how these factors are being transformed by the new technologies. In each case, however, management theorists and others have lined up on both sides of the issue. How will the new technologies affect worker skills? Some see deskilling—the "dumbing down" of jobs; others argue that the skill content of most jobs is being driven up. What about the impact on organizational structure? Some see in information technology a tool enabling the organizational center to exert more control over the periphery; others see the opposite trend—more decentralization, and greater autonomy for individuals and small work teams. Will firms grow or shrink? Again, there are voices on both sides. Some argue that advanced computer and communications networks are expediting the rise of huge, globe-spanning corporations, able to coordinate multinational activities far more efficiently than before; others predict that the same technologies will cause the dissolution of large corporate bureaucracies and the emergence of "virtual" enterprises—flexible networks of small businesses (often sole proprietorships) rapidly forming, dissolving, and re-forming almost at will as new opportunities come along.

The empirical evidence on these issues is inconclusive. In each case there are persuasive examples on both sides. Consider, to take one such example, the impact of the bar-code-scanning, change-making, inventory-keeping electronic cash register on the skills of supermarket checkout clerks—surely an unambiguous case of job deskilling. But think also of what programmable automation has done to at least some machine operator jobs in factories. Workers who once were primarily engaged in repetitive physical activity now monitor and analyze streams of data, schedule machine maintenance, and even write software programs to operate the machines.

Evidence of the impact of computerization on centralization is similarly mixed. Immediate access to detailed financial and operating information allows small executive offices at the apex of large corporations to wield enormous authority, bypassing divisional managers who were once empowered to act on the corporation's behalf. On the other hand, distributed vendor databases eliminate the need for centralized procurement departments in many firms, while point-of-sale information systems installed by giant retail chains like Wal-Mart support a decentralized decision structure that gives individual store managers more authority to set prices to match local competitors.

The question of firm size is also unresolved. Even as the rapid rise of the World Wide Web opens the way for thousands of small new businesses to sell their wares over the Internet, some of America's largest corporations—huge firms like Microsoft, Hewlett Packard, and Motorola—are using their expertise in information technology to grow faster than almost all other firms, regardless of size.

What does such seemingly contradictory evidence imply about the availability of choices for individual firms? There are several alternative interpretations, all consistent with the data. One possibility is that appearances are deceiving: the sheer number of distinct technologies and business situations leads to a range of outcomes that is broad enough to make it *look* as though there are choices, but in reality there are none. In any particular situation there is only one "right" way to proceed. This is a version of what is often called the "technological imperative" argument.

An opposing view holds that the new technologies simply reinforce the existing predilections of firms and their managers. In this view, firms do what they do for other reasons, and the introduction of the new technologies doesn't fundamentally alter organizational outcomes. Indeed, from this perspective what really matters is the way that the technologies are molded by the organizations that use them, rather than vice versa. This is the "organizational imperative" perspective.

An intermediate possibility is that the new technologies influence choices, but don't determine them. The huge reduction in the costs of processing, storing, and communicating information makes certain types of organizational practices relatively more attractive than before, but what firms choose to do also depends on other factors: for example, the nature of their competition; their strategic objectives; and their endowments of "complementary" capabilities—forms of knowledge, managerial preferences, existing routines, and so on. Since these factors vary from one company to another, different companies will come to different conclusions about how best to organize. This, too, is consistent with the available empirical evidence.

A more radical variant of this argument is that the new information technologies are acting as a kind of "universal solvent," dissolving constraints that had previously limited the organizational choices that were available. In the limit of costless information, almost any organizational solution is possible. But even before this limit is reached, a much wider range of organizational practices will exist, and be observed, than ever before.

Deciding which of these interpretations is closest to the truth is not merely an academic exercise. There are practical consequences. Take the question of skills, for example. The conventional wisdom—for which, indeed, there is considerable hard evidence—is that computers are eliminating lower-skilled jobs and causing firms to upgrade the average skill level of their work forces. Will this continue in the future? Is it true of all occupations? And to the degree that it does continue to be true, will individual firms still have some flexibility to choose different strategies around the mean? The answers, moreover, have important implications for society as a whole. If firms have choices, and if the choices have consequences for society (in this case the need for skills), the public will perceive itself to have a stake in these choices, and will likely seek to influence them in a particular way.

Recent research by Professor Frank Levy of MIT and Professor Richard Murnane of Harvard sheds further light on these complex issues. Their study tracked the influence of computerization on the workforce of a single, large bank. They focused on one of the bank's lines of business—a "custodian" unit that sells accounting services to other financial institutions, particularly pension and mutual funds.

One of these services involves providing up-to-date calculations of the value of mutual fund shares, a task that the mutual fund managers themselves find convenient to outsource. The bank recalculates these values daily for its mutual fund clients and for the stock tables that are published in the newspapers each day. Levy and Murnane wanted to know how the jobs of the accountants who calculate these share values had been affected by computerization. Although their study covers only a tiny slice of the American workforce—one type of worker in one business unit of a single firm in one industry—the story they tell is a microcosm of the forces now sweeping across the economy as a whole.[10]

The bank, already well known throughout the industry for its forward-looking use of computers, had made a strategic decision in the early 1980s to target the accounting needs of other financial services firms. Its timing was impeccable. This was the beginning of a period of extraordinary growth in the investment management industry, especially the mutual fund sector, whose combined assets grew twenty-fold between 1980 and 1994. The bank's custodian business expanded rapidly to meet the new demand, and employment in the custodian unit grew fourfold during this period. The average educational qualifications of the workforce also rose sharply; four out of every five new hires had at least four years of college education, so that by the end of the period nearly three quarters of the employees were college-educated, compared with only 40 percent at the start.

The influence of computers on these developments was pervasive. On the demand side, computerization of the financial markets—initially of back-office paperwork, and later of trading itself—fueled a phenomenal increase in the volume of financial transactions, which in turn helped stoke the demand for the bank's accounting services. As Levy and Murnane point out, whereas three decades ago the New York Stock Exchange often had to close early if the trading volume exceeded 10 million shares in the course of a single day, today 10 million shares commonly change hands within minutes of the opening bell. Computers have helped expand market activity in other ways, too, by making it possible to value (and therefore to trade) a host of complicated new financial instruments, including increasingly complex financial derivatives. All of this helped drive up the demand for the bank's external accounting services.

Meanwhile, as the computerization of the financial markets was helping to create more accounting jobs at the bank, its own computer investments were changing the character of those jobs. Twenty years ago, the accountants did their jobs manually or with an adding machine. The introduction of mainframes, followed by stand-alone personal computers, and most recently networked PCs, has eliminated the most routine parts of the job like data entry, and today the accountants spend more of their time on the more challenging aspects—those that involve reasoning by analogy, communication with others, and the ability to track down information.

The computers have greatly increased the accountants' productivity—a single accountant today can handle the reporting requirements of up to six mutual funds, compared with one or two fifteen years ago—but demand for the custodian unit's services has been growing even faster. To fill the new accounting positions, the bank has recruited mostly from local four-year colleges. Its recruiting strategy seems to have remained largely unchanged over this period. It has never focused on straight-A accounting majors ("we're not competing for people with the Big Eight"), instead targeting "the 'B' students in second-tier colleges and the 'A' students in third-tier colleges." The bank relies mainly on its own training to provide the necessary accounting knowledge, and has continued to recruit some people with little or no accounting background. However, as the demands of the job have increased, the bank has upgraded its training programs, and now all new recruits go through an eight-week training course before starting work. This is estimated to cost about $10,000 per trainee.

But the upgraded training may have raised expectations faster than the job itself has changed. The accountants are handling more funds than before but, as Levy and Murnane note, "it is not clear that [they] are thinking more deeply about issues involved in any single fund. Rather, they are doing what always were the more difficult parts of their job . . . at a standard level of intensity for a greater number of funds." New recruits describe the job as alternatingly boring and tension-filled, much as their predecessors did. And although the first-line managers generally welcome the higher skill levels of the trainees, some have not adjusted their own practices to accommodate the increased expectations that go along with this.

Turnover among the new recruits remains fairly high, and because of the upgraded training programs is becoming increasingly expensive to the firm. At a time when increased competition in the custodian service market is eroding profit margins, this may yet become a serious problem for the bank. As Levy and Murnane conclude, "the challenge will be to redesign the . . . accountant job so that it is attractive to individuals who have the skills to evaluate increasingly complex financial instruments, and who will not be satisfied to stay very long in jobs that consist primarily of feeding information about exceptions into a computer system."

Several important lessons with broad applicability emerge from this case:

1. *Computers do not eliminate management choices.* In this case, the bank chose to recruit four-year college graduates from second- and third-tier institutions. But it might also have considered junior college or even high school graduates, at least some of whom could certainly do the work. (Indeed, the bank experimented with this option in the mid-1980s when labor markets were briefly very tight.) Its decision to go with four-year college graduates seems to have been motivated by a combination of factors: the preference of its first-line managers, almost all of whom have four-year college degrees themselves, for hiring people like themselves; the lack of reliable information on the quality of high school and junior college graduates, which increases the risk and cost of hiring from this pool; and the relative abundance of four-year college graduates in the bank's home city. But in other locations or at other times, or perhaps even at the same location and the same time in another firm, the decision might have been quite different.

2. *Computers are part of an organizational system.* The adoption of computer technology opened up major new business opportunities for the bank. The new technology was the *sine qua non* of entry into the custodian market. But the bank's ability to exploit those opportunities *profitably* depended on a host of other actions regarding recruiting, training, job design, and management development. Moreover, these factors interacted with each other and with the technology in complex ways. Indeed, the concern over high turnover suggests that even now the bank may not have worked out an ideal mix of practices. On the other hand, it also suggests that there is no unique solution to the problem, and that the same technology could support different combinations of job designs, skill requirements, and recruiting and training strategies.

3. *The aggregate impact of computers on employment and skill levels is extremely difficult to predict.* Levy and Murnane's research shows that several competing effects were at work in this case, and makes clear that there was nothing preordained or predictable about the outcome. The bank's investment in computer technology increased its relative demand for skilled versus unskilled labor. But those same computers increased the productivity of its (now generally more skilled) accountants, therefore reducing the de-

mand for such people below what it might otherwise have been. On the other hand, computer investment elsewhere in the financial services sector was driving up the demand for these people, by helping to expand the market for the bank's accounting services. Finally, all of these factors were interacting with other economic developments unrelated to computers—the rapid rise in the popularity of 401(k) pension plans, for example, which greatly increased the flow of money into mutual funds—to determine the overall demand for entry-level accountants at the bank. But even this is not the full story, since management decisions and practices at the bank affected both the kinds of people who were recruited to fill these positions and the rate of turnover in those positions.

The complexities of this single case are a salutary reminder of the difficulties of trying to predict the impact of computers on skills and jobs. At the very least, it is clear that all categorical claims about such matters need to be taken with a pinch of salt. Moreover, the idiosyncrasies of the case, the dependence of the outcome on the specifics of the company—its history, its location, the preferences of its managers—also point to the limits of broad-based public interventions intended to produce particular results. The bank's need to upgrade the skills of its accountants is certainly consistent with the general picture of "skill-biased technological change" in the economy as a whole. But *how* it chose to respond—the particular combination of internal training practices, relationships with external educational institutions, technology choices, business strategies, and so on— would not necessarily have been emulated by any other institution.

The new technologies of the information age are presenting firms with previously unimagined possibilities and enormous challenges. Few things are more unnerving than the unknown, and in the face of it there is a natural tendency to try to search for order, for predictable patterns, for dependable maps and blueprints to guide the way forward. A large and rapidly growing industry of experts has sprung up to help firms understand the new technologies and how to manage them. Much of this advice is very valuable. But the time of golden rules and universal principles is fast running out. The range of technological applications is already so broad that it defies generalization. Computer-controlled continuous casting, computer-aided design, and computer-generated financial derivatives may all rely on microprocessor technology, yet from a management perspective they have next to nothing in common. As a category, "information technology" is becoming less and less useful. To refer back to Paul David's analogy, it is about as meaningful today to speak of "doing IT right" as it would be to talk about "doing electricity right."

One general need remains, however. There is an old adage that you can't manage what you can't measure, and by any standard the ability to measure and value flows of information is poorly developed. As firms shift more and more of their investment capital toward systems and technologies whose principal output is information, the consequences of that deficit are becoming increasingly serious. Not long ago, during a long airline flight, I watched a promotional video for some expensive, high-end office computer equipment. Though obviously unintended, it was in fact a parody of this sort of communication—the narrator moving smoothly from meaningless recitations of technical specifications, gigaflops, MIPs, and all the rest, to breathless predictions that his sleek new product would "change everything about your business," without ever suggesting even one way in which it might actually help a prospective customer. It was a performance that a vendor of mere washing machines could certainly never get away with.

As I watched, I was reminded of an earlier conversation I had had with the director of a European engineering concern who had been given the important assignment of selecting and purchasing the information systems that were to enable his firm to effect a major strategic repositioning. It was a vital task for the company, for which an ample budget had been provided, but the manager complained that he had no way to choose among the competing claims of the IT vendors, that in fact he had no basis for evaluating what they were saying to him. The language they used did not speak at all to his needs as the manager of a going concern. This individual, highly qualified in engineering and management and technologically sophisticated by any measure, gave every indication of being intimidated. It was not a healthy situation. Nor, it can safely be assumed, is it an unusual one.

Professor Erik Brynjolfsson has found that firms investing in certain classes of computers do so with one of two broad strategies in mind. Some have as their primary objective improving quality, customer service, and speed of response to customer needs. The others are mainly interested in using the computers as a cost-cutting tool. Significantly, the customer-oriented firms appear to have realized a higher return from their computer investments than the cost cutters. But because the benefits of quality, flexibility, and service are so difficult to measure, Brynjolfsson finds that even these firms tend to base their formal investment decision analyses on estimates of the cost savings that they expect to realize. The conclusion is inescapable: Until better methods are developed for measuring the economic value of information flows, there will be little basis for judging whether the current rate of investment in the new information technologies is too little or too great, and any correspondence between what firms are actually investing in information technology and the optimal level of those investments will be coincidental.

On the foregoing evidence, then, the question with which we began Part III of this book, the question of best practice in a volatile economic environment, remains wide open. Total quality management; reengineering; bundles of progressive organizational and human resource management practices; strategic investments in information technology—each one of these approaches has revealed its limitations. In different ways, and for different reasons, each has promised more than it has delivered, and none is the silver bullet that differentiates the most successful firms from the rest. Indeed, this cannot be true by definition. The very popularity of these innovations would seem to rule it out. If everyone is adopting them, it is axiomatic that they cannot be the secret of success. (Perhaps an important difference lies in *how* they are implemented, but of course this merely begs the question of why some firms have been more successful at implementation than others.)

Moreover, the popularity of these ideas is clearly transient. That is not necessarily a bad thing; the business environment is constantly evolving, and firms must always be on the lookout for new methods and practices to deal with the changes. But the fact remains that many of today's leading American firms—General Electric, Hewlett Packard, Motorola, Procter & Gamble, to name a few—have managed to remain successful for decades, far longer than the average lifespan of whatever happens to be the leading business innovation of the day, proof once again that the fundamental explanation for success must lie elsewhere.

To explore the question of best practice further, my colleague Suzanne Berger and I decided to revisit some of the firms that the MIT Commission on Industrial Productivity had identified in the late 1980s as being among the most innovative and successful companies in their industries. We wanted to find out how the general strategies and processes that we ourselves had identified several years ago as "best practice" had in fact influenced competitive outcomes in the interim. How would these firms define best practice today? Had the experiences of the intervening years confirmed the merit of these ideas? Or had these firms found it necessary to rethink them—a response, perhaps, to the prospect of more or less permanent volatility in their economic environment? Would they point to a different or more specific set of tools and techniques? What did *they* think of TQM, reengineering, and the other popular business ideas of the last several years?

CHAPTER 12

Best Practice Revisited

Not all of the companies that were identified in 1989 in *Made in America* as paragons of best practice have continued to fare well. Some that did not, such as IBM, have struggled for reasons that we might have anticipated based on our own analysis (we didn't, unfortunately); others because of more contingent factors—poor business judgments, or just plain bad luck. But most of these companies—firms like Motorola, Hewlett Packard, Levi Strauss, Nucor, Chaparral Steel, Milliken—are still doing quite well; in some cases, very well indeed. To what do they attribute their more recent successes? How, if at all, does their assessment today differ from that of several years earlier?

In many important respects, the experience of the last few years has validated our earlier findings about best practice. (These are summarized in Appendix III.) All of the firms that we revisited remain strongly committed to the principles and processes of organizational transformation that we saw previously. Traditional hierarchies are disappearing; walls between functions and departments are being eliminated; and small, autonomous units, capable of responding rapidly to new market developments, are springing up everywhere. The shift from "vertical" to "horizontal" organizational structures still appears very much on track.

All of the firms also remain committed to the idea of upgrading the skills of their front-line workers, even as the head count declines. Training in and out of the workplace, and compensation policies promoting learning, are also the norm. Most of the companies remain committed to multiskilling as a source of both flexibility and economies.

There is also a continuing emphasis on building stronger and deeper relationships with valued suppliers and customers. These firms are looking everywhere along the value chains to which they belong for ways to extend their competitive advantage, not just those stages that they themselves control directly. They are committed to working cooperatively with their suppliers (and often, their suppliers' suppliers) to improve the performance of the entire value chain. And they are committed, too, to developing closer ties with key customers. The idea of the "extended enterprise" is alive and well.

Also alive and well is the global perspective that had been so apparent during our initial research. A recent conversation with a General Electric executive aptly illustrates the degree to which the realities of global competition have been absorbed into the daily routine of these firms. The executive was describing a business proposal that had recently been submitted by GE's Plastics division. The quote was to supply a particular kind of plastic to a Japanese customer, whose plant was located in Germany. The plastic was to be produced at a GE plant in Australia. The price was quoted in deutsche marks, pegged against the Dutch guilder, and the customer was informed that he would have the right to qualify the material in Japan before accepting it at his German facility. For big corporations like General Electric, the ability to deal with such international complexities as a matter of course has become an important source of competitive advantage.

Smaller firms, too, though lacking the resources for a fully fledged global production or distribution network, continue to expand their horizons. Chaparral Steel, pushing ahead with the historic project to rewrite the steel industry's scaling laws, is developing the technology for a new "micromill," significantly smaller even than today's minimills, which it plans to introduce first in the Far East.

In all of these dimensions of practice, our earlier conclusions were confirmed. But as we went back to these firms, we were also struck by some things that hadn't been as evident to us the first time around. At that time we had been puzzled by the slowness of other companies to emulate the patterns of the successful companies. After all, most of these firms were well known, and the best practices we had highlighted were not new even then. Our conclusion at the time was that what distinguished these companies was their ability to see these practices not as independent solutions but rather as part of a coherent system. They had understood the strength of the linkages between business elements that others saw as separable. Whereas most firms were taking a piecemeal approach to organizational change, focusing first on one thing and then another, our leading firms seemed to have recognized the need for systemic change and the importance of aligning their organizational practices with each other.

But this explanation, though consistent with the evidence we had collected, still seemed incomplete. What was it about these firms that had led them to embrace the idea of systemic organizational change? *Why* had they seen the need for this, when so many others had not? So, on revisits to these companies, we focused on the sources of change and the processes through which these had been translated into pressures for internal reform. We anticipated that this would provide important additional insights into what distinguished these firms from their less successful counterparts.

Our expectation was that market pressures would turn out to be the strongest impetus to transformation. To our surprise, however, we found that the sources of transformation that top managers pointed to frequently could not be directly traced to changes in markets. Even though the market is never absent from the manager's mental screen, market perturbations seemed to be playing a less direct role than we had imagined. More often, the driving force for change seemed to be coming from within.

Inner Voices

The injunction to "listen to the voice of the customer" is today one of the most common forms of advice to business firms. For many firms, indeed, listening to the voice of the customer has attained an almost religious significance. It is the way they define themselves: "our mission is to satisfy our customers"; "we will be whatever our customers want us to be."

Yet, as we revisited the firms in our group, we could not help noticing that, while listening very carefully to what their customers were saying, the people in these firms—at every level—also seemed to have an understanding of what they were doing and of their mission that transcended the customer's voice. It was as if they were also listening to an *inner* voice, a voice that was not always in perfect harmony with the voice of the customer, a voice often distinguished, in fact, by its conviction that the world will soon want what it may not yet even know exists. As the former Motorola CEO William Weisz once observed: "When you are pioneering in something the world doesn't even know it wants, you have to have a belief that the world is going to want what you have, and that it will start falling over its feet to get it."[1]

Similarly, though these firms were paying very close attention to what their competitors were doing, their actions in the marketplace were not purely reactive. Their strategies were shaped by a core belief in what they were trying to accomplish as much as by the drive to preempt or mimic the competition. In short, on reexamination, these companies appeared to us to be distinguished not only by the diligence with which they were pursuing a particular set of organizational practices, but also by the strength of their internal convictions. We saw more clearly that their goals and aspirations were derived as much from a kind of inner compass as from the external pressures that are imposed on them by the marketplace. These are companies that seem never to stop thinking hard about who they are.

Consider Boeing, a firm with a history of taking huge financial risks, of "bet the company" dimensions, to build the next generation of planes. The best-known example is the Boeing 747, the world's first commercial wide-bodied jet, which eventually became extremely profitable, but which in its early years nearly drove the company into bankruptcy. Widely regarded as the greatest gamble in aviation history, the development of the hugely expensive 747, like other big Boeing projects before and since, was not really a response to a competitor—no other company was then seriously entertaining such a project—and was not justified purely on the basis of return on investment. Indeed, given the risks that were involved, it is quite unlikely that such a decision could ever have been justified on purely financial grounds. Profitability considerations were obviously an important part of the decision; but by most accounts it was Boeing's sense of itself as an aviation pioneer, as a company that pushes the envelope of aeronautical technology, that "eats, breathes, and sleeps" the world of aeronautics, that was a critical factor both in determining whether to proceed at all and in driving this historic project to completion.[2]

None of this is to understate the importance of competition as a driving force for change at Boeing. Making and selling commercial airliners is one of the most competitive businesses in the world, and Boeing did not get to where it is today by ignoring what its competitors were doing. But a preoccupation with the competition is not enough to explain what has differentiated Boeing from McDonnell Douglas and its other great rivals over the years. To understand fully why Boeing has consistently been willing to take risks that have kept it ahead of its competitors, we must also keep in mind the company's deeply held beliefs about its fundamental purpose and what it stands for—coupled, of course, with an exceptionally well developed ability to act on those beliefs.

Another example of a rather different sort is provided by Levi Strauss & Company. One of the few unequivocal success stories in the struggling American apparel industry over the past decade, Levi Strauss's emphasis on the long term, on building its organizational capabilities, and on increasing the contribution made by its workers to the business, has set it apart from the volatile, highly reactive, often exploitative norm in the rest of the industry. When a top Levi's executive laid out for us the sequence of events that had led the company to invest more heavily in training and to reorganize assembly-line style garment manufacturing into team-based "modular" production, enabling teams of sewers to coordinate their production and to gain much more control over their work environment, he kept returning to two issues that had driven the process. First, management was haunted by the prospect that new rulings on company liability for carpal tunnel syndrome—a work-related injury common in sewing machine operators—might astronomically escalate their health costs. So the company needed some way of reorganizing work in order to reduce the incidence of this injury. Second, even though Levi's was doing better than ever, the rise of lower-cost competitors and the availability of overseas production possibilities made workers and managers alike anxious about the future of jobs and willing to experiment with new patterns of production.[3]

These clouds on the horizon made top management focus on the question of what distinctive value was added to the company's products when they were manufactured in the United States. The managers (in this case with the cooperation of the union) looked within for inspiration, drawing on the company's history of commitment to worker empowerment and advancement to craft a solution to their business problem. They said, in effect: This is what we stand for; this is what makes us special. Or, as Levi's CEO Robert D. Haas put it: "We are not doing this because it makes us feel good—although it does. We are not doing this because it is politically correct. We are doing this because we believe in the interconnection between liberating the talents of our people and business success."[4] Once again we see a potent mixture of commercial calculation and internal values at work in a critical business decision.

Levi's commitment to its employees was affirmed in its corporate Aspiration Statement, adopted in 1987, which states in part:

We all want a Company that our people are proud of and committed to, where all employees have an opportunity to contribute, learn, grow and advance based on merit, not politics or background. We want our people to feel respected, treated fairly, listened to and involved. Above all, we want satisfaction from accomplishments and friendships, balanced personal and professional lives, and to have fun in our endeavors.

The statement also emphasizes the importance of ethical behavior: "We will conduct our business ethically and demonstrate leadership in satisfying our responsibilities to our communities and to society."

Many companies include this kind of language in their mission statements, of course, but not all of them act on it, and Levi's has gone much further than most in inculcating the underlying principles and values into its organization.[5] Remarkably, the luster of these values was undiminished by the company's decision in late 1997 to cut a third of its North American workforce in the face of low-wage competition from overseas. Its handling of these cuts has been widely praised, even by union officials at the company. One called the severance package "phenomenal"; another described it as "by far the best severance settlement apparel workers have ever gotten."[6]

Another tough test of the company's commitment to these values has been posed by its network of overseas subcontractors—some six hundred of them sewing Levi's in thirty-five countries. Not all of these countries are known for respecting the rights of their citizens to work in safe conditions, and some have also demonstrably failed to meet international norms regarding the protection of basic human rights.

How should the company apply its ethical standards in such cases? To insist on a universal standard of behavior among its suppliers would rule out production (and probably also sales) in some of these countries, with an immediate negative impact on the company's bottom line. Moreover, the loss of jobs would almost certainly be a severe blow to the employees of the affected subcontractors, for whom risky work might well be preferable to no work at all. On the other hand, for Levi Strauss to waive its ethical standards in its overseas dealings would smack of hypocrisy, and would risk alienating its U.S. workers, already fearful of losing their jobs to cheap foreign labor. Besides, rumors of child and prison labor do not help sell jeans.

In 1992, the company introduced new guidelines governing its dealings with overseas business partners. The guidelines specified the "terms of engagement" under which it would be willing to pursue business relationships with foreign contractors and suppliers, and also laid out criteria for selecting the countries where it would consider sourcing. The new policy noted that Levi Strauss

> has a heritage of conducting business in a manner that reflects its values. As we expand our sourcing base to more diverse cultures and countries, we must take special care in selecting business partners and countries whose practices are not incompatible with our values. Otherwise our sourcing decisions have the potential of undermining this heritage, damaging the image of our brands and threatening our commercial success.

When we reconnected with Levi's soon after the publication of its new sourcing policy, the company was struggling to decide what to do about its operations in China, a decision that involved balancing the Chinese government's human rights violations against the costs of losing access to the potentially enormous Chinese market. Eventually, Levi's decided to discontinue all production, sourcing, and sales in China, a decision that a top executive described to us as one of the toughest it has ever had to make.

Once again, the point here is not that Levi Strauss's decision was driven by purely altruistic motives. The company was clearly also very concerned about the risk to its brand image posed by Chinese labor and human rights policies. Nor is it the case that Levi's strong commitment to upholding ethical standards is matched by all "best practice" companies. (Indeed, some of the other companies in our own sample are very active in China.) The point is rather that the company's decision to terminate its Chinese operations grew out of a deeply held sense of what Levi's stands for, in which issues of commercial brand, corporate values, and self-image are all intertwined. It is a decision that would not—indeed, *could* not—have been made if the company had only been reacting to the external market pressures imposed by its customers and competitors.

Yet another example of this internally driven behavior is provided by Motorola. The successes of Motorola in a wide range of electronics and communications markets cannot be ascribed purely, or even primarily, to a goal of beating the competition, even though that has very often been the outcome. Again, this is not to understate the intensity of competitive pressures in these markets, or the company's attention to its competitors. But a visitor to Motorola cannot help but notice the relentless self-criticism and drive to improve on its own past performance that exists at every level of the company. It is the objective of always trying to do better than before, the impossible quest for "perfection before the customer," that seems most to animate this unusual firm. Mobilizing the whole company around seemingly impossible-to-achieve goals has long been a central part of its leadership strategy. Targets such as the famous 6-Sigma quality goal, and the more recent goal of reducing all cycle times tenfold, create a common vocabulary and a sense of common purpose for a company that is considerably more decentralized than most others its size. Even more important, stirring the pot in this way keeps the organization moving and searching. As longtime chairman Robert Galvin explained in an interview, "It doesn't really matter what the goal is exactly. As long as it is reasonable. The point is to stimulate. To catalyze."

Galvin, who chooses his words carefully, is of course perfectly aware that these goals have struck many people as being anything but reasonable, especially when first mooted. But the idea of Motorola as a company that is driven by a long-term vision to pursue the seemingly impossible is integral to its self-identity. As he so often does in explaining a contemporary practice or purpose at the firm, Galvin in this case invokes the influence of his father, Motorola founder Paul Galvin, who counseled decades earlier that it is important always to have something to shoot for. And as the younger Galvin (whose own son Christopher recently took over the leadership of the company) has himself advised: "at times we must engage in an act of faith that key things are doable that are not provable."[7]

The Virtue of Values

Skeptical readers might be put off by this emphasis on inner values and vision in explaining the origins of corporate success. To those schooled in hard-nosed quantitative analyses of competitive situations and strategies, it will no doubt all seem very "soft." And there are other reasons for skepticism, too. These few examples certainly do not prove that every company with a strong sense of identity and internal values is successful, or that every successful company has succeeded *because* of them. And indeed, neither our latest round of corporate visits nor even the original assessment of the MIT Commission on Industrial Productivity could be described as scientific. Though the industries from which these firms are drawn—and the firms themselves—differ widely in age, size, and technological sophistication, it is not likely that the sample would satisfy a rigorous test of representativeness; nor did we impose a uniform template on our data-gathering activities that might have ensured strict comparability of results. As was pointed out in *Made in America,* "there is no algorithm that could take as input our mosaic of testimony, observation, cross-national comparisons, statistical analyses, and case histories and produce as output a number characterizing the performance of [a] national economy."[8] And what is true of national economies is also true of individual firms. Drawing general conclusions about "best practice" on the basis of this kind of evidence is necessarily an exercise in judgment.

But now there is other, more systematic evidence to support these judgments. The evidence comes from a detailed study of eighteen companies with a record of exceptional achievement extending back over many decades (and in some cases well over a century). This pioneering study, conducted by James Collins and Jerry Porras of Stanford University, posed the question of how these "visionary" companies—firms like Procter & Gamble, Motorola, Merck, 3M, Wal-Mart, and Hewlett Packard—have managed to thrive over such long periods, and what has distinguished them from the other companies in their industries. The question has a particular resonance for us because at various points in their long lives these firms have dealt with business and technological uncertainties that, though probably more localized, were as radical in nature as any that confront our firms and industries today. That they were able to survive and indeed prosper in spite of this suggests that we can learn much of practical value by studying them.

In their excellent book *Built to Last: Successful Habits of Visionary Companies* (1994), Collins and Porras carefully compared each of these firms over their entire histories with one other company of comparable vintage which, at least in its early days, had pursued similar products and markets.[9] The firms in the comparison group were themselves no slouches. All of them had achieved significant successes at various points in their lifetimes, and as corporate performers they were above average in many respects. But they had not been able to match the accomplishments of the visionary companies, and they had not attained the same stature. Table 12.1 shows the matched pairs of companies, and Figure 12.1 compares the stock market performance of the visionary and control groups with each other, and with the general market, over a period of more than six decades.

Table 12.1: Matched Pairs of Companies in *Built to Last*

Visionary Company	Comparison Company	Visionary Company	Comparison Company
3M	Norton	Johnson & Johnson	Bristol-Myers Squibb
American Express	Wells Fargo	Marriott	Howard Johnson
Boeing	McDonnell Douglas	Merck	Pfizer
		Motorola	Zenith
Citicorp	Chase Manhattan	Nordstrom	Melville
Ford	GM	Philip Morris	RJR Nabisco
General Electric	Westinghouse	Procter &Gamble	Colgate
		Sony	Kenwood
Hewlett Packard	Texas Instruments	Wal-Mart	Ames
IBM	Burroughs	Walt Disney	Columbia

Source: James Collins and Jerry Porras, *Built to Last: Successful Habits of Visionary Companies* (New York: HarperBusiness, 1994), p. 3, table 1.1.

The device of using matched pairs of companies goes a long way toward eliminating the problem of "survivorship bias" that plagues many studies focusing solely on successful companies—the problem

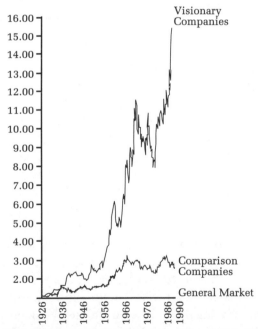

Figure 12.1 Ratio of Cumulative Stock Returns to General Market 1926–90

Source: James Collins and Jerry Porras, *Built to Last: Successful Habits of Visionary Companies* (New York: HarperBusiness, 1994), p.8, figure 1.B.

that the characteristics supposedly associated with their success might also have been found in other, less successful companies if the researchers had only bothered to look. Even the more diverse sample of companies in *Built to Last* doesn't completely avoid this problem. Though admittedly unlikely, we cannot rule out the existence of a third category of firms: firms that failed despite sharing all the characteristics that Collins and Porras associate with the success of the visionary companies.

Yet in spite of these lingering methodological questions, Collins and Porras's book is full of valuable insights and well deserves the wide readership it has attracted. In the process of differentiating the visionary companies from the others, the authors undermine many pervasive myths about effective corporate management—for example, that business success requires a single-minded focus on maximizing profits and market share; that it requires visionary, charismatic leadership; and that it requires brilliant, sophisticated strategic planning. In general, these characteristics were no more likely to be found in the visionary companies than they were in the others; indeed, they were often entirely absent from the most successful companies, and so could not be implicated in their success at all.

So what *does* explain the difference? The answers provided in *Built to Last* confirm, clarify, and amplify many of the conclusions discussed previously. Four points in particular deserve emphasis:

The Primacy of Organization: Many readers of the chapters on best practice in *Made in America* commented on their emphasis on organizational processes and structures. Some felt that it all seemed a bit too prosaic. What about the role of strategic foresight, of innovative products, of visionary leadership? they wondered. And indeed, with a popular business press full of reports of charismatic, farsighted corporate leaders and breakthrough products, it is not hard to understand this reaction.

But Collins and Porras's findings confirm the importance of organizational structure and process. Compared with the control group, the leaders of the eighteen visionary companies were not distinguished by a greater ingenuity in devising new products, or by the power of their strategic insights, or by their force of personality. Rather, they consistently devoted more attention to establishing, sustaining, and renewing the processes and mechanisms needed to build an outstanding organization. By focusing on the inner workings of their firms, successive generations of leaders at companies like 3M, Hewlett Packard, and Procter & Gamble have built robust, adaptable enterprises with the capacity to *keep on* producing outstanding products (and outstanding leaders). They are "clock builders" rather than "time tellers." Their true legacy is an outstanding *organization*, whose productive and competitive capabilities have long outlasted the contributions of any single product, no matter how innovative, or any individual leader, no matter how creative and visionary.

A Core Ideology: Our more recent conclusion on the importance of the "inner voice" of the leading companies is similarly reinforced and valuably amplified by Collins and Porras. In each of the eighteen visionary firms, the authors observed a set of core beliefs—an "ideology"—that had remained essentially unchanged over long periods and that had mobilized and inspired people at all levels of the organization. They found, moreover, that in almost all cases the visionary companies had been more ideologically driven and less purely driven by profit than the comparison firms, even though, paradoxically, they had been more profitable over the long haul. These core ideologies—and Collins and Porras insist that they are unique to each company, that there is no single, "correct" version—are understood by everyone in these companies, and infuse everything that they do. They generally consist of a small set of essential values, the things that most matter to the company, and a purpose, a reason for existing beyond just making profits. Examples include dedication to serving the customer (Wal-Mart, Nordstrom); commitment to staying at the cutting edge of technology (Boeing); respect for individual employees (Hewlett Packard); and innovation (3M).

Many of these values are found in several of the visionary companies. But there is no common set, nor even a single idea to which all of the eighteen companies subscribe. What matters is not the correctness of the ideology but rather its *authenticity*—the strength of the belief within the firm that this is what it stands for and that this is how it should do business. Usually first enunciated by the founders, these values and purposes endure for decades, guiding and inspiring successive generations of employees. They shape the company's practices and strategies and its behavior in the marketplace, yet they are by and large independent of the external environment.

To those who consider all this to be too "soft," Collins and Porras point out that for the people who actually work at such companies, it makes for an environment that is not soft at all. On the contrary, because these companies "have such clarity about who they are, what they're all about, and what they're trying to achieve, they tend to not have much room for people unwilling or unsuited to their demanding standards."[10] The culture of these companies is tight-knit, almost cultlike. People who do not fit in usually leave; as one observer put it, they are "ejected like a virus."[11]

A Relentless Drive for Progress: Though the core ideology may remain unchanged for decades or even longer, virtually everything else in the visionary companies *does* change. "It is essential not to confuse core ideology with culture, strategy, tactics, operations, policies, or other noncore practices," say Collins and Porras. "Over time, cultural norms must change; strategy must change; product lines must change; goals must change; competencies must change; administrative policies must change; organization structure must change; reward systems must change." Indeed, one of the main distinguishing features of the visionary companies is their unwillingness to be satisfied with the status quo, and their constant tinkering and experimentation with new techniques, strategies and products—an internally generated, never-ending drive to do better. Once again, there is nothing soft or comfortable about this, at least for the employees. Typically, these companies "install powerful mechanisms to create *dis*comfort—to obliterate complacency—and thereby stimulate change and improvement *before* the external world demands it" (emphasis in the original).[12]

An Aligned Organization: Finally, Collins and Porras reinforce the argument in *Made in America* that the processes and practices we observed in the best practice firms ought not to be thought of as independent solutions, but rather form a coherent system, in which the individual parts reinforce each other. They argue that what differentiates the visionary companies above all is their achievement in converting their core beliefs into a set of concrete, mutually aligned strategies, practices, and processes: "A visionary company creates a total environment that envelops employees, bombarding them with a set of signals so consistent and mutually reinforcing that it's virtually impossible to misunderstand the company's ideology and ambitions."[13] Summing up the organizational alignment at three such companies, they write:

> Taken in isolation, each fact about Ford, Merck, and HP would be trivial, and certainly wouldn't account for their visionary status. But in the context of hundreds of other facts, they add up to a consistent overall picture. . . . Notice the clustering at Ford: statistical quality control methods *reinforced by* employee involvement programs *reinforced by* participative management training programs *reinforced by* promotion

criteria based on participative management skills. Notice the clustering at Merck: recruiting of top scientists *reinforced by* allowing them to publish *reinforced by* allowing them to collaborate with outside scientists *reinforced by* the "Merck Campus" *reinforced by* the dual career track. Notice how it would be impossible to work at HP and not get the message that managers had better treat their people well or that divisions had better make profits by technical contribution (emphasis in the original).[14]

Built to Last convincingly captures the essence of this select group of outstanding enterprises. But some may wonder how useful its lessons are for lesser mortals. After all, not everyone can build a company that remains at the pinnacle of performance for fifty or a hundred years. Many firms, probably the vast majority, have more modest goals. Others are fiercely but less durably ambitious: managers may prefer to grow their businesses very rapidly in the short run and then cash out; investors may prefer a higher-risk strategy of investing in a succession of shorter-term, high-growth opportunities, seeking always of course to time their exits before the bloom comes of the rose. An interesting question is whether the most successful examplars of rapid short-term growth have pursued a fundamentally different model from the outset, or whether instead it was their premature abandonment of the habits of the enduringly successful companies that caused their success to be shorter-lived. This is a proper subject for further research.

In the meantime, perhaps the best answer to those who doubt the visionary companies' relevance to their own experience was given by Robert Louis Stevenson more than a century ago. "To travel hopefully is a better thing than to arrive, and the true success is to labour," wrote Stevenson—a lesson that few have understood better than the visionary companies themselves.

PART IV

Living with Ambiguity:
A Path to
Faster Growth

CHAPTER 13

Investment, Growth, and Uncertainty

The most interesting thing about the companies in the previous chapter is the longevity of their success. They thrived and grew even as everything about them was changing. Exceptionally, they found a way to flourish in spite of encountering what must have been frequent periods of great turbulence and uncertainty along the way—conditions that helped finish off many lesser rivals. That, in a sense, is also the challenge facing the U.S. economy as a whole. As we saw in the first two parts of this book, America today confronts both a serious problem of weak productivity growth and an increasingly volatile economic environment. Measurement uncertainties obscure the exact dimensions of the former problem, and pending revisions to the official statistics may brighten the gloomy picture they paint of lackluster productivity performance and stagnating or at best slowly improving living standards for most Americans. But, as discussed in chapter 2, the central fact of a sharp and prolonged productivity slowdown that began sometime in the early 1970s is not in doubt.

What is needed for an advanced industrial economy like the United States to sustain a healthy rate of productivity growth? The question can be answered on many levels, but at root three things are essential. First, business enterprises must continually improve the efficiency of what they are already doing, enabling them either to make do with less or to produce more with what they have. Second, they must improve their existing products and services, by adding new features to them and by improving their quality—and, to the degree that the markets for these products and services are contested internationally, to do all this ahead of their international competitors. Third, they must develop new, more highly valued products and services and find new markets for them, both at home and abroad. Robust productivity growth requires that all three processes operate simultaneously.

For much of the past decade the first of these processes dominated

America's business headlines, and, to a large extent, the attention of its firms. But sometime in mid-1990s, a new conventional wisdom began to emerge. Executives, their consultants, and business writers started to declare the need for a new focus. The emphasis on cost cutting, consolidation, downsizing, and efficiency had been necessary to deal with the bloated and uncompetitive condition of many American companies, they explained, but now it was time to change course. As one executive put it, "you can't shrink to greatness."[1] The new message was partly a tactical response to the wave of criticism that had been directed at U.S. corporations over the human costs of downsizing (when the going gets tough, change the subject). Still, many firms, perceiving rapidly diminishing returns from downsizing, seemed serious about their new emphasis on growth.

But this new focus presented a problem. It meant placing more emphasis on developing new products and finding new markets—the third of the growth processes mentioned above. And this is almost always a riskier and more expensive proposition than finding new ways to reduce the cost of what firms are already doing. A leading exponent of reengineering, insisting on his technique's relevance to the new growth agenda, pointed out that reengineering, by improving the efficiency of the enterprise, frees up the resources that it needs in order to grow. This is perfectly true, of course, but the statement perhaps unintentionally also revealed how little reengineering has to say about growth itself.

What *is* known about growth, whether the unit in question is an individual business or a national economy, is that it requires investment. Firms may be able to improve the efficiency of what they are already doing without major capital outlays. But finding new markets or commercializing new products *always* entails new investment. Similarly, studies of productivity growth at the national level all point to the importance of investment—both tangible investment in plant, equipment, and physical infrastructure and less tangible investment in new knowledge and skills.

Private, profit-seeking business firms account for most of the investment in the economy, and if the nation is to invest more, it is they who will have to come up with most of the new funds. Firms will commit resources today if they have reason to expect that adequate profit will flow from their investments in the future. Private investment is therefore more likely if conditions are stable and if there is a feeling of optimism about the economy's prospects, and is correspondingly less likely during periods of uncertainty.

These intangibles are brought to bear on individual investment decisions in a quite particular way. Firms acquire the resources to make investments from different sources—by borrowing, by selling equity, or by accumulating retained earnings. Whatever the source of capital, there is a cost of using it, which represents the threshold that must be overcome if an investment is to be viable. The higher this threshold rate of return, the fewer investments will qualify. Most firms evaluate investment opportunities by comparing the expected rate of return with a "hurdle" rate, which incorporates both the cost of capital and an allowance for the risks associated with the particular investment in question.

The cost of capital in a society will generally be higher when the supply of capital is scarce, as occurs when the national rate of savings is low. The cost of capital also increases at times of high economic uncertainty—for example, when fears of inflation are running high. For particularly risky projects, moreover, the hurdle rate may be as much as several times greater than the average cost of capital to the firm. In this way, perceptions of risk have an impact on the rate of investment, and thus, eventually, on the rate of productivity growth.

By almost any measure, America's recent investment record has been unimpressive:

- Gross private investment as a percentage of gross domestic product (GDP) has ranked below that of almost all other major industrialized economies for more than two decades (see Table 13.1). The alarming downward trend in the rate of investment throughout much of the 1980s appears to have been reversed, but even today, at about 16 percent of the GDP, it still remains well below its (mediocre) average for the last twenty years (see Figure 13.1).

Table 13.1: Nonresidential Fixed Investment Including Government Expenditures (% of GDP)

	United States	Japan	Germany	France	Canada	United Kingdom
1970–74	13.8	27.9	17.2	16.7	16.4	15.4
1975–79	14.2	24.2	14.7	15.5	16.8	15.0
1980–84	15.1	24.0	14.6	14.6	16.5	13.2
1985–89	13.8	23.5	14.3	14.8	14.5	14.4
1990	13.1	25.7	15.3	16.1	14.7	15.7
1991	12.3	26.0	15.6	16.0	13.8	13.7
1992	11.8	25.3	14.7	15.0	12.4	
1993	12.2	24.2	12.7	13.9	12.2	
1994	n.a.	23.0	11.9	13.4	12.6	

Source: OECD, Annual and Quarterly National Accounts.

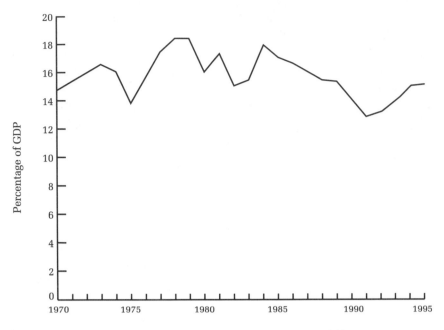

Figure 13.1 U.S. Gross Private Domestic Investment/GDP (%), 1970–95

Source: BEA, National Income and Product Accounts.

- Almost all of this private investment has been used to replace old and obsolete plant and equipment. The *net* rate of new private investment has declined nearly to zero in recent years, meaning that there has been very little net expansion of the nation's physical capital endowment for the last decade.
- Public investment in education and training, research and development, and infrastructure has also been declining, even as public "consumption" programs like Social Security, Medicare, and Medicaid have continued to grow. As a percentage of GDP, public investment has fallen from about 2.5 percent before 1980 to less than 2 percent today.[2] And in recent years the volume of public investment has also been declining in absolute terms.
- In the key category of research and development, both public and private investment have been declining as a percentage of GDP.

Blame for America's poor investment record has mainly been directed at macroeconomic causes, especially the nation's low rate of savings and the pressure this has exerted on the supply of capital. The federal government has been a major contributor to the national savings problem because of its big budget deficits—a form of negative saving—and attempts to cut the deficit have dominated the political agenda in Washington throughout the first half of the 1990s. But as Table 13.2 shows, savings by private households and businesses have been declining, too, and there has been much discussion of policies that would reverse these trends, notably including tax reforms that would shift the tax burden away from savings and investment toward consumption.

Table 13.2: Net Rates of Savings in the United States (% of GDP)

	Net Personal Savings	Corporate Savings	Government Savings*	Net National Savings
1960–64	4.4	3.4	-0.1	7.8
1965–69	4.9	3.6	-0.2	8.3
1970–74	5.9	2.3	-0.5	7.7
1975–79	5.0	2.8	-1.1	6.8
1980–84	5.8	1.4	-2.6	4.6
1985–89	3.6	1.9	-2.4	3.0
1990	3.9	1.8	-2.7	2.9
1991	4.4	1.9	-3.3	3.0
1992	4.6	1.8	-4.4	2.0
1993	3.5	2.0	-3.6	1.9
1994	2.9	2.1	-2.3	2.6
1995	3.4	2.2	-2.0	3.6
1996	3.6	2.5	-1.6	4.6

*Gross Federal, state, and local government revenues minus expenditures (including investment expenditures).
Sources: Bureau of Economic Analysis, U.S. Department of Commerce, National Income and Product Accounts, various years; Survey of Current Business, May 1997.

Other macroeconomic policies also have an important bearing on the investment problem. The interaction of fiscal and monetary policies affects interest rates; and the government's general performance in macroeconomic management importantly affects the level of business and consumer confidence in the future, which in turn affects the inclination of firms to invest. All of this is discussed extensively in the technical literature on macroeconomics, as well as in policy debates and political campaigns.

In recent years, macroeconomic trends have generally been in a direction to favor increased private investment. Inflation and interest rates are at historically low levels. The federal budget deficit has fallen sharply since 1992, and this has helped to raise the nation's chronically poor gross savings rate, although, at 14.5 percent of GDP, this still remains well below the OECD average of 20 percent. The

1997 budget agreement between the Congress and President Clinton calls for the federal budget to be balanced by 2002 (though many budget projections anticipate a dramatic increase in the size of the deficit shortly thereafter if the growth of the huge federal entitlement programs is not addressed).

But other influences on the rate of private investment are less amenable to macroeconomic management. As we have seen, the turbulent energies released by the combined forces of globalization, deregulation, and technological innovation are transforming traditional patterns of microeconomic behavior, and are bringing new risks and uncertainties in their wake that conventional macroeconomic policies can do little to mitigate.

People have a well-known tendency to exaggerate the historical significance of their own experiences, and popular claims that today's economic climate is unprecedentedly volatile warrant a healthy dose of skepticism.[3] Yet there may indeed be something extraordinary about the present situation, about the fact that three such powerful economic driving forces should have come together at more or less the same historical moment. Globalization, rapid advances in information technology, and the deregulation of many industries at home and entire economies abroad would each on their own have had far-reaching effects on the U.S. economy. In combination, their effect has been to leave almost no corner of the economy untouched. The question is what impact these changes are having on the rate of investment. Is the increase in business volatility inhibiting the new investment that is needed for growth? Or is this negative impact being overwhelmed by the enormous opportunities for the development of new products, services, and markets that these same forces of change are opening up?

There are two ways to look at the turbulence associated with these developments. In one view it is a temporary phenomenon, the by-product of a great structural transition from the industrial era to the postindustrial or "information" age. Like the great transformations that came before—the shift from an agrarian to an industrial economy at the end of the eighteenth century and the Second Industrial Revolution a hundred years later—this is a time of unusually rapid change, as obsolete economic structures are torn down to make way for the new demands of the information era. The processes of creating new institutions and developing new ways of organizing economic activity might take decades—as happened on both previous occasions—but eventually, in this view, the turbulence will subside, and a new phase of relatively smooth, stable growth will begin.

In an alternative view, the volatility of today's economy is not so much a precursor as an intrinsic condition of the information age. The new risks and uncertainties are a permanent fact of economic life, an unavoidable consequence of technological innovation and global economic integration, of the capabilities that make it possible for firms to segment and cater ever more precisely to evolving and inherently unpredictable consumer desires and to coordinate ever more complex chains of economic activity across vast distances. In this view, the heightened uncertainty of today will never really diminish.

As a practical matter there is not much to choose between these two interpretations, for even the transitional view suggests that the current economic turbulence will likely not be over soon. The historical record shows that economic transformations of this magnitude take several decades to run their course, and by that standard the transition to the information age—at this point still only twenty or thirty years old—is relatively young.

The fundamental question in either case, therefore, is the same: How can faster growth be achieved in spite of the prospect of a continuation—and perhaps even an intensification—of economic volatility? More specifically, what changes—in corporate strategies, in government policies, in public attitudes—are most likely to produce a higher rate of productive investment in a climate of increased uncertainty?

This question takes on special significance when it is applied to investments in "intangible" assets: ideas, information, skills, and organizational capacities. For it is when change is most rapid that the fruits of these investments—new products and processes, better-educated employees, more flexible business organizations, new market possibilities—are most critical. Yet it is also during periods of rapid change that this sort of investing comes under the greatest pressure. Even under normal circumstances activities such as training, research and development, and the development of new markets pose special problems for investors. Part of the difficulty is that, unlike investments in tangible assets like new equipment, buildings, land, and physical infrastructure, investments in intangibles do not create collateral and their returns are inherently more difficult to measure. These same characteristics make them especially vulnerable when uncertainty about the direction of economic activity is high.

Some of the most important questions facing American industry today have to do with these so-called intangible investments. At a time of rapid economic change, when the bonds of loyalty between enterprises and their employees are subject to maximum stress, how will our society come up with the investment needed to upgrade the skills of the workforce? At a time when many companies find it difficult to say with any confidence which markets they will be competing in and who their competitors will be even five years from now, who will finance the R&D activity that will lay the foundation for the new products and services of the twenty-first century? And at a time when so much of the energy and attention of our business organizations is still focused on improving efficiency and effectiveness, how will these organizations find the creativity and imagination needed to strike out in new directions?

We shall examine each of these questions in turn in the next three chapters. Chapter 14 considers the changing character of employment relations, and what this implies for investment in the development of human resources. Chapter 15 explores new possibilities for financing investment in R&D. And chapter 16 suggests an alternative way to think about the work of business organizations that sheds new light on activities that are critical to organizational creativity but usually overlooked in conventional management thinking. Taken together, the insights developed in these three chapters point the way toward a new agenda for economic growth in the United States. The last chapter adds a critical final ingredient to the mix.

CHAPTER 14

Redefining the Employment Relation

Judging by both their rhetoric and their actions, many firms today value the benefits of flexibility over the virtues of consistency and stability. They emphasize the development of nimble, agile organizations that can anticipate and react quickly to changes in the marketplace. And they want a workforce that is as flexible and adaptable as possible.

Chapter 10 described what might be called the "high road" to a flexible workforce. The evidence presented there showed that increased training, participative forms of work organization, less hierarchical and more open organizational structures, and the other elements of high performance work systems can yield handsome gains in performance, including substantially greater flexibility.

But the evidence also showed that relatively few firms have implemented these practices in a comprehensive way. Often the absence of trust has been too big a hurdle to overcome, sometimes also the belief that the transition costs are too high. Any change of this magnitude creates losers as well as winners: supervisors concerned that self-directed teams will mean no jobs for them; union representatives unable to conceive of a role for themselves in a nonadversarial environment; workers worried that they will lack the skills to function in high-performing teams and unable to afford the cost of retraining themselves.

Paradoxically, the biggest obstacle on the high road to workforce flexibility may be the very conditions that seem in theory to make it such an attractive route. Periods of rapid change tend to undermine both the commitment of firms to their employees and their employees' commitment to them. In the aftermath of AT&T's widely noted announcement in early 1996 of its intention to cut 40,000 of its 300,000 workers over the next three years, a vice president of human resources at the company explained that "people need to recognize that we are all contingent workers in one form or another . . . we are all victims of time and place."[1] But will workers whose employers see them as contingent, and who see themselves in those terms, be prepared to subscribe to the values of a "high-commitment" workplace? And will employers be willing to make the necessary investments—in recruiting, training, and so on—in employees to whom they are unwilling or unable to make a long-term commitment?

For firms who are not prepared to take the high road, there is a well-traveled alternative: "outsourcing," subcontracting in-house work to external suppliers, and relying on contract workers to staff internal operations, with both internal and external workplaces organized along traditional Taylorist lines. The flexibility to hire and fire at will that such a strategy offers (as well as its generally lower costs) has proved very attractive to many American firms. But this path, too, has its drawbacks. Firms that follow it are often constrained to producing low-end products and services because the human resource base on which they depend lacks either the skills or the motivation to achieve the levels of innovativeness, quality, and service needed to compete in higher-value, more profitable product markets.

Some of the world's purest practitioners of this low-road strategy can be found in Hong Kong, and their experiences are instructive.[2] Following the opening of China in the late 1970s, Hong Kong electronics, garment, and plastics manufacturers outsourced much of their manufacturing activities to neighboring Guangdong province in South China, to take advantage of the enormous supply of much lower cost labor there. More recently, as labor costs in Guangdong have risen, another wave of outsourcing has led to new manufacturing beachheads being established in even lower wage countries like the Philippines and Vietnam. The workers in these factories are typically short-timers; the companies make no effort to keep them for more than a couple of years, and often for much less. The high turnover helps keep wage costs down, and the firms reckon that this is more important than building up workforce skills and loyalty. (In one country, the workers are all routinely fired after five and a half months to avoid unionization, which, according to local labor laws, is only permitted after employees have been on the job for more than six months.)

One Hong Kong entrepreneur has described this strategy, inelegantly but accurately, as "low commitment, high hustle." It has worked very well over the years, but now some Hong Kong manufacturers are concerned that the huge pool of low-cost Chinese labor may have been a poisoned chalice. They worry that by coming to rely so heavily on this sort of labor, they may have unwittingly locked themselves into a low-end product strategy, even as their rivals in the other East Asian Tiger economies try to move upmarket into more innovative, higher-value, and more profitable goods and services.

Most U.S. firms occupy an intermediate position between these two extremes, between the low road of labor-cost minimization and minimal commitment and the high road exemplified by Aaron Feuerstein's Malden Mills. But is there a third alternative, a genuinely different approach to the employment relationship that is not simply a watered-down version of one of the other two? A promising place to look is in the workplaces of firms that have subjected themselves to restructuring and reengineering (a category that by now includes nearly all large American firms), on the theory that in the artificial as well as the natural worlds, stressful environments not uncommonly yield up a broader range of possibilities than are typically found in more stable conditions.

A standard litany about restructured workplaces has developed: that they are unhappy places, whose remaining employees feel bereft, overworked, insecure about their own prospects, and fearful of the future. But this stereotype quickly breaks down into two contradictory images. In one, the remaining employees, anxious and challenged as never before, are driven to levels of achievement far above their performance in earlier, more comfortable times. In the other, the insecurity and the loss of morale have the opposite effect: employees feel betrayed and embittered; their loyalty to the firm is shattered; productivity suffers. Which of these versions of events is closer to the truth?

One of the most thorough investigations of the effects of corporate downsizing on behavior and performance in the workplace has been conducted by Charles Heckscher, a professor of labor studies at Rutgers University. Over a period of several years, Heckscher studied fourteen different organizations in eight companies—including Du Pont, AT&T, General Motors, Wang Laboratories, and Dow Chemical. He focused in particular on middle managers, a group that has been targeted in much of the latest restructuring activity. (A recent survey found that middle management accounted for 19 percent of all workforce reductions between 1988 and 1993, despite making up only 8 percent of the workforce.)[3]

The results of Heckscher's research, presented in his book *White Collar Blues* (1995), are revealing. They show that many of the restructured organizations are indeed troubled places, but not for the reasons we might have expected. There is much less internal conflict and open resistance to change than is generally assumed. The surviving managerial employees have retained a surprising amount of their original feelings of loyalty to the company, with many apparently hoping for a return of the values of community and loyalty their employer once held. But these employees have also retreated into a kind of "cautious individualism," focusing only on doing their own jobs well, while waiting for the turbulence around them to subside.[4] The result has been to disrupt the network of informal personal contacts and unofficial relationships that coexisted with the formal bureaucratic structures in the original organization, and that were at least as important in getting its work done.

Paradoxically, then, restructuring has often created more of precisely what it was designed to eliminate. Organizations that were supposed to have become more flexible have instead become more rigid and bureaucratic. Managers who once worked well together no longer do so. In Heckscher's words:

> At the start is an organization with a significant level of trust based on shared loyalty. As this is threatened, people pull back into a more isolated and narrow focus on their own particular roles. Decentralization, which is typically a major part of the shift, only increases this fragmentation; links across the decentralized units fail to establish themselves. And the end result is a more bureaucratic organization than before: "bureaucratic" in the sense of rule-bound, conservative, unable to mobilize people around a common task.[5]

Other evidence points in a similar direction. A recent study of the effects of downsizing on the product innovation process found that it had disrupted the informal network of relationships that in-house innovators typically exploit in order to integrate their innovations into the routines of the firm—a critical step that makes it possible for the new products to compete effectively for cash and people with the firm's existing product portfolio.[6]

But perhaps the most interesting result of Heckscher's study was his conclusion about the limitations of loyalty as a force for organizational improvement. Heckscher found much stronger residual feelings of loyalty and goodwill toward the firm among the remaining managerial employees than he expected. But these employees also recognized that their loyalty was not being reciprocated, and it was to cope with this painful realization that they had headed for the trenches, hoping to wait it out—not resisting change exactly, but not willing to open themselves up to it, either—and narrowing their focus to their own jobs. And as they retreated into themselves, they lost touch with the bigger picture.

Indeed, Heckscher found evidence of a willful ignorance of the company's competitive situation among these managers, a refusal to look outward and to grasp the magnitude of the challenges confronting the firm. (Many had an unrealistically rosy view of their firms' marketplace performance.) By clinging to the hope that the firm would reemerge as a paternalistic, benevolent employer, the managers were simultaneously denying *their* need to rethink their own roles. The loyalty of these managers, concluded Heckscher, was getting in the way of change: "The usual assumption in current writing on this topic is that loyalty is being destroyed by the downsizing wave, and that this is harmful to managers and their companies. The responses of the managers I talked to, however, suggested that the opposite was closer to the truth: loyalty is not being destroyed, and *that* is harmful."[7]

But if loyalty in these organizations has indeed become, in Heckscher's words, a "trap," how might firms and employees be able to break out of it? Is there a plausible alternative to reciprocal loyalty as a basis on which to build the employment relationship?

Heckscher thinks that one such alternative might now be emerging. In a few of the organizations that he observed (all but one of which were succeeding in the marketplace), the firms and their managerial employees seemed to be trying to replace the traditional community of reciprocal loyalty with a different kind of community—a new way of working together—that he terms a "community of purpose." In these organizations, employer and employee are joined not by a paternalistic/dependent relationship, but rather by a shared sense of mission, based on a joint understanding of the firm's strategy and the nature of its competitive environment.

The employees in these firms are dedicated to accomplishing the current mission, and to working with others who are similarly dedicated, but they do not necessarily see themselves as staying with the company throughout their careers. They are "professionals," not "loyalists." They derive their identity less from the particular firm that is employing them than from the nature of the assignment they are working on. They judge their success less on who they work for than on what they do. They are committed to achieving a set of long-run professional and personal goals, and if at some point they are no longer able to contribute to the organization in a manner that is consistent with those goals, it will then be time to move on.

This attitude, says Heckscher, is not to be confused with the pure individualism of free agency, where the agents are constantly looking to hire themselves out to the highest bidder. These professionalized employees are strongly committed to the firm in which they are working, and to cooperating with other employees to achieve its goals. They also have high expectations of their employers; but these expectations have changed. They do not expect guarantees of job security, and they do not expect their association with the firm to be permanent. But they *do* expect to have interesting and important work to do. And they do expect to accumulate experience and training that will make them employable in the future, whether at their current firm or elsewhere.

The employers, for their part, no longer expect unconditional loyalty from their employees. But they *do* expect a high level of initiative and autonomy, and that employees will no longer be content simply to be told what to do. And they are prepared to give more resources and more authority to those who are themselves willing to be more entrepreneurial both in finding ways to add value to the firm and in managing their own careers. If pressed, they would probably say that this kind of contribution is more important than unconditional loyalty.

Jack Welch, CEO of General Electric (not one of the companies studied by Heckscher), is one of those who has embraced this idea, going so far as to suggest that the whole concept of loyalty itself should be redefined. According to Welch, the commitment to lifetime employment in the old General Electric produced "a paternal, feudal, fuzzy kind of loyalty" that is poorly suited to today's environment:

> My concept of loyalty is not "giving time" to some corporate entity and, in turn, being shielded and protected from the outside world. Loyalty is an affinity among people who want to grapple with the outside world and win. . . . The new psychological contract, if there is such a thing, is that jobs at GE are the best in the world for people who are willing to compete. We have the best training and development resources and an environment committed to providing opportunities for personal and professional growth.[8]

Welch and other corporate advocates of this more open employment relationship believe that most companies are no longer well served by the old implicit employment contract, and that only the new arrangement can provide the kind of flexibility that is needed to accommodate the demands of constant change and of diverse employees, while also bringing forth a high level of effort and cooperation. Heckscher (who has his reservations about it) sums up the differences between this arrangement and the traditional employment relation in the following way:

> The older form of loyalty seemed to be based on a sense of shared destiny—that we are all in this together through thick or thin. In the organizations more successfully making the transition, there seemed to be a sense not so much of being in this together as of working together toward a common purpose, one based on a collective definition of a strategy and of the demands of the environment. It is a far more contingent and voluntarist form of community than the old; some might also say it is colder and less fair. But it can also be seen as less paternalistic, more capable of responding to and developing individual capacities.[9]

Heckscher found this "community of purpose" in only a few of the organizations he studied, and the obvious question is, what were the factors that differentiated them from the rest? One difference was that the middle managers in these organizations were far more knowledgeable about their firm's business strategy, about the rest of the firm's operations, and about what their competitors were doing. In the other firms, most middle managers weren't able to talk nearly as intelligently about these subjects. Usually this was not for lack of information; *every* company seemed to be trying hard to provide this. The difference was that in the organizations with "professional" managers, this information was truly *needed.* These firms had pushed the process of organizational change much further than the others. Many of the original hierarchical structures had been dismantled, and much more emphasis was placed on formal (but temporary) cross-functional teams.[10] The middle managers could not function effectively in this environment without a deep understanding of the firm's business strategy. They had to know the bigger picture because they were constantly in decision-making situations which involved other parts of the firm.

In short, Heckscher's research suggests that the organizations in which an apparently successful alternative to the traditional employment relation has emerged are also those in which the process of organizational change has gone the farthest:

> The most successful companies so far—those that have best maintained enthusiasm and a positive outlook among their managers—are those that have made the biggest changes. They have dismantled many of the structures of bureaucratic hierarchy and replaced them with flexible teams; they have opened their boundaries wide to the outside. They demand far less unconditional loyalty from their managers, encouraging independence and mobility.[11]

Heckscher's findings raise many questions. How stable is this new, professionalized employment relation? And how generalizable is it? Heckscher found it in only a few of the organizations in his sample, and even in those it did not seem to have been present for very long. And though it was evidently capable of producing effective team-work on a small scale, whether it could match the capacity for large-scale cooperation of the best bureaucracies of the traditional, loyalist sort remains an open question.[12] Moreover, though many midlevel managers seemed exhilarated by the new environment, and were plainly thriving, some were finding it difficult to adjust to a situation in which traditional loyalty counts for less than independence and initiative. Will there be a place for such people, or will they be left be-hind? And even for those who do successfully make the transition, what happens if it is the company, rather than they themselves, who decides that they should move on (perhaps because younger, better-trained candidates have come on the scene)? And what happens if, when it is time to move on, they aren't able to find a new job?

Employers like GE's Jack Welch talk about the need for companies to shift from providing guarantees of lifetime employment to provid-ing a commitment to "lifetime employability," but it is not clear ex-actly what this means, and it is easy to imagine some employers invoking the rhetoric of responsibility toward their workers while relinquishing most or all of it in practice. Indeed, if helping employ-ees prepare themselves for a lifetime of change means making them more attractive to another company, it is not at all clear why any ex-isting employer would be motivated to do this. Firms will generally invest in training if they can see a benefit to themselves. Faced with a choice, they are much more likely to spend money on developing skills that are useful to them but of little value to other employers.

One model that may fit Welch's conception is the program that the semiconductor manufacturer Intel has implemented for redeploying its workers. Rapid technological change in the semiconductor in-dustry creates a constant demand for new skills, and the company spends nearly $3,000 per employee on training each year, more than double the national average. Workers who find themselves out of a job are given four months at full pay to find a new one within the firm. If they are unsuccessful, they are generally asked to leave. Much of the responsibility for gaining the necessary skills rests with the work-ers themselves. According to one of Intel's human resources special-ists, "Our message to our employees is that they are responsible for gaining new skills so they can continue to be employable either in-side or outside the company."[13] As one of the fastest-growing firms in one of the nation's most rapidly expanding industries, Intel, of course, is far from typical. With its voracious demand for new employees, the company's willingness to spend more than the average amount on internal training is only to be expected, given that it is usually much cheaper to redeploy an existing worker than to hire one from the outside. Most firms are not likely to see the same benefits from training investments, however, and will spend correspondingly less on them.

But probably the biggest question associated with the professionalized employment model is whether it could be extrapolated to nonmanagerial personnel. It is one thing to contemplate an entrepreneurial, mobile, professionally oriented managerial workforce, but it is quite another to think that the majority of blue-collar or hourly employees could redefine their relationship to the firm in similar terms. To be sure, for certain groups of workers with highly specialized and transferrable skills, this is by no means an unthinkable prospect. Indeed, there are precedents—unionized craft workers in the construction industry, for example, who move from project to project and employer to employer as their skills are called for. But for the majority of hourly employees, whose knowledge and skills are less marketable, a professionalized employment relation seems much less plausible. For these workers and their employers, the basic options are the familiar ones: traditional, Tayloristic work systems— the "low road"—on the one hand; and "high performance" work systems built on trust and reciprocal loyalty such as those described in chapter 10 on the other.

Many firms are now trying to have it both ways. Some are pursuing a "core-periphery" model of employment relations, outsourcing certain functions to firms that are often organized according to Taylorist principles, while organizing their own remaining permanent employees into high performance work systems to carry out "core" operations in house. Others, like NYNEX, AT&T, and Bank of America, are increasing their reliance on temporary help firms and contract employees to fill some jobs that used to be performed by the permanent workforce, in effect creating a two-tier workplace in house.[14] The number of temporary workers supplied by agencies to American companies has risen fourfold over the past decade, and many big firms are forming close, long-term relationships with major agencies.[15] Almost all of the temporary jobs and many of the outsourced jobs pay less and offer fewer health and employment benefits than the jobs they replaced.

Still other firms are pursuing high-road and low-road strategies simultaneously with different groups of permanent employees, either because they are of two minds about what to do and have yet to re-solve their confusion, or because they have concluded that they do in fact need both approaches.

Whether these different patterns of employment relations will turn out to be stable in the long run remains to be seen. Over time, com-petition in the periphery may cause at least some of the jobs there to be reorganized along high performance lines. Conversely, attempts to introduce participative work organization, management-labor col-laboration, upskilling, and the other elements of high performance work systems on a limited scale may be swamped by simultaneous moves to downsize, automate, and deskill. Recent research on the telecommunications industry sheds light on what can happen when firms try to have it both ways.

Since the divestiture of the old Bell System in the early 1980s, first AT&T and later the Regional Bell Operating Companies (the RBOCs, or "Baby Bells") have been busily transforming themselves from highly bureaucratic, monopoly providers of public goods to more streamlined, entrepreneurial enterprises. Today, these firms are trying both to fend off competitors and maximize profits in their tra-ditional markets and to enter potentially lucrative new businesses like cellular wireless and multimedia services. At the same time, technological innovations have been rapidly changing the way that traditional telecom service is provided, as well as greatly expanding the range of services that are available.

From the perspective of the employment relationship, the former Bell System companies have responded to these developments in contradictory ways. On the one hand, they have experimented with innovations aimed at strengthening employee commitment, broad-ening jobs, and decentralizing decision making. On the other, they have implemented changes which in many respects go in exactly the opposite direction, dividing jobs into more specialized functions, dis-placing labor with automation, deskilling many of the remaining jobs, centralizing decision making, and ending the Bell System tradition of lifetime employment security and predictable career patterns.

In research conducted while still a doctoral student at the Indus-trial Performance Center, Rose Batt (now a professor at Cornell Uni-versity) made a detailed study of what has happened at the RBOCs since divestiture.[16] A few examples from her rich trove of findings suffice to illustrate how, at least in these companies, the status of high-commitment work systems is still very much unresolved.

Take, for example, customer service employees—office workers who handle orders for new service, billing queries and adjustments,

and collections on overdue accounts. Prior to divestiture, the majority of customer service representatives were located at thousands of
local business offices scattered across the country. These were mostly
"universal representatives," who would typically handle the full
range of customer issues. Many requests demanded customized responses, and the representatives routinely exercised their discretion
and enjoyed a fair measure of autonomy. At the higher levels of the
career ladder, the jobs were fairly complex and quite diverse. Especially in smaller communities, it was not uncommon for the representatives to know their customers personally. Though the phrase
had yet to be invented, these were in many ways quintessential "high
performance" jobs.

Since divestiture, though, the jobs have changed radically, becoming more specialized and faster-paced, and with less autonomy
and less variety. In most cases, the old "one stop shopping" model has
been abandoned. Customer service jobs have been divided into sales
and service, partly in the expectation that separating "positive" (i.e.,
sales) and "negative" (e.g., problem calls) customer interactions will
help sales. Jobs have also been divided by market segment: residential, small business, and large business accounts. As more and more
products have been added (e.g., call forwarding, call waiting, fax,
voice mail), jobs in both sales and service have become more technical, requiring more training. Pressure on the sales force to sell more
has also increased, while regulators have imposed increasingly elaborate requirements on what sales representatives must say in order to
explain the new services fully. In parallel, business offices have been
consolidated as an efficiency measure; service calls are now automatically distributed to offices around the region, eliminating the
possibility of personal relationships between representatives and all
but the biggest customers.

The companies have also added telemarketing departments to handle high-volume sales solicitations. These are repetitive, short-cycle-
time jobs, and have typically been staffed by low-wage, often
part-time workers, paid on a commission basis. Turnover here has
been particularly high.

Jobs are also being changed by new technology. Automatic call
distribution systems control the flow of incoming calls to service employees. Previously, workers were able to pace themselves to some
degree, but now the pace of work is set at state or regional headquarters. Not even local managers have the discretion to schedule breaks
or assignments. Expert systems provide immediate information about
the background of customers and help identify sales opportunities,

but representatives are also required to go through a formally pre-scribed set of questions with prospective customers, with no oppor-tunity to depart from the script, even if some variation is clearly called for. The new technology also allows calls to be electronically monitored by managers.

Many employees say these organizational and technological inno-vations are reducing their sense of control, increasing the pace of work, and raising their stress levels. As one representative told Batt:

> Our job is constantly changing as the system does more and more for you. The old system was USOX—this was the traditional Bell system-wide language that you had to learn to put in an order . . . you had ser-vice order codes. It used to be that the telephone would ring and you'd pick it up. Now they come on the line automatically. We have no con-trol of the pace. It's a speed up. It used to be you'd finish writing up an order while waiting for the next call. Now you can't. As soon as you get off the line, another one comes on. You can't ever adjust your mind . . . so to manage, you have to keep the customer on the line longer—make them sit there while you write everything down because you won't have the chance once you get them off the line—or you put the new customer on hold while you finish the prior customer.[17]

Yet while all this has been going on, the RBOCs have also been ex-perimenting with self-managed teams. The new customer service teams absorb many of the administrative tasks for the group and the representatives assume the responsibility—traditionally exercised by their supervisors—for consulting experts elsewhere in the organiza-tion to find out the answers to nonroutine questions that may come up. The employees like the increased respect and autonomy that comes with the new job, and the satisfaction of solving problems on their own. They also like working as part of a team. Said one:

> As for our work, it's not that different. The difference is that we work together. If I need help with an order, my teammates will help me so we get everyone's work done at the same time. We're family. . . . We work differently because of the training in team building we received. We make sure we're here at 8 AM. We now have the right to call different departments—marketing reps, frame engineering. Now we decide who among us handles special projects. Now we're also in on coordinators' meetings and conference calls.[18]

The popularity of these teams is confirmed by survey results show-ing that 75 percent of workers who aren't in them would volunteer to join one if given the opportunity, while only 6 percent of current team members would choose to return to the traditional form of supervision.

The self-managed customer service teams also improve performance. Batt systematically compared the performance of traditional work groups and self-managed teams at one RBOC. After controlling carefully for other sources of variation, she found that members of the self-directed teams (who received no additional pay and were covered by the same labor contract provisions as other workers) achieved sales revenues that were about 15 percent higher than workers in the traditional work groups, or about $9,000 in additional sales per year per employee.

This particular RBOC has enjoyed generally cooperative labor-management relations over the years, and is relatively advanced in experimenting with decentralizing innovations like self-managed teams. Even so, only about 5 percent of the workforce is actually participating in these teams. At other companies, the status of these experiments appears even more precarious, as downsizing and the introduction of labor-saving technologies act to limit their scope. For the customer service teams, for example, the faster pace of work, with more calls to be answered and less time on the phone, means less time to attend to team business. At another regional Bell company, U.S. West, a two-year effort to reintegrate customer service jobs by cross-training employees in multiple skills and rotating job assignments was overtaken by events and never implemented. The experiment was halted following a major companywide consolidation of business offices across the entire multistate region.

On the available evidence, it seems certain that no single pattern of employment relations will come to dominate the landscape in the years to come. Professionally mobile, lifetime-loyal, and contract and part-time workers; Tayloristic, high performance, and two-tier workplaces: all will coexist for the foreseeable future. But in what proportions? The question is a crucial one, if only because the answer will determine the collective working experience of millions of Americans. Some proponents of the high-road approach advocate a role for public policy in shaping the outcome. They argue that the spread of the high-trust, high-commitment, high performance workplace model beyond the current, fairly limited group of practitioners would bring considerable benefits to firms and employees alike.

Some proposals would provide financial rewards to companies that offered their employees enhanced job security, above-average training opportunities, and the like. Others would penalize those that didn't. But these schemes would effectively involve the government directly in the business decisions of hundreds of thousands of individual firms, and for that reason seem unwise. As we have seen throughout this book, the choices that firms make with respect to the development and management of their human resources are *strategic* choices, with vital connections to other strategic decisions regarding markets, products, and technology. In many cases—indeed, in the vast majority of cases, in this author's judgment—the high performance workplace approach is likely to deliver the best results. But there are certain to be some situations in which this is not so. In any event, the government should not be in the position of anticipating or second-guessing those decisions. The choice is best left to individual firms, with appropriate input from employees and their representatives.

Instead of attempting to influence the outcomes of these decisions directly, the government's main concern should be to relieve the burden of public policies that may distort outcomes today. The main constraint here, ironically, comes not from public policy obstacles to greater job security, but rather from the converse: labor market institutions that reduce the mobility of the workforce. The United States is generally regarded as having one of the most flexible labor markets of any advanced industrial country. Nevertheless, important labor market structures are still largely based on the assumption that lifetime employment with a single company is the norm. Pensions, health insurance, and other benefits have typically been dependent on the number of years of service with a single company, for example, and the result has been to elevate the risks to individuals of moving between firms. These benefits should be made much more portable. Individual skill grants, or tax-deductible individual training accounts modeled after today's individual retirement accounts would also help to increase workforce flexibility. A stronger unemployment insurance system should be created to meet the needs of employees who are between jobs. Some of this might be accomplished by private firms working cooperatively, some of it perhaps by a revivified union movement in which pensions, training, health insurance, and other fringe benefits are tied to unions or employee associations rather than to particular companies. But it is difficult to imagine that the necessary changes can be made without government intervention of some sort.

Beyond this, there is one other domain in which government can and should intervene directly to shape the future of employment relations in America. This, of course, is to improve the quality of the nation's basic education system. Ensuring an adequate supply of well-educated workers is the surest way for government to influence firms deciding whether to take the high road or the low road to flexibility. And a workforce equipped with the basic skills and positive attitudes that the primary and secondary education system ought to be providing (but all too rarely delivers) will be better prepared to thrive in an increasingly volatile economy. In particular, a better-educated workforce will be better prepared to cope with the constant renewal of the corporate stock, the continuous process of enterprise formation and failure that is such an important source of economic flexibility today, and that may well become even more important in the future.

CHAPTER 15

Investing in Science and Technology

Beginning with the pioneering studies of MIT professor Robert Solow in the 1950s, economists have been able to document the dominant role of technological advance in long-term productivity growth. Indeed, in a fundamental sense, advances in technological knowledge account for *all* gains in total factor productivity. (Here "technology" is defined broadly to encompass ways of organizing social as well as physical processes.) New knowledge is generated in many ways, of which organized research and development activity is only one. It is disconcerting, nevertheless, to discover that the U.S. research and development system—especially the part that is concerned with longer-term research—is today contracting, and indeed is likely to undergo deeper cuts during the next several years than at any time in the last half century.

This unwelcome development is the product of two independent trends. Under intense competitive pressures to cut costs and shorten development lead times, firms are redirecting R&D resources away from longer-term, more speculative activities toward development projects that are more likely to produce near-term commercial payoffs. (The recent pattern of funding at several research-intensive U.S. companies is shown in Figure 15.1.) At the same time, federal support for R&D is also contracting. The total federal R&D budget has actually been falling in real terms since 1988 (see Figure 15.2), but until now most of the cuts have been on the development side. Further reductions are projected for the next few years, and every category of R&D will be affected.[1] Pressures to reduce the federal budget deficit are partly responsible, as are the continuing cutbacks in defense R&D—traditionally the leading source of government R&D funding. Another contributing factor is a rather widespread loss of confidence in some

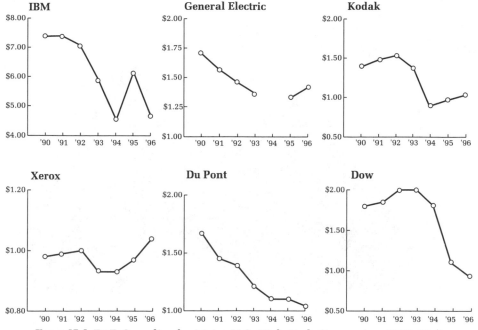

Figure 15.1 R&D Spending by Major U.S. High-Tech Companies, 1990–96 (in billions of 1996 $)

Sources: Compiled from company annual reports: Moody's *Industrial Manual* (various years), *R.D. Magazine* (October 1997); *Wall Street Journal,* 22 May 1996, B1.

of the mechanisms that have been used to allocate federal research dollars.

These developments are not uniformly bad news. Corporate R&D may indeed be getting more risk-averse, but it is also becoming more efficient. Firms are getting quicker results from their smaller, more focused R&D investments. Irrelevant research and poorly targeted development programs have been cut. R&D organizations are becoming leaner and more market-driven.

In parallel, the cutback in federal R&D funds is forcing a long-overdue shakeout of the federally funded R&D infrastructure. The scale of the federal laboratory system, especially, can no longer be justified by its current missions. Federal laboratory consolidations have already begun. The process of allocating the shrinking budget is by no means perfect, and political considerations often loom large. Nevertheless, the average quality of the federally funded R&D effort should be quite a bit higher after the cuts have been implemented.

Moreover, the decline in U.S. funding for longer-term R&D is to some extent being offset by increases elsewhere, especially in Japan.

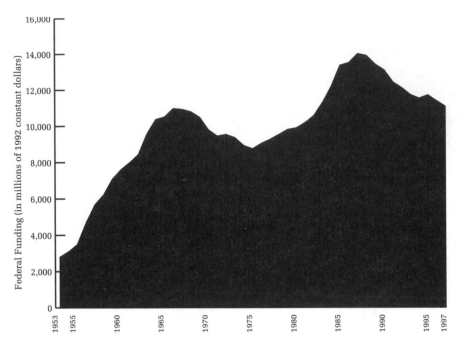

Figure 15.2 Federal Government Funding of R&D

Source: National Science Foundation (1997).

There, despite the economic slowdown and the growing budget deficit, government spending on long-term research is growing rapidly, and is expected to exceed American spending for the first time in 1997.[2] In the meantime, many American firms have begun to look more systematically at non-U.S. sources of new technology, including their own overseas affiliates, other firms, independent contract research organizations, and universities. One reason for sourcing R&D overseas is to take advantage of what are often much lower costs. (The cost of a software engineer in Bangalore, India, where many Western companies are locating new software development activities, is reported to be just 20 percent of an equivalent American engineer.)[3] In other cases firms are required to contribute to a foreign nation's R&D base as the price of doing business there.

It is difficult, nevertheless, to be sanguine about the reductions in U.S. R&D. The facts remain: (1) a preponderance of evidence points to new technology as the dominant engine of productivity growth; and (2) even when overall investment in R&D was on the rise, U.S. productivity growth was disappointing. So it does not seem likely that a reversal of this trend will be a positive development.

Is there a "correct" level for a nation's investment in R&D? Unfor-

tunately, there is no basis, either in theory or in empirical fact, for determining such a thing. Partly this is because R&D, like any investment, involves a trade-off between current consumption and future
consumption—a matter of individual and social preference for which
there is no right answer. But another problem is the lack of precision
in even the best estimates of just how much growth a given level of
investment in R&D will generate. Much about this subject remains
poorly understood. So, in the absence of anything better, the debate
about how much R&D is enough has tended to focus on simple rules
of thumb, such as the ratio of R&D spending to economic output
(GDP). This ratio has declined sharply in the U.S. in recent years (see
Figure 15.3), and on this scale the United States lags well behind
other major industrialized countries (see Figure 15.4).

President Clinton recently called for an increase in this ratio from
2.5 percent to 3 percent (though it is notable that his own budget
plans call for a reduction in federal R&D spending of about 14 percent
in real terms between 1998 and the year 2002). But aside from the fact

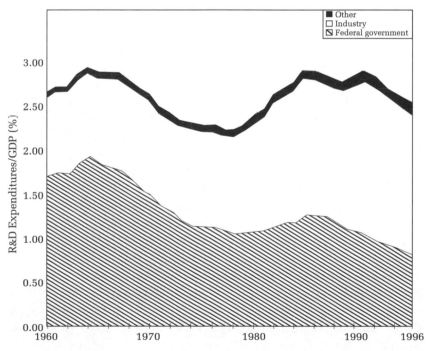

Figure 15.3 R&D Expenditures as a Percentage of GDP by Funding Source,
1960–96

Source: National Science Foundation, *Natural Patterns of R&D Resources: 1997 Data Update.*

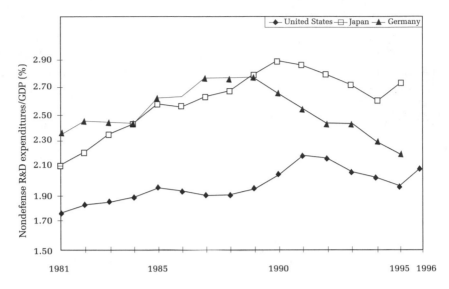

Figure 15.4 Nondefense R&D Expenditures as a Percentage of GDP

Source: National Science Foundation (1996).

that it would match Japan's current spending rate, the rationale for this target is unclear. Why not 2.8 percent, or 3.2 percent, or 3.5 percent? And how is the optimum ratio in the United States affected by the rise of R&D spending in other countries? Should the United States be investing more to stay ahead, or less now that the burden is being shared by more countries? And does the ratio of R&D spending to GDP matter more than the absolute size of the R&D establishment? (In the aggregate, the United States still outspends Japan, Germany, and France combined.)

Convincing answers to these questions are hard to find. A more useful approach is to look in further detail at the different kinds of activities that are conducted under the broad heading of research and development. As we shall see, the most serious implications of the current retrenchment revolve around one particular subcategory of R&D.

The late Princeton University professor Donald Stokes suggested two distinctions that are helpful in understanding the various components of the R&D system. The first concerns the broad purpose of the research: Is the new knowledge being pursued entirely for its own sake, or rather with some practical considerations of use in mind? The second distinction has to do with the nature of the work that is being undertaken: Does it advance the frontiers of fundamental scientific knowledge or not? Stokes used these distinctions to create the two-by-two matrix shown in Figure 15.5. The upper-left cell refers to fundamental research that is pursued purely for its own sake, without thought of practical application. Stokes invoked Niels Bohr's studies of atomic structure early in the twentieth century as an example of this class of research. The lower-right quadrant is epitomized by the work of Thomas Edison, who took existing knowledge and converted it into practical inventions while paying almost no attention to the deeper scientific implications of his discoveries. The upper-right cell contains research of a fundamental nature that is stimulated by practical concerns. One of Stokes's examples is the research of Louis Pasteur, whose very practical objectives of treating specific diseases in humans and animals and preventing the spoilage of milk and other foods motivated him to undertake investigations into fundamental scientific questions. (Examples of work in the lower-left quadrant that neither seeks to explain at a fundamental level nor has any practical purpose in mind can be imagined—Stokes cited Roger Tory Peterson's taxonomic studies of birds—but it is not, for our purposes, a significant category and we need not consider it further.)

A crucial consideration for any kind of R&D activity concerns the ownership of the knowledge—the "intellectual property"—that it creates. Here there are two basic possibilities. Either the knowledge is freely available to all, or it is held proprietary by a private firm or in-

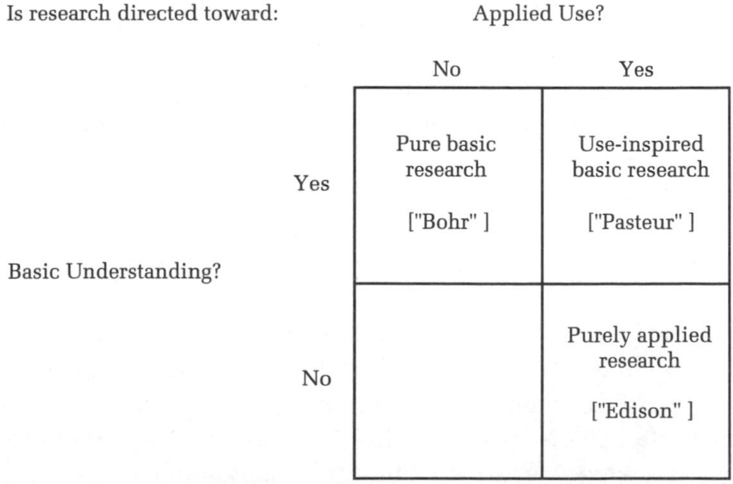

Is research directed toward:		Applied Use?	
		No	Yes
Basic Understanding?	Yes	Pure basic research ["Bohr"]	Use-inspired basic research ["Pasteur"]
	No		Purely applied research ["Edison"]

Figure 15.5 Stokes's Matrix of Research and Development

Source: Donald E. Stokes, "The Impaired Dialogue Between Science and Government and What Might Be Done About It," in *AAAS Science and Technology Policy Yearbook 1994*, edited by Albert H. Teich, Stephen D. Nelson, and Celie McEnaney (Washington, DC: American Association for the Advancement of Science, 1994), pp. 123–46.

dividual. A good way to think about this choice is to ask whether society is likely to benefit more from being able to harness market forces to develop the new knowledge (in which case "strong" private property rights are preferred) or from having unrestricted public access to the new knowledge. As we shall see, the answer depends on where the knowledge sits on Stokes's map.

Private firms will generally invest their own funds in R&D on new products and processes if the expected returns are commensurate with the risks involved. Technological and market risks are obviously central to the calculation. But the investment decision is also influenced by how confident the firm is of being able to prevent its competitors from gaining access to the results. Firms that fear losing control of the knowledge they have paid to acquire will naturally be less inclined to spend money acquiring it. Others, so-called free riders, will not invest at all. (Why pay if you can get it free?)

Some of what firms learn in the course of their R&D is so particular to their own internal routines and capabilities that it is of little interest to would-be poachers. This tends to be especially true of some of the work in the "Edison" quadrant, but it may also be true in quite fundamental areas of science if the firm already has particular strengths there. In other cases, the knowledge may be valuable to others but firms can maintain control by keeping it secret. Secrets rarely last for ever, of course, but usually they need only be kept for as long as it takes to introduce the next generation of technology, after which their value will probably decline rapidly anyway. In industries where products have short life cycles, speed of new product development is often the firm's best defense against knowledge leakage. By the time its rivals have figured out what it is doing, the firm has moved on to a new product.

But sometimes neither speed nor secrecy are viable options. This is true, for example, of most pharmaceutical products. A commercially available drug that costs hundreds of millions of dollars to develop, test, and license might be analyzed and reproduced by a competitor for a tiny fraction of this sum long before the developer has had a chance to recover the original investment. For products like these, private rights to intellectual property are protected by the patent system. This assigns to the inventor (or the inventor's designee) a monopoly of limited duration to exploit the patented knowledge. Society is willing to grant these monopolies because without them many inventions would be much less likely to be made.

In theory, there is an alternative to this arrangement: research and development could be financed with public funds, and the results, instead of being patented, could simply be given away. This would certainly ensure that the new knowledge was more widely disseminated. But for R&D on new commercial products and processes, the disadvantages of such a scheme are overwhelming. Even if the necessary public funds were forthcoming (unlikely), the scheme would still suffer from two crippling drawbacks. No firm would have a strong incentive to exploit the results of the research, since every other firm would have access to the same information at the same price (i.e., free). Moreover, the public authority would be placed in the position of having to choose which technology to develop in the first place.

So, for R&D that leads directly to commercial products and processes, the choice is clear. Far better that decisions on what to do be made by private firms, who know much more about the marketplace, and far better that these firms be given strong incentives to invest their own resources in the R&D. Even though diffusion of the knowledge will be restricted, society will be better off as a result.

Exactly the opposite choice is made for the sort of research that is carried out in the Bohr quadrant, where fundamental knowledge is pursued for its own sake. In this case, society judges that the benefits of unrestricted dissemination and free exchange of information are paramount.[4] So this type of research is mainly financed by the government, and the results are given away to all. Decisions about what research to undertake within a given field and who should do it are delegated by the government to the scientific community itself, through the mechanism of peer review of competitive grant proposals. Much of this research is carried out by the universities, in the course of which the next generation of scientists and engineers is trained—a combination that the universities are uniquely able to accomplish.

Not all federally funded fundamental research is of the Bohr type. A good deal of it, in fact, is conducted in support of one or other of the government's missions—national security, public health, safety regulation, space exploration, and so on—and so more properly belongs to the Pasteur quadrant. Sometimes peer review is heavily relied on here, too (this is true of the National Institutes of Health research program), but in other cases government bureaucrats play a more active role in resource allocation decisions, though usually with input and advice from the scientific community.

To summarize, for much of the research on Stokes's R&D map, the institutional choices are clear. R&D that is undertaken with the purpose of developing or improving a specific product or process (usually in the Edison quadrant) is almost always paid for by for-profit firms responding to market forces; and where appropriate, the knowledge is held secret or is protected by patents. Most of the fundamental research in the Bohr quadrant and some in the Pasteur quadrant involves government funding, peer review, and unrestricted dissemination of information.

For an important category of commercially relevant research straddling the Pasteur and Edison quadrants, however, no satisfactory institutional arrangement has ever been devised. This category consists of work that is relevant not just to a specific product but to a broad *class* of products (or services) and that is typically of interest to multiple firms. It tends to be longer-term—a time horizon of five to ten years is typical—and can range from fundamental studies (i.e., in the Pasteur quadrant) to the development of prototype technologies (i.e., Edisonian). The problem in this case is that neither the Bohr-type fundamental research model nor the Edisonian market model is really suitable for funding and resource allocation. Private firms, if left to their own devices, will underinvest in this kind of R&D because of the free rider problem.[5]

On the other hand, the government, which (at least in principle) could overcome that problem with public funds, can't be relied upon to allocate those funds among the alternative research possibilities wisely. Delegating these decisions to a scientific peer review process—the strategy used for pure fundamental research—won't work in this case, since commercial relevance is a key consideration along with the intrinsic technical merits of the alternatives. But *not* delegating the decisions is equally problematical, since government bureaucrats and their congressional overseers are too distant from the marketplace to be able to judge effectively which alternatives offer the potential for the highest return on investment. At best, such decisions are likely to be influenced by political considerations; at worst, they will be tainted by log-rolling and pork barrel politics.

Historically, this sort of work has been funded partly by industry and partly by government with a variety of ad hoc approaches of varying effectiveness. As long as the R&D system was expanding, the special problems it posed could be fudged. But in the current climate of retrenchment in both the public and private sectors, this critical link in the R&D chain is particularly vulnerable.

Much of the industry-funded portion of this class of R&D has traditionally been carried out at central corporate research laboratories.

But many of these great laboratories have been dismantled in recent years, and those that have escaped this fate have mostly been repositioned to do shorter-term, product-specific work. Reports from AT&T's Bell Laboratories, from IBM's Yorktown laboratories, from Du Pont's central research organization, and from many other large American corporations with a strong tradition of long-term research, all tell much the same story. As the head of one major industrial research laboratory commented recently: "I have been told every day that 18 months is my horizon. If you can't help in 18 months, they don't want to see you."[6]

There are some counterexamples. Microsoft Corporation, for one, has announced plans to establish a new laboratory for long-term research.[7] But Microsoft is the exception that proves the rule in more ways than one. Consistently one of the world's most profitable technology-based companies for fifteen years, Microsoft has pursued a technology strategy that until now has mainly consisted of incrementally improving upon and successfully marketing technologies invented by others—an Edison-type strategy that many firms now downsizing their long-range R&D programs would dearly love to emulate.

Government funding of "generic" industrial R&D is also coming under particularly heavy pressure—the target of deficit reduction and ideological disputes over the proper role of government in the economy. Throughout the postwar period, public funds have actually paid for a good deal of this sort of R&D under the umbrella of one or other of the government's statutory missions—mainly national security and public health. The record is mixed. There have been successes, occasionally of spectacular proportions, as well as periodic embarrassments. A strikingly successful intervention was the development of the basic Internet architecture and protocols by the Defense Advanced Research Projects Agency (DARPA) and other government agencies: a public investment of $250 million over a period of twenty-five years that leveraged a far larger private investment and has spawned a multi-billion-dollar industry.[8] In this case, farsighted government technocrats saw an opportunity that would never have been grasped by private industry on its own, justified the government's intervention on the grounds that the Department of Defense's R&D costs would be reduced by a system of electronic links between computers that would facilitate the sharing of computational resources and research results, and designed and managed a highly effective research and development program.[9] There are other, similar examples, many of them also originating with DARPA.

But there is also a long list of failures. Linda Cohen and Roger Noll of Stanford University recently studied six large federal technology commercialization projects, including the Clinch River Breeder Reactor, the synthetic fuels program, the supersonic transport, and the space shuttle, and reached a gloomy conclusion: "The overriding lesson from the case studies is that the goal of economic efficiency—to cure market failures in privately sponsored commercial innovation—is so severely constrained by political forces that an effective, coherent national commercial R&D program has never been put in place."[10]

How could the same system have produced both the Internet and the synfuels program? Part of the answer has to do with scale. Synfuels and most of the other technologies in Cohen and Noll's study were all very big projects—too big to avoid direct congressional involvement in resource allocation decisions. DARPA's projects were typically much smaller. Even more important, the agency itself operated with an unusual degree of independence from congressional oversight: its mission was politically unassailable during the cold war years, and its activities were mostly conducted in secret anyway.

But if this indeed explains DARPA's successes, it is a formula that was never likely to evolve into a workable strategy for generic industrial R&D as a whole. The operative lessons—keep the programs small, squirrel them away from congressional oversight whenever possible, and always stress the link to national security—were inherently self-limiting, even when the cold war was at its height. And as the cold war faded and funding for defense R&D became scarcer, the DARPA formula became still less plausible.

Instead, when industrial performance and international competitiveness emerged as major national issues during the 1980s, a series of government R&D initiatives explicitly directed at helping civilian American industries was launched (see Table 15.1). Some of these, like the SEMATECH consortium, were partly justified on the basis of their expected contribution to national defense. But others had as their sole rationale the strengthening of specific sectors of the civilian economy. Though many of these programs originated with the Republican administrations of Presidents Reagan and Bush, the scale of activity was greatly increased in the early years of the first Clinton administration. Existing programs such as the Commerce Department's Advanced Technology Program and Manufacturing Extension Program and the industrial partnership programs of the Department of Energy's national laboratories were expanded dramatically. Many new initiatives were also announced. (Even DARPA was caught up in the new enthusiasm. In a sign of the times, the word "Defense" was dropped from the agency's name in 1993 to reflect its new emphasis on civilian as well as military applications, making its acronym ARPA.)

Table 15.1: Government-Sponsored Industrial R&D Programs

Program	Sponsoring Agency	Govt./Industry Cost Sharing	Number of Projects
Advanced Technology Program	National Institute of Standards and Technology	~ 50:50	280
Cooperative Research and Development Agreements (CRADAs)	Department of Energy/National Laboratories	~ 50:50	>1000
Manufacturing Extension Partnership	National Institute of Standards and Technology	~ 50:50 (industry component can come in form of local govt. aid)	60 regional centers
SEMATECH	DARPA	50:50 (federal support ended in 1996)	n.a.
Small Business Innovation Research Program	11 federal departments/Small Business Administration	Phased, tiered competitive grants	~ 4000/yr
Technology Reinvestment Program (renamed Joint Dual Use Program)	DARPA	Industry contribution at least 50%	131

But the elevation of the federal budget deficit to the nation's highest policy priority following the 1994 congressional elections brought much of this activity to a halt. The new focus on the deficit created intense pressures to cut domestic discretionary spending, and the administration's civilian technology initiatives were singled out for elimination by the new congressional leadership, which was inclined to see them as unwarranted government intrusions into the marketplace. (In 1995, "Defense" was duly restored to ARPA's name.)

And there the matter stands today. Democrats and Republicans, though differing on details, agree broadly on the need for federal government funding of basic research in the Bohr quadrant. There is also agreement in principle on the appropriateness of federally funded applied R&D in support of the government's own missions. But on the question of federal R&D support for private industry, deep divisions persist. Advocates argue that only the government can compensate for industry's chronically short time horizons. Opponents insist that government intervention will inevitably be wasteful and inefficient—just another form of "corporate welfare." But each side overlooks a key point. Opponents seem unwilling to recognize that an important category of industrially relevant R&D is likely to be neglected without collective action, and that because of free rider problems such action is not likely to be sustainable without some form of government involvement. Advocates, on the other hand, are unwilling to acknowledge that even well-intentioned collective action is likely to go awry if it is implemented through existing political institutions.

Is there a way out of this dilemma? An intriguing solution has been proposed by the Stanford economist Paul Romer.[11] Romer's scheme recognizes that government must intervene to secure the funds necessary for collective R&D, but places decision-making authority for allocating R&D resources firmly in the hands of industry, completely removing the flow of funds from Congress and the executive branch. The scheme has the following features:

- The initiative for taking collective action would come from industry itself. If a group of firms within a given industry decided that there were opportunities for new scientific or technological advances that individual firms would not address on their own because they could not appropriate the results (e.g., the development of new standards, or new manufacturing principles for the industry), they would create one or more "industry investment boards" to pursue these opportunities.

- The government would be required to certify that the investment board would meet a genuine public need, i.e., that it would generate knowledge that would not be provided through the private actions of individual firms.

- If the plan passed the test, all of the firms in the industry would then vote on whether to levy a tax on sales to fund it. If a majority of the firms voted for the tax, it would then be imposed on the entire industry as a legal requirement. (The authority to do this would require general enabling legislation.)

- The tax would be levied on all sales in the United States, whether they were produced by domestic or foreign firms. Foreign firms would receive equal treatment. They would pay their taxes, vote in the elections, allocate their contributions, and participate in the governance of the boards they supported, like any U.S. firm.

- The proceeds from the sales tax would not go to the government. Instead, each firm would have the right to direct its share of the tax to the industry investment board that it felt was doing the most important work. If a firm didn't like what a particular investment board was doing, it could redirect its contribution to another board. Alternatively, in conjunction with other firms it could form a new board. The boards would thus compete with each other for the tax contributions of the firms in the industry. If a board failed to perform well, it would quickly find itself without resources.

- These boards would operate as nonprofit, private foundations, with a board of directors answerable to the firms that funded them. They would not be overseen by an executive agency or Congress. The only requirement would be that they invest in activities that would benefit the entire industry, and that all of the firms in the industry would have equal access to the results.

Romer's proposal resembles a number of existing schemes, but there is no exact precedent for it. Like SEMATECH, the initiative for new R&D investment would come from industry itself under Romer's scheme; but unlike SEMATECH (at least in its original form), none of the funding would come from a government agency. Also unlike SEMATECH, participation in the scheme would be mandatory for all firms in the industry. Firms that were unhappy with SEMATECH's agenda could still refuse to contribute to it; but instead of opting out completely, as some did with SEMATECH, they would instead establish an alternative investment board to pursue research closer to their own interests.

The financing mechanism envisaged by Romer also bears a resemblance to the Electric Power Research Institute (EPRI). EPRI has traditionally been funded by contributions from electric utilities, whose state regulators have typically allowed them to include these costs in their customer ratebase. In effect, the R&D has been financed by a government-approved sales tax on electricity that is collected and allocated by the utilities themselves (though in this case the utilities have been free to choose whether or not to participate). But unlike Romer's proposed scheme, utilities that did not approve of EPRI's performance or agenda have had no alternative outlet for their R&D tax dollars. And it is likely that the lack of competition has helped to foster a culture at EPRI that many have criticized for being inward-looking and unimaginative.

In short, Romer's scheme potentially solves the two key problems that are at the heart of the institutional dilemma. It invokes the authority of government to overcome the free rider problem, while delegating resource allocation decisions to individual private firms, who are far better judges than the government of what kinds of investment will yield maximum returns. It also has the virtue of building competition into the process. The freedom to form new industry boards and to choose among existing boards means that R&D laboratories with the most to offer would prosper, while the weakest would not survive.

Romer's scheme does have several disadvantages. One of the biggest has to do with how one would define the boundaries of the industry. Because of the coercive nature of the scheme (everyone has to pay the tax), deciding who is in and who is out is critically important. This will not always be obvious. A related problem is that the opportunities for collective action don't always fall neatly within industry boundaries, even when these are well defined; cross-industry collaborations may make more sense in some cases. And if, as we have already discussed, the boundaries between industries are becoming increasingly fluid and unstable, these problems will only be compounded. Indeed, many of the most revolutionary technological developments seem to occur in domains that lie at the boundaries of very different and traditionally noncooperating industries. Two fairly recent examples are the development of optical fibers and of video cameras; looking ahead, the development of computers based on biological processes at the molecular level may turn out to be another example. For these and other reasons, the scheme would only be implementable in some cases. But even partial coverage would be preferable to none at all.

From "Technology Transfer" to R&D Integration

The development of new ways to finance "generic" industrial research is one of two key challenges facing the nation's R&D system today. The other is to find ways to couple the various parts of the system more closely together.

It is actually impossible to understand the science and technology enterprise without an appreciation for the mutual dependences linking the different R&D categories in Stokes's matrix. Many years or even decades may elapse before these linkages work themselves out, and often the outcomes are entirely unexpected. Harvard University professor Harvey Brooks has illustrated this point with an example from the semiconductor industry. Much of the instrumentation used in wafer fabrication plants today is derived from instruments that were conceived many decades ago for investigations in nuclear and high energy physics. Thus one of the "purest" of fundamental research programs, firmly rooted in the Bohr quadrant, turned out to have, as an incidental by-product, an industrial relevance that could not even have been imagined at the time. Another example is Harvard professor Norman Ramsey's seminal contributions to the development of atomic clocks, work for which he was awarded the Nobel Prize in physics. These advances led subsequently to the development of the global positioning system, and to the synchrotron radiation used in integrated circuit manufacture. Yet none of these benefits was evident when the original research was carried out. As Ramsey himself has observed, "I would have had difficulty justifying most of my research on the basis of future applications either I or anyone else would have foreseen."[12]

Ramsey's research was part of a long line of work that began in Isidor Rabi's laboratory at Columbia and was also carried on by Felix Bloch at Stanford and Nicolaas Bloembergen and Edward Purcell at Harvard, all of whom would also subsequently win the Nobel Prize. Purcell's fundamental discoveries in the field of nuclear magnetic resonance paved the way for today's thriving medical imaging industry, but, like Ramsey, he didn't anticipate this development at the time. Some twenty-five years later, in a letter thanking Raymond Damadian for sending him a copy of a whole-body nuclear magnetic resonance image, the first such image ever obtained, Purcell wrote: "I congratulate you and shall keep the picture as a perpetual reminder of how little one can foresee the fruitful application of any new physics." To add another layer of complexity to the story, it turns out that several of the members of this closely interacting community of physicists had worked closely together during World War II at MIT's eminently worldly and mission-driven Radiation Laboratory, and drew on these relationships in their later, fundamental research.[13]

The richness and complexity of the interactions between fundamental, applied, public mission—oriented, and industrial research are suggested by the two brief case histories, one in drug discovery and the other in information technology, that are reproduced in the boxes at the end of the chapter.[14] The cases reveal a flow of knowledge that is at odds with the stereotype of a linear progression from the laboratory to the marketplace.

In the linear view, the R&D process begins with fundamental research, which sometimes leads to a discovery; then comes a search for applications, followed by a period of applied research during which the feasibility of alternative applications is explored; the most promising of these are developed further, products and production processes are designed, and the process ends with marketing and production. It is a tidy model that has, among its virtues, the great advantage of being easily understood even by those to whom the details of science and technology often seem impenetrably mysterious. But as the two case studies make clear, the reality is typically much more complicated, with knowledge flowing back and forth between the different stages of the process in a highly nonlinear fashion. There are, to be sure, prominent cases of innovations that *do* broadly conform to the linear model—nuclear power, lasers, and genetic engineering, for example. But often it is a practical invention that sparks a fundamental research investigation rather than vice versa, or it is a shift in the marketplace that stimulates the development of a new product feature that in turn triggers more fundamental advances.

It is often pointed out that two of the most momentous inventions of the last two centuries *preceded* the discovery of many of the fundamental scientific phenomena on which they depend: the development of the science of thermodynamics took place only after the invention of the steam engine; and more recently, the tremendous growth of the field of condensed matter physics followed—and was stimulated by—the invention of the transistor. In each case, of course, the subsequent elaboration of the underlying scientific ideas in turn supported an extraordinary outpouring of related inventions and applications. But initially, at least, one could say that these were instances of technology leading science.

The differences between the linear and nonlinear views of the innovation process have important practical consequences. For most of the postwar period the linear model dominated the organization of research and development in the United States. Research was science-driven; priority was given to discovery; and the nation's achievements in basic science were outstanding. But less attention was paid to the downstream activities of product and process realization, of design, development, and manufacturing. The rapid gains of Japanese industry in the 1970s and 1980s revealed America's deficiencies in those areas. Yet even then, many of the responses were shaped by the still widespread view of product development as proceeding in a linear series of discontinuous steps—a view that naturally led to an emphasis on strengthening the mechanisms of "technology transfer" from one stage to the next.

More recently, the nonlinear model has been gaining ground. A 1994 presidential statement on American science policy reflected the shifting consensus:

> We acknowledge the intimate relationships among and interdependence of basic research, applied research, and technology, appreciate that progress in any one depends on advances in the others, and indeed recognize that it is often misleading to label a particular activity as belonging uniquely to one category.[15]

The nonlinear model of innovation has profound implications for the organization of R&D, and indeed of the entire firm. If useful knowledge can be generated anywhere in the value chain, including the firm's customers and suppliers, what becomes critical is the ability to bring to bear the full range of capabilities—in R&D, manufacturing, marketing, design, and so on—that are needed to convert this knowledge into something of value to the firm's customers as quickly as possible. This argues for a flexible organization, for closer links with customers and suppliers, and for a research effort that is integrated as fully as possible into the business enterprise. Even fundamental researchers cannot afford to define success purely in terms of what their fellow researchers deem important. They can no longer concentrate solely on making significant research advances, throw them over the wall, then sit back and place the blame on other parts of the firm when something goes wrong.

A story told to an MIT seminar not long ago by IBM's director of research at the time, Jim McGroddy, illustrates what is at stake here. The story was about a series of events that was partly real and partly imagined. During the 1970s, IBM's Research Division made many pioneering contributions to computer science and technology. One was the invention of reduced instruction set computing (RISC) technology, now the dominant architecture for certain types of computer systems, including workstations. At around the same time, IBM researchers were developing some of the world's first microprocessors, and were also pioneering the development of the DRAM memory chip. This part of the story is true. But now comes the fictional part. The developers of RISC technology joined forces with the researchers who had learned to put an entire processor on a single chip. Then it was immediately recognized that the IBM RISC processor could be combined with IBM memory chips and an IBM data-storage device (another field where the company was very strong) in a small box. The box was called a personal computer. Along the way, the company developed a new operating system for the computer (something else it was very good at). And so a new industry was born. IBM's personal computer business became phenomenally successful.

Its domination of yet another computer market was too much for the Justice Department, which forced the company to break up. One company, called Macrosoft, split off and made the operating system. The microprocessor unit was also spun off and named Extel.

As everybody knows, of course, the real story was different. IBM purchased the microprocessors for its first commercial personal computers from Intel (which used the less advanced complex instruction set computing, or CISC, architecture in its design) and obtained the operating system from Microsoft. IBM's enormous presence in the computer industry enabled it to dominate the personal computer business for a while, but it soon lost control of the business to Intel and Microsoft (and it was later Microsoft that would attract the attention of the Justice Department's antitrust department). Perhaps, in the end, the greater good was served by IBM's failure to retain control of the personal computer market. Set that question aside, though, and a puzzle remains: Why was McGroddy's story only a fable when it could all too easily have come true? According to McGroddy himself, a big part of the problem was that IBM's Research Division conceived of its role in overly narrow terms. It defined success in terms of the world of the researchers' peers rather than the world in which it was embedded, the world that actually supported its work. It failed to take responsibility for capturing the full value produced by its research.

Many firms, under pressure to reduce costs and with similar stories of their own, are now trying to tie their laboratories more closely to the needs of their business units. A staple of such efforts is the formation of cross-functional teams, in which researchers who were previously involved in fundamental research now work directly with manufacturing, engineering, and marketing personnel on new products and processes.

Most companies have found these teams to provide good value, but there are risks attached that often go unrecognized. Serving the needs of today's customers is too narrow a vision for corporate research. It excludes too much. It runs the risk of ignoring what is latent in the marketplace—the products and services that consumers *will* want but aren't yet aware of; and its emphasis on what *is* risks driving out the creative impulse to think about what *might* be. Thoughtful R&D managers still value the researcher who follows his nose. They do not want to eliminate serendipity from the R&D process entirely, and they recognize how evanescent a phenomenon that is. They speak instead of trying to change the *context* within which researchers exercise their curiosity, to broaden it to reflect the company's business strategy and the needs of the marketplace, not just the peers in the research community. At Xerox's Palo Alto Research Center (PARC), a prolific laboratory with a famous history of missed connections with the rest of the company, researchers now learn the language of competitive strategy. IBM's McGroddy talks of the need for more "worldly" researchers, of "Franciscan monks in the street, not Capucin monks on the hill."

Even firms as large as IBM and Xerox are also recognizing that their in-house laboratories cannot provide the necessary research inputs on their own, and that they must increasingly rely on external R&D resources. New products are thus being generated in processes that span many kinds of boundaries: disciplinary, corporate, industrial, institutional, and national. Think of chapter 3's description of how automobile firms go about developing new cars today. Or, to take a quite different example, think of how Levi Strauss came up with its hugely successful Docker's brand of khaki pants. The Dockers concept actually originated in Argentina, where the Levi's affiliate was the first to use the name (for a not very successful khaki product). It was later picked up by a visitor from Levi's Japan, which modified the design and came up with a logo for the new concept. Only afterwards did the product find its way to the United States, when a visiting American Levi's merchandiser spotted it in a Tokyo showroom and persuaded product development colleagues to try it out back home. Examples like these make clear that at the heart of the modern product development process are encounters between different communities of practice, each with different styles, norms, and vocabularies. These interactions are placing extraordinary new demands on the integrative skills of managers. The central problem is that the conventional tools and techniques of management are poorly suited to the task.

Our prevailing ideas about integration derive from the basic assumptions that the elements that are to be integrated are well-defined and the objectives of the integration are clear. But in the case of new product development almost everything about the task of integration is uncertain and changing rapidly. The process is open-ended; it is enveloped in ambiguity and uncertainty. Indeed, it is here that the opportunities for creativity arise. But the thrust of many of our most popular management tools is to respond to uncertainty by trying to control it, by trying to minimize its effects, and where possible by trying to eliminate it altogether. Too often the effect is to promote a false sense of clarity. By purging our organizations of what is ambiguous, we risk losing our sense of what is possible. And as volatility in business conditions increases, it is exactly this ability to recognize multiple possibilities, to coexist with them, and to adapt continuously as new ones emerge and old ones fade, that is becoming the key to the health of many—perhaps most—of our business organizations.

In the next chapter we will explore an alternative framework for dealing with the problem of managing under conditions of great uncertainty. Our focus will be on the organization of new product development. But we will see that this new approach offers insights that can be extended to the organization of other functions and areas of economic activity in which volatility and uncertainty are present too. In this sense, product development provides us with a vantage point from which to rethink what is fast becoming a very general business problem—indeed, perhaps the dominant business problem of the era.

Case History: Antihypertensive Drug Discovery*

From the 1930s to the 1960s, research funded by private nonprofit groups, the Veterans Administration, and the National Institutes of Health revealed dietary and behavioral risk factors associated with high blood pressure. An early and important step was finding a way to measure blood pressure quickly and cheaply, and to correlate those measures with diseases. Rigorous epidemiological studies confirmed suspected links between high blood pressure, stroke (and later, heart disease), and premature death. Parallel clinical trials demonstrated that treatment for lowering blood pressure prevented stroke, death from heart disease, and cardiac and renal failure. The National High Blood Pressure Education Program, built on these findings, commenced in 1972. Since then, changing social norms, individual exercise and diet decisions, and better medical management have reduced the incidence of hypertension by more than a third, and reduced stroke mortality by over 60%, a remarkable achievement. For millions of Americans, a broad base of research—spanning the full range from social and behavioral research to molecular biotechnology—has meant the difference between life and death.

As epidemiological and behavioral research progressed, a complex web of biological factors also was uncovered through clinical investigations and basic biological research. This line of research was funded predominantly by the federal government, and supplemented by hospitals and private sources. Private pharmaceutical firms made investments comparable in magnitude to federal funding, but focused on narrowing the search for specific agents and clinical testing to prove their worth. Drugs lower blood pressure by reducing fluid retention (diuretics), by influencing nerve impulses transmitted to the heart and blood vessels (beta-blocking agents), and by reducing resistance to blood flow in small peripheral arteries (calcium antagonists and angiotensin converting enzyme, or ACE, inhibitors).

*Sources: Committee on Criteria for Federal Support of Research and Development, *Allocating Federal Funds for Science and Technology* (Washington, DC: National Academy Press, 1995), Supplement 4, "Interactions between Federal and Industrial Funding and the Relationship Between Basic and Applied Research." The committee's principal sources for this case history were: Rebecca Henderson, "The Evolution of Integrative Competence: Innovation in Cardiovascular Drug Discovery," *Industrial and Corporate Change,* 3 (Winter, 1994): 607–630; the historical research of Harriet Dustan (University of Vermont), Edward Roccella (National Heart, Lung, and Blood Institute), and Howard Garrison (Federation of American Societies for Experimental Biology); National Heart, Lung, and Blood Institute, *National High Blood Pressure Education Program: 20 Years of Achievement* (Bethesda, Md.: National Institutes of Health, 1992); and Thomas P. Gross, Robert P. Wise, and Deanne E. Knapp, "Antihypertensive Drug Use: Trends in the United States from 1973 to 1985," *Hypertension,* 13 (Supplement 1, 1989): I-113–I-118.

The use of calcium channel blockers came from clinical tests of various compounds that were first made by pharmaceutical firms. Knowledge of how these compounds worked and how they could best be used came years later, mainly through federally funded research. In contrast, the ACE inhibitors were developed by drug companies through a logical progression of discoveries that built on decades of publicly funded research. Private investment was essential, but federal investment was equally important at many stages, both leading and following privately funded research. Almost all the important technical decisions, in both public and private sectors, were made by those educated in research universities and trained at least in part through federally funded research.

Case History: The Development of Information and Communications Technology*

Lynn Conway of Xerox and Carver Mead of the California Institute of Technology in the 1970s conceived of "silicon foundries," where graduate students, their professors, and others could have computer chip designs fabricated into integrated circuits. Their idea won federal support and became the heart of the very large scale integrated (VLSI) circuit program supported by the Advanced Research Projects Agency in the Department of Defense. NSF joined the program, broadening access to VLSI fabrication services: the foundries. On a parallel track, the network that later became the Internet (first as ARPANet) was used to send designs to the foundries, which then created and shipped the chips, reducing cost and increasing speed. What once took months now took days. The impediments to chip design diminished; graduate students felt free to experiment and innovate; even radical designs for chips became practical.

The foundries and other components of ARPA's VLSI program had spectacular results: a renaissance in computer design, universities creating VLSI programs, the beginnings of three-dimensional graphics, and initial efforts in reduced instruction set computing (RISC), now in use in millions of computers. RISC computing originated at IBM but was adopted only after a period of federally funded research that made its applications readily apparent, at which point several firms in addition to IBM invested in it. Several major corporations grew directly out of the VLSI program.

Decades of federal and industrial investments in information technology led to the creation of the elements—from three-dimensional graphics to windows to local networks—now embedded in the way we work, obtain and share information, and teach our children. The dynamic interactions between federally funded academic R&D and industrial R&D made the United States dominant in information technology, which strengthened the nation's competitiveness and also provided advantages in other sectors throughout the economy that depend on information technologies, such as finance, entertainment, communications, education, and transportation.

*Sources: Committee on Criteria for Federal Support of Research and Development, *Allocating Federal Funds for Science and Technology* (Washington, DC: National Academy Press, 1995), Supplement 4, "Interactions Between Federal and Industrial Funding and the Relationship Between Basic and Applied Research." The committee's principal source for this case history was the report of the Computer Science and Telecommunications Board, National Research Council, *Evolving the High Performance Computing and Communications Initiative to Support the Nation's Infrastructure* (Washington, DC: National Academy Press, 1995).

CHAPTER 16

*The Creative Organization**

Pressures for shorter product development cycles, lower project costs, and greater product variety have once again brought to the fore an old problem: how to organize product design and development. The central issue is, as it has always been, the "creative spirit" and the way it seems to conflict with the efficient management of virtually every other aspect of the business. We have a well-developed set of tools for managing other business functions, but creativity is a "black box."

The impenetrability of the black box encourages extreme solutions. One extreme is simply to give creativity free rein. A famous example is Xerox and its Palo Alto Research Center. PARC, generously funded by its parent and located close to a thriving university research community, was a prolific source of new ideas for computing and communications products, including the personal computer, local area networks, the graphical user interface, laser printers, and the computer mouse. But the Palo Alto facility, three thousand miles away from Xerox headquarters on the East Coast, lacked working connections to the rest of the company. Nobody inside Xerox was prepared to pick up these ideas and bring them to market, and they ended up being sold off (or in some cases walking out of the door with their inventors) and commercialized by other firms.

The opposite extreme is to suppress or circumvent creativity entirely. Even in a fashion-driven industry like garments there are ex-

---

*This chapter is adapted from a paper by Richard K. Lester, Michael J. Piore, and Kamal M. Malek, "The Sources of Creativity in New Product Development," MIT Industrial Performance Center Working Paper, MIT IPC 96-011WP, November 1996. A related article by the authors, "Interpretive Management: What the General Manager Can Learn from Design," appeared in the March–April 1998 issue of *Harvard Business Review*.

amples. Camaïeu, a French retailer comparable to The Gap in the United States, has no designers whatsoever. It simply tests a range of patterns and styles it has acquired from small manufacturers in its lead stores and produces in volume those that sell. The result is a collection that, compared to the products displayed in Gap stores, is a hotchpotch of different items, with no coherence. It is a marketing strategy which may appeal to Frenchwomen who come into the stores with a strong sense of fashion of their own, but it bars the company from entering major markets overseas.

What is needed is to find a balance between these two extremes. But this balance will remain elusive until we have a useful theory of creativity. We need to open up the black box and see what is inside. At MIT's Industrial Performance Center, we have embarked on a series of case studies of product design and development in an attempt to find out what such a theory might look like and how it could actually be used. The case studies compare design and development organizations for different types of products and for the same product in different companies located in different parts of the world. The products include cellular telephones, denim jeans, medical devices, automobiles, and software. From each of these cases the imbalance between managers' ideas about how to organize and manage efficiently and about how to foster creativity in design and development emerges quite clearly. But by carefully comparing these two types of activities, it is also possible to pinpoint the differences between them more exactly, and to develop a way of thinking about creativity that can hold its own with conventional, efficiency-driven theories of management. With these new insights there is a chance to establish a working balance between efficiency and creativity in our business organizations.

The critical distinction is between an *analytical* and an *interpretive* approach to product development. These two approaches call for quite different sets of organizational strategies and managerial skills. The analytical view dominates managerial thinking today. It leads us to think of the design of a new product as a "problem" that must be "solved." We seek to define a clear goal, identify the resources available to meet that goal, and establish the constraints that limit the solution. We then divide the problem into a series of discrete and separable components, and assign each one to a knowledgeable specialist. The approach is closely related to the idea of the division of labor. And it presumes a clear and unambiguous notion of what the pieces of the problem are and the specialists to whom they can be assigned.

The role of the manager in this process is captured by two images: the *technician,* splitting up the problem into its pieces and distributing them among his or her subordinates; or the *negotiator,* resolving conflicts among the goals of the organizational constituencies so as to create the clarity needed for efficient problem solving to proceed. This approach to design is really no different from the way we think about business organization in general. It is the same approach that leads us to separate accounting from production and production from purchasing in corporate organizations, to separate the engine from the chassis in building a car, and to make each station on the assembly line a separate operation.

The division of labor is necessarily followed by a process of integration, in which the pieces are brought back together to form a whole. But this form of integration is purely mechanical. It works perfectly well for the ongoing operation of the business organization, or in the assembly of standard products. It can also be important for bringing design and development projects to closure. But the aspect of design that we refer to as "creative" is more often about a different kind of partitioning and integration. It involves breaking up familiar objects into novel pieces and bringing together familiar pieces in new and surprising ways. It plays upon the very ambiguity that the analytical approach seeks to eliminate. The cellular telephone grew out of the marriage of telephone and radio technologies. And the fashion jean industry was created by the unexpected effects of washing what had until then been the most standard piece of industrial clothing first with acid and then with stones. In both cases, the eventual outcome was, at the outset, unpredictable. The forcing of design into an analytical mode would have risked the reification of insight, the premature freezing of ideas—the elimination, in fact, of the very conditions that are needed for creativity to flourish.

A good way to understand the limits of the analytical approach to design and product development is to think about how we use language to communicate with each other. One view of language is very closely aligned with the analytical approach. In that view, words have unambiguous meanings and convey a clear message that requires no interpretation to be understood. It is like communicating in Morse Code. But in another view, these sorts of messages are relatively rare. More commonly, the message must be interpreted. Think, for example, of the message carried by the word "bird." Generally, this word calls to mind something like a robin. But ostriches are birds, too. If someone says "bird" when he really means "ostrich," a good deal of confusion and misunderstanding is likely to result. That kind of confusion occurs all the time in ordinary conversation. In most conversations the participants somehow work through and resolve it.

Working out this ambiguity in the course of the conversation is often a fruitful activity. Through a process of interpretation, the participants come to understand each other better than before. And the meanings of both the broader category "bird" and the specific member of that category "ostrich" have been changed in the process. Together, the participants have invested these words with new meaning.

This process is a far better analogy to the communication that occurs among designers and between designers and customers during the sort of product development activity that we tend to think of as creative than is the exchange of unambiguous, Morse Code–like signals. In this analogy, the "ostrich" is to the "bird" what the "cellular telephone" is to the "telephone" and the "fashion jean" is to "jeans." And from this perspective, the way to understand the creative alternative to the analytical approach is as an *interpretive* process.

Pushing the linguistic analogy a bit further provides some useful new insights into what is required to manage these processes. We can think of the specialties that were integrated in the development of cellphones and fashion jeans as different *language communities.* The people within each specialty have their own way of going about their business; they think and talk differently from people in other specialties. The creation of the fashion denim product category involved the fusion of ideas drawn from several specialties, each with a different way of operating: conventional jeans manufacturers, the laundries that finish the jeans by stonewashing, laundry equipment manufacturers who build machines able to withstand a hundred pairs of jeans being washed for twenty minutes with a ton of stones, and textile manufacturers who rework denim to survive a process that would take off as much as 80 percent of the life of conventional cloth.

The linguistic analogy also gives us insights into the development of cellular telephones. The telephone industry has been dominated historically by large, bureaucratic organizations, which emphasize order and expertise. The industry has also placed enormous emphasis on quality: when you pick up the phone, you always get a line; once you are connected, you never lose a call. Compared with the telephone industry, the radio sector is more like the Wild West. Radio engineers operate empirically in an informal, ad hoc way. The industry is used to tolerating wide variation in the quality of reception; transmissions fade in and out. Getting radio and telephone people to work together to create the cellular industry in the beginning was like getting the French to talk to the Chinese. Ultimately, it involved the generation of a new language, which could then evolve as the industry developed.

This linguistic model suggests two additional roles for the manager that are quite different from the analytical roles of technician and negotiator. In one, the manager is literally an interpreter or translator, who makes it possible for different organizational units to communicate with each other across linguistic boundaries. As anyone who has attempted a conversation across a language barrier well understands, an accomplished interpreter does much more than mechanically apply rules for translating individual words. The conversation hinges on the interpreter's skill in making sense of each word in its context, and ultimately on his or her understanding of the different world views of the speakers. (In one firm we studied, the managers and engineers who performed this function were referred to as "alloy people.") But if what is involved in product design is the invention of a *new* language, the parties will ultimately have to learn to communicate with each other directly. To make this happen, the manager is no longer functioning as a translator, but rather as an orchestrator of conversations. The manager's role here can be compared to that of a host at a cocktail party.

At most cocktail parties, the guests are relative strangers. They come from different backgrounds. They are invited because they might have something interesting to say to each other, but only the host really knows what that is, and even she is not always sure. To make the party a success, she will often invite enough people that it doesn't really matter if any pair of them fails to hit it off. Once the party is under way, her job is to make sure things flow smoothly, introducing new people into groups where conversation seems to be flagging, intervening to suggest a new topic when the people do not seem to be able to discover what they have in common on their own, and breaking up groups that don't seem to be working or are headed for an unpleasant argument.

To equate the apparently idle conversations of a cocktail party with the serious business of developing new products might seem to be a stretch. But product development, too, can be thought of in terms of a set of ongoing, intersecting conversations—in this case about customer needs and technical possibilities. Like any good cocktail party, these have a life of their own; at the outset, it isn't possible to say exactly where they are headed. And like all real conversations, they are characterized by ambiguities and misunderstandings, at least to begin with, and especially when, as is usually the case in product development, they involve people of different backgrounds. At a cock-

tail party, where nothing of importance is at stake, people are prepared to work through these ambiguities until they arrive at a common understanding. And if they don't, it doesn't really matter. But in
a business situation, where the stakes are high and there are potential
conflicts of interest, the ambiguities can lead people to break off the
conversation altogether.

The conventional analytical approach to management typically as-
sumes that the ambiguities have already been eliminated; or, if they
still remain, its basic thrust is to eliminate them. But by purging our
organizations of what is ambiguous, we risk losing our sense of what
is possible. In design and development, it is the ambiguities that
make the conversations worth having. It is by working through them
that we arrive at new insights. What is needed are approaches that are
as useful for managing these ongoing, interpretive processes as our
analytical tools are for bringing projects to closure.

The virtues of the interpretive perspective (and the limits of the analytical approach) are particularly obvious in the case of fashion garments. Fashion is not a problem that is "solved" or "optimized" in the
course of a discrete project. Rather, the sense of what is fashionable
emerges from a series of interactions—conversations—among fashion
designers, key customers, manufacturers, and fashion writers. The
conversations have neither a beginning nor an end. The question of
fashion has no final answer. On the contrary, the whole idea is that
the answer keeps changing. New creations—new garments—emerge
continually, *drawn out* of an unfolding process like fish pulled from
a stream. From the interpretive perspective, what is important is the
firm's position within this process, and its ability to anticipate and influence the direction the process is taking.

The fashion apparel industry is hardly typical, of course, but in
this sense it is not as different as one might think. Other industries
also produce a flow of products that evolves more or less continuously in response to changes in customer tastes, or in technology, or
in the relative price of inputs. Many consumer product industries
have this characteristic, as do many service industries. Even in industries in which product development seems to be dominated by
large projects, there are usually distinct processes going on in the
background. Andrew Grove of Intel, the archetype of the technology-
driven, analytical firm, whose product development activities are
dominated by a series of huge design projects, with thousands of people racing against tight deadlines to get the latest generation of chips
to market, recently disclosed "a deep-seated conviction that our business has some of the characteristics of the fashion industry."[1] For all

of these industries, the problem posed by the analytical approach to management is the same. It does not provide us with a way of thinking about these ongoing, interpretive processes. And without a framework for thinking about them, they tend to be overlooked, or regarded as just another form of "overhead."

To make the interpretive approach more concrete, we next consider three issues that are familiar to all practicing product development managers today: (1) "listen to the voice of the customer"; (2) partnering with suppliers; and (3) strategic alliances. By contrasting the analytical and interpretive views of each issue, we can gain a fuller understanding of the interpretive approach.

"Listen to the Voice of the Customer": The familiar injunction to the designer to "listen to the voice of the customer" might at first seem to be quite consistent with the interpretive view of product development. But in fact it is usually understood in analytical terms. It is taken to mean that customers know what they want and can articulate what it is, and that the designer's job is to create products that conform to this as closely as possible (and, of course, to do so as efficiently and quickly as possible). Yet products typically do not stand alone, like pieces of art. They fit into an ongoing activity, an activity which people often do not think about consciously. With new products, moreover, the question is not just how the product fits into an ongoing activity but *which* activity. Early in the history of the cellular telephone industry, for example, it was unclear whether the market would be for car phones or handheld instruments. This is hardly the exception. In all such cases, the customer has no "needs" until they are articulated. This is what the conversation between the designer and the customer is all about. The interaction is not analytical; the designer and the customer are together discovering something new about the customer's life and how the product will fit into it.

For customized products, the designer is engaged in a conversation with the consumer quite literally. Think of the architect and his client. In other cases, the designer is talking to the client not just about what the client wants but also about what the ultimate consumer wants. Consider the conversation between the cellular infrastructure supplier and the telecom service provider, or between the medical imaging equipment manufacturer and the physicians in the teaching hospital. Firms in these equipment supply industries invest heavily in lead clients. A good lead client is demanding, but is also a good *interlocuteur.*

In mass production, the notion of a conversation with the customer has to be understood more metaphorically. For many companies, though, it is a strong metaphor. Levi Strauss divides its market into age segments. A designer is assigned to each segment. She visits the stores where the members of that segment shop, eats in their restaurants, dances in their clubs, listens to their radio stations. The conversation is then extended into Levi's itself in meetings where the designers discuss what they have seen and what they think it means, and what the events in one segment might imply for what will happen in another.

The way in which design is a conversational process even in a mass consumption industry is illustrated by the case of baggy jeans. This was a fashion trend that came out of the ghetto and was spread by rap music. Levi's picked it up early and invested heavily in designs rooted in the trend. But the market began to level off long before anticipated. At that point Levi's considered abandoning the line, but instead launched a major advertising campaign for its baggy jeans around the rap theme, and to its relief succeeded in generating a second, larger fashion wave. But its success came about because Levi's advertising is as much a part of youth culture as the rap music with which baggy jeans were originally associated. Did Levi's "create" the baggy jeans fashion for suburban teenagers? Not exactly. Company managers were unsure why the advertising campaign had worked, and they by no means viewed its success as preordained. To the analytical eye, Levi's success would seem to be the product of a mysterious chemistry, an unmanageable chain of serendipitous events. But the fact is that Levi's, by pursuing an open-ended, unstructured form of interpretive management, instigated and guided that chain of events to create a winning product.

Not all garment companies use the conversational mode. As we saw earlier, Camaïeu escapes the need for this through its test store procedure. At the other extreme, the need for conversation is sometimes circumvented by attempts to control the entire activity in which the garments will be used. When the big Japanese apparel firm Onward Kashiyama decided to enter the market for nautical sports clothes, it designed and built an entire marine resort complex. The idea was that the resort would teach its tourist-consumers the context in which the new garments were to be worn and used.

Partnering with Suppliers: At Levi's the conversations about and with customers have been enlarged to include its laundries, which perform a diverse repertoire of finishing operations on denim garments so as to achieve the desired "used" look and feel. A recurring problem is how to translate the designers' ideas about finishes into an actual garment that can be produced reliably in volume. Designers know what they want, but frequently don't know how to get it, while laundries and their equipment suppliers are continually coming up with new finishing ideas that may or may not have commercial appeal. An equally difficult problem is how to reproduce the effects that are achieved at one laundry at the several others that typically work on the same garment.

The owner of the most innovative of Levi's contract laundries plays a classic interpreter's role in managing these conversations. A trained chemist who grew up in the family textile business, this executive moves easily between the highly technical world of the laundries and the commercial world of the designers. He stays current technically by traveling widely, visiting and exchanging ideas with laundries all over the world. But in addition to this technical knowledge, it is his sense for the styles and finishes that are likely to sell in the retail market, and his ability to interpret new technical developments from this perspective, that have made him such a highly valued supplier to Levi's.

At the request of Levi's, this entrepreneur is now also beginning to orchestrate conversations among the company's other laundries, which Levi's believes are too isolated from each other and from the company's laboratories. This problem has arisen partly because Levi's has in the past encouraged them to think of themselves as competitors. Thus, when one laundry develops a new finish, it doesn't fully communicate the process to others; and when it faces a problem, it may try to hide its existence. The analytical approach to the problem would be to standardize knowledge and procedures among the laundries. But the laundry executive himself understands his role in interpretive terms. He sees himself as a catalyst of wide-ranging conversations among the laundries in which the point is not so much to eliminate the variations in finishing as to exploit them as a continuing source of new ideas and insights.

Yet even in an industry that is as driven by fashion as denim jeans, analytical thinking remains the ideal in some quarters. One of Levi's design managers, despite having the highest regard for the laundry executive's skills, nonetheless saw the latter's role as temporary. He hoped that in the long run Levi's would cross-train its designers in chemical engineering so that they could develop and standardize new finishes "scientifically . . . the way they do it in biotechnology." Ironically, though, our parallel research at one of the nation's leading biotechnology companies was simultaneously revealing that its approach to new product development had much in common with the ad hoc, empirical approach that Levi's laundries were using to develop new finishing techniques. Indeed, managers at the biotechnology company were worried that the analytical rigor that was beginning to be imposed on its product development process by the need to comply with the FDA's regulatory procedures could formalize its relations with the medical research community to the point at which creative interactions would be stifled.

Strategic Alliances: Because of concerns about the leakage of important technical ideas, Levi's insists on exclusive relationships with its laundry contractors. (To compensate for the loss of outside contacts, it is seeking to increase communication among its laundries, as we saw.) Italian jeans manufacturers have adopted the opposite solution, deliberately seeking out laundries that work simultaneously for a wide range of different firms, even including their immediate competitors. From an analytical perspective, the trade-off is straightforward: the benefits of having more ideas flowing in from the outside must be weighed against the risks of giving up proprietary information to competitors. But the interpretive perspective sheds a different light on the choice. The Italians with whom we spoke insisted that laundries can only remain innovative if they come into contact with a wide range of clients. One laundry felt compelled to give out new ideas for finishes selectively so as to hold as broad a client base as possible. It was clear, though, that the company did not see this as an "exchange," but rather valued the stimulation of constant conversation with a broad range of clients.

A remarkably similar strategy was articulated by a senior executive at the American biotechnology company. This company has deliberately sought to position itself at the center of an extensive network of university and corporate researchers. Echoing the European denim laundry, the executive explained that in carving out this position it had "given" first and often, and that it had sometimes received particular ideas in exchange. But for both companies, the strategic benefits of drawing in firms this way stemmed from the breadth and diversity of the conversations that ensued. It is these qualities, rather than discrete information transactions, that are the real fountainhead of new ideas.

To recapitulate: There are two alternative ways to organize design and development activities. The analytical approach works best when alternative outcomes are well understood, when they can be clearly defined and distinguished from each other. The interpretive approach is more appropriate where the possible outcomes are unknown— where the process is one of "creating" those outcomes and determining what their properties actually are. Until now, the analytical approach has been dominant. The problem is not that it is wrong. But because managers have not had a way of thinking about the alternative, their actions have tended to be folded back into an analytical framework, even when the circumstances might have called for an interpretive approach.

The analytical perspective teaches us that organizations need closure, otherwise nothing will be accomplished. But the interpretive perspective enables us to see in ambiguity the seeds not of paralysis but of opportunity. Even though a product development organization may need to emphasize one approach more than the other at different times, at *every* moment what it is actually doing can be understood in both analytical and interpretive terms. Just as modern physics instructs us to think about light as both particles and waves, a product development organization can be looked at from either the analytical or the interpretive perspective. As in the particle-wave duality, the two perspectives seem logically contradictory. But it is not true to say that the organization is either one thing or the other. Rather, it is both. Depending on the circumstances, one perspective may be more immediately useful; but viewing the organization from both angles gives us deeper insights into what is going on, and this in turn opens up new possibilities for action.

The implications of the analytical/interpretive distinction extend beyond product development activities. As we have seen throughout this book, the changing business environment over the past two decades has created increasing incentives for firms to develop much greater flexibility—the flexibility continually to adjust their product portfolios, the ways in which the products are produced, and the markets they compete in. The result has been to produce a dramatic shift in organizational forms: a wholesale abandonment of the bureaucratic, hierarchical corporation, with clean functional divisions and clear lines of authority, and a movement instead toward flat, decentralized structures, network organizations, and matrix management practices.

A central problem in these new organizations is how to manage across organizational boundaries and disciplinary borders—the same problem that design and development organizations have also encountered. But if the process of managing across these boundaries in design and development is central to the realization of creativity, it follows that the question of creativity need not be confined to design and development. Rather, we can think of it as pervading business organizations. And to the extent that the interpretive approach is the key to the question of creativity in design and development, it is an approach that should be applicable to a very broad range of other business problems, too.

The consequences of these findings are far-reaching. The implications for education are especially important. Management education, and indeed education in general, places enormous emphasis on analytical, problem-solving skills. A frequent criticism is that this approach fails to imbue in students—or, worse, actually "breeds out"—the creative skills necessary for effective leadership, the skills that successful leaders tend to describe not in analytical terms but rather in terms of vision and inspiration. The most common response to this critique is essentially to shrug it aside—"the most creative designers and managers are born, not made." But the interpretive perspective suggests practical ways in which creativity might be fostered in an educational setting. It shifts attention away from individualistic notions of creativity, from "isolated genius" theories of innovation, toward the creativity of *organizations.* It focuses on the management of ambiguity, and the importance of interpretation and orchestration as leadership styles in these organizations. And as these attributes become relevant to an increasingly wide range of business organizations, it predicts that the focus of educational preparation for leadership will need to shift from the problem-solving skills traditionally taught in engineering and the management sciences to the more interpretive fields of literature, history, and anthropology.

This brings us full circle, to the problem with which this chapter began. We see now that the problem of organizing product design and development is indeed an old problem, but not the one we thought we were dealing with. At the outset, we defined the problem as one of creativity. Now, however, we see it in terms of the gap between the scientific and humanistic cultures, the same problem that was so memorably described by C. P. Snow forty years ago.[2] And the interpretive approach, intriguingly, begins to suggest a way of bridging that gap.

CHAPTER 17

Toward a New Economic Citizenship

Throughout this book I have argued that nothing is more important to the current and future prosperity of Americans than productivity. Yet a casual observer of the popular conversation about the economy could be forgiven for reaching the opposite conclusion. Compared with the state of the stock market, or the federal budget, or the size of the trade deficit, productivity languishes in the rear, a wallflower at the pundits' slamdance. One reason is the difficulty of bringing this complex, rather dry subject to life; even in the most skillful hands, a discussion of productivity is unlikely to set pulses racing. Nor does it help that there are no obvious villains on hand when things go wrong. Weak productivity growth—unlike, say, the trade deficit or the budget deficit—cannot be blamed conveniently on predatory foreigners or vacillating politicians.

But other reasons for productivity's low profile are more fundamental. The problem of slow productivity growth is one of the great unsolved mysteries of American economic life. Even those who might be expected to know most about it have had relatively little to say. In spite of its far-reaching impact, economists have been unable to come up with a convincing explanation for what caused the productivity slowdown of the early 1970s. All agree on the broad requirements for healthy growth: ample supplies of capital at reasonable cost; high levels of private investment; continual infusions of new technology; and a well-educated workforce. Beyond this, however, there has been no consensus on either the causes of the problem or the solution, save perhaps for the belief that there is no quick fix, no panacea. This, of course, is yet another reason for the relative obscurity of the issue; politicians and pundits alike tend to be more comfortable talking about problems with simple, quick solutions.

Our reading of the problem in the preceding chapters has confirmed that there is indeed no quick fix. But it has also revealed several other insights into the obstacles that must be overcome, which, taken together, begin to suggest the outlines of a new national agenda for productivity growth.

1. *There is no evidence that the wave of corporate restructuring and downsizing during the first half of the 1990s has made a significant contribution to the nation's overall productivity performance.* Even though downsizing has sometimes helped the productivity and competitiveness of individual firms, it has had no discernible effect on the nation's productivity growth. This should come as no surprise. Even if all downsizing actions produced productivity gains for the firms that undertook them—and as we have seen, they do not—a one-time effect at the national level would not be guaranteed. An overall gain equal to the gain by the individual firms would occur only if those whose jobs were eliminated found other work in which they were as productive as before.

2. *There is also no sign that total quality management, reengineering, and the many other strategies for improving operational effectiveness adopted by U.S. companies over the past decade have produced a significant overall productivity benefit for the U.S. economy.* Once again, this is not to say that these measures did not yield important productivity and competitiveness gains for individual firms. But it is difficult to find any evidence that they have produced a one-time gain in aggregate productivity, let alone an increase in the overall rate of productivity growth.

3. *Even for individual firms, the benefits delivered by the tools and techniques for improving operational effectiveness have often fallen short of expectations.* There are many reasons for this, including exaggerated claims by their advocates, and incomplete or faulty implementation by firms. Sometimes, too, different prescriptions have run afoul of each other. Efforts to implement cooperative "high performance work systems" have sometimes been undermined by the legacy of damaged trust and battered morale left by downsizing and reengineering efforts. And the organizational requirements of reengineering and TQM are so different that it has been difficult for the same organization to pursue them simultaneously.

4. *The most successful firms understand "best practice" not as a collection of independent techniques, but rather as a coherent system of mutually reinforcing processes, practices, and strategies.* These

firms understand the strength of the linkages between business elements that other firms see as separable, and recognize the critical importance of aligning these elements with each other.

5. *For both individual enterprises and aggregate economies, a strategy of improving operational effectiveness is not enough to sustain productivity growth over long periods.* Finding ways to do things better—to improve existing products and services and to carry out existing processes more efficiently—is a necessary but not a sufficient condition for long-term productivity growth. Business enterprises must also constantly find new markets and develop new products and services and processes. It is often possible to make improvements in operational effectiveness without major capital outlays. But finding new markets and commercializing new products *always* requires new investment.

6. *By almost any measure, recent U.S. investment performance has been below par.* Gross private investment; net new private investment; public and private spending on research and development; public investment in infrastructure: in every case, the record is unimpressive—either a negative trend, or a historic low, or sometimes both. The poor record of aggregate investment independently points toward the same explanation for the nation's productivity problem that the preoccupation of American managers with improving operational effectiveness also suggests: a lack of investment in new products, services, and markets. A strategy of increased investment in specific new product and market opportunities, and in the underlying capability to keep generating these new opportunities, must be at the heart of a national program for productivity growth.

7. *Although macroeconomic conditions appear stable, other economic uncertainties are proliferating.* Private investment is more likely to be forthcoming when economic conditions are stable and predictable. At a time when the need for new investment is great, however, the combination of globalization, deregulation, and rapid technological change is transforming traditional patterns of microeconomic behavior, and bringing not only new opportunities but also new risks and uncertainties in its wake that conventional macroeconomic stabilization policies can do little to mitigate.

8. *During periods of rapid change, investment in* intangible *assets— knowledge, ideas, skills, organizational capabilities—takes on special importance.* The results of these investments—ideas for new products and processes, knowledge of new market possibilities,

more competent employees, nimbler organizations—give the economy the flexibility to keep adapting and reconfiguring itself to new supply and demand conditions. They are the lubricants of the economic machinery. But while these kinds of investments are especially important during periods of rapid economic change, it is also during these periods that they are most likely to be neglected.

Economic volatility affects ordinary people as well as profit-seeking firms. The great forces of change at work in the world economy today—rapid technological innovation, the opening and rapid development of new markets around the world, the progressive lifting of government controls on economic activity—hold enormous promise for the American workforce. Yet the very forces that create such great potential for future growth are simultaneously inspiring widespread feelings of apprehension. Every economic change creates losers as well as winners, and for some, the price of change will be high. But even many who stand to gain have come to equate change not with opportunity but with disruption and a loss of control over their lives. In democratic societies, the fear of economic dislocation may be strong enough to compel governments to act in ways that are intended to reduce economic anxieties and promote social stability but whose actual effect will be to inhibit private investment and growth. In America, and throughout the industrialized world, the fear of rapid economic change has already brought increasingly strident calls for protectionist trade policies, for other forms of what has come to be called "economic nationalism," and for more stringent regulation of corporate behavior. To people who are nervous about the future direction of the economy and their place in it, such policies have considerable appeal.

These anxieties abated during the expansion of the mid-1990s, but they never entirely disappeared, and they will gain new force when the economy turns down, as it inevitably will. And at that point the pressure will build on policymakers to do more to relieve the anxiety, whatever the cost in terms of foregone investment and long-term growth. The solution to the problem of productivity growth will therefore turn partly on how much uncertainty ordinary people are willing to bear before a backlash against the forces of change sets in.

For many, the uncertainty is made tolerable by the expectation of greater material rewards for themselves and their children. But for many others, an improvement in living standards remains a distant and uncertain possibility, whereas the threat of economic dislocation is immediate and real. If the price of protection against this threat is merely the postponement of an already unlikely prospect, it is a price that is likely to seem well worth paying.

Could anything change this calculus? Here the successful companies whose experiences we explored in chapter 12 may offer useful insights. To some, such a connection will seem implausible. The study of why firms succeed and the study of how and why national economies grow are like two parallel but separate conversations. The participants in each are aware that the other exists, and will even eavesdrop on their counterparts from time to time, but mostly they have little to say to each other. Indeed, some have argued that the less said the better. The MIT economist Paul Krugman has forcefully reminded us that nations are not firms, and that to speak of the performance of national economies in the language of corporate competitiveness is to confuse two fundamentally different ideas. "The idea that a country's economic fortunes are largely determined by its success on world markets is a hypothesis, not a necessary truth; and as a practical, empirical matter, that hypothesis is flatly wrong."[1] Krugman is quite correct, of course. Still, if one thinks of the firms that have managed to prosper and grow over several decades in spite of frequent, often radical changes in their environment, it is not so farfetched to imagine that their experiences might contain some lessons relevant to the problem of national economic growth.

Recall that one of the most striking features of these companies has been their ability to combine a highly developed, almost protean ability to transform themselves to take advantage of new technological opportunities or market developments with an enduring, deep-rooted commitment to a handful of core beliefs (different in every case) about their identity and purpose. For the people in these firms, these ideas have served at once as a powerful motivator, as a credo giving meaning to their individual efforts, and as a framework within which to organize rapidly changing and often confusing information about the external environment. In a sense, these ideas have been the "glue" that has held these firms together and enabled them to grow steadily over long periods.

The lesson such companies teach is that a strong sense of direction and purpose is critical. The employees of these firms were left in absolutely no doubt about what was important to their firms and what they were trying to achieve, and how their own individual actions and decisions could contribute to the realization of these more general goals. Throughout these organizations there was a clear and concrete understanding of core goals and values, and this had the great benefit of helping employees remain focused on what needed to be done even while almost everything else around them was changing.

In this respect, at least, the employees of a company may not be so very different from the citizens of a country. Just as a strong sense of identity and of purpose beyond profit has helped the most successful companies navigate through confusing and unpredictable territory, so too might a shared sense of *national* direction and purpose help advance the prospects for improving the nation's overall growth performance.

Today, though, such ideas barely feature in the national conversation about growth. The debate is dominated instead by discussion of the rate of savings, the rate of investment, the budget deficit, and so on—macroeconomic abstractions that for most Americans have no obvious relation to any conception of national identity and purpose. As long as this persists, the analogy with firms suggests that the public's tolerance for the instabilities that are part and parcel of the growth process will be in short supply.[2]

At one time the general alarm over the nation's declining competitiveness *vis-à-vis* Japan and other advanced economies might have provided the missing sense of purpose. Notwithstanding the well-founded reservations of Krugman and others about the shortcomings of "international competitiveness" as an intellectual category, the Japanese challenge actually did galvanize significant sections of American industry and the American workforce for the best part of a decade. It elicited a broad-based and vigorous search for new sources of competitive advantage and an openness to experimentation—in sharp and welcome contrast to the complacency and myopia that had become the hallmarks of American business practice by the 1970s. But as a vision of what the U.S. economy might become, international competitiveness is hardly the animating force that is needed today. For one, the problems now besetting the Japanese economy would surely disqualify it from such a role in the eyes of most Americans. And in the final analysis the goal of international competitiveness, in addition to its intellectual shortcomings, offers a parched, crabbed view of the nation's economic future. (Is the main point of the U.S. economy really to outperform Japan?)

Today, a different economic vision is needed. If people are to be persuaded to embrace change rather than resist it, if they are to be convinced of the need to live with the heightened volatility and ambiguity of the new economy rather than to fight against it, they must see the beneficial possibilities of such a stance. They must have a positive reason to open themselves up to economic forces that will sometimes seem arbitrary and out of control. They must, in short, have a sense of direction and purpose. For many in the workforce, perhaps even the majority, the promise of greater material compensation will not suffice. What is also needed, I believe, is a coherent vision of the place of work in society and what the work experience itself might become for the majority of contributors to the new economy—a vision that is almost totally absent from the current debate.

Take the new information technologies, for example. Job-destroying, occupation-reshaping, wage-polarizing "agents of change"? Perhaps. But that is only one side of the story. The other emphasizes the unprecedented opportunity afforded by these technologies to move beyond the production systems of the past, systems that offered intrinsic satisfactions only to people at the top of the pyramid. This aspect of the story highlights the potential of these technologies to eliminate much of the rigid, narrow, repetitive work of today, and more broadly to provide personal and professional satisfaction for a far greater number of workers than ever before. Whether this happy outcome eventually comes to pass will depend not on some uncontrollable technological force but on the exercise of conscious choices. As individuals, and as a society, we may choose to use technology in such a way as to diminish the human contribution—to pressure, to downskill, or to demean. Or we may choose to use it to augment human capabilities and to enhance the work experience.

The key point is that such a choice exists, and is one of the things at stake in the debate about growth. Yet that choice is hardly acknowledged in the debate today. By divorcing the question of what economic growth is *for* from the question of how to achieve it, the possibilities of growth are much less likely to be realized. By seeking instead to articulate a vision of what the workplace can become, and by establishing norms of technological usage on the basis of this vision—for example, that technology will be used not to compromise but to protect the dignity of work, that workers should expect to be in control of their working environment, that they should expect their own endeavors to be appreciated, and so on—our society stands a far better chance of realizing the full potential of technological advance.

Consider also the implications of an economy in which lifetime careers with a single employer are becoming the exception rather than the rule. To many people, a varied career path with multiple employers will seem daunting, a prospect to be endured rather than welcomed. But once again, the possibilities need to be more fully articulated. The continuing transformation of the economy is making it possible to imagine a future in which individuals not only take on more responsibility for managing their own careers but also obtain more control over the resources with which to exercise that responsibility. This is the larger implication of current proposals for portable pensions and benefits, individual skill grants, tax-deductible individual training accounts, and the like, and indeed of the movement for greater parental choice regarding schooling for their children. As Anthony Carnevale, chairman of the National Commission on Employment Policy, has pointed out, these new career development and benefit structures, by promoting individual autonomy and private choice, would have the effect of bringing the world of work into closer alignment with our society's individualistic and participatory values.[3] In this view, too, these individually tailored resources would begin to provide a true alternative to today's social institutions, to "the standardized offerings of the welfare state on the one hand and the increasingly rare and uncertain embrace of corporate paternalism on the other."[4]

Taken together, the rights, responsibilities, and resources identified in the preceding paragraphs significantly expand the idea of a "new economic citizenship" with which this book began. I do not claim that these are the only possible elaborations of that concept, or that they are the best of all possible alternatives. I *do* believe, however, that these are the kinds of issues we should be talking about when we debate how to achieve stronger economic growth. The problem of growth remains the central question facing the American economy. But it is a question that cannot be separated from the challenge of maintaining a healthy relationship between industry and society, a relationship without which neither can survive, let alone thrive. Modern industrial enterprise stands today as a glorious, living monument to society's powers of cooperation, ingenuity, and imagination. If this book has demonstrated anything at all, it is that the solution to the problem of growth at the dawn of the new millennium will hinge on the success with which those same powers are applied to the design of the world of work.

APPENDIX I

Measuring Productivity Growth

Conceptually, the measurement of productivity is quite straightforward. All of the outputs produced by the economy for final consumption during a specified period are summed up, and then divided by the total amount of input required to produce them. (Intermediate goods and services that are used in the production of the final products are not included so as to avoid double counting.) If the objective is to determine the productivity of labor, the input measure will be the total number of employees in the labor force, or the total number of hours worked. The productivity of capital can be determined in much the same way, except that the input in this case will be some measure of the use to which the nation's total stock of capital has been put during the period in question. A third measure of productivity, multifactor productivity, is a composite measure of how efficiently an economy is using both capital and labor inputs.

The measurement of output, the numerator in the productivity ratio, is more complicated. If the economy only produced one type of product, the calculation of output would be very simple. If every firm produced only bread, for example, all that would be needed would be to count the number of loaves produced in a given period. For a real economy, however, it is necessary to find a common yardstick with which to measure the output of bread and computers and hundreds of thousands of other products. That yardstick is money. Total output in a multiproduct economy is calculated by multiplying the money price of each product in the market by the amount sold and then taking the sum over all products.

There is a problem with using money as the yardstick: prices can (and usually do) go up and down from year to year. So productivity comparisons between years must be normalized such that output is expressed in dollars of the same purchasing power. Suppose, for example, that the money measure of output increased from $100 billion in one year to $110 billion in the next, but that average prices increased by 5% over the same period. The *real* increase in output would be less than $10 billion; in fact, it would be [110 x (95/100) - 100] = $4.5 billion.

Another complication is that products usually do not remain the same from year to year. Technological innovations and other improvements may substantially increase the benefit that consumers derive from a given type of product over time. The improvements in quality and service and functionality might be reflected in an increase in the market value of the product. If so, they would be automatically factored into the measurement of output. (The calculation would work something like this. Suppose there was a breakthrough in the design of beds, and from one year to the next all consumers switched from buying traditional box spring mattress beds to the newfangled orthopedic specials. Because of their superior quality, the latter were able to command a 10% price premium [after correcting for inflation]. Then, even if the total number of beds sold annually remained the same, the measured real output of the bed industry would have increased by 10%, simply by virtue of the improvement in quality.)

But market price changes are often not a reliable barometer of such improvements. A spectacular case in point is computers, where technological innovations occurring in that highly competitive industry have led to dramatic reductions in the market price per unit of computational power. In principle, economic statisticians could adjust the measured output of each product to account for changes in quality over time; but in practice, this is a very unwieldy task, especially where technological change is rapid, and the statisticians acknowledge that it is not performed very well, even for manufacturing industries. The problems are compounded in service industries like health care and financial services—now the biggest slice of the economy—where the job of accounting for changes in the quality of delivered services is still less well understood and usually barely even attempted.

The official system used to measure output and productivity is gradually being overhauled. But progress is slow, and in the meantime the economy continues to shift toward the kinds of activities that the current system has most difficulty in handling. It is disconcerting that the measurement of these most basic features of economic performance should rest on such shaky foundations. Perhaps the best that can be said is that every country has similar measurement problems, and even though the estimates for each country may be significantly in error, the relative ranking of countries that emerges from these estimates is probably still fairly reliable.

APPENDIX II

A Brief Guide to Wireless Services

Though still in early adolescence, the wireless communications industry already offers a wide range of services, with many more on the horizon. Some of these may never materialize; others will surely fade quickly; and some of the most successful services a decade from now might not yet even have been invented. For now, the main categories of services include the following:

Land Mobile Radio: The oldest of the mobile wireless technologies, two-way land mobile radio was originally introduced to meet the dedicated mobile communication needs of police and other security services. Today, it provides voice dispatching and other communication services for police, fire, and ambulance services, as well as taxi and trucking fleets.

Cellular Telephony: Cellular telephone service allows individual subscribers to use the public telephone network to make and receive calls without being tied to any particular location. In countries with well-developed landline infrastructures, cellular networks supplement the fixed network by providing both *portability* (the telephones can be carried around by individuals) and *mobility* (uninterrupted communication with users on the move). In some other countries, cellular networks also serve as less expensive alternatives to landline service.

Paging: Wide-area paging service, a simpler and lower-cost alternative to cellular telephony, offers nonspeech personal calling capability. The communication may simply be an alert, or it may also involve limited numeric or alphanumeric messaging. The newest paging services now offer two-way paging, allowing users to acknowledge a beep or a page directly, without having to use a telephone. In another new variant, the pager serves as a wireless pocket answering machine.

Cordless Telephony: Cellular wireless transmissions typically occur over kilometer-scale distances, but other wireless applications entail much shorter range transmissions, of 50 to 100 meters or less. Cordless phones in the home and high-capacity cordless PBX (private branch exchange) systems for office buildings are examples. Another short-range application is "telepoint"—a form of wireless public payphone service restricted to high-traffic public places like shopping districts or airports. This scheme involves the use of small, inexpensive cordless handsets that can operate within a limited range of a base station that is linked to the fixed network. The first generation of telepoint systems, introduced experimentally in the United Kingdom and Asia, allowed only outgoing calls (and partly for that reason was not a success in the U.K.). On the other hand, the restriction to outbound calling eliminates the need to locate subscribers, making for less costly service than cellular. A newer, two-way variant—the so-called personal handy phone system (PHS)—is proving to be enormously popular in Japan.

Still another short-range wireless scheme, the "wireless local loop," links household or business subscribers to the landline network without having to string wire to each building—the most expensive part of installing a landline infrastructure. This is an attractive option in much of the developing world, where many people do not currently have home phones. Wireless local loop connections are also cheaper than the alternative of putting cellular phones in each house, partly because there is no "roaming" capability, i.e., subscribers cannot use their phones away from their homes.

Personal Digital Assistants (PDAs): These pocket communicators allow users to exchange fax and E-mail messages and to receive stock market, sports, and other news. The wireless networks that support these devices are optimized for data rather than voice. The market performance of the first generation of PDAs has generally been disappointing, partly because of poor handwriting recognition and other software problems, and partly because the demand for mobile online services did not materialize as quickly as expected.

Mobile Satellite Communications: Satellite systems are supplying a wide range of wireless communication services to maritime, aeronautical, and terrestrial travelers. For more than two decades, satellites have been providing oceangoing travelers with telephone service, navigation and weather information, as well as vital communication links during search and rescue operations. Satellite communications are also increasingly being used by airlines to provide outbound telephone service for their passengers, and data communications, facsimile, and two-way telephone service are now being added.

On land, satellite systems are already providing two-way communications and position-tracking services for long-distance trucking and rail car fleets, and a wide range of new services is under development. Some are designed to provide mobile voice and data communications to people with wireless handsets anywhere in the world; they would, for example, enable international business travelers in areas with unreliable or undeveloped telecommunications infrastructure to communicate directly with their home office. Others would serve fixed locations, for example, allowing computer users to use satellite links to bypass the local telephone network and connect directly to the Internet. Plans are also under way to use dedicated satellites to provide local telephone service in sparsely populated regions and in developing countries lacking reliable terrestrial systems.

Personal Communications Services: In 1994 and 1995, the U.S. Federal Communications System auctioned off licenses to use the spectrum around the 2-gigahertz frequency to provide a new set of wireless services known as personal communications services, or PCS. (Current cellular services operate in the 800-megahertz range.) The higher operating frequency reduces the power requirements for transmissions, which in turn will allow both the handsets and the base stations to be smaller. It is still too early to know what services will eventually be offered by PCS licensees. The networks will almost certainly be all-digital, and some predict that it is here that the wireless vision of a handheld communications device that can handle voice, data, Internet, and video transmissions with a single personal telephone number that is usable anywhere will ultimately be realized. Others expect less difference between PCS services and the digital cellular services that are beginning to be offered in the 800-megahertz range. (The first PCS network, offering a combination of telephony, paging, and voice-mail services, began operating in the Washington, D.C.–Baltimore area in late 1995.)

A portion of the PCS spectrum will also be allocated for devices like cordless home and business telephone systems and wireless local area computer networks (wireless LANs)—applications that do not require licenses because their use of the spectrum is confined to the owner's premises.

Vehicle Information Systems: Another promising application of wireless technology is in providing traffic-related communications services, including traffic management, vehicle identification, speed sensing, collision warning and prevention, and digitized map information and navigation.

Wireless Cable: The first large-scale application of wireless cable has been to broadcast cable television programming from a transmitter to houses within a radius of about thirty miles, a service that is also known as local multipoint distribution service. Today, there are about 900,000 wireless cable TV subscribers in the United States. This "fixed wireless" technology can be easily converted to carry digital broadcasts, and is also capable of supporting individualized two-way Internet communications. The Federal Communications Commission recently announced a plan to allocate spectrum in the 28-gigahertz region for these services.

APPENDIX III

"Best Practice": Lessons
from Made in America's
Leading Companies

Nearly a decade ago, in an attempt to discover whether there were certain fundamental patterns of thought or practice that linked the world's most successful manufacturing firms, the MIT Commission on Industrial Productivity studied the leading firms in each of eight industries. The differences among them could hardly have been greater: there were aging steelmakers and sleek young computer companies; huge airframe manufacturers and small, family-owned machine-tool firms; process-oriented businesses like chemicals as well as discrete parts manufacturers like the auto companies.

Despite this diversity, the commission discovered striking similarities in what the most successful firms in these industries were doing. In its book *Made in America,* the commission concluded that these firms had all developed a broader view of what leads to success than most of their competitors, a view that stressed the contribution made by the firm's human resources at every level of the organization. Whereas in the traditional mass production model, labor had been seen essentially as a cost that had to be minimized, in the new model the workforce was an asset to be cultivated. The successful firms had understood that they could not achieve the levels of quality and responsiveness necessary to compete successfully without committed, knowledgeable, and responsible workers. Building on this foundation, these firms were proceeding to transform practically every aspect of their production processes. The commission identified seven crucial areas of "best practice" in the leading firms:

1. *Simultaneous pursuit of continuous improvement in cost, quality, service, and speed of new product introductions:* Whereas most firms focused on only one of these aspects of performance, or consciously traded one off against the others, the leading firms were

337

seeking improvements in all of them simultaneously. Inevitably, there were differences in emphasis, reflecting differences in strategies, markets, and production processes. Compared with a commodity steel producer, say, a manufacturer of fashion apparel would obviously pay more attention to the task of getting new products to market quickly, and less to improvements in process efficiency. But none of the best practice firms, regardless of what industry they were in, thought that they could compete by focusing exclusively on one performance goal and ignoring the others. And all of them dedicated themselves to a continuous, never-ending drive for improvement.

2. *Breaking down organizational barriers:* The successful firms were vigorously dismantling organizational walls between functions and departments, by relying increasingly on cross-functional teams and by broadening the responsibilities associated with individual jobs. They were finding ways to involve manufacturing and marketing people early in the design process in order to speed the development of new products. They were reorganizing the workplace to eliminate the costly and inefficient "hand-off" phenomenon, in which individuals and departments had responsibility only for a narrow slice of the production process, and no stake in what happened once the work was transferred to the next stage. And they were much less likely to tolerate the presence of inward-looking specialists who were unable to see beyond their immediate area of expertise.

3. *Eliminating layers of management:* The leading companies found that by flattening organizational hierarchies and pushing responsibility down lower in the organization, they could not only save on overhead costs but also enhance their flexibility and responsiveness to changes in markets. A customer with a problem could speak directly to the group that was responsible for producing the product. And with fewer intermediaries to get in the way, top managers would hear much more quickly about opportunities or problems arising on the shop floor, and so be able to target the resources necessary to deal with the issue right away.

4. *Closer relations with customers and suppliers:* The leading companies had developed ties with their customers that enabled them to pick up more detailed signals about differences within and between customer groups and how these were changing over time. They had also implemented closer and more tightly coordinated relations with their suppliers. The traditional, arm's-length approach to contracting had been abandoned in favor of much closer

coordination of product design, quality, production scheduling, and training. The benefits included more rapid product introductions, lower inventory costs, and fewer defects in the final product.

5. *Intelligent use of technology:* The commission observed a recurring pattern of firms seeking and failing to gain competitive advantage through the rapid introduction of advanced technology. Perhaps the most dramatic example was that of General Motors, which invested billions of dollars during the 1980s in automating its assembly plants in an attempt to improve their performance. In what was a generally unhappy decade for the automaker, this vast program stood out as a particularly miserable experience. Simply getting the technology to work proved to be enormously costly and disruptive. Worse, the eventual productivity benefits were meager at best. It was a classic case of "paving the cowpaths"—taking an inefficient process, automating it, and getting a process that was automated *and* inefficient.

    In contrast, the most successful firms had understood that a business strategy that was based on throwing new technology at performance problems was rarely the answer. These firms had learned to integrate the new technologies with their manufacturing and marketing strategies, and to link them more closely to organizational changes that promoted teamwork, training, and continuous learning. Technological innovation was thus only one component of a larger set of changes.

6. *Global reach:* In virtually all of the successful firms, even the smaller ones, there was an eagerness to embrace international opportunities. These firms routinely scanned the world for new technological developments, compared their performance in each functional area with best practice wherever it happened to be in the world, and strongly encouraged their marketing divisions, purchasing agents, and production managers to become more knowledgeable about conditions abroad.

7. *Innovative human resource policies:* The leading firms were all committed to continuously upgrading and broadening the skills of their employees, and had devised a variety of innovative hiring, training, career development, and compensation strategies in support of these goals. In these firms, the workplace was a place of learning as well as a place of production, and in different ways they were breaking down the barriers that had traditionally separated organizations for education from organizations for production.

Not all of the leading firms were pursuing each of these practices with equal fervor. Nevertheless, the similarities between them along these seven dimensions of practice were clearly evident. But this was only half the story. What was most striking about these firms was that at some level they understood these practices not as independent solutions, but rather as a part of a coherent *system,* in which changes in each domain reinforced the others. Firms like Motorola and Chaparral Steel and Hewlett Packard had understood that each approach on its own would yield only limited benefits—that, for example, a strategy of investing in workforce training was unlikely to be effective without a parallel redesign of career development and compensation strategies to provide more incentives for learning on and off the job; or that investing in the latest programmable machining centers would likely be for naught if the only people with the skills to operate them were the managers, who ought instead to be concentrating on developing new products or finding new markets for the company. These firms implicitly understood the strength of the linkages between business elements that others saw as separable—between market strategies, production techniques, the organization of work, training practices, compensation schemes, sourcing policies, and even accounting systems.

But for every firm that had recognized the need for systemic change and the critical importance of aligning their organizational practices and processes with each other, many others were taking a piecemeal approach, focusing on one thing for a while and then moving on to another. Most of these firms seemed eventually to stall out; the problems they faced were too pervasive and interconnected to be attacked in a piecemeal way.

NOTES

Chapter 1

[1] "Japan's Companies Moving Production to Sites Overseas," *New York Times,* 29 August 1993, 1.

[2] See Lester Thurow, *Head to Head: The Coming Economic Battle Among Japan, Europe, and America* (New York: Morrow, 1992).

[3] *New York Times,* 27 February 1994, Section 3, 1.

[4] In mid-1997, the *New York Times* reported that some Japanese companies have even begun to adopt the American practice of compensating their senior managers with stock options, a practice that some of these same companies had condemned just a few years earlier on the grounds that it resulted in obscenely large incomes for the beneficiaries and an unhealthy focus on short-term results. (See Andrew Pollack, "Japanese Companies Take a New Look at Western Management Ideas," *New York Times,* 23 May 1997, C1.)

[5] *Fortune,* 9 June 1997, p. 74.

[6] *Wall Street Journal,* 10 April 1996, A12.

[7] *Time,* 24 October 1994, pp. 50–56.

[8] Henry Farber, "The Changing Face of Job Loss in the United States, 1981–1993," NBER Working Paper 5596, (Cambridge, MA: National Bureau of Economic Research, 1996). For a similar conclusion, see President's Council of Economic Advisors, "Job Creation and Employment Opportunities: The United States Labor Market, 1993–96," The White House, 1996.

[9] A widely reported study by the National Commission on Employment Policy seemed to provide more support for the belief that job security has been declining. The study concluded that employees with "strong" job stability, defined as only one or no job changes in a ten-year period, decreased from 67% in the 1970s to 52% in the 1980s, while the percentage of employees with "weak" stability, defined as those changing employers at least three times during a ten-year period, doubled to 24% in the 1980s. See Stephen J. Rose, "Declining Job Security and the Professionalization of Opportunity," National Commission for Employment Policy, Research Report 95-04, May 1995.

[10] Dan Rodriguez, Department of Economics, MIT, personal communication, December 1996.

[11] Michael L. Dertouzos, Richard K. Lester, and Robert M. Solow, *Made in America: Regaining the Productive Edge* (Cambridge, MA: MIT Press, 1989), p. 135.

Chapter 2

[1] Paul Krugman, *The Age of Diminished Expectations: U.S. Economic Policies in the 1990s* (Cambridge, MA: MIT Press, 1994, revised and updated edition), p. 15.

[2] W. Baumol, S. Batey Blackman, and E. N. Wolff, *Productivity and American Leadership: The Long View* (Cambridge, MA: MIT Press, 1989), p. 9.

[3] Until recently this argument was a rather low-profile affair, conducted mainly by a small circle of experts. At the end of 1996, the issue surfaced briefly in the popular press following the release of a report by a commission led by Stanford University economist Michael Boskin, a former chairman of the President's Council of Economic Advisors. The Boskin report criticized the government's method of measuring inflation, arguing that it overstates the real rate of increase of prices and correspondingly underestimates the real rate of productivity growth.

The report attracted wide attention partly because of its implications for the federal budget deficit. About one third of all federal budget outlays are automatically escalated from year to year by an amount equal to the measured inflation rate. If this has been systematically overestimated, the government's inflation-indexed welfare and pension benefits must have been increasing too rapidly, thereby adding large amounts to the federal budget deficit unnecessarily.

[4] Indeed, if, as is sometimes the case, bank output is measured in terms of the number of checks processed, the measured impact of ATMs on bank productivity would be *negative.*

[5] Bruce Steinberg, chief economist at Merrill Lynch, cited in the *New York Times,* 13 August 1997, D1.

[6] *Challenge* (November–December 1995): 32.

[7] On this point, I am indebted to Stephen D. Oliner and William L. Wascher, "Is a Productivity Revolution Under Way in the United States?" *Challenge* (November–December 1995): 18–30.

[8] During the 1970s and 1980s, real investment in computers and peripherals increased at an annual rate of 37.8% and 26.7%, respectively. See Oliner and Wascher, op. cit., p. 24.

[9] For recent rosy accounts of the contribution of information technology, see "These *Are* the Good Old Days," *Fortune,* 9 June 1997, p. 74–86; and "New Thinking About the New Economy," *BusinessWeek,* 19 May 1997, p. 150.

[10] Stephen Roach, chief economist of Morgan Stanley, has been a particularly prominent contributor to the debate about U.S. productivity. Roach's views could easily fill a chapter by themselves. Until recently, he was most closely associated with the idea that the productivity statistics grossly underestimate actual performance, and that U.S. productivity growth was much stronger than most people appreciated. While continu-

ing to espouse the view that the statistics are biased downward, Roach now argues that too much of the productivity gain is the result of short-term fixes like downsizing. Now, according to Roach, "the miracles of the so-called productivity revolution of the 1990s are starting to ring hollow." See Stephen S. Roach, "The Hollow Ring of the Productivity Revival," *Harvard Business Review* (November–December 1996): 81–89.

11 Frank Levy, "Where Did All the Money Go? A Layman's Guide to Recent Trends in U.S. Living Standards," MIT Industrial Performance Center Working Paper, WP-96-008, July 1996.

12 The younger families whose husbands had only a high-school education saw their total money income increase from $40,000 to $48,000 between 1979 and 1996 (the husband's income declined slightly during this period), while the families with more highly-educated husbands saw their incomes rise from $48,000 to $72,000. (See Levy, op. cit. All incomes are expressed in 1994 dollars.) During the most recent five-year period (1989–94), three of the four types of families experienced a decline in total household money income; only the younger families with college-educated husbands recorded an increase in money income over this interval.

13 See Levy, op. cit. As before, all incomes are expressed in 1994 dollars. The income data reported here are all pre-tax; moreover, they do not include noncash income, such as health insurance and other fringe benefits. Levy's calculations show, however, that even when adjustments are made for these factors, the conclusions do not change fundamentally.

14 *New York Times,* 20 June 1996, A1. Other studies suggest that income inequality has actually been accelerating during the 1990s. See, e.g., Lynn Karoly, "Anatomy of the U.S. Income Distribution: Two Decades of Change," *Oxford Review of Economic Policy,* vol. 12, no. 1 (1996): 76–95.

15 Lawrence Mishel, Aaron Bernstein, and John Schmidt, *The State of Working America 1996–1997* (Armonk, NY: M. E. Sharpe, 1996, for the Economic Policy Institute).

16 Department of Commerce, International Trade Administration, Office of Trade and Investment Analysis, *Business America,* biweekly.

17 John F. Welch, "A Matter of Exchange Rates," *Wall Street Journal,* 21 June 1994, A22.

18 During the 1973–81 business cycle, real wages for production workers in manufacturing fell by almost 0.6%/year on average; during the 1981–90 cycle, the average rate of decline was about 0.4%/year; and during the 1990–95 period (not a complete business cycle), the rate of decline was less than 0.1% per year.

19 Office of Technology Assessment, *Technology and the American Transition,* 1988, p. 6.

20 Between 1980 and 1995, annual personal expenditures on services increased from $7,352 to $9,804 per capita, while expenditures on manufactured products increased from $5,931 to $7,624. Of the latter, expenditures on *durable* manufactures increased from $1,244 to $2,210, or 78% in real terms. Data from the National Income and Product Accounts published by the U.S. Bureau of Economic Analysis (all amounts are expressed in 1992 dollars).

Chapter 3

[1] *Time,* 13 December 1993, p. 62.

[2] James P. Womack, Daniel T. Jones, and Daniel Roos, *The Machine That Changed the World* (New York: Rawson Associates, 1990).

[3] The most authoritative description of the Toyota Production System is by its inventor, Toyota's production chief Taiichi Ohno, in *The Toyota Production System: Beyond Large Scale Production* (Cambridge, MA: Productivity Press, 1988). Interested readers may also want to consult Michael Cusumano, *The Japanese Automobile Industry: Technology and Management at Nissan and Toyota* (Cambridge, MA: Harvard University Press, 1985).

[4] Susan Helper and David I. Levine, "Long-Term Supplier Relations and Product-Market Structure," *Journal of Law, Economics, and Organization,* vol. 8, no. 3 (October 1992): 561–81.

[5] Malcolm Salter, seminar presentation, Harvard Business School, June 1994.

[6] Kim B. Clark and Takahiro Fujimoto, *Product Development Performance: Strategy, Organization and Management in the World Auto Industry* (Boston: Harvard Business School Press, 1991).

[7] Charles Fine, "The World's Quietest Factory," unpublished paper, June 1994.

[8] *Automotive Industries* (June 1993): 34.

[9] *Ward's Auto World* (December 1993): 44.

[10] Ibid. See also Jeffrey H. Dyer, "How Chrysler Created an American Keiretsu," *Harvard Business Review* (July–August 1996): 42–56.

[11] *Automotive News,* 18 April 1994, p. 3.

[12] For a full description of the Saturn organization, see Saul Rubenstein, Michael Bennett, and Thomas Kochan, "The Saturn Partnership: Co-Management and the Reinvention of the Local Union," in Bruce Kaufman and Morris Kleiner, eds., *Employee Representation: Alternatives and Future Directions* (Madison, WI: Industrial Relations Research Association, 1993).

[13] Keith Bradsher and Andrew Pollack, "Falling Yen Puts Car Makers in Japan in the Driver's Seat," *New York Times,* 15 July 1996, A1.

[14] "GM Building Plants in Developing Nations to Woo New Markets," *Wall Street Journal,* 4 August 1997, A1. See also *Wall Street Journal,* 11 September 1997, A3.

[15] Bill Sharfman, "The Long View: Six top executives make some pretty surprising predictions about the state of the auto industry in ten years' time," *Automobile,* vol. 11, no. 1 (April 1996).

Chapter 4

[1] This evocative phrase was first used by Donald F. Barnett and Robert W. Crandall in their book, *Up from the Ashes: The Rise of the Steel Minimill in the United States* (Washington DC: Brookings Institution, 1986).

[2] Richard Preston, *American Steel* (New York: Prentice Hall, 1991).

[3] Kenneth Iverson, seminar presentation, Harvard Business School, 29 November 1990.

[4] F. Kenneth Iverson, *American Metal Market,* 2 August 1991.

[5] Louis Schorsch, *American Metal Market,* 31 August 1992.

[6] *Wall Street Journal,* 10 March 1995, A4.

[7] Gordon Forward, interview by author.

[8] "Changing the Rules of the Game," *Planning Review* (September–October 1993).

[9] F. Kenneth Iverson, "Effective Leadership: The Key Is Simplicity," in Y. K. Shetty and Vernon M. Buehler, eds., *The Quest for Competitiveness* (New York: Quorum Books, 1991).

[10] Preston, op. cit., p. 6.

[11] Ibid., p. 50.

[12] *Wall Street Journal,* 27 October 1992.

[13] Forward, interview.

[14] *New Steel,* (May 1995): 25. In early 1996, Garvey was appointed chairman and chief executive officer of North Star's rival, Birmingham Steel—*Wall Street Journal,* 8 January 1996, B5.

[15] *American Metal Market,* 24 February 1994.

[16] A notable exception is Oregon Steel. According to its CEO, Thomas Boklund, "quotas were the worst thing that ever happened to Oregon Steel, absolutely the worst. What they did was they gave Korea and Japan quotas, and of course they shipped to what was the shortest distance—the West Coast—with complete openness to the market at any price"—See *Iron Age* (April 1993): 25.

[17] *Iron Age* (April 1993): 25.

[18] In 1994, the share of total steel output produced in electric arc furnaces was 37.7% in the United States, 31.6% in Japan, and 21.8% in Germany—*Iron and Steelmaker,* 15 July 1995, p. 10.

[19] Donald F. Barnett, "Factors Influencing the Steel Work Force: 1980 to 1995," Organization for Economic Cooperation and Development, Directorate for Science, Technology and Industry Working Paper, OCDE/GD(96)127, 1996.

[20] Harvey Katz, "Nucor," Valueline Investment Survey, 4 July 1997, p. 600.

[21] *New York Times,* 13 October 1994, D1; *Wall Street Journal,* 1 November 1995, A1.

[22] *New York Times,* 13 December 1995, D1.

[23] *Automotive News,* 23 May 1994, p. 33.

[24] Standard and Poor's, *Steel and Heavy Machinery: Basic Analyses,* 6 January 1994, vol. 162, no. 1, sec. 1, p. S35.

Chapter 5

[1] Report of the Defense Science Board Task Force on Defense Semiconductor Dependency, February 1987, p. 1.

[2] *New York Times,* 5 January 1987, A1.

[3] Cited in *Standard and Poor's Industry Survey* (Electronics), 9 June 1994, E40.

[4] *A Strategic Industry At Risk.* Report to the President and Congress from the National Advisory Committee on Semiconductors, November 1989, p. 14.

[5] Kiyohisa Ota and Hunt Macnguyen, "Semiconductors and Computers: A Study of U.S. Industry and Company Competitiveness in the World" (New York: Nomura Research Institute America, June 1991, English version), cited in James Fallows, *Looking at the Sun: The Rise of the New East Asian Economic and Political System* (New York: Pantheon Books, 1994), p. 44.

[6] Fallows, op. cit., p. 5.

[7] Ibid., p. 51.

[8] *Wall Street Journal,* 4 January 1993, R3.

[9] Data cited by Craig R. Barrett, Chief Operating Officer, Intel Corporation, at a presentation at MIT on 10 May 1995, based on studies by VLSI Research.

[10] U.S. Department of Commerce, "U.S. International Trade in Goods and Services," August 1994.

[11] The Apollo computer specifications are reported in Fredrick H. Martin and Richard H. Battin, *Computer-Controlled Steering of the Apollo Spacecraft,* MIT Instrumentation Laboratory, Cambridge, MA, August 1967, p. 5, and Eldon Hall, *Case History of the Apollo Guidance Computer,* MIT Instrumentation Laboratory, Cambridge, MA, June 1966, p. 19.

[12] Robert W. Keyes, "The Future of the Transistor," *Scientific American* (June 1993): 70.

[13] *BusinessWeek,* 4 July 1994, p. 86.

[14] Paul Valentine, *Electronics Basic Analysis,* Standard and Poor's, vol. 162, no. 23 (June 9, 1994): E41.

[15] "Science and Business," *Scientific American* (July 1994): 97.

[16] Keyes, op. cit., p. 72.

[17] Franklin M. Fisher, James W. McKie, and Richard Mancke, *IBM and the U.S. Data Processing Industry: An Economic History* (New York: Praeger, 1983), p. 14.

[18] Howard Aiken, "The Future of Automatic Computing Machinery," *Elektronische Rechenmaschinen und Informationsverarbeitung* (Vieweg, Braunschwing, 1956), pp. 32–34. Cited by Paul Ceruzzi, "An Unforeseen Revolution: Computers and Expectations, 1935–85," in *Imagining Tomorrow,* edited by Joseph Corn (Cambridge, MA: MIT Press, 1986), p. 197.

[19] *BusinessWeek,* 6 March 1995.

[20] From data provided by the Semiconductor Industry Association.

[21] "And in the wake of this government 'interference,' through the semiconductor agreements and Sematech, the fortunes of the American semiconductor industry finally brightened," Fallows, op. cit., pp. 64–65. Also, see quote on p. 33 about the impact of the trade agreement.

[22] *Wall Street Journal,* 18 June 1996, B6.

[23] G. Dan Hutcheson, president of VLSI Research, cited by Katie Hafner, "Does Industrial Policy Work? Lessons from SEMATECH," *New York Times,* November 1993, Section 3, p. 5.

[24] *New York Times,* 6 October 1994, D1.

[25] David P. Hamilton, "Sematech: Techno-Policy in Action," *Science,* 5 April 1991, p. 23.

26 *Electronic Business,* 18 May 1992, p. 58.

27 Hafner, op. cit., p. 5.

28 Michael L. Dertouzos, Richard K. Lester, and Robert M. Solow, *Made in America: Regaining the Productive Edge* (Cambridge, MA: MIT Press, 1989), p. 10.

29 Charles Ferguson, "Computers and the Coming of the U.S. Keiretsu," *Harvard Business Review* (July–August 1990): 66.

30 *The Economist,* "Computer Industry Survey," 17 September 1994, p. 4.

31 The market penetration of personal computers in Japan was also held back by the vertically integrated Japanese manufacturers' practice of making machines that were incompatible with other brands. The software for one brand would not run on the others; and since most brands did not have a large enough share of the market to attract many software developers to write for them, the range of applications available to users was much more restricted than in the U.S. market.

32 *Wall Street Journal,* 14 March 1995, A11.

33 Anton Peisl, "Can a Keiretsu Work in America?" *Harvard Business Review* (September–October 1990): 180.

34 *Wall Street Journal,* 7 June 1995, A1. See also *Intel 1996 Annual Report,* 8 April 1997, available at http://www.intel.com.

35 Apple Computer's unwillingness to adapt to this new structure, and its insistence on exclusively bundling its (superior) operating system with its own hardware, is generally believed to have been responsible for its rapid decline in the 1990s.

36 *Electronic Business* (April 1993): 62–65.

37 James McGroddy, "Industry, Government, Universities, and Technological Leadership—An Industry Perspective," Honeywell/Sweatt Lecture, University of Minnesota, 29 April 1993 (available from the Center for the Development of Technological Leadership, University of Minnesota, Monograph 22).

38 *New York Times,* 6 February 1996, D17.

39 Semiconductor Industry Association, "Global Semiconductor Market Should Grow 4.6% in 1997," Press Release no. 16, San Jose, 12 May 1997.

40 Andrew Rappaport and Shmuel Halevi, "The Computerless Computer Company," *Harvard Business Review,* (July–August 1991): 73.

41 Chaur-Ming Chou, "Dedicated IC Foundries: An Assessment of Strategy and Prospects for Contract Manufacturing in the Semiconductor Industry." S.M. Thesis, MIT Sloan School of Management, June 1995. Among the most successful foundries are Taiwan Semiconductor Manufacturing Company and Chartered Semiconductor Manufacturing of Singapore.

42 Andrew Grove, letter to the editor, *Harvard Business Review* (September–October 1991): 140.

43 *Electronic News,* 31 October 1994, p. 70.

Chapter 6

1 In cogeneration plants, heat produced as a by-product of power generation is captured (typically in the form of steam) and used as an energy source in its own right (e.g., in a chemical plant, or for district heating purposes).

The overall energy efficiency of cogeneration plants is often greater than electricity-only power plants.

2 This issue has been a long-standing bone of contention between investor-owned utilities on the one hand and municipals and consumer-owned cooperatives on the other. Many of the latter are primarily or exclusively distribution utilities that rely on fully integrated utilities for generation. They have long sought the flexibility to buy power from their supplier of choice, but their efforts to secure the requisite transmission capacity from their immediately neighboring utilities have often been resisted.

3 After several years of interpreting the law on a case-by-case basis, in 1996 the Federal Energy Regulatory Commission adopted a rule that would require all utilities to post transmission charges that would apply to everyone who used their facilities (including their own wholesale transactions).

4 A. E. Columbia and I. C. Bupp, "Essex Development Associates, Inc.," Harvard Business School case no. 0-682-101, Harvard Business School, Boston, MA, 1982.

5 Two weeks prior to the NEES–U.S. Gen agreement, PG&E had announced its intention to purchase Bechtel's interest in U.S. Generating Company.

6 *Power Markets Week,* 2 June 1997, p. 1.

7 *New York Times,* 3 February 1995, D1.

8 Robert Michaels, "Unused and Useless: The Strange Economics of Stranded Investment," *Electricity Journal* (October 1994): 12–22.

9 Ibid.

10 *The Economist,* 6 January 1996, p. 21.

11 Lester Baxter and Eric Hirst, "Estimating Potential Stranded Commitments for U.S. Investor-Owned Electric Utilities," Oak Ridge National Laboratory Report, ORNL/CON-406, January 1995.

12 Paul Joskow, "Competition in the Electric Power Sector: Some Recent Developments," MIT Center for Energy and Environmental Policy Research Working Paper, MIT-CEEPR 94-008WP, October 1994.

13 The legislation also preserves subsidies for renewable generation, energy efficiency, and R&D investments, as well as low-income customers. It is not entirely clear how all of this will be paid for. The assembly authorized the issue of a new class of "rate reduction bonds" to finance part of the package, but the eventual allocation of costs among the shareholders and different ratepayer classes is not made transparent by the legislation.

14 Other gas-and-electric mergers are also taking place. In the largest to date, Duke Power of North Carolina agreed in November 1996 to purchase PanEnergy, a Texan natural gas firm, for $7.7 billion.

Chapter 7

1 The estimate for the year 1999 is from the Cellular Telephone Industry Association web page at http://www.wow-com.com (14 August 1997).

2 As of this writing (August 1997), the American cellular industry, with 50 million subscribers, is the world's largest, and growing at about 50% per year (see http://www.wow-com.com). But the growth rate is even higher elsewhere—60% per year in Western Europe, 70% per year in Australia

and Asia, and more than 200% per year in South America's largest markets. See George I. Zysman, "Wireless Networks," *Scientific American* (September 1995): 68–71.

3 From a report in *Electrical World,* 9 October 1915, quoted in W. R. Maclaurin and R. Joyce Harman, *Invention and Innovation in the Radio Industry* (New York: Macmillan, 1949), p. 93. Not long afterwards came the first experiments with one-way radio communication to vehicles on land. This required more compact and more rugged equipment than the naval radio telephone. The Detroit Police Department introduced the first such system in 1921. This was one-way only; messages were broadcast to mobile receivers in police cars The next step was the development of the mobile transmitter, and by the early 1930s a crude two-way mobile radio system had been deployed by the Bayonne, New Jersey, police. See George Calhoun, *Digital Cellular Radio* (Norwood, MA,: Artech House, 1988), p. 26.

4 Ibid., p. 40.

5 Data compression techniques are continuously improving. Good-quality speech can be transmitted today at a rate of 8 kilobits per second. Better quality, which not long ago required 32 kilobits per second, now only requires 13. See Zysman, op. cit, p. 69.

6 CDMA was originally developed by Qualcomm, Inc. of San Diego. Qualcomm has since licensed its technology to large cellular equipment manufacturers, including Motorola and AT&T.

7 The first PCS network began operating in November 1995, in the Washington, D.C.–Maryland–northern Virginia area.

8 Rohit Sakhuja, "Air Interface Standards for Digital Mobile Cellular Systems in the U.S., Europe, and Japan." S.M. Thesis, Department of Electrical Engineering and Computer Science, Massachusetts Institute of Technology, 1995.

9 The FCC did require that all carriers allocate part of their spectrum to analog; since all U.S. analog systems use the AMPS standard, this ensured that subscribers with analog phones would still be able to "roam" across networks.

10 PCS networks will operate in the 2-gigahertz range, while the current generation of cellular networks use spectrum in the 800-megahertz range.

11 CDMA technology has also recently been adopted by some operators of the current generation of cellular networks.

12 Sakhuja, op. cit., interviews.

13 Jeffrey L. Funk, "The Success and Failure of Firms in the World-Wide Mobile Communication Market." Research Institute for Economics and Business Administration, Kobe University, 15 May 1997 (mimeo).

14 The material on which the following section is based was obtained mostly from a series of interviews at Motorola conducted by the author and his colleagues during the mid-1990s. The author has also drawn on several published accounts of Motorola's business practices. Particularly useful sources are Joseph Morone, *Winning in High-Technology Markets: The Role of General Management* (Boston: Harvard Business School Press, 1993), and James C. Collins and Jerry I. Porras, *Built to Last: Successful Habits of Visionary Companies* (New York: HarperCollins, 1994).

[15] The company's other main businesses include semiconductors, pagers, and land mobile radio.

[16] The average Motorola employee receives forty hours of training a year, and the company spends about 4% of its payroll cost on training and development, compared with about 1.2% for the average U.S. company—*BusinessWeek,* 13 February 13, 1995, p. 69.

[17] Morone, op. cit., p. 110.

[18] Motorola sold GSM equipment in fifteen countries in 1994.

[19] Cited in *U.S. News & World Report,* 24 June 1991.

[20] The new federal rules permitted two cellular service providers in each local market, one of whom was the local wireline operator, and the other an independent carrier drawn from outside the ranks of the wireline companies. The second licensee was selected by lottery, and the early population of cellular operators ranged widely in technical capabilities, from large telecommunications companies to small, unsophisticated cable operators. Many of these new customers had no choice but to rely on their cellular equipment suppliers to install complete working systems.

[21] Motorola's ability to provide this flexibility recently helped them to regain GTE as a cellular infrastructure customer, five years after they had been displaced by AT&T. A GTE spokesman reported that the company selected Motorola in this round of infrastructure procurement because Motorola's equipment would allow it to operate in a variety of transmission modes until CDMA is fully ready for the market—*Wall Street Journal,* 18 September 1995, A3.

[22] I caught a glimpse of what this is likely to mean on a recent nighttime drive through the central district of Hong Kong, one of the world's hottest markets for consumer electronics. Across the harbor in Kowloon, dominating all other advertising messages, was an enormous neon sign announcing: MOTOROLA. Another indication that the company is taking consumer marketing issues increasingly seriously was its recent appointment of John Pepper, a former CEO of Procter & Gamble, to its board of directors.

[23] For a comparison of product development practices in five leading cellular companies, see M. Piore, R. K. Lester, and K. Malek, "The Organization of Product Development: A Case Study of the Cellular Industry," MIT Industrial Performance Center Working Paper, WP-95-008, July 1995.

[24] In June 1997, Lucent Technologies and Philips Electronics announced that they were merging their consumer communications products businesses. The new company, to be called Philips Consumer Communications, will be the world's leading supplier of corded and cordless phones, and will also house the two companies' wireless phone products.

[25] Zysman, op. cit, p. 69.

[26] Ibid., p. 71.

Chapter 8

[1] James Brian Quinn, *Intelligent Enterprise* (New York: Free Press, 1992), p. 21.

Chapter 9

[1] "Reengineering Reviewed," *The Economist,* 2 July 1994, p. 66.
[2] Kathryn Troy, "Recognizing Quality Achievement: Noncash Award Programs," Conference Board Research Report 1008, New York, 1992.
[3] Bruce Rayner, "Trial by Fire Transformation: An Interview with Globe Metallurgical's Arden Sims," *Harvard Business Review* (May–June 1992): 117–29.
[4] U.S. Department of Commerce, private communication.
[5] *The Economist,* 18 April 1992, p. 67.
[6] *Wall Street Journal,* 19 April 1993, B1.
[7] Noriaki Kano, "A Perspective on Quality Activities in American Firms," *California Management Review,* vol. 35, no. 3 (Spring 1993): 14.
[8] George Easton, "A Baldrige Examiner's View of U.S. Total Quality Management," *California Management Review,* vol. 35 (Spring 1993): 32–54.
[9] Guillermo Gomez del Campo and Richard K. Lester, "Total Quality Management in the U.S. and Japan: Lessons from Deming Prize and Baldrige Award Winners," MIT Industrial Performance Center, Working Paper 93-006WP, August 1993.
[10] Joseph M. Juran, "Made in USA: A Renaissance in Quality," *Harvard Business Review* (July–August 1993): 47.
[11] Michael Hammer, "Reengineering Work: Don't Automate, Obliterate," *Harvard Business Review,* (July–August 1990): 104–12.
[12] Rose Batt, Ph.D. Thesis, Part II: "Internal Labor Markets in Telecommunications Services" (1995), p. 123, available from the MIT Industrial Performance Center.
[13] Michael Hammer and James Champy, *Reengineering the Corporation: A Manifesto for Business Revolution* (New York: HarperBusiness, 1993).
[14] Michael Hammer, "Beating the Risks of Reengineering," *Fortune,* 15 May 1995, p. 105.
[15] *BusinessWeek,* 7 November 1994, p. 6.
[16] *Boston Globe,* 9 July 1996, p. 31.
[17] Hammer, "Reengineering Work: Don't Automate, Obliterate," op. cit., pp. 105–06.
[18] Gene Hall, Jim Rosenthal, and Judy Wade, "How to Make Reengineering *Really* Work," *Harvard Business Review* (November–December 1993): 119–31.
[19] James Champy, *Reengineering Management: The Mandate for New Leadership* (New York: HarperBusiness, 1995).
[20] *Wall Street Journal,* 6 July 1993, A1.
[21] *Wall Street Journal,* 17 January 1995, B1.
[22] See Champy, *Reengineering Management,* op. cit.
[23] *Wall Street Journal,* 17 January 1995, B1.
[24] Ibid.
[25] Ibid.

Chapter 10

[1] *Boston Globe,* 9 June 1996, p. 85.

[2] *New York Times,* 16 March 1997, A49.

[3] Alan S. Blinder, ed., *Paying for Productivity: A Look at the Evidence* (Washington, DC: Brookings Institution, 1990).

[4] For a review of this research, see Casey Ichniowski, Thomas Kochan, David Levine, Craig Olson, and George Strauss, "What Works at Work: Overview and Assessment," *Industrial Relations,* 35 (1996): 299–333.

[5] Casey Ichniowski, Kathryn Shaw, and Giovanni Prennushi, "The Effect of Human Resource Management Practices on Productivity," unpublished paper, Columbia University, New York, 1993 (a revised version of this paper was published in 1995 by the National Bureau of Economic Research, Working Paper 5333).

[6] Kathryn Shaw, presentation at the Fourth Annual Sloan Industry Studies Conference, Pittsburgh, 17 April 1995.

[7] Data provided in the paper by Ichniowski, Shaw, and Prennushi, op. cit., suggest that a 7 percentage point increase in uptime in this particular part of the steel mill corresponds to an increase in sales revenues of $2.5 million per year.

[8] Arthur, Jeffrey, "Effects of Human Resource Systems on Manufacturing Performance and Turnover," *Academy of Management Journal,* vol. 37, no. 3 (1994): 670–87.

[9] John Paul MacDuffie, "Human Resource Bundles and Manufacturing Performance: Organizational Logic and Flexible Production Systems in the World Auto Industry," *Industrial and Labor Relations Review,* vol. 48, no. 2 (January 1995): 197–221.

[10] This interpretation was initially suggested by Lee Dyer and Todd Reeves in a paper entitled "Human Resource Strategies and Firm Performance: What Do We Know and Where Do We Need to Go?" prepared for presentation at the Tenth World Congress of the International Industrial Relations Association, Washington, D.C., 31 May–4 June 1995.

[11] Cited in Christopher Bartlett and Sumantra Ghoshal, "Changing the Role of Top Management: Beyond Systems to People," *Harvard Business Review* (May–June 1995): 133.

[12] Ichniowski, Shaw, and Prennushi, op. cit., p. 43.

[13] Kathryn Shaw, presentation at the Fourth Annual Sloan Industry Studies Conference, Pittsburgh, 17 April 1995.

[14] Casey Ichniowski and Kathryn Shaw, "Old Dogs and New Tricks: Determinants of the Adoption of Productivity-Enhancing Work Practices," *Brookings Papers: Microeconomics* (Washington, DC: Brookings Institution, 1995), p. 50.

[15] Ichniowski, Shaw, and Prennushi, op. cit., p. 42.

[16] See Ichniowski, Kochan, et al., op. cit.

Chapter 11

[1] Quotation from C. P. Snow, "Government, Science and Public Policy," *Science,* 151 (1966): 650–53.

[2] Stephen S. Roach, "The Hollow Ring of the Productivity Revival," *Harvard Business Review* (November–December 1996): 84.

[3] According to one recent estimate, only 5% of firms even have complete inventories of the hardware and software in their possession—*Fortune,* 9 September 1996, p. 108.

[4] *Wall Street Journal,* 22 November 1995, A7.

[5] See E. Brynjolfsson and L. Hitt, "Is Information Systems Spending Productive? New Evidence and New Results," *Proceedings of the Fourteenth International Conference on Information Systems,* Orlando, Florida, 1993; and "Computers and Economic Growth: Firm-Level Evidence," MIT Industrial Performance Center Working Paper, WP-94-005, August 1994. The later analysis covered the period between 1988 and 1992. The 367 U.S. firms in the data set accounted for average annual sales of nearly $2 trillion during this period.

[6] See, for example, *BusinessWeek's* cover story of 14 June 1993, "The Technology Payoff."

[7] *BusinessWeek,* 19 May 1997, p. 150.

[8] Paul A. David, "The Dynamo and the Computer: An Historical Perspective on the Modern Productivity Paradox," *American Economic Association Papers and Proceedings,* vol. 80, no. 2 (May 1990): 355–61.

[9] Researchers at Harvard University's Center for Textile and Apparel Research have shown how the application of information technology is transforming the clothing industry's distribution channels. (See Frederick Abernathy, John Dunlop, Janice Hammond, and David Weil, "The Information-Integrated Channel: A Study of the U.S. Apparel Industry in Transition," *Brookings Papers: Microeconomics* (Washington, DC: Brookings Institution, 1995), pp. 175–246.

[10] A more detailed account is given in Frank Levy and Richard J. Murnane, "With What Skills Are Computers a Complement?", MIT Industrial Performance Center Working Paper, WP-96-001, January 1996, presented at the Annual Meeting of the American Economic Association, San Francisco, January 1996.

Chapter 12

[1] Cited in Morone, *Winning in High-Tech Markets,* p. 71.

[2] See, for example, Robert J. Serling, *Legend and Legacy: The Story of Boeing and Its People,* (New York: St. Martin's Press, 1992), and John Newhouse, *The Sporty Game* (New York: Knopf, 1982). The reference to Boeing being a company that "eats, breathes, and sleeps" the world of aeronautics is attributed to its long-serving chief executive officer, William Allen, who was presiding over the company when the decision to proceed with the 747 was made. Cited by Collins and Porras, in *Built to Last,* from articles in *Time,* 19 July 1954, and *Nation's Business* (August 1967).

[3] Another source in the company mentioned the management's nagging discomfort over conflict and bitterness stirred up when it closed a Texas plant with bad labor relations problems and transferred production to other plants, some in Mexico. The pickets that remained in front of com-

pany headquarters were a constant irritant and reminder of the costs of old ways of dealing with the workforce.

[4] *BusinessWeek,* 1 August 1994, p. 46.

[5] See Robert H. Waterman, *What America Does Right,* (New York: W. W. Norton, 1994), pp. 137–68.

[6] *Washington Post,* 4 November 1997. The severance package includes eight months' notice, three weeks' pay for every year worked, and $6,000 in benefits to cope with the dislocations of job loss. The affected workers will also continue to participate in a company plan that could provide each of them with one year of extra pay by the year 2000.

[7] Robert W. Galvin, *The Idea of Ideas* (Schaumburg, IL: Motorola University Press, 1991), p. 24.

[8] Michael L. Dertouzos, Richard K. Lester, and Robert M. Solow, *Made in America* (Cambridge, MA: MIT Press, 1989), p. 8.

[9] See Collins and Porras, op. cit.

[10] Ibid., p. 121

[11] Ibid.

[12] Ibid., p. 187.

[13] Ibid., p. 201.

[14] Ibid., pp. 212, 214.

Chapter 13

[1] The quote is attributed to Jim Stanford, president of PetroCanada—*Wall Street Journal,* 5 July 1995, A1.

[2] "Winning Markets Abroad While Raising Living Standards at Home," Report of the Competitiveness Policy Council to the President and Congress, 1995, p. 3.

[3] On the pace of innovation, the Harvard economic historian Claudia Goldin has drawn parallels between the present period and the early part of the century. As she and a colleague observed in a recent paper: "We are often told that ours is a time of extraordinary technological change. Yet consider the changes that took place in the two decades around 1915. Barely 10% of American households had electricity in 1905 but 50% did by 1925. . . . The electric refrigerator was virtually unknown in 1909, yet was a separate category in the 1919 census of manufactures. The automobile was in its infancy in 1905, but eight years later Ford created the assembly-line for its production. . . . The Wrights completed their first successful flight in 1903, yet airplanes were used in World War I. . . . Commercial radio made its debut in 1920, yet 8 million households had a radio just eight years later. Only one broadcast station existed in 1921 (George Westinghouse's) but there were 681 in 1927." (Claudia Goldin and Lawrence Katz, "Technology, Skill, and the Wage Structure: Insights from the Past," paper presented at the American Economics Association Session on Technology, Human Capital, and the Wage Structure, San Francisco, 7 January 1996.)

On the question of globalization, Paul Krugman has observed that the United States, which still produces almost 90% of what it consumes, is far less exposed to international trade than the United Kingdom has been since the nineteenth century. (Paul Krugman, *Pop Internationalism* [Cambridge, MA: MIT Press, 1996], p. 120.)

Chapter 14

[1] *New York Times,* 13 February 1996, D1.

[2] For a more extensive discussion of Hong Kong's manufacturing industries, see Suzanne Berger and Richard K. Lester, eds., *Made by Hong Kong* (New York and Hong Kong: Oxford University Press, 1997).

[3] American Management Association, "1993 Survey on Downsizing: Summary of the Key Findings," New York, 1993. Another study, by the U.S. Department of Labor, found that managerial and professional workers accounted for 24% of all layoffs during 1991–93, compared with only 13% during the 1981–83 recession—*BusinessWeek,* 11 September 1995, p. 26.

[4] Charles Heckscher, *White Collar Blues: Management in an Age of Corporate Restructuring,* (New York: Basic Books, 1995), p. 53.

[5] Heckscher, op. cit., p. 69.

[6] Deborah Dougherty and Edward Bowman, "The Effects of Organizational Downsizing on Product Innovation," *California Management Review,* vol. 37, no. 4 (1995): 28–44.

[7] Heckscher, op. cit, p. 11 (italics in the original).

[8] Cited in Christopher Bartlett and Sumantra Ghoshal, "Changing the Role of Top Management: Beyond Systems to People," *Harvard Business Review* (May–June 1995): 141.

[9] Heckscher, op. cit., p. 12.

[10] Other firms talked about the importance of teams, but had accomplished much less with them.

[11] Heckscher, op. cit., p. 171.

[12] Ibid, p. 159.

[13] *New York Times,* 9 March 1996, p. 12.

[14] As a reporter for the *Boston Globe* noted of NYNEX: ". . . two groups of workers could be found working almost side by side at this company's Braintree offices: One making up to $19 an hour and employed full time with benefits; the other earning a starting salary of just $8 an hour with no benefits or job guaranteed. . . . NYNEX rejects any idea it is not a fair employer, insisting its full-time workers make top pay, and the new temporary workers earn competitive wages given today's market place. The problem is there are fewer and fewer full-time workers and more and more lower-paid temporary ones"—*Boston Globe,* 31 December 1995.

[15] See Barnaby J. Feder, "Bigger Roles for Suppliers of Temporary Workers," *New York Times,* 1 April 1995, A37; also, *Wall Street Journal,* 4 June 1996, B2.

[16] This discussion draws from Rose Batt's Ph.D. thesis, "Performance and Welfare Effects of Work Restructuring: Evidence from Telecommunications Services," Sloan School of Management, MIT 1995; available from the Industrial Performance Center. The results of Batt's research are summarized in "The Performance Effects of Teams in Customer Services," School of Industrial and Labor Relations, Cornell University, October 1996.

[17] Ibid., p. 133.
[18] Ibid., pp. 135–36.

Chapter 15

[1] According to analyses of the president's fiscal year 1998 budget plan and the congressional FY 1998 budget resolution conducted by the American Association for the Advancement of Science, federal funding for R&D will decline by 14% or more in real terms by the year 2002. See AAAS *Report XXII: Research and Development FY 1998,* April 1997 (updated May 23, 1997), available on the World Wide Web at http://www.aaas.org/spp/dspp/rd/rdwwwpg.htm.

[2] See *Science,* vol. 271, 5 January 1996, p. 22; *New York Times,* 9 November 1995, D2.

[3] *The Economist,* 23 March 1996, p. 67.

[4] This consideration also figures prominently in U.S. patent law. U.S. patents are held to a strict standard of appropriate subject matter, which requires that acceptable inventions be man-made. Basic knowledge and laws of nature are not patentable.

[5] One of the most outstanding industrial practitioners of this kind of directed fundamental research was Bell Laboratories during its golden age prior to the breakup of AT&T in 1984. In this case, of course, there *was* no free rider problem, since AT&T was to all intents and purposes a national monopoly. The work of Bell Labs was supported by contributions from the Bell operating companies, which recovered the costs from their customers under billing provisions approved by their regulators. In fact, AT&T was required by the government, as a condition for preserving its monopoly, to license any invention coming out of Bell Labs to anybody desiring to apply the invention outside the field of telecommunications. Thus, a few years after its invention of the transistor, Bell organized a series of meetings to explain to all comers everything that was known at the time about transistors and their methods of manufacture, and to offer the technology for licensing at a fair price.

[6] The laboratory in question was Bellcore, the central research laboratory of the regional Bell operating companies (the Baby Bells). Bellcore has since been sold by the Baby Bells to the research and consulting firm Science Applications, Inc.

[7] *New York Times,* 11 December 1995, D1, D5.

[8] See Vincent G. Cerf, "Research Pays Off," *Science,* vol. 271, 8 March 1996, p. 1343. The market for Internet-related products in 1996 has been estimated at $12 billion. See *Fortune,* 25 November 1996, p. 77.

[9] It is widely believed that the development of ARPANET, the progenitor of the Internet, was motivated by the desire to create robust communication networks capable of surviving a nuclear attack. But although an interest in survivable communications did influence the development of the network, it was not the primary motivation for the ARPANET initiative. An illuminating account of these events has been provided by Katie Hafner and Matthew Lyon in their book *Where Wizards Stay Up Late: The Origins of the Internet* (New York: Simon & Schuster, 1996).

[10] Linda Cohen and Roger Noll, *The Technology Pork Barrel* (Washington, DC: Brookings Institution, 1991), p. 378.

[11] Paul M. Romer, "Implementing a National Technology Strategy with Self-Organizing Industry Investment Boards," *Brookings Papers: Microeconomics 2* (Washington, DC: Brookings Institution, 1993), pp. 345–90.

[12] Committee on Criteria for Federal Support of Research and Development (Frank Press, Chair), *Allocating Federal Funds for Science and Technology* (Washington, DC: National Academy Press, 1995), Supplement 4.

[13] The quote from Purcell's letter is included in James Mattson and Merrill Simon, *The Pioneers of NMR and Magnetic Resonance in Medicine: The Story of MRI* (Ramat Gan, Israel: Bar-Ilan University Press, 1996 (see http://www.mribook.com/index.html). I am grateful to Harvey Brooks for pointing out the MIT Radiation Laboratory's part in this story.

[14] See Committee on Criteria for Federal Support of Research and Development, op. cit.

[15] President Bill Clinton, *Science in the National Interest* (Washington, DC: Office of Science and Technology Policy, Executive Office of the President, 1994), p. 17.

Chapter 16

[1] "A Conversation with the Lords of Wintel," *Fortune,* 8 July 1996 (cover story).

[2] See C. P. Snow, "The Two Cultures," *New Statesman,* 6 October 1956.

Chapter 17

[1] Paul Krugman, *Pop Internationalism* (Cambridge, MA: MIT Press, 1996), p. 5.

[2] Indeed, it is the advocates of the "no-growth" view who today are more likely to invoke value-based arguments in support of their position.

[3] National Commission for Employment Policy, "Declining Job Security and the Professionalization of Opportunity," Washington, DC, 1995, foreword by Anthony P. Carnevale (Chair).

[4] Ibid.

INDEX